DIARY OF A DECADE
1939–50

DIARY OF A DECADE
1939–50

Edward Stebbing

The Book Guild Ltd
Sussex, England

The Book Guild Ltd
25 High Street,
Lewes, Sussex

First published 1998
© Edward Stebbing, 1998
Set in Times
Typesetting by
Keyboard Services, Luton, Bedfordshire

Printed in Great Britain by
Antony Rowe Ltd,
Chippenham, Wiltshire

A catalogue record for this book is
available from the British Library

ISBN 1 85776 274 6

To MF and LF

CONTENTS

PREFACE

The greater part of this book was written more than 50 years ago, by an ex-grammar-school boy born in Essex – two huge disadvantages according to modern thinking. How it came to be written, and the repercussions from it after the war, can be traced back to two social phenomena whose birth almost coincided in the late 1930s and which ran a parallel course through the war years and up to the late 1950s. *Picture Post* magazine was one of these phenomena; it came into existence in 1938, but it had been preceded by a little more than a year by Mass-Observation, which aimed to study the way people behaved by scientific methods.

Both of these institutions were to have a significant effect on my own life. At the time of their beginnings I was still in my late teens and finding it rather difficult to make my way in the world. I was of humble origins, had had a conventional Church of England upbringing, and was living in what was then a country village, but I had received a good secondary education and I had an enquiring mind. When Mass-Observation appealed for volunteers to help in their research, by answering questions about their own lives, I became an early member of their panel. The experiment seemed to catch on with the public; I suppose it gave people the idea that the lives of the *hoi polloi* could be equally interesting and meaningful with those of more famous figures. M-O was not a political organisation, but class attitudes certainly entered into it.

As a Mass-Observer myself I was sometimes rather unsure of my role. They seemed to be mainly interested in pubs and

ix

factories, neither of which I knew much about. There did not seem to be much scope for that sort of enquiry in a country village, but then in 1939 the war came and everybody's lives changed completely. Perhaps we, the ordinary inhabitants, were of some importance after all.

For nearly six years, day in, day out, the war was with us – though the war as it seemed to ordinary people was perhaps far different from the war as it seemed to those fighting and running it, responsible for policy and strategy. What is difficult for historians to convey, and perhaps for readers to grasp, is that such a multitude of different events were happening simultaneously. The academic advantage of this record is that it was all written at the time it happened, an authentic account of what those (including myself) who bore the everyday burdens of wartime duties thought and said about the war, how they reacted to the many pressures that were put upon them.

At all events, both Mass-Observation and *Picture Post* – in a rather curious, but fortuitous, way – seemed to be in the right place at the right time when war broke out. Both were really unusual types of journalism, though *Picture Post*, with its team of brilliant photographers and professional writers, could obviously reach a wider public. As well as being a Mass-Observer, I was a regular reader of the magazine and there are quite a few references to it in my war diary. Alongside its eye-catching photo-journalism, however, it also featured serious articles by well-known writers and its letter pages were a valuable forum for public opinion. It was in the latter function that it printed a letter from me about war aims, which was to have an unforeseen result after the war, and led to some fresh thinking about it. This episode, recounted through letters received from a Dutch girl in the immediate post-war era, should help the reader, as it did the author, to a better insight into what the war had meant to ordinary families in occupied Europe. Some letters describe the harsh reality of their existence and they show what it undoubtedly would have been like for us, if the war had not been won. While we in Britain had to withstand the constant threat of death and destruction from the skies, those living under Nazi rule had to face a different threat, one of a more sinister and relentless nature – apart from the bombing. In the aftermath, much more information about this came to light.

This was brought home to me with added force when, on a visit to Germany in 1950, I stayed with a couple who had suffered much persecution for their religious beliefs. Whilst there I was told the story of how the husband had survived three years in Buchenwald concentration camp. This was really oral history, albeit not very pleasant, and again my Mass-Observation instincts and habits prompted me to keep another diary, which is the basis for the second part of the 'Aftermath' section. Both the Dutch and German experiences, in fact, hark back to wartime events, and allow us to understand why all that we endured in this country had been necessary.

Mass-Observation

Mass-Observation was started in about 1936 by a man named Tom Harrisson. He and a few others began with a case study of one town, Bolton in Lancashire. I think it was 1938 when I joined, by which time war was already looming and the M-O idea seemed to catch on, so that by the time war started there were, I imagine, several thousand observers covering the whole country.

Observers were asked to send in reports as often as they could about the way in which ordinary people were reacting to events. Those directing the scheme issued guidelines quite frequently on questions which might be of particular interest, but we were by no means confined to those topics. Every observer was different and had different experiences. Doubtless some of them died during the war, but those that survived kept on sending in reports for the whole six years of war.

In my case I wrote the reports in a duplicate book, sent out the top copy and kept the duplicate. Later I made fair copies of these into exercise books. Thus what you read is all authentic, written down first-hand at the time it happened. Much later, long after the war was over, I typed it all out (it is all my own typing!), omitting only a few passages which were of little interest.

One or two other points need emphasising. I was only quite young when war started, and therefore some of my judgements may seem immature, but I could not help that. Also, I reported faithfully what other people said or thought, but this should not be taken to mean that I necessarily agreed with what was said. It was a commonly expressed opinion of the man in the street – I have recorded it more than once – that the Germans should be exterminated. I would not have gone so far, for I was inclined to a pacifist viewpoint, but I wonder whether such views could be openly expressed today? Of course, we did not then know what was going on in Germany (only vaguely), but by the time the war ended and we saw the terrible pictures coming out of the concentration camps – a big exhibition was shown in London – it was at least permissible to think that perhaps those who advocated extermination had a good argument. On the whole, though, I had come to accept, as most people did, that Hitler could only be stopped by force.

The diary only covers this corner of Hertfordshire (or Middlesex as it then was) from towards the end of 1941, when I came to work at Clare Hall, but from then covers all the rest of the war. The first two years refer, somewhat disjointedly, to parts of Essex, Aldershot, London, Yorkshire, and Scotland.

After the end of the war I think the M-O concept rather lost its momentum, although it carried on for some time afterwards. Tom Harrisson eventually found other projects abroad, and so the observer network came to an end. The M-O archives, containing a great deal of primary source material, were acquired by the University of Sussex, where as far as I know they still are. During and after the war a few books were published making use of this material. I have one entitled *Living Through the Blitz* (published in 1976).

I have had mixed feelings, at different times, about the value of my own records. At one time I came close to throwing them out, as I did not think they would be of much interest to others and also, too, because so many books have been written about the war. On the other hand, in a 'local historical' context there are many interesting bits – how small my (our) wages were, how little one could pay for a meal, how people managed with the food and clothes rations, and so on. And how did people live without television? And I must confess that I had almost forgotten about the rocket which fell at Potters Bar! Attitudes to the V1 and V2 weapons still make interesting reading, I think. So I have decided now that it is worth keeping.

1939

Aug. 30th   After tea a friend of the family – a girl of about 26, a factory worker – comes round and says she has been at home all day because she feels so down. She wants to know if we think there is going to be a war.

My sister's young man comes round and starts talking about an aeroplane that came over very low during the day. My sister says that she thought it was going to drop a bomb.

I try to get my gas mask changed, as it doesn't fit very well, but the warden isn't in. Later, as we are going to bed, we hear another aeroplane. I have an interesting conversation with my sister B, which I give as nearly as possible verbatim.[1]

B: 'I hope it isn't one of the enemy.'
Me: 'They wouldn't let it fly about like that if it was.'
B: 'How could they stop it?'
Me: 'Why do you think we've got our own aeroplanes and anti-aircraft guns?'
B: 'Oh.'
Me: 'Anyway, if an enemy aeroplane was coming this way, they'd know a long while before it got here.'
B: 'How?'

I explain about direction-finders and that watchers were sure to be on the look-out in a time of crisis.

Me: 'Anyway, if it was an enemy bomber we would have heard the air-raid signal.'

B: 'Have we got one?'
Me: 'I hope so. It'll be a poor lookout for us if we haven't.'
B: 'What should we have to do?'
Me: 'Get under cover.'
B: 'Where?'
Me: Indoors, or in an air-raid shelter.

Then I say something about having a refuge room and making it gas-proof.

B: 'If there was a gas attack, how would we know when to come out?'
Me: 'There's a signal for that, too.'
B: 'Oh, is there? But how would they know when the gas had cleared away?'
Me: (almost losing my temper) 'What do you think air-raid wardens are for? What do you think they have had gas courses for? They can test for gas.'
B: 'Oh.'
Me: 'That shows what a lot you know about it. Why don't you read the leaflets? It's all in there.'
B: 'I will. I'll read them tomorrow. Put them in a conspicuous place and I'll take them to work with me tomorrow.'

Aug. 31st   In the morning there is a radio announcement to say that evacuation is to take place. War seems nearer, I think.

After tea I help my father measure the windows to see how much material we shall need for dark blinds. I make a list of things we might want should war start, such as first-aid supplies, etc.

One of my cousins comes up. My sister asks him if he thinks there will be a war. He says 'Yes'. She says she was hoping he'd say 'No'. There is a political discussion.

I succeed in getting my gas mask changed.

Sept. 1st   The wireless announces that hostilities between Germany and Poland have begun. Now I am sure that we shall be at war in a short time. But I think this is Hitler's final fling; he had to go down fighting. Most people are unanimous in wishing a bad end to Hitler. Examples: 1. 'Now he ought to go and get himself killed.' (Also, 'I felt like sitting down and crying when I heard they'd started,' said the same lady.) 2. Girl: 'I hope the same bomb kills the lot of 'em (Hitler and his appointed successors). 3. 'I'd like to shoot him.'

I buy some first-aid things, torch, etc. Total cost 3/4d. In the evening we make temporary coverings for the windows from an old tablecloth, quilts, brown paper, etc., as we have not yet purchased dark blinds.

Sept. 2nd   Get stuff to cover windows and a little more extra food. I have to wait in all the shops as there are a lot of people all getting emergency requirements. There is a big rush on electric torches in Woolworths.

In the evening we make and fix blinds for the most important windows.

There is a storm in the night and a great clap of thunder which many people think is a bomb.

Sept. 3rd   The declaration of war is received calmly for the most part. I feel rather glad that we are going to get it over with. It would have had to come some time. Mr. Churchill's statement that 'in our hearts this Sunday morning there is peace' is true for me at any rate.

In the afternoon we finish making and fixing window blinds. An uncle of mine, who lives near, has not got his gas mask yet, so goes and gets one from the warden. My cousin, who thought that there was going to be a war, has still not got his.

There are a good lot of people about in the evening, about half carrying their gas masks, half not. In a pub some people sing a song about ARP with complete lack of concern.

Sept. 4th   The air-raid warning goes in the early hours of the morning. My father wakes me up. I half-dress in a hurry, with a feeling of resentment at being pulled out of bed at such an hour, and grope downstairs in the darkness. We do not put the light on as chinks still show at the sides of the window; we sit in the

3

dark. The darkness makes it worse. I admit that I was in a funk and my sister was trembling with fear. After the 'Raiders passed' signal has gone we go back to bed and it is difficult to go to sleep again.

In the morning I offer my services for the food-rationing scheme. Am told they don't know whether they will want me or not. Practically everybody is now carrying a gas mask. What a reflection on our civilisation!

In the evening I hear some stories about the 'air-raid'. Most people were scared and think the weird siren made it worse. As a friend of ours remarks, 'You think your house is the only one.' My aunt was too frightened to get up, says she would have fainted if she had. Some humorous stories too. Some get out of bed, some don't. Some hear handbells after they have gone back to bed, some don't hear them at all; one family waits until nearly 5 o'clock as they think they can't go back to bed until they've heard them, then they don't hear them. Somebody says that one warden was blowing a whistle and ringing a bell at the same time. Another blew his whistle as hard as he could and shouted, 'Get your gas masks out. I'll tell yer when to put 'em on.'

We make sure that no chinks of light show at the sides of windows.

Sept. 5th   Nothing of interest to note.

Sept. 6th   The air-raid warning goes again at about 6.45 a.m. I get up and dress. It is not half so bad this time as it was on Monday morning, as it is daylight. We have our breakfasts, do a few chores, and go out to look when aeroplanes go over. I feel quite calm now. The 'All clear' goes at about 9 o'clock.

Sept. 7th   Sidelights on evacuated children: 'Did you have a bath before you came away?' 'No, I had a haircut.' Same child (aged seven), as though announcing a marvellous discovery, 'I heard a cow moo last night.' Another child had never seen a cow before and thought ducks never walked on land, but always swam on water. This seems almost unbelievable to me.

My sister is three-quarters of an hour late home from work as the bus service is unreliable. 'All old Hitler's fault,' she says. 'I'd like to be taken out there and shoot him myself.'

Several people I have met have remarked how tired they feel today. I do myself. I expect it is the effect of yesterday's early disturbance.

Sept. 8th   One of Judge Rutherford's pacifist disciples, a woman, comes to the door, and we have an argument. She says we should have nothing to do with the present war and runs on about Armageddon. ('This silly little scuffle will be nothing compared to what is coming after.' Apparently all those who have taken part in any sort of national service will be destroyed and we shall not be able to say that we have not been warned (by Judge Rutherford). The gist of my argument is that we are acting as a police force to keep world order (and I was nearly a pacifist once). In the end she gives me a final warning and departs without having sold me any of her literature.

Sept. 9th   Nothing of much interest to note. Except for gas masks and newspaper placards one would hardly think there was a war.

Sept. 13th   The last four days have seen nothing in connection with war reactions. We seem to have slipped into wartime conditions very easily. In fact, life goes on much as before, except for carrying gas masks, obscuring lights, and talking about the war. Of course, the war is much talked about and rumours float about rather vaguely. Today I went out without my gas mask again. I don't seem to be able to get used to taking it with me everywhere I go.

Sept. 14th   Talking to my aunt and she says she is always awake at night hearing, or thinking she can hear, aeroplanes.

My sister's young man says he knows a man who actually saw bombs drop and heard them explode during the 'air-raid' some days ago. In fact, no bombs were dropped, but this shows how rumour can spread so easily and why it is so readily believed; it is hard to disbelieve a man who says he actually saw such things happen.

Sept. 15th Bought a copy of Hitler's 'Will' in the street. It contained some dozen 'bequests', all of which were insulting and some rather coarse, but on the whole witty, especially that which says: 'On my death I proclaim the annexation of HELL which I have tried to give to my German people and rightfully belongs to the Fatherland.' I think the worst thing we can do to the dictators is to laugh at them.

Sept. 17th When I heard that Russia had invaded Poland I felt very depressed and bewildered. Since the signing of the German-Soviet pact I have been puzzled by Russia's apparent reversal of policy. Yet we must not despair. My sister was very perturbed by the news. 'We ought to start bombing Germany as hard as we can,' she said.

Afternoon. Had a long argument with a pacifist, lasting well over an hour. The main difference between him, as a pacifist, and myself, as a semi-pacifist, is that he would rather be killed than kill, while I would rather kill, much as I hate killing, than be killed. The vicar came up while we were talking and spoke to my friend (who is about 22), having heard that he was a pacifist and apparently not too pleased about it. The vicar thought that we were quite right in waging the war and that we must fight for all we are worth. He was very emphatic about this. This seems a strange view for a priest, but he is an old army chaplain and is always enthusiastic about the views of retired military people and about military life in general. The pacifist thinks that Russia invaded Poland to keep Germany off her own doorstep. I am inclined to agree with this and I hope it is right.

Sept. 25th Met a soldier friend of mine, home on leave. He says he is very tired (only two hours sleep per day) and fed-up and 'will be jolly glad when the war is over.'

Sept. 27th Budget day. One of the men who works with my father, on hearing the terms of the budget, said, 'I shall give up drinking and I shall give up smoking.' My father: 'Well, you're not very patriotic. Somebody's got to pay for the war.'

Sept. 30th I went to visit my brother, who is a policeman stationed some distance from home. From where he is one can see some of the balloons around London. They look very small in the distance. It was the first time I had seen them, and I had not expected them to be so numerous. I could not see what protection they offered against enemy planes. My sister's fiancé explained that the raiders would be forced to fly high, or else risk being caught in the cables of the balloons, and flying high brings them within range of the anti-aircraft guns.

The people with whom my brother lodges are upset about the prospect of food rationing. The lady of the house, having heard that the sugar ration would be ½lb per person per week, said that it was ridiculous to expect people to manage on that small amount, as she always used 8lb a week (rationing would reduce it to 2½lb), so she had been getting a little store in. Talking about sugar in tea, she said, 'I could drink it without sugar, but I'm not going to while I can still have a little.' About her husband she said, 'Even if I put two spoonfuls in he always takes a little more.' Her husband, being told that my sister and her young man do not take sugar in tea, jokingly suggested that they save their rations and send them to him.

On the way back we stopped for petrol (the last lot, as S is not running the car after today). The woman at the garage said that one lady thought she did not have to pay as she had the petrol coupons!

I went to the cinema in the evening. Only the highest price (1/6d.) seats were left, and these were quickly filled. Outside another cinema I saw the longest queue I had ever seen there.

Oct. 1st   Listened to Churchill's broadcast in the evening. A reassuring speech, just what we want. Getting tired of the diluted news we get on the radio.

Oct. 2nd   My chief concern at present regarding the war is to find a job of some service to the country. I have offered my services at various places without success, but am still trying. I thought it would be easy to get a job now, but it isn't. They seem to be employing a lot of married women, which is decidedly unfair when there are plenty of men out of work.

Oct. 4th   In the afternoon I went to the pictures without my gas mask. I did not discover I had left it behind until I was on the bus, so decided to risk going without it, which made no difference, as it happened.

Oct. 5th　　My father and S were talking about pacifists. Some of the remarks: 'Some of them will do anything to get out of it.' 'Most of them object on religious grounds.' 'I don't know where we should be if everybody was like that.' 'If your country is not worth fighting for I don't know what is. I don't know of any other country where they'd be so free.' 'It's not the true British spirit.' 'It certainly isn't.' My sister: 'Why don't clergymen have to fight?' 'Because they are exempted.' 'Yes, but why? They're only human beings.' These views dismayed me considerably, for they show a complete lack of understanding of the pacifist point of view, which, though I do not agree with it, I understand and respect. What is the good of fighting against the persecution of people because they hold different opinions from their rulers, if we are going to have the same sort of thing in this country? The future outcome of the war does indeed seem dark if people are already adopting this attitude towards those who are upholding Christian principles. The views of my own family and friend surprised and distressed me so much that I found difficulty in getting to sleep through thinking about it.

Oct. 6th　　Listened to *Adolf in Blunderland* on the radio. I thought it a brilliant satire and thoroughly enjoyed it. The BBC deserve great praise for this.

Oct. 7th　　Went to the cinema. Many people using torches in the black-out, some of them looking very bright. People seem to take the black-out cheerfully and laugh when they nearly bump into one another.

Oct. 11th　　Conversation at home:

My sister:　　'Shall I get a tin of soup in case we can't get any meat?'
My father:　　'Yes, if you like.'
My sister's fiancé:　　'Some of those tinned soups are very good.'
Myself:　　'That won't be much instead of meat, will it?'

Sister:	'But we might not be able to get meat. You don't seem to realise we might not be able to get things.'
Me:	'I don't see why we shouldn't get any meat.'
	Sister: I don't say we shan't get any, but we shan't get so much.'
Me:	I know. Meat will be rationed. But you usually have soup before anything else.
Sister:	'Yes, but we can have it with potatoes...'
Father:	'Tomato soup's very nice. A plate of steaming hot tomato soup will warm you up on a cold day.'
Sister:	'What sort shall I get?'
Her fiancé:	'What's that one with a funny name?'
Me:	'Mulligatawny?'
S:	'Yes, that's the one I was thinking of.'
Father:	'It's very good too.'

Conversation gets round to what kinds of soup there are and my father telling us what they had to eat in the trenches in the last war, etc.

This is what we now have in out food store, built up gradually week by week: two tins of sardines, two of herrings, two of salmon, one of crab, one of pilchards, two of paste, two of cream, three of condensed milk, one of soup, six of fruit, three of peas, one of baked beans, two of corned beef, and 8lb of reserve sugar (saved without buying extra).

Oct. 13th   More talk about evacuees. One girl, fairly old, had never seen a knife and fork. A man who had taken two boys in chased one upstairs for bad behaviour and he jumped out of the window. The boy expected the man to be sorry for him, but he rather bitterly remarked that it was a pity he hadn't broken his neck. There have been several cases of children with lice in their hair. One woman took in two children with this complaint and caught it herself. The mother came on a visit and treated the matter lightly. 'Fancy, I've had it all my life and now you've got it.' Apparently they don't bother about it. The woman 'told her off' and got rid of the children. My sister said, 'I never thought people went about with dirty heads nowadays.' If good can

9

come out of evil, then this war is surely doing good in showing people how other people live. There is no doubt that folk in this district have been taken aback by the habits and conditions of life of slum children (which many of them are), and many clean, decent country people have been shocked and hurt at the way in which some of them act in their new homes. 'Disgusting' the headmaster of the local school called it, having had experience of it in his own house. 'If I had my way I'd give them a jolly good hiding.' The behaviour of some near here was so bad that they had to be put in an empty house by themselves. 'Isn't it awful, though!' my aunt said.

Oct. 14th   Saturday night. Walked up the town. Plenty of people about, but not so many as in peacetime. I went in the public library. When I came out it seemed so dark by comparison that I walked straight into a soldier as though he wasn't there. 'Sorry,' I said. 'Sorry,' he said 'you can't see where you're going.'

There was a dance on, so I went in. The place was crowded, no room to dance properly. There were few soldiers, the majority being civilians; plenty of girls. No war talk.

Voices, as we go out: 'Have you got a torch?' 'No.' 'It would be useful if you had.' Came home in a dimly-lit bus; how dreary it seemed! I gave the conductor 3d. for a 2¹/₂d. fare. Apparently he misunderstood me and gave me 3d. ticket. I did not think it worth while to bother about the halfpenny, as he was obviously working under difficulties. 'This is a good show, isn't it?' someone said to me.

Oct. 15th   Glanced at an article in a Sunday newspaper, called 'Hitler is Mad'. I think this sort of article does more harm than good and, though the writer claims to be able to prove it, is probably without foundation. It is merely an excuse for abusing Hitler. No doubt the latter's mind is abnormal, but his actions by no means show that he is mad. I simply do not believe stories about him having fits.

Oct. 16th   Applied for a job at a fruit farm. No luck. Called in at my aunt's. Another elderly lady, Mrs S, was there. Mrs S: 'I don't bring my gas mask with me. I don't think he'll come. I don't think he'll bomb us – no.' 'He' presumably refers to Hitler. They talked about butter, how much they would get when it was rationed.

Oct. 17th   Saw the blue Government poster, 'Don't help the enemy, etc.' in the post office. I entirely agree with it, but thought how difficult it is for some people to hold their tongues.

The air-raid warning went at 1.35. I was alone and didn't notice it until the woman next door came and said, 'That is the warning, isn't it?' I listened and could hear it faintly. I wasn't sure if it was our warning. Mrs C said I could go in with her if I liked, but I said, 'No, it's all right.' I went and shut the windows. One upstairs would not shut, as the sash was broken. Everything deathly silent. I had my gas mask near at hand and undid the waterproof case, so that I could get it out more quickly if necessary. One or two people on bicycles went by; an occasional car. I did some typing until the 'All clear' went at about 2.30. I could only just hear it, but knew by everything coming to life, cars starting, voices talking, people going by, etc.

My sister, who is a typist at a factory, in accordance with instructions to staff, took refuge in a nearby cemetery (!) when the warning went. My father went on working. Mrs S did not hear the warning, so didn't know anything about it until the 'All clear' sounded.

Oct. 18th   I was waiting for a bus and spoke to Mrs K, a middle-aged woman. She said, 'I expect we shall feel funny when we don't have to carry our gas masks. Still, the sooner we can give 'em up the better. I wouldn't mind if it was tomorrow. But we might be out without them and get caught. He might try it. Some of them think he'll try it. But he tried it yesterday, didn't he, and he didn't have it all his own way.' 'No,' I said, 'he got the worst of it.' (Strange, how many people identify Hitler with his raiders.) 'Yes, he got the worst of it, but we must expect some losses. That's what makes it so hard.'

I had a lift in a car. The man driving asked me if I was looking forward to being called up. I said I didn't mind and expected I should be next year. 'Still, it'll all be over next year, we hope,' he said.

I went to see my aunt (not the one previously mentioned). 'It's a beastly business, this war,' she said. 'The trouble is we don't know how long it'll last. It might be short and it might be long. But I certainly can't see how it can be short.' Talking about air-raids: 'If we've got to have it, I'd rather it was in the daylight. You can see what you're doing then.' About butter: 'We might as well make the most of it while we've got it. We might not be able to get it soon.' Me: 'We shall have to have margarine.' 'Oh, I hate the thought of it. Of course, uncle would rather have margarine. He likes it better than butter.'

Oct. 21st   Went to a football match. An oldish man next to me was carrying his gas mask loose in his overcoat pocket.

Oct. 22nd   Went to see Mrs S. One of her daughters, about 27, was looking at a magazine. 'Look, there's old Hitler,' she said, pointing to a photograph of him. 'What would you like to do to him?' her mother asked. 'I don't know what I should like to do to him,' was the reply, as though nothing bad enough could be thought of.

Oct. 25th   Two snatches of conversation at home:

My father: 'I hear that butter is going to be severely rationed. Three ounces, they say.'
My sister: 'Whatever shall we live on?'
Myself: 'Margarine.'
My father: 'Margarine hasn't got any vitamins.'

My sister: 'How long do you think this war is going to last?'
My father: 'Four years.'
Her fiancé: 'I think so, too.'
My sister (to me):   'Do you think it'll last four years?'
Myself: 'No, not so long ... a year or two.'
My father: 'This war is not going to be won on the battlefield.'

Oct. 27th   My sister and I were talking to Mrs S.

My sister: 'Have you got any extra butter in?'

12

Mrs S:	'Yes.'
My sister:	'How much? A pound?'
Mrs S:	'Yes.'
My sister:	'Ought I to get any extra?'
Mrs S:	'How much do you use a week?'
My sister:	'A pound and a half.'
Mrs S:	'Well, you'll get half that, won't you? I should get an extra pound, or a pound and a half, before rationing starts. Mrs B went all over the town and got three pounds, all in half-pounds.'

Oct. 28th   Conversation between my sister and her fiancé:

He:	'Do you think I was bold to come without my gas mask?'
She:	'Yes, I do. All that time … you ought to have brought it.'
He:	'I don't think we shall have any gas attacks yet. They'll use it at the front before they use it here.'
She:	'Don't you be so sure. You can't prophesy anything.'[2]

Oct. 30th   Went to see Mrs M. She agreed with me that it doesn't matter much about carrying one's gas mask when going only a short distance.

Nov. 1st   Evacuee, when asked by his mother if he'd like to go back with her, said no, he didn't want to.

Nov. 2nd   Preparations for Christmas. Mrs S has cooked her Christmas puddings today. We have got the ingredients for ours, as they will probably be hard to get later.

Nov. 3rd   Overheard a man and a woman talking in a bus. The man had been listening to a wireless commentary on the war the night before. He: 'As he said, those who fought in the last war … it's their sons who are fighting in this.' She: 'Oh, I think it's dreadful. I saw some of them marching in the street this morning. I'm sure some of them weren't more than

13

seventeen.' The conversation turned into a political discussion, including comments on the Maginot and Siegfried lines, all of which I could not hear. Then, 'Why did Baldwin hand over the reins to Chamberlain?' 'Because he knew he couldn't do it himself.' 'Yes, because he wasn't strong enough. Chamberlain is old, but he's got more fighting power.' (!)

Nov. 4th   Black-out time half an hour later. House next door not blacked out at 6.20 p.m.

My sister, as we are about to go to bed: 'Do you remember at the beginning of the war? ... I used to take my gas mask up with me every night.'

Nov. 7th   My sister's intended, on riding a bicycle in the black-out: 'There are so many people about and so many lights, you don't know which is the road and which is the pavement. Some are one side, some the other, and some crossing – you don't know where you are.'

Nov. 9th   An elderly man spoke to me in a shop: 'I expect they'll be saying this bomb was Churchill's work, won't they?' 'Yes, I expect so,' I answered. 'Pity it didn't get him.' 'If it had there would be someone else,' said the man. 'I've lived in Germany and I'm one of the few people in Chelmsford who knows what he's talking about. Don't you believe we're not fighting the German people, because we are. They're all the same – full of hatred and envy for Britain. I'm no jingo; I have no politics. But you can take it from me that all nations envy the British, even our friends the French.'

I heard at least two people say that it was a pity the bomb did not kill Hitler.

Nov. 11th   Armistice Day. Bought a 6d. poppy. At 11 o'clock I was writing a letter to join Federal Union, which I believe is the only way to lasting peace. I did not observe the silence. My sister's young man said he did, also several others in his office.[3]

Nov. 12th   Mrs S: 'I don't worry about air-raids now. I used to at the beginning of the war. But we've had so many false

14

alarms, haven't we? I don't worry about them now.'

Joke told by seven-year-old evacuee: 'A little boy was being washed by his mother and he got some soap in his eye. His mother said, "You're lucky to have soap in your eye. The little German boys haven't got any soap."'

Nov. 13th   On Friday I had bought the White Paper concerning the treatment of Germans in Germany.[4] The undoubted truth of the statements make this wonderful propaganda. I think this war will have done some good if it stamps out the evil in Germany itself, as shown in the White Paper. Today my sister read a few pages, but said she was not going to read any more – it was too dreadful. 'You wouldn't believe such things could happen, would you?' she said. 'It's a wonder the Lord above allows it.' It was her opinion that Hitler ought to be put in one of his own concentration camps and have the same things done to him.

Nov. 15th   Two remarks of interest:
My sister: 'I don't know what we shall do if the war lasts five years. Lots of people think it will last a long while. There'll be a change in everybody. We shall be a different race of people.'

My father: 'I saw some torches in a shop window and I looked to see if there were any batteries as well and the torches, what you'd usually pay about 9d. for, were 2/3d. each.'

Nov. 16th   Filled in our ration books. None of us was very clear about how to do it. My father put his name on the coupon page for meat, which is not to be rationed yet; I thought we ought to fill in our names in the spaces provided in the middle of the pages, but eventually left them blank; my sister wasn't sure whether to put the date; my father forgot to fill in his name on the last page but one and put down the name of his retailer for cooking fats, which also are not to be rationed. Clearer instructions should have been given.

Nov. 19th   My sister asked us if we knew that ammunition was kept under——. S: 'You shouldn't have told us that. That's a secret. Haven't you read the notices?' 'What notices?' Myself: 'The blue ones. "Don't help the enemy. Careless talk may give

away vital secrets." ' My father: 'That means in public.' Myself: 'You might say something at home and then one goes and tells someone else – it soon gets round.' My sister: 'Don't tell anyone else then.' General discussion on spies.[5]
S began to read the White Paper which I mentioned the other day, but after reading about 16 pages also gave it up. 'I don't think I'll read any more; it's terrible.'

Nov. 22nd   I was in the butcher's when a man came in and registered for meat. My aunt said she had already done so. 'Why?' I asked. 'Well, they all are.' 'We haven't been told to.' 'No, but we shall be.'

About 9.55 p.m. the air-raid alarm was sounded. I was at a dance in the parish hall, not far from my home. Girls had to bring their clothes out of the cloakroom, which is a first-aid post. The dancing went on. Hardly anybody left; those who had gone out at the interval came back. Nearly everybody was still there at the end. Nobody seemed upset. 'My poor little dog is all on his own,' was the chief concern of one woman. One of the dancers went and put on a nurse's uniform, then came back and watched the dancing. 'Do you feel annoyed?' she said to one of the men. 'No, I'm going on with this.' 'I wish I could.' 'Well, why can't you? Don't be so silly. You can dance like that. There's no sense in stopping unless you're wanted.' Someone said something about gunfire, but dancing went on as though nothing had happened and half an hour later the 'All clear' went.

Nov. 24th   I heard a girl in a restaurant say, 'I like the Germans.'

Nov. 25th   Went to the cinema. The electricity supply was cut off owing to a barrage balloon breaking loose and its cable fouling some overhead electric cables. We sat in darkness for about an hour. Someone played a piano and the audience sang. Some of the songs were: 'There'll Always be an England', 'Run Rabbit Run', 'Wish Me Luck', 'Tipperary', 'South of the Border', and other popular songs, old and new.

Nov. 26th   Listened to Chamberlain's speech. Though no

Chamberlain fan, I almost completely agreed with what he said. I didn't like what he said about entering the war 'to establish peace', which always sounds silly to me.

Nov. 28th   Mrs S says that lard is unobtainable in the town unless you are registered at one of the shops. My sister had tried to get butter on Saturday and found the same difficulty, but said she was registered at one shop, which was a lie, and obtained half a pound. It is the same everywhere: shops will not serve you with rationed goods unless you are registered there.

Mrs S is making sure of her Christmas cards by buying them today. In the evening we make our own list to see how many we shall want. It seems rather ironical, to me at any rate, to send Christmas cards in these times. Mrs S's daughter calls in for a few minutes and Christmas shopping is mentioned. 'You won't go shopping in London this year,' said my father, for she and my sister used to go shopping in London just before Christmas. 'No, it's upset everything,' she replied.

My sister makes some remark about Russia and Finland. 'I reckon they'll invade Finland,' I said.

Nov. 29th   Bought ten Christmas cards; my sister had already bought five. The cards are the conventional kind. I think they ought to have some bearing on the special circumstances in which we are living.

Nov. 30th   My prophecy about Russia proves correct. With every new aggression I feel gloomier than ever and always feel depressed, but it soon passes off. But this is a blow to us, because Finland is a true democracy. I do not feel that Finland can last long.

Talking about last week's air-raid, my father says that one of the men working with him did not hear the warning, but heard the 'All clear'. He must have mistaken this for the warning, as he sat up until 1.30 a.m., but didn't hear any more so went to bed.

Dec. 4th   The local Co-op have introduced temporary ration cards, as some people send their children, evacuees, or neighbours to the shop when they have already been themselves, thus getting more than their fair share. Now each purchase of butter, bacon, or sugar has to be entered on a card which bears the customer's name. One cannot obtain more than a quarter of butter or bacon per person per week, so that we are now as good as rationed.

Dec. 7th   Effects of rationing begin to be felt, as is shown by my sister saying to me, 'Will you have a boiled egg for breakfast tomorrow, to save a rasher of bacon?'

Dec. 9th   Christmas drawing near – my sister has bought two boxes of dates, one of figs, one of chocolates; Christmas cake being made tomorrow; two chickens to be ordered next week; my sister starts Christmas shopping, says the best time is in the evening, as there are not many people in the shops then.

Dec. 13th   Christmas preparations still going on:

Myself:	'Aunt N wants you to tell her if you would like a little bit of bacon for Christmas, so she can order it.'
My sister:	'What, might they have some?'
Myself:	'They will have some, I think.'
My sister:	'Yes, I would like a bit. And would you like a piece of Stilton for Christmas, Dad?'
My father:	'No, I don't think so.'
My sister:	'Why not? Economising?'
My father:	'Yes.'

Dec. 14th   My sister comes in from the shop. 'I saw a lovely box of chocolates in the shop – ten and six. I wish someone would buy me one like it.' My father: 'I have seen the time I might, but not this year.'

My sister goes upstairs to black out. She calls down, 'Is there a light on in the front room?' (We don't use the front room much, so it is rarely blacked out.) Myself (going to see): 'Yes.' 'Who left it on?' 'I don't know.' 'I went upstairs to black out, and when I went to my window I saw a light shining right across the lawn.' 'I believe Mrs S went in there to get some apples. She must have left it on.' 'And all that time! It's a wonder we haven't had a policeman up here. The light must have been on for more than two hours since black-out time and we didn't know!'

Dec. 18th Mrs S: 'I think Winnie (her daughter) would marry if it wasn't for the war, but if he's going to be called up, it don't seem much good, does it?'

Dec. 19th Went Christmas shopping. Crowds of people, which shows that though the atmosphere may not be as merry as usual, people are determined to keep up outward customs.

My father says that he has heard that the Germans have invented a new gas against which our gas masks are useless. It is in powder form, he says, and after a time gives off a vapour. The gas is called 'Arthur'! I do not believe it and say so.

Later we talk about war aims. My father and my sister's fiancé, S, both say the Germans must be kept under. S thinks it silly to say that we're not fighting the German people. My father says if Hitler had not come to power there would have been someone else. S says that Germans have an aggressive nature, and his ideas are so distorted that he says the German people *put* Hitler into power. After some argument I make him agree that Hitler wangled and forced his way into power. My sister is with me in thinking that the Germans are really decent (but rather stupid) people and were led by unscrupulous leaders into a war they did not really want. S produces as evidence for his 'aggressive nature' theory the fact that Germany has been in five wars in the last hundred years. My father agrees with him.

Dec. 21st Listened to the programme about Poland, 'Thy Banner Torn, but Flying', on the radio. Are such programmes deliberately planned to stir up hatred? I wondered. My sister, who, the other night, was saying that the Germans were fundamentally nice people, was so appalled that now she thinks they are fundamentally brutal. 'The Germans can't have souls,' she says. S says they are pagans.

Dec. 25th Celebrated Christmas in the usual way. We went to S's house to tea and played games afterwards. We listened to

19

Gracie Fields' broadcast; everyone thought she was wonderful. We arrived home at about 12.45 a.m. and noticed that the Cs, next door, had apparently just arrived also, having been out all day, and had not bothered to black out. The light shone out shamelessly. We had blacked out before we went out. Otherwise our Christmas was not affected in any way.

Dec. 26th   Had a party at home, as last year. All passed off normally and, except for a few remarks about evacuees and black-out ('One of our evacuees has put on nine pounds since he's been here.' 'Do you think they'll come back after Christmas?' 'Yes I think so.' 'I've got a dynamo on my bike and, of course, when I get to traffic lights my lamp goes out. I got spoken to by a policeman about it.' 'I've got a dynamo, but I just lift up the back wheel and tread on the pedal.') the war was forgotten.

Dec. 30th   Mrs S: 'I don't think he'll come over here much – to bomb us, I mean, because I expect we should go and bomb them if he did ... It don't seem much good, does it?'

Notes
[1] At the outbreak of war, our family household consisted of my father, a builder's foreman then aged 57; my sister Elizabeth (usually known as Bet or Betty), who was some four years older than I; and myself, aged 19. My elder brother Jack was serving in the police force and lived away from home. My mother had died, from illness, in 1936. My sister was employed in a secretarial capacity at the Crompton Parkinson factory in Chelmsford, where they made electric motors and other equipment. Her fiancé (sometimes referred to as her 'young man') also worked as a draughtsman at the same factory. Since my sister was out at work during the day, a friendly widowed neighbour, Mrs S (Swallow), helped with some cleaning and cooking, for which my father paid her a few shillings a week. However, a good deal of responsibility fell on my sister's shoulders. I myself was unemployed at the time, but that situation did not last long.

Our home was in a village about two miles from Chelmsford in Essex.
[2] The possibility of gas attacks dominated people's thoughts during the early weeks of the war, but this fear later receded.
[3] Federal Union was a new political movement whose star burned brightly for a time, but then faded out.
[4] Government White Paper on treatment of Germans in Germany. Evidently our eyes had been opened to some of the evils of Hitlerism quite early in the war, although the full scale of the horrors was not revealed until the liberation of the death camps towards the end of the war. Unfortunately, I did not keep my copy of the White Paper.
[5] My sister's remark was a classical example of what was meant by 'Careless talk costs lives'. I cannot now remember where the ammunition was supposed to have been stored.

1940

Jan. 6th   Lard being unavailable, we have to use vegetable cooking fat. Mrs Swallow has not a very good opinion of it. 'It's no good for frying,' she said.

My sister said that some of the men where she works thought that Hore-Belisha was not liked because he is a Jew and that was why he resigned.

Hardly anyone carries a gas mask now. At a football match this afternoon, the only people carrying them were soldiers. I have not touched mine for weeks.

Jan. 7th   My Uncle A came over to see us and told this story about evacuees. A woman took in two little girls. All they had were the clothes they had on and some plimsolls. The woman bought them some clothes and shoes, deciding to tell the parents when they came down to see the children. Later, the parents came, or rather they wrote to say that four people would be coming, but in the end seven came. She told them what she had done. No offer of payment was made; one of them merely said 'Thank you'. The woman also had to feed all the visitors, and the next day there was nothing to eat in the house.

Jan. 12th   Went to see about a job as assistant in a men's clothing shop. There was some difficulty about my age, as I am almost 20. I explained that my health, which has not been robust, would probably bar me from military service. I was told that I shall know definitely in a day or two.

Jan. 13th   The local British Legion held their annual party as usual. First there was a concert and afterwards there were games, one of the prizes being a half-rasher of bacon, a lump of sugar, and a small piece of butter.

Jan. 17th　　Was informed that I had got the job at the shop. My wages will be 25/- a week to start with. This seems a fortune to what I have been getting. If I can do no military service, this is at least of more service to the public than mere idleness. I am glad to have found a job in these difficult times. It will bring a little more money into the house; it will be needed now that prices are going up and my father has very little work in the building trade.

Jan. 21st　　Conversation at home:

B:　　'Did you hear on the news about those two Germans who were sent to prison for listening to a broadcast other than German?'
S:　　'No I didn't hear the news.'
B:　　'The man got five years and the woman one.'
My father:　'The other day I read about a woman who killed herself through listening to Lord Haw-Haw.'
B:　　'She must have believed what he said, then?'
My father:　'Of course she did... Of course, this war business affects a lot of people like that.'

Jan. 22nd　　I started work.
In the shop are two other youths, one a little younger, the other a little older, than myself. The younger tells me that the other, S, is a conscientious objector. Then he gives me his views on pacifists: 'I shouldn't want to be one... I can understand them, but I don't agree with them... There's a lot in what they say, but...' etc.

Jan. 23rd　　Smith (the conscientious objector) says that he has had to cancel his holiday. He was going to Scotland with some others in a hired car. Two have been called up, and he will soon have to take up non-combatant duties.

Jan. 24th   Smith asked me if we had an air-raid shelter in our garden. 'No,' I said, 'have you?' 'No... We haven't had an air-raid alarm lately, have we? It would be a change just to have one.'

Feb. 2nd   The opinion of a fairly old male customer, who was in the last war, about the picking up of German sailors at sea: 'We never ought to pick them up. That's the only way to do it. They don't pick our men up.'

Feb. 3rd   Mrs C, from next door, asked if I had any old coats her two evacuees could have – they have only got two ragged ones. She had had a note saying that parents must not be approached. She had told a woman who came to the door and the children's mother, when she came down, also told the teacher, but nothing has been done. Yet some evacuees have had clothes.

Feb. 4th   The news announcer tells of the rescuing of shot-down German airmen. My sister remarked, 'Some of those whom they had probably been bombing rescued them.'

Feb. 5th   Customer in the shop: 'Funniest sort of war I ever came across. The manager: 'Most difficult at times to know there is a war on.'
    I had to walk home in the black-out, as there were no buses because of fog. I walked all the way home (two miles) behind someone with a torch. Saw a few buses crawling back at less than walking pace. One of them and a lorry had removed all dimming apparatus from one headlight; it was strange to see the headlights as bright as in peacetime. One car went on to the pavement.

Feb. 6th   Through a letter which I wrote to *Picture Post* about war aims, I received a letter today from a native of the Gold Coast.[1] I copy it here exactly as written:

Dear unknown friend,
    You will be very surprised to receive a letter from me, whilst I do not know you or written to you before.
    Not because of anything, but I was one day having a

review of one of the war pictures, when I came across your name and address, about your war aim: your aim which charms me to write you is this: 'We must see that a sane system of government is established in Germany. Then when Europe is free from the fear of aggression we can begin to construct a United States of Europe and, eventually, a United States of the world.'

For this reason I want to be your intimacy as we all are under the British Flag. My age is just the same as your age.

Please when replying me, try to send me some of your war news and pictures, for I am thinking deeply of the war, especially on British boys and girls. I remember in the beginning of the war, I heard the British boys and girls in the radio, going to some town (? evacuees) and were singing the 'Lambeth Walk', how sad I became when they sang this song.

Reply again to tell me how things go on and believe me
Your affectionate friend,
I. Newton Adu.

The remark about the 'Lambeth Walk' puzzles me. Why was he sad?

Feb. 8th   A railway carrier came into the shop and began to talk about the war. 'I'm beginning to wonder whether it's all worthwhile, whether we didn't ought to have kept our noses out of it, that's what I'm beginning to wonder,' he said. He supposed I would soon be called up. 'Damn rotten, ain't it, taking all the best of the young men.'

The 9 o'clock news gave some information of the atrocities being committed against the Poles. 'If they're doing that to them now,' my sister said, 'whatever would they do to us?' Her fiancé: 'That's what we're fighting against.'

Feb. 11th   The news announcer reads a comparison by an American of food consumed by rationed Britain and unrationed America, in which he states that each person in England receives 2lb of meat per week.[2] My father commented, 'I don't know how we're going to get 2lb each at 1/10d. a pound.' A long pause, then my sister said, 'What will happen about meat? It s going to be awkward.' My father: 'Yes.' My sister: 'We shall have to have sausages one day a week, if we can get them.'

Feb. 12th   War talk has died down to a minimum in the last few weeks, probably because there has been nothing very interesting to talk about. Hardly anybody makes more than a casual remark about the war, often without any significance. Typical conversation: 'More enemy planes over the East coast today.' 'Oh, were there?' End of conversation. News in the papers and on the radio is almost of no interest. Except for a few things, which have now become so familiar that they no longer serve as reminders that a war is on, one might not think that there was a war on at all.

As for myself, I am beginning to feel a little disillusioned about our war aims. Indications in speeches, etc., seem to show that vindictiveness against Germany is growing. I am tired of the inactivity in almost every department of the war. I would rather there were a big flare-up and get it all over with. This long drawn-out war is bound to have a more ruinous effect on morale, economic affairs, war aims, and social conditions and a greater toll in human life and material destruction. On the other hand I think it would be worse still to make a 'patched-up' peace with the Nazis. Sooner or later we would have to fight them again.

Feb. 13th   Smith: 'Have you seen the new posters – you know, the "Careless Talk" ones?' Myself: 'No, have you?' S: 'Yes, a friend of mine s got a business in London Road. He's had two. One with Hitler hiding under a table in a restaurant and one with heads of Hitler all round a telephone kiosk.'

Spent part of the morning and most of the afternoon tying together pieces of string, which had been saved, to use in the shop, as we hear that string may be hard to get. We made two huge reels.

Feb. 16th   The manager and Smith were talking about the blacking-out business. Manager: 'I suppose we shall get used to it as the years go on.' S: 'As the *years* go on! You sound

26

hopeful.' Manager: 'I'm not very hopeful. I reckon it will be a long, long time before it's finished.'

Feb. 17th   After the 9 o'clock news we put Haw-Haw on to hear what he had got to say about the Altmark incident – we do not usually listen to him. We all laughed at his indignant remarks about our 'brutal violation of neutrality'.

Feb. 19th   Smith: 'I don't think Hitler really wanted it. He didn't think we should go in. He's making poor old Poland suffer for it now, isn't he? They are trying to wipe out the Polish nation.' We discussed the capture of the Altmark. S says Norway was in the wrong, Germany was in the wrong, and we were in the wrong, but the real fault lay with Norway for not searching the ship properly.

Feb. 25th   My father, my sister, her fiancé, and I went to visit my uncle and aunt, who live about four miles away. My uncle is head gardener at a big house, where some evacuees are billeted. My aunt told us how one of them said to her: 'What do we want with a butler, a nurse, and servants to wait on us and then have to go up to the attics to sleep?' My aunt (to us): 'To think such things go through children's minds! Surely they can't be children's words – they must have heard their parents talk about it.' Other points from the talk about evacuees: parents walk in the house without knocking when visiting their children and almost take charge of the house, bring friends without warning or invitation, make no offer to pay for damage done by children or for clothes bought for them (at one house evacuees ripped up three sheets, but parents made no offer to make good the damage. My aunt said, 'If our children did that, we should offer to make good the damage as a matter of course, shouldn't we?'). Some parents avoid buying clothes for their children, as they know that if they leave it long enough they will get them free from the authorities. There are cases of evacuees returning to billets late for meals and telling lies to cover up their misdeeds; my married cousin's method of dealing with this, my aunt told us, was to refuse to give her evacuee any food unless he came in at the proper time – this worked after one try-out. At another house two Jewish boys were billeted, and one Sunday the hosts had pork for dinner. The Jews said they could not eat it. Their host's reply was: 'You can either have a bit of pork or damn well go without.' One of the Jews: 'Would it be possible to have chicken sometimes? That's what we have at home.' Host: 'You won't get no damn chicken here.' This and other evidence shows that the evacuation is, psychologically at least, a failure: hosts resent advantage being taken of their hospitality, and there seems to be a tremendous gap between the mentalities of hosts and parents.

Almost the whole evening's conversation was about aspects of the war – prices, evacuees, rationing, profiteering, increased taxation, comparisons between this war and the last, etc. The definite note, however, cropping up again and again in the conversation, was one of dissatisfaction with the way things are being handled on the home front. Taxation, for instance. My uncle (61) says the rich are no worse off than before, as they dismiss employees and pay extra tax with the wages thus saved. My sister: 'It's always the poorer people who suffer, isn't it?' My uncle agreed. 'I don't reckon there's 5 per cent of the working class really satisfied and happy,' he said. He thought there was as much profiteering now as in the last war. He and my father recalled memories of the last war and agreed that the life of soldiers today is much easier than it was for them.

These were the main topics of conversation. There was very little mention of the war itself, none of Hitler's speech of the day before.

Feb. 28th   Went to a dance at the local parish hall. The war is having its effect on dances. There are not so many young men to patronise them now. In my experience, the women outnumber the men by about three to one, and the dances in consequence are not so enjoyable. Many of the girls have to dance with each other, instead of with men. In view of the recent bad weather it is hard to say whether there is such a big demand for dancing as in pre-war days, but, apart from the men who are serving, I should say that attendances are roughly the same.

Feb. 29th　　Smith, a conscientious objector (though rather an inconsistent one) who works with me, brought in an evening paper. 'What's the news?' I asked. S: 'Nothing much. Only the Finns' military position is serious – it'll soon be over now.' Myself: 'I reckon we ought to have given Finland as much help as we could.' S: 'Yes. It would have been worth it. Russia will be another Germany before she's finished.' He said he could not understand Sweden's attitude and would not be surprised if Russia turns on her next. I agreed.

Mar. 3rd　　My sister's friend mentions that two girls who live in the village got married yesterday. As my sister and her friend are going to a wedding next Saturday, it seems that weddings are on the increase rather than decrease. The two girls mentioned and the one to whose wedding my sister is going are all young girls, one about 17. My sister's friend also remarked on the weather: 'Isn't it lovely, though. You wouldn't think there was a war on – everything is so peaceful.'

In the afternoon I went for a walk. It was a beautiful sunny afternoon; everything was quiet. The drone of four aeroplanes alone reminded me, unpleasantly, that there was indeed a war on. On days like this one wonders how men can hate and seek to destroy each other.

Mar. 5th　　S, who works with me, my employer, and I were talking about the effect of the war on the clothing trade and about the mind of the customer. Customers do not yet realise that the war affects the retailers in that goods cannot be obtained, either so quickly or in anything like such large quantities, as they could in peacetime. Underwear, whether woollen or cotton, is especially hard to get. But when customers are told that we have none of a certain article in stock, they look at you as though you are telling them lies, as much as to say that we've got the stuff but are holding it back. If we have a little to show, they say, in a surprised tone, 'Is that all you've got?' or 'You can still get woollen things, can't you? It isn't as bad as all that?' When told that it is as bad as all that, the usual remark is something like: 'What, have we got to go about without clothes?' Of course, the trouble is that the manufacturing firms

29

have to turn out so much for Government requirements each week. If they fail to turn out the required amount, the Government threatens to take over the firm. So the firms, who do not want that to happen, do the Government work at all costs and production for civilians suffers in consequence. First comes production for the Government, then for export, then, a poor last, for home trade.

Mar. 8th   My sister and a friend of hers were talking about gas masks. Her friend, a girl of about 25 who works in a factory canteen, said, 'I take mine every day.' My sister said, 'I shall start taking mine soon. They say we shall get the air-raids in the spring.'

Mar. 9th   I saw a Fougasse poster for the first time today when I went to register. There were two, one with Hitler leaning out of a window over the heads of a sailor and an airman, the other with Hitler under a restaurant table. That was the most interesting thing that happened. For the most part, the young men waiting to be registered sat or stood not speaking much and with somewhat solemn faces. We were all registered without any fuss, except that those who were not working in the afternoon had to go and come back at the official time, according to their initials.

Mar. 12th   Was in the barber's today and saw another Fougasse poster there. I thought it was the best of the three I have seen. It showed two men talking in a railway carriage. One of them is saying '... of course, this mustn't go any further...' On the racks above one sees the lower halves of two bodies, Hitler and Goering. The way in which the identity of the listeners is conveyed without showing their faces is masterly and in the case of Goering especially amusing. However, I do not know whether it was because the poster was in an inconspicuous position or because the poster itself was not very attractive, but I did not notice it until I had been waiting for twenty minutes.

Mar. 14th   Two women behind me in the bus were having

a conversation. One mentioned that her brother had been home on leave from France. 'It s nice coming,' she said, 'but not so nice going back.' The other woman: 'I suppose by the end of the year everybody'll...' She left the sentence unfinished, but presumably she meant that all the men would be called up. 'Yes... It don't look like ending, does it?' said the first speaker. 'I wish they'd make a start and get it over,' her companion replied.

Mar. 16th   Someone brought a Fougasse poster into our shop for us to hang up. It showed two men talking in a pub. One of them is saying, 'Be careful what you say,' or some such words (none of the words seem to stick in one's brain), and there are heads of Hitler on all the bottles, etc. We all thought it was very good.

My father said he had been asked today if he wanted to give anything to the War Loan, but he had said, 'No, your job is not safe enough now for that sort of thing.'

Mar. 20th   I came down to breakfast this morning and my sister told me they had been bombing Sylt all night. 'Good Lord!' I said, 'That's the stuff to give 'em,' but do not know whether I really meant it. Today I have to go for my medical exam and as I went towards the railway station I kept being reminded of the Sylt raid. A placard said: 'Biggest raid of war. Full story.' A newspaper seller was shouting 'Bombs over Germany.' In a waiting-room at a junction a negro soldier was reading a midday paper with the headlines: 'RAF bombs Sylt for seven hours.' I saw several Fougasse posters at railway stations; I must have seen nearly all of them by now.

After some waiting about at the medical centre with a few other chaps, who did not talk much, I went in to be examined and passed Grade 1. I was never so surprised in all my life, as I did not expect to pass, having lost my first job through failure to pass the medical exam. I was not disappointed or sorry that I had passed – just flabbergasted. I had even ordered a new suit and raincoat on the strength of my certainty of not passing (I cancelled the order next day). I feel rather pleased, in fact, that I have passed, as if three doctors passed me Grade 1 there can't be much wrong with me. This is encouraging, and pleasure at the fact that I am Grade 1 overrides all other emotions.

All my friends were surprised at my passing, especially Smith, who works with me, who expected to pass but didn't.

Mar. 25th   Went to London for the day. My sister told me to take my gas mask, but I couldn't be bothered. When I got there I went first to book a seat for a show in the afternoon. Afterwards I watched a barrage balloon being moored down near the Embankment; I had previously had lunch. Then I made my way to the theatre and enjoyed C. B. Cochran's *Lights Up.* Allusions to various aspects of the war seemed to me original, amusing, and in good taste.

Getting tea was a long job, and by the time I had finished it was nearly seven and it had begun to rain. I wandered about for a while, looked in one or two amusement places, but could not see much of interest. This was the first time I had been in London since the outbreak of war, and its dreariness in the black-out struck me forcibly. Where there had been bright lights and plenty of life there was now a uniform gloom and practically nothing to do besides go to cinemas or theatres. Finally I became bored and caught the 8.45 home. The journey home was also dreary, the compartment being in semi-darkness. Why can't the trains be blacked out so that brighter lights can be used? Total darkness would be preferable to the dim blue light which is used at present.

Apr. 4th   I read about the Government reshuffle and am glad that Churchill is to have more scope. I do not approve of Hoare as Air Minister; I never had much respect for him.

Our electric light went off for about two hours in the evening. We sat and did almost nothing by the light of four or five candles. When the lights came on my father said 'I'll go and see if Mrs C knows it's on. She might not have had her switch on.' My sister said 'You can soon tell if it is on. Their black-out is never very efficient.' My father went to have a look, came back and said 'It was on. I could see.'

Apr. 8th   Talking about the British laying of mines in

Norwegian waters, my father said 'I reckon this set-out will intensify the war now.' My sister's young man: 'I shouldn't be surprised.' My father (later): 'We must be prepared to hear surprises of any sort any time now.'

Apr. 9th   Almost as soon as he arrived in the morning the manager asked me, 'Did you hear the 8 o'clock news?' 'No,' I said, 'was there anything special?' 'Germany is supposed to have invaded Denmark.' S said, 'I wonder if that's right. If they have, I'm afraid it'll mean...' Myself: 'What?' S: 'Well, the start of everything.' We had a discussion on what Germany and the Allies will do. S thought we would send troops to Norway and the fighting would start there. (We had discovered that both Norway and Denmark had been invaded by seeing a newspaper-seller's placard as he passed by the shop.) 'Poor little old Denmark!' was the manager's remark and seemed to be a fairly general sentiment. Everyone was wondering what the next move would be. Would there be a sea-battle off Denmark? S said Germany could walk through Denmark and Norway and we couldn't do much about it. Everyone eager for news. The manager went out and bought an early evening paper in the morning, a rare occurrence, and S and myself crowded round to read it. Later there was a group round the radio shop across the road when the Government statement was given out. The manager and I went to listen to the later bulletins. We were discussing the matter most of the morning. I found myself hoping that the Allies would take strong action, yet trying to resist that desire. The reason was that anything which will help to bring the end nearer is welcome; on the other hand I dislike the thought of countless numbers losing their lives and small countries being made battlegrounds.

The invasion of Norway and Denmark seems like a desperate action to break the blockade and to raise the morale of the German people. It may, in fact, be a sign of weakness. S changes his opinion almost every half-hour. Later he said this will pass over, nothing will happen, and it won't mean the start of hammer-and-tongs fighting after all. But everyone I met seemed rather bewildered. I was myself, as I had expected that if

Germany was going to attack anyone it would be Holland or Belgium, and not Norway or Denmark.

Apr. 10th   Our manager said, 'It looks as though we're too late again. Still, I suppose we shall be in front one day.' There are rumours that the *Bremen* has been sunk.

Apr. 11th   A man came in the shop, said he felt 20 years younger. He said half the German fleet had been sunk. Smith: 'Old Churchill's a hot-headed old blighter, I bet, when he gets going.' There are rumours about an air-fight in which 1000 German and 800 British (one version said 500) took part. My chief feeling was one of excitement, mixed with a kind of depression that all those lives were being lost. 'Bodies floating in the sea' was a phrase which seemed to horrify me more than any other.

Apr. 12th   Talk has died down somewhat through lack of news.

Apr. 14th   More excitement over the new battle at Narvik, but I have not heard much, as it is Sunday and I have not been out.

Apr. 16th   S, my workmate, says he reckons it will take at least four months to drive the Germans out of Norway and thinks they might attack Sweden. I say I shouldn't be surprised if they attack somewhere in the Balkans. Reasons: important Turkish official says he doesn't think Turkey will be neutral much longer; Rumania has stopped all oil exports and Germany covets Rumanian oil and wheat; pressure has been brought on Holland and Belgium by Germany, everyone is wondering whether they will attack there, but Hitler's policy is to distract attention and take by surprise. If he does attack in the Balkans, I say to S, I think Italy will join in to make sure of getting her share (and Italy's anti-British propaganda strengthens this theory). S doesn't think Italy will join in and says that Russia would not like Rumania to be attacked, as they are friends. He says Russia has guaranteed Rumania, but I disagree. I say I wonder whether Russia would like Germany to invade Sweden.

S says perhaps Russia would like Sweden herself. We both agree that Russia is a mystery.

9.20 p.m. Gracie Fields on the radio. My sister's fiancé says, 'I'm afraid "The Voice of the Nazi" (on the Home Service) won't get much attention tonight.'

Apr. 20th   I mentioned to my sister the fact that it was Hitler's birthday. She said, 'Oh, the old goose! What did he want to be born for?' She and her young man went to London today, brought back two new gas-mask cases (2/11d. each). 'What's the use of buying these?' I said. 'You never carry them.' My sister: 'I shall.' Myself' 'When?' She" 'When I think we shall have raids – in the summer.'

Apr. 21st   Conversation between me and my sister:

She: 'Did you think the Maginot Line was just a trench?'
Me: 'No.'
She: 'I did, until I saw it in *Picture Post*. It's like a big house, or a big hotel. It goes five storeys underground.'
Me: 'It's not just a single line, though. It's wide as well as long.'
She: 'I thought it was just a trench they sat in. So did Mrs S.'

Apr. 22nd   In the street I saw a woman trying to get a small parcel into her gas-mask case (one of the zip-fastener type), which presumably did not contain her mask. 'It won't go in,' she said to her friend. 'It takes such a lot of things sometimes.'

I went out to buy a paper. I told Smith there had been another RAF raid on Stavanger. He said the first raids could not have been very successful or it would have been completely destroyed. Then I said the Navy had shelled Narvik (according to a German communiqué). S was under the impression that Narvik had been captured by us; so was I. If so, why shell it? We both agreed that Germans have probably still got Narvik. S said we can tell as big lies as the Germans.

Apr. 23rd   Spoke to a young man about to register. I asked him if he had any preference. He replied, joking, 'I'd like to be a spy and get sent to Berchtesgaden and be Hitler's personal bodyguard. If he wasn't dead in a week it wouldn't be my fault.' Actually, he has no particular preference, but wants to be where there's action. While we were talking a man came out and said that a British troopship had been sunk. I told S, who said, 'That's pretty rotten, isn't it?' but only casually. Later I learnt that the report was not true. 'What do you think of the Budget?' 'Well, I expected something like that.' 'Yes, I suppose we've got to pay for it somehow.'

Apr. 30th   Our manager, speaking to me about the war: 'How long has this war been going on now?' Myself: 'Eight months.' He: 'Eight months come Sunday.' Me: 'It seems a long while, doesn't it?' He: 'It does. It would be nice to hear it was over.' Me: 'It won't be over yet awhile, I know that.' He: 'I don't see how it can.'

May 1st   Our manager says there were 100 killed and injured when the German plane came down. Right in the centre of Clacton, he says. (This was early in the morning.) He goes out to get a paper, but can't get one. He comes back and says he has been talking to a man who has seen a paper and he says the plane came down near Clacton station. It was full of mines and damaged two rows of houses and 100 were actually killed, according to him. In the afternoon Mrs S and her daughter both tell me it was mostly children who were hurt. Mrs S remarks that in yesterday's paper it had an advertisement saying: 'Come to Clacton for holidays. It is safe here: no air-raids, evacuees sent here.' My aunt tells me that someone told her it was a little place outside Clacton where the plane crashed.

May 2nd   My sister says she thinks the German plane crashed in Clacton on purpose. They knew they had got to come down, so thought they would do some damage in the process. They could have landed in the sea.

The effect of Chamberlain's speech is negative, disappointing, however much I try to look on the bright side. (When my sister told me about the evacuation of southern Norway yesterday, I did not believe her.) Chamberlain seemed all the time to be trying to make excuses for weak policy. It's a loss of prestige for us, says my father.

May 7th   Some comments by S, who works with me: 'I reckon old Chamberlain will get the push soon.' 'The Government are all old.' 'We're losing the war so far.'

There again seems to be a shortage of war talk and reactions.

May 8th   Noticed a large poster, in white letters on a red ground, similar to the Govt. posters about 'Your Courage...' etc.: 'Your courage and cheerfulness will be strengthened by a knowledge of Spiritualism.'

May 10th   This morning, first thing, my sister came in my bedroom and said, 'They're in Holland,' which told me all I needed to know. A little later the postman brought my calling-up papers. I arrived at work a little before S, who had not heard the news and appeared surprised when I told him. 'The old devils,' he said. 'They do what they like, don't they?' And another (age about 36): 'It's this terrific air power that worries me. It seems to terrify everyone.' S saw a newspaper headline: 'Britain sending all help we can', and quipped, 'All help we can't.' Curiously, the wording of the phrase had conveyed exactly the same sense to me as soon as I saw it. Our manager came back from lunch carrying his gas mask. S and I thought the cancelling of the Bank Holiday ridiculous. Just because Germany has marched into another small country is no reason to get the wind up. In my view, this disappointment will be a setback to morale.

S remarked that the placards said: 'Bombs on Kent'. Our manager said, 'I'll be glad to hear "Bombs on Berlin". That's what they want – a taste of what they've been giving everybody else.' By evening there is a noticeable increase in gas mask carrying, but there is still a majority who do not.

I thought Chamberlain's speech a good one. My opinion of him is that he is a brave man, a good man, even a great man, but unimaginative, weak, and inefficient. I think that Churchill is the best choice as successor.

May 11th   The manager of our shop said to a customer,

'Everyone's more cheerful today than they were yesterday. Have you noticed it?' Early in the evening numbers of mechanised troops went through the town. Many people all along the street stood and watched.

May 12th   Went down to Clacton to see some relations and to say goodbye before I join my unit. Of course, I went to see the damage done by the German plane. The main area was roped off, but I could see that damage was considerable. What I find hard to believe is that men sat and had their lunch on one of the unexploded mines, not knowing what it was. One of my cousins gave me a piece of the aeroplane as a souvenir, of which he had several. The general feeling seemed to be optimistic, not so much from the change of Government, but because we can now get to grips with the enemy. I heard two or three opinions that the war would not last much longer. 'This country's not dead yet,' as my cousin's husband said, but he also said he did not sleep so well now.

May 13th   What has happened to Norway? The complete lack of news seems ominous.

July 28th   My first entry since I was called up on May 16th.[3]

I came here (the RAMC depot at Crookham) rather looking forward to some new experiences in a strange life, and I came with an open mind, not knowing whether I should like or dislike it. At first I liked it, and wrote home to say so. I found the food, living conditions, provision for entertainment, etc., beyond my expectations and the routine by no means hard. This opinion seemed fairly general too, during the first two or three weeks, among the others who had arrived at the same time as myself. It was all so new and different from what we had been used to that many of us came to the conclusion that the new life was better than the old. But after a while opinions began to change. It seemed as though the authorities deliberately made it pleasant for us during the first weeks. Then we began to encounter many instances of red tape, official pettiness which seemed, and still does seem, ridiculous, little rules and regulations which went under the name of 'discipline', but which did not make sense. Nothing, in my view at least, seemed to be done sensibly or smoothly, but unmethodically and with an unnecessary waste of time. Some did not like the work, which, of course, is non-combatant, and wished they could have a gun in their hands. Saving life did not seem so exciting as destroying it, though that was not my own feeling. Besides that we found that there were extra duties which sometimes meant working all day Saturday and Sunday. This caused resentment. Leave had been cancelled from the first, but no-one seemed to mind this at first. After several weeks, however, without leave, most of us began to feel homesick and, by some process of wishful-thinking, all kinds of rumours about leave being resumed began to spread around.

Yet there are hardly any complaints about the food or material things and only in a few cases about the training itself. It is the taking away of liberty and individuality, the rules without reason, and the boredom which so fester as to override all consideration of material (including financial) well-being. I know that most of us would be glad to lead a much rougher life for the sake of a little more freedom and self-respect. I should say, however, that nearly everyone realises that he must make the best of things as they are and that grumbling will only make things worse. But underneath, the truth is as I have stated it.

The surrender of France was a complete and bewildering surprise. Up to the time of the actual surrender nobody thought it possible. 'France will never give in,' was the general opinion, and when the armistice terms became known no-one thought that France would so humiliate herself to sign them. Even when the papers printed it in black and white it was hard to believe; many thought that further details would be revealed which would show that France had not really given in after all.

A point of interest is the attitude to conscientious objectors, of which there are several here. As far as I have observed, the majority seem to think that there ought not to be any. One of the men said to me last week that he thought all conscientious objectors ought to be stood against a wall and shot, and asked me whether I didn't think so too. I said I didn't, as I didn't think that that would alter their consciences. He differentiated, however, between those who agreed to do non-combatant work and those who refused to do any form of military service, and thought that the latter were in the majority and that hardly any of them were sincere, on both of which points I disagreed.

There have been a few air-raid warnings, which have seen received calmly for the most part. We have to go to surface shelters, and when inside the men either try to go to sleep or joke together. Once, when five small bombs fell near, there were arguments as to whether they were bombs or anti-aircraft fire.

Another point of interest, which perhaps might be gone into more deeply, is the frequent jokes and remarks about homosexuality. One often hears a man call another 'darling', 'sweetheart', 'my precious', or some other term of endearment which a man might employ towards a woman and which, although used in fun, I never came across in civilian life. Perhaps this is to be expected when men are separated from their womenfolk.

July 31st   Overheard conversation between a corporal and a private:
Corporal: 'He said, "The only difference between Germany and England is that England has a King and a Government while Germany has a dictator and the Nazi Party." I said, "That's all the difference in the world. The difference between a king and a democratic government and a dictator and the Nazi Party is the difference between a shilling and a thousand million billion pounds. We vote for our Government. We vote for a Conservative Government because we think it'll be good for the country. If they don't do the country any good, we chuck 'em out and put some other party in power."' Then they got talking about jobs and the private said that he was getting £4 a week before he was called up. Corporal: 'You're fighting for that four pound a week. If we don't win, when the war is over, you won't be able to go back to that four pound a week. In Germany you'd get about four marks.'

Aug. 2nd   I read in the paper about the debate on the 'doorstep quiz'. The motives of those for and against are not

40

clear. One does not know whether the supporters of the Press want to prevent the people expressing their opinions or whether they want to prevent the Govt. using their opinions against them or whether they think it is unnecessary spying into people's private affairs; and one does not know whether Duff Cooper and Co. really want to know public opinion in order to assess morale, or whether they want to use their knowledge in Gestapo fashion, or whether they have some other ulterior motive. On the one hand the Press seems to be frightened that it may lose its influence, that its own opinion may be ignored; on the other hand Duff Cooper seems to be sincere, but why does he not make public the information gained?

I noticed an evening paper on the counter of a shop, with a big headline saying that German planes had dropped leaflets. I also noticed that they were being sold to aid the Red Cross, which, apart from other things, struck me as sheer impudence.

Aug. 3rd   One soldier this morning remarked that leaflets had been dropped over Southern England, but I spoke to another at dinnertime and he had heard nothing about it.

Aug. 5th   I had not heard or observed any more about the leaflets since Saturday morning, but this evening the same soldier mentioned above said that more leaflets had dropped in SW England, but that most of them had fallen on a sewage farm! Then another said that he had met someone who said that some had fallen in Portsmouth. I then spoke to a soldier, who was formerly a teacher in a country town, who said he would like to read one of the leaflets, as the German idea of English grammar was sometimes very amusing, to go by German seed catalogues he had seen. I asked him if he had heard anything about leaflets being dropped near here, but he had not. He asked me if I wanted to get hold of some. 'Yes,' I said, 'one would be enough.' 'Subversive literature,' he said. 'No,' I said, 'I'd just like to see one. Still, you wouldn't be able to read them in Germany.' 'You won't be allowed to here,' he said (incidentally he is a conscientious objector), 'I expect they will be collected and burnt.' I told him that some people had been selling them in aid of the Red Cross and that extracts had been printed in the

41

papers, and he seemed surprised. So far, I have not been able to discover much about the leaflets. Where they fell seems obscure, but it was not near here.

The chief concern of soldiers about here seems to be whether they will get cheaper cigarettes and tobacco.

Aug. 8th   There has been much excitement here for the last few days, as posting orders come through. Those who have been posted were glad to go, although this was in some cases lessened by the fact that they were going farther away from home. Some of them went out to the local pubs, and when they got back amused themselves by turning over several beds in the barrack room. Most of them were exchanging addresses, so that they could keep in touch with their special friends. Several of them said they did not like losing friends they had only made a short time before. Those of us who are left behind feel nervy at hanging about in more than half-empty barrack-rooms.

Talk about the war has been at a low ebb. I have noticed that when you are actually taking part in the war it is much more difficult to look at it with the detachment of a spectator, and you cannot talk about it in the same way. I myself do not take so much interest in the war news as I did before I was called up. You are always thinking about what is going to happen to *you*, about your home, whether you are going to get any leave, etc.

Aug. 9th   More have received their posting orders, but I have still not received mine, as I have been recommended for special training (as laboratory assistant) and expect to be the last to go, perhaps not for some time. I am very fed-up and disappointed at the thought of lingering on here without any leave. I am in that state when I feel irritable with everybody and everything and thoroughly sick of life.

The soldier who was a schoolteacher said that he thought our propaganda was ten times as good as German propaganda, but yesterday he remarked, 'Germany must have a marvellous spy system in this country. Look at the things Haw-Haw says on the wireless – it's nearly all gospel truth.' It seems probable that the intelligent are duped as easily as the non-intelligent, but not by the same methods, the intelligent being more inclined to believe intellectual arguments against his own country, the non-intelligent more inclined to believe rumours, threats, and exaggerations, in part, if not whole. The only alternative is that Haw-Haw is really speaking the truth.

The rise in pay for the troops, as was to be expected, has met with general approval.

Aug. 14th   About 20 of us have been posted to another company in the same camp. Here the rules are stricter and the NCOs less friendly, and this, together with the fact that we are instructed with other men who have not reached the same standard of training and the anxiety of not knowing what our future will be, increases resentment, boredom, and depression in most of us. And still there is no leave. How I begin to hate the Army!

Aug. 15th   Two of the men in our room were talking about what they would do after the war. Both were decided that they would not stay in the Army.

'Then I suppose we shall all be out of work.'

'I don't care. I shall go on the dole.'

'Yes, we shall be able to say we fought in the Great War.'

'The *Second* Great War.'

'Supposing you're still alive,' I said.

'Oh, we've got a cheerful bloke here.'

'Well, you don't know,' I said.

'They can't kill a good soldier.'

'Both good and bad soldiers get killed,' I said.

One of the others made some remark about not being in the actual fighting and concluded, 'I'm not going to do anything brave or daring. I'm going to save my skin.'

Aug. 16th   12.45 p.m. The air-raid siren went just as we were about to start dinner. We filed out of the dining-hall table by table. Few bothered to run to the shelters until told to do so. There were no incidents, and once in the shelter the men talked or dozed. Our chief reaction was annoyance at being interrupted just at mealtime. (We had already had a warning at breakfast-time on Tuesday.) The 'All clear' went about 1.45 p.m.

5.10 p.m. Just at teatime the siren sounded again. Went down to the shelter, read *Picture Post*, and smoked. Some crowded the entrances – against the rules of safety – to see what was going on outside. Nearly everyone was talking, but when aeroplanes or some other noise was heard, there were shouts of 'Quiet!' and 'Listen!' There would be a brief silence, then a renewed outburst of talking, so the others had to shout 'Quiet!' louder; consequently no-one could hear anything. Several planes went over and someone would say, 'That's a Spitfire,' or 'That's a bomber,' or 'That's a Jerry.' We heard some muffled explosions, then after a time the 'All clear' went at about 6.25 p.m. I was very hungry and had two helpings of tea.

Aug. 17th   I had to wear my gas mask (civilian) for about an hour in a practice. I felt almost suffocated and can imagine some people taking their gas masks off through sheer discomfort even in a gas attack.[4]

Aug. 18th   Another warning just after dinner. I was glad that the Germans had been considerate enough to let me finish my dinner. Walked to the shelter, taking a book with me to read. The alarm was completely uneventful, and we came out of the shelters in just under an hour. I strolled back (it is much too hot to run to or from shelter) and wrote this.

Aug. 23rd   Show at the Garrison Theatre, in which all the artists were feminine. The most popular turns were a conjurer and an accordionist. The best known and most loudly sung song was 'Roll Out The Barrel', which wherever there is a soldiers' sing-song seems to be the most popular and to date may claim to be the song of the war.

Aug. 24th   The siren sounded while I was in the cinema, about 4.30 p.m. Several got up and went out; one man, probably a warden, ran out. The rest remained and the film went on. There was no further incident during the period of warning.

Aug. 26th   Warning about 1.30 a.m. I put my uniform on

over my pyjamas and went to the shelter. A few minutes later the 'All clear' sounded. 'They only gave the warning so they could sound the "All clear",' said my friend when we got back. 'What do they want to sound the "All clear" for?' I asked. 'So that the people where bombs have been falling know when it's all over and they can go back to bed.' We had, in fact, heard bombs falling earlier in the evening.

Two more warnings later in the day – one just before dinner which did not last very long, another just before tea which lasted just over an hour. Neither warning was marked by any special incident, but the frequency of warnings just at meal-times and at other awkward times is becoming annoying.

Yet another warning just before ten, when I was coming back from a dance. I hurried to my room and found that most of the others had gone to the shelter, but some had been told to go back to their rooms, so I stayed in my room with three or four others. We stayed there until a bomb exploded rather near, then we went to the shelter. I stood at the entrance and watched the many search-lights. A group inside the shelter told dirty stories by the dozen. About midnight we were told to go back to our beds, which we thankfully did, although the 'All clear' had not gone. It did not go until 4 a.m., but I did not hear it, being asleep. We were all late getting up in the morning.

Aug. 27th   Moved to a hospital to start a course of training as laboratory assistant. Things promise to be easier here: parade at 8.30 instead of 8, no drill, less so-called 'discipline', allowed out until midnight unless on duty, possibility of leave, etc., are welcome improvements. Food, however, not so good. Being on the outskirts of the town will make it more convenient for amusement.

Aug. 28th   Have had two letters this week from relations saying how good it will be when the war is over and everybody can go back to their homes and people.

Sept. 3rd   There has been a strange dearth of material the last few days and today, the first anniversary of the outbreak of war, is not marked by any interesting event. In the evening I went to the cinema and saw *Let George Do It*, which was somewhat topical. George Formby's fight with Hitler produced a mixture of laughs, cheers, and boos. There was also a Gaumont-British review of the war and, in this, shots of RAF men were easily the most loudly applauded, while the glimpse of Churchill did not give much chance for response. The evacuation of Dunkirk was fairly well applauded.

Sept. 4th   The transfer of 50 US destroyers has caused some interest, and opinion seems to be that we have got the better of the bargain, because, besides our getting the destroyers, America will be giving some measure of protection to our own territory, as well as to hers.

Sept. 5th   Opinion overheard while waiting in the basement during an air-raid warning: 'The more raids he makes against this country, the more the people will be incensed against him, and won't rest until he *is* bumped off. I know this much – this country will never give in until we've smashed them or they've smashed us. Personally, I can't see them smashing us.' The speaker was a young soldier, aged about 20.

Sept. 7th   About 4.45 p.m. the air-raid siren sounded. In the market, where I was, the people gradually deserted the stalls and the stall-holders closed down business, although at one stall some of the people asked the seller to carry on. I walked along to a shelter. A good many, mostly soldiers, were sheltering in shop entrances and similar places The shelter was near a small park, in which all the seats were empty, but a lot of people were standing round the edge. I decided to go in the shelter. Some who were lingering on the steps were told by an air-raid warden to go right inside. The shelter was almost full and there were many more women than men. Light was provided by three or four hurricane lamps hanging up. Nobody spoke much and when they did it was usually to complain about the heat, or the light, or the lack of air, or the length of the air-raid. 'I'd rather see what's going on outside,' said a girl sitting opposite me. Once it was said that the 'All clear' had gone and everyone started going out, only to find that it was a false alarm and we all went back again. After a while I went to have a look outside. Several soldiers had gone back to the park seats, and there was still a good crowd standing on the pavement looking at any aeroplane that might go over. I went back into the shelter. Three women were having a discussion. 'We've got faith in our leaders,' one of them said, 'that's why we go into the shelters. We've got faith in our leaders and in our Army, Navy, and Air Force. I don't like people who talk defeatism. The others appeared to be in agreement. Just before the 'All clear' went some more people came in. 'We've all got to come inside,' said one. 'It's serious.' Not long afterwards, at about 6.30 p.m., the 'All clear' was heard.

In the evening I went to a dance in the town hall of a nearby town. There was a big crowd there, and I saw some jitterbug dancing for the first time. A notice said: 'Jitterbug dancing only allowed when announced.' During the interval four girls came round with collecting-boxes for the 'Spitfire' fund. One cannot go to many places now without seeing these collectors.

Sept. 8th   Several rumours floating round the hospital this morning – rumours that the church bells had been ringing in the night and that there had been an attempted invasion, that all leave was stopped, that a great fire had been visible in the night (this probably true), that there had been big movements of troops. None of the patients had actually heard the church bells, but one of the orderlies had. He also said that a general alarm had been given all over the country. (Where he obtained his information I do not know.) 'I said things would break before winter, didn't I?' he said to one of the patients. 'And you know what some of the officers think – if they get cracking now the war will be over in six months, one way or the other.'

The general atmosphere is one of excitement.

During the day an official notice was put up, saying that we are confined to barracks until further notice. Later in the day this was altered so that those not on duty may leave barracks, but all leave is suspended.

Sept. 9th   If they try to invade us, it'll be another Dardanelles, only ten times worse,' a soldier said to me today.

Sept. 10th   The *Daily Sketch* today says, 'Six hundred enemy aircraft came and made heroes of our Londoners ... on Saturday.' How the fact of being bombed makes anyone a hero I fail to understand. The nonsensical emotionalism which some papers are printing now is annoying and disturbing. The emphasis on the fact that our Air Force is confining itself to military objectives and at the same time doing more serious damage seems to be good propaganda, and the fact itself good policy.

Sept. 11th   Listened to Churchill's speech and, as usual, found his determination and his mastery of words not a little inspiring. The 'All clear' went just before he finished, but those of us who were listening waited until the end of his speech before going off duty.

Sept. 13th   Was in a dance-hall when the siren wailed at 9. The hall was crowded and several went out, either to the shelters or home. The MC said that dancing would continue, but the hall authorities said that dancing could not go on. Someone was sent to a higher authority to get a ruling. During the interval some Canadians got on the platform and sang. After a few minutes permission was obtained to continue the dancing. The hall still seemed as crowded as it was before. Two loud bangs were heard, possibly bombs, causing some mild alarm, but not enough to stop the dancing, which then went on uninterrupted. When the MC announced that the dance would have to finish at 11 o'clock there were cries of disappointment. As I walked back I could see the anti-aircraft artillery barrage round London, like big sparks in the sky, and felt somehow reassured.

Sept. 14th   This morning a corporal said that it was a fact that the Germans tried to invade England last Sunday. Later today a private told me that he had heard that there had been several attempted invasions.

Sept. 18th   Was again told that there had been two attempted invasions and that not a single German escaped alive, owing to electrified wire defences, but that we had also suffered 5,000 casualties. One of my companions doubted this, as I did also, as he thought that the authorities would have boasted about it. This started a discussion on the authenticity of news given out by the English and by the Germans, propaganda, and the relationship between the Press and public opinion. It was agreed that the news we were given was probably not always true, but that we were allowed more of the truth than the Germans were and than the French had been. I and one of the others, however, thought that the Press did not represent public opinion, but only the opinion of those behind the Press, falsely represented as being the people's opinion, and that the majority were easily tricked and led, while the other two thought that the Press, having to deal with people, could not help expressing their opinion, that the public were not really fools and if they were it wasn't their fault. One said that the Government had to listen to public opinion quite often, and gave the demand for deep shelters as an example. I said that the demand for deep shelters was not an expression of opinion, but an obvious necessity. I said that as a rule the public did not know what it wanted and was content to let the leaders do all the thinking. One of the others agreed, but the other two did not, and one said that even in Germany the Nazis had had to take notice of public opinion. I said that the Nazis had used their propaganda to make the people think what they were wanted to think. We agreed that Nazi propaganda was better than ours – the British leaflets were threats, not appeals.

In the evening I visited the cinema. A film showing an attack on a British lightship was shown. There was much laughing and cheering when one of the lightship men called the Nazi airmen 'You dirty bastards!' and more laughs when one of the men twice used a swear word.

Sept. 19th   Heard two of our unit talking about the war, saying that we had definitely got the upper hand and that the war in Africa would be the decisive factor. One of them was already thinking of a ten-year army of occupation.

At dinnertime one of my companions started grumbling because the Post Office (and other Government departments) left off work during air-raids while factories carried on, and began an argument on whether work should go on during air-raids. The complaint about long-delayed letters is pretty general, however.

The wife of a friend of mine came down from London this evening, and he asked her what her impression was of what the people of London were thinking about the air-raids. She said they didn't think it could go on much longer; this wasn't war, it was just horrid. She said that Battersea had been almost blown to pieces and that land-mines had been dropped by parachute. Disturbing news.

Sept. 22nd   Went to a concert given by Polish artists for the local Spitfire fund. The artists were a pianist, a violinist, three accordionists, and a ballet dancer. They gave a very good programme of Polish and English music and songs, with two ballet dances, which was very well applauded in spite of the fact that most of the Polish music was unfamiliar. During the interval over £50 was collected for the fund, partly by auctioneering and re-auctioneering several times a few pieces of a German bomber, partly by plain begging.

Sept. 23rd   A good deal of talk today about the sinking of the liner carrying children to Canada. Suggestions as to what ought to be done were varied, including these: send 2,000 bombers over Germany and 'bomb it to hell'; shoot 85 German prisoners; float a shipful of German prisoners about the Atlantic for five weeks, or sink it. The Germans have been called 'pirates' and 'bastards'.

Sept. 24th   One man of this unit said that he wished the Germans would attempt to invade, as if they did and failed, he thought the war would be over. But if they waited until next year there would be a winter campaign in Africa and the war would be prolonged. The idea of the invasion *succeeding* did not seem to occur to him!

Sept. 25th   The same soldier said that the situation at Dakar was an interesting development, as it was the first real offensive the British had made, and that it looked as if de Gaulle had 'turned yellow' on us by withdrawing. There was a good deal of discussion among several of us about what was actually happening at Dakar and who was fighting, but no-one was very clear about it. I said that I shouldn't have much faith in the British Army if they do not soon have some success.

Sept. 26th   Several have expressed disappointment at the British failure to take Dakar. The list of withdrawals is growing long: Norway, Belgium, France, Somaliland, Dakar, and even in Egypt there has been some withdrawal. It is felt that the statement that we did not want to fight the French is an excuse, and a feeble one, to cover up weakness and incompetence. In any case, why was the expedition sent at all?

Oct. 3rd   Satisfaction that Chamberlain is going seems to be pretty general. He was distrusted by many. I have heard two people in the last two days, when discussing the likelihood of this country giving in like France, suggest Chamberlain as the man who might be the one to start negotiations. The inclusion of Anderson and Wood in the Cabinet, however, almost cancels out the pleasure at Chamberlain's departure.

Oct. 4th   Comment on the Hitler-Mussolini meeting: 'Why the hell don't they bomb them?'

Oct. 7th   A friend of mine in this unit, who is a Communist, said he thought the German move into Rumania was a move against Russia. I thought it was chiefly to get hold of Rumanian oil, but there might be other motives.

Oct. 10th   A soldier (age about 50) returned from leave in London and brought back violent anti-German views. He said that even when the war is over, wherever he is, if he should meet a German he would want to murder him. He would hear of no comparison between what RAF bombers are doing and what German bombers are doing. 'There is no comparison between a civilised people and an uncivilised people,' he said. 'All Germans are pigs; all Germans are brutes. They only understand the mailed fist.' He advocated random bombing of Germany. 'We shouldn't be so sympathetic and lenient. Then there wouldn't be any war.' He told an atrocity story of how a little girl was killed and her head and two parts of her body found in different places.

Oct. 15th   A visit to one of the two theatres in this town tonight proved that the unclothed female form is the biggest attraction in the way of entertainment that can be offered to the troops. In the 1/- seats, which I always patronise, there are usually some empty ones, but tonight there were several people standing. The main attraction was 'The Confessions of a Fan Dancer' (billed as 'The Girl the Lord Chamberlain Banned').* The act consisted of two recitations, one of them a satirical commentary on her own profession, followed by four nude poses and a dance in some occasionally revealing drapery. To me it all seemed in good taste – there was nothing objectionable about the poses; the jokes, though suggestive, were witty rather than broad; and she did really seem to be making fun both of the audience and of herself. She showed a good understanding of the psychology of the audience (which, not surprisingly, was nearly all men) as, for instance, she realised that some of us had stopped to see it twice, by saying the second time, 'I will now introduce myself – in case there is anyone who wasn't here at the first performance.'

Oct. 16th   I asked one of my Communist friends whether he thought that Russia would fight against Germany. 'No,' he said, 'not yet, anyway.'

Oct. 23rd   Overheard opinion on whether France would fight against us: 'She's in a position where she can't very well do anything else. Of course, what they're doing it for is to get the French fleet. It's been somewhat reduced, but combined with the German and Italian fleets would be very effective.'

Nazi diplomacy moves at tremendous speed and we are left miles behind. As one soldier said the other day, 'Isn't our

*This was Phyllis Dixey.

Government slow!' If France is persuaded to fight us it will surely be the biggest double-cross in history.

Oct. 28th   The announcement that the *Empress of Britain* had been sunk brought forth some criticism of the Government news service. 'Why couldn't they tell us before? The German radio gave it out three or four days ago. Why can't they tell us the truth?' One man said it might have helped the enemy to give the news before the survivors had been landed, as it might have endangered their lives. Two others criticised the Government's frequent statements that air-raids have caused little damage and few casualties. 'It is surprising – the number of people that have been killed,' said one.

Oct. 29th   Rumours this morning that British troops had occupied Crete.

Oct. 30th   A young soldier declared, 'If we lose in Greece nobody will believe in us. If we can't save Greece we can't save anyone. If we don't mean to fight in Greece we shan't fight anywhere... We've got to stop this retreat, retreat, retreat business. We've got to fight somewhere.'

Nov. 8th   Roosevelt's re-election seems to have been taken for granted, and as nothing much happens in Greece there is not much comment about that either.

The popularity of striptease is proved by a return visit this week of the same artiste I mentioned before. Tonight the theatre was more crowded than previously, people standing at the back and at the sides all through. The show was entirely altered, and I thought it more daring and sexier too. The striptease act appealed to me because there was as much emphasis on the tease as on the strip. The performer's digs at the audience were amusing because true.

Nov. 9th   Soldier's comment on Chamberlain's illness: 'That's it, you old b—, die.' Another soldier: 'Why, is he ill?' Reply: 'I hope so.'

Nov. 11th   In a letter from home my sister says: 'Aren't you glad Roosevelt got in? We all are, for we do know how he feels about things and I'm sure he will help us all he can.'

Observed the two minutes silence, but only thought how futile the last war was and how futile this one is. Reluctantly bought a poppy.

Of four papers read today, only the *News Chronicle* seemed to be sincere in its comments on Chamberlain. The *Daily Mail* and *Daily Sketch* seemed to be making desperate efforts to white-wash Chamberlain. The *Daily Mirror* printed its usual mush (how the paper sells I can't understand), and one soldier, himself anti-Chamberlain, deplored it for attacking him while alive and making 'oily platitudes' about him when dead.

Nov. 14th   I have heard a good many members of this unit say that they wished the war would end, whether we win or lose, or that they would be glad to get out of the Army. If there were only one or two of this opinion I would not take much notice, but almost every day I hear some variation of the same idea, the common reason being that most of us are fed-up with the whole business.

The Government is criticised for its lack of aggressiveness, and the attack on Taranto came as a welcome bit of excitement. Concentrate on Italy – in Greece, in Egypt, in the Mediterranean, with air attack – seems to be a widely-held view.

Nov. 16th   Overheard at breakfast: 'I hear Churchill is talking about a campaign in 1944.' 'Of course, I think most of that is propaganda.' I had been thinking the same thing myself for some time – and very clever propaganda too.

I notice that nothing is said in the papers about the damage which must have been done to factories and other military objectives in Coventry.

Nov. 21st   A soldier who is fond of airing his opinions said that this country still lacks imaginative leadership. Although the help given to Greece was an improvement on Norway, the Government should have had plans ready supposing Greece were to be invaded, whereas it seemed that they did not start making plans until after the invasion. Also, he thought that instead of being driven out of Somaliland we should have driven the Italians out of Abyssinia, Eritrea, and Italian Somaliland. If the plea was that our forces were inferior, why were they inferior, when we are supposed to have a big army in the Near East and we have all our Dominion troops to call on?

Sir Neville Henderson's astonishing statement that before September 1938 we had no Spitfires and few anti-aircraft guns is considered by two of my friends to be a lie, invented as an excuse for the 'deliberately planned Munich scare'. My opinion is that whether it is true or not it is no excuse for the Munich policy, but only a further condemnation

Nov. 22nd   The best news I have heard today is that I am going on leave next week. After six months of army life without a break, the thought of going home and not having to do anything I don't want to is a tremendous relief. For the last few months my idea has been, whenever possible, to escape from it all. I have spent more money at the cinema, theatres, and dances than I have ever spent in an equal period in civilian life. This escape is, of course, only temporary, and I would not wish it to be permanent. The facts, ugly as they are, of the present situation must be faced if they are to be abolished. I still read as much as I can – am now reading Sir Richard Acland's *Unser Kampf* and so far am almost completely in agreement with him. I still spend about the same amount on tobacco, allowing for the rise in prices. Yet I also manage to save more, since I have food and clothes provided, do less travelling, have things sent me which I might have bought myself in civilian life, entertainment is fairly cheap, and I do not indulge in so many little luxuries. Now that I shall get 1/- a day extra, having qualified as a laboratory assistant, I shall probably save still more.

Nov. 27th   Randolph Churchill's maiden speech in the House of Commons attracted my attention today. In my opinion it was a stupid speech and the papers made an unnecessary fuss over it. What does he, as an officer, know about what the men talk about in the barrack-rooms? It is true that the main aim of many of them is simply to defeat Hitler, but there are just as many who think that this war will be worth fighting only if there is a new order of things to follow. Merely to fight to salvage all that was good in the old world, which wasn't much, is a restricted outlook, showing a poor imagination of what is necessary to make the world a better place. I have detected signs of suspicion (on the part of ordinary people) that we may not be fighting for all that we are supposed to be, of fears that the peace may be much more difficult to win than the war, of hopes that we may never go back to the pre-war state of affairs.

I arrived home on leave in the afternoon. I found it more or less unaltered, except that the black-out has been improved and my father and sister now sleep downstairs. My sister says she has not been to a cinema or other entertainment all the time I have been away. My father comes home late from work, and by the time he has had his evening meal and everything has been cleared away there is not time to do very much. Saturday night's radio programme seems to be the main entertainment of the week. The radio is not listened to so much at home, however, because reception is often poor in the evenings. As regards air-raids, the noise of enemy aeroplanes droning about seems to disturb some people more than the actual bombs, which have not done extensive damage in this area.

Nov. 28th   Visited an uncle and aunt this afternoon. Talk was mostly about air-raids (this subject seems to crop up in nearly all conversations) and food. My sister remarks that some things are hard to get now: 'One day you have to run about all over the place for cheese, the next day it's something else.' 'People are beginning to notice it now' said my uncle. 'Before, they had a little to fall back on, now they haven't got it.' Cheese, soap-flakes, lard, biscuits, chocolate, are all in short supply.

I went to a dance in the evening. There was a good crowd, plenty of soldiers. A special late bus to town encouraged people to stay late. Nearly all were strangers to me, but by good luck I met a friend who was on leave also, whom I had not seen for a long while. I went and had my first drink for months with him. He said he would be glad when it (the war) was all over. We talked about air-raids, food, and girls.

Dec. 1st   Just before 11 o'clock tonight we heard a whistling noise. I did not realise what it was, but my father said 'Look out!' and dived under the table. I followed suit, just as a bomb exploded not far away. My sister came running downstairs and got under the table too, where we stayed for a little while. I could not help seeing the absurdity of the situation. My sister said, 'I was going back upstairs to sleep, but I shan't now.' She is almost afraid to go upstairs when there is a warning on. I still sleep upstairs.

Dec. 3rd   My leave goes much too quickly. Tomorrow I shall have to go back. I wish that I had never got to return.

Everyone says it won't be much of a Christmas this year, that nobody will keep it as usual. My father says he is going to have a chicken for Christmas dinner.

A walk round the village shows little sign of change. I noticed surface shelters in the school playgrounds, a huge heap of scrap metal on a piece of waste ground. The bomb the other night caused considerable damage but no deaths. One woman, whose house was damaged, thought the miraculous escapes 'an act of God'.

We were talking about the war and my sister asked, 'Can we stick all this bombing?' and with reference to the shipping losses, 'Can we hold out?' This is the first time I have heard doubt expressed about our ability to win. Nobody, of course, could give definite answers to the questions, except that if we can destroy the Italian fleet we can spare more ships to attack the U-boats.

Dec. 8th   In an overheard conversation amongst four or five men of my unit the following conclusions were more or less unanimously reached: That Chamberlain would have surrendered after the first big raid on London; that Churchill has saved this country from defeat; that Russia would be the only one to benefit from this war; that Hitler was mad, but a genius, and the chief victories of the war had been Hitler's diplomatic victories; that all Germans should be exterminated (shoot them, sterilise them, etc., also make them work for us as slaves).

Dec. 9th   This slogan, burnt on a piece of wood, was seen in a restaurant: 'Act victory, think victory, talk victory. Otherwise b— well shut up.'

Dec. 12th   Received a letter from my sister, saying that she is going to be married: 'We had been thinking about it since last summer – when we postponed the plans we had made between us because of the war – but as it seems the war is going on for years we are not going to wait.'

Marriages seem to be on the increase now. Several of my friends and acquaintances have been married recently, as well as my brother. Another couple are going to be married as soon as they can find a house, which is a big problem for newly-weds nowadays.

First sign of Christmas in the hospital – patients making paper-chains.

Dec. 14th   Drunk soldier in a fish and chip café: 'Let's hope when this war's over, it'll be the last one. Let's hope there'll be no more fighting.'

Dec. 18th   All the wards now are showing Christmas decorations of some sort, but in spite of this the Christmas atmosphere seems to me to be entirely absent. It is difficult to explain this feeling of it not being Christmas-time, but the feeling is definite. Christmas is perhaps the time of year I like best, it always seems different, but this year there is no difference. It is the same as any other time. It has come, so to speak before I am ready for it. I did not realise until today that Christmas was only a few days away. The arrival of a parcel for Christmas made me realise its nearness. People were right when they said, 'It won't be much of a Christmas this year.'

Dec. 20th   Sent off my Christmas cards, which will be almost my only Christmas shopping this year. This is not only, nor chiefly, a measure of economy. I simply have not got the time nor the inclination to go hunting about for presents and then packing them up and posting them. At home this would have been one of the most exciting Christmas preparations.

Dec. 23rd   Soldier's remark on the appointment of Lord Halifax as ambassador in the US: 'I hope he gets torpedoed on the way.'

Dec. 24th   It still doesn't seem like Christmas and I am wondering what sort of a Christmas Day it will be tomorrow. The atmosphere is everything at Christmas time; yet it will not be easy to keep up appearances even.

My feeling about Christmas is shared by others of this unit. One opinion was: 'How can you celebrate Christmas when there's a war on? Season of peace and goodwill – and we're battering each other with aeroplanes and guns! It's a mockery, like Armistice Day.' This, not from a person of great intelligence, but from an ordinary, rather aggressive young soldier. Others complained that there were no facilities for celebration, nothing to do. The lack of special arrangements, as most have been used to at home, is felt.

Dec. 25th   It would not be true to say that today has not seemed a little more like Christmas, but it still does not compare with other Christmases. No presents, no games, no visitors. Actually, 'no presents' is not quite true, as there was one present from the sister of the ward, which came as a pleasant surprise. And two extremely good Christmas dinners, one at midday, the other at teatime, helped to mark the occasion. After dinner someone came round dressed in the red robes and white beard of Father Christmas – how that custom still clings, even among grown-ups! – and gave each patient a present off the Christmas tree. Each ward had devised its own decorations, and there were some very bright efforts.

In the afternoon a few of us had an argument about the merits of Socialism and Conservatism. Four out of five of us would vote Labour.

I feel that Christmas can never be the same without friends or family. My sister says, in a letter, that she worries because I am to be moved farther away from home. Also she says 'Oranges are scarce round here, as are most things now. We are definitely feeling the effects of the war now, but it is true that you can generally make up with something else if you can't get what you want.' She hopes I will be able to get time off for her wedding. In another letter, my cousin, who was evacuated, says, 'I'm just longing for the time when we can all get home again.'

Dec. 29th–30th   Managed to get home for a few hours before being moved to another unit in Sheffield on January 2nd. Going home and coming back I saw the shelterers in the Underground for the first time. I noticed how they seemed to accept all this business of carrying bundles of bedding, food, etc. down to the tubes and spending the night there as a normal part of their existence, without fuss, without excitement. All this was strange to me and rather wonderful.

At home the most interesting observation was that there is a pretty general opinion that the war will end next year, or that the worst part of it will be over.

Next year I may be a long way from home, perhaps in a more active theatre of war, perhaps under worse conditions. Everything is uncertain.

Notes
[1] *Picture Post* was not merely a picture magazine; it was also a useful forum of public opinion. Some weeks previously they had run a series of statements and letters about war aims. My letter on the subject had been published with several others in the issue of 11 November, 1939. The full text of my letter will be found in the section of the book called 'Aftermath'.

Though not expecting any replies, I in fact received two – with a gap of some years in between. I am sure that I answered my correspondent from the Gold Coast (now known as Ghana) to the best of my ability, but I am sorry to say that I received no further communication from him. In wartime circumstances there may have been all sorts of reasons for this.

A second letter came, out of the blue, much later.
[2] Meat 1/10d. a lb. 1/10d. was equivalent to 9p in decimal currency. Though 2lb for each person would have been rather a large amount, by our standards, the meat bill for three persons would therefore have been 11/- (55p) weekly, a sizeable

proportion of our income. Offal. of course, was cheaper, but not always obtainable.

[3] My call-up was responsible for a gap of about three months in my diary entries. I was posted to the RAMC depot at Church Crookham in Hampshire and had little opportunity at first to continue with the diary. As it happened, this period coincided with the defeat of France and the British withdrawal from Dunkirk, so I was unable to report on those significant events.

After completing basic training at Crookham I was posted to the Connaught Hospital at Aldershot for a special course, and most of my diary entries in the next few months refer to the Aldershot area. At that time there were two military hospitals in Aldershot: the Cambridge was the main one, while the Connaught was smaller. Due to the demands of the war I had now effectively left home: except for one short spell and occasional visits to see my family. I did not live in the parental home again.

[4] My breathing difficulty while wearing a gas mask was to be a relevant factor in my eventual discharge from the Army.

1941

Jan. 5th   Life in Sheffield so far has not been very inspiring. I slept the first night in a draughty school and the next day found myself billeted with some others in an empty house without water, light, or palliasses to sleep on. We have to walk to the school for meals, so I probably shall not bother to have any breakfast, which is at 7.30. Food is poor anyway.

One of my Aldershot comrades is billeted in the next house but one, so I shall not have to make all new friends. In that house they have water and light and we go there to wash. When we get the water and gas turned on in our own billets, and something softer than the floor to sleep on, it should not be too bad.

We are here to form a unit to go abroad, so there is nothing much to do. The main job is to keep warm.

Sheffield has suffered much from the blitz, although it has had only two raids. Before then, I am told, it was one of the liveliest places you could wish to be in. The damage, though not so widespread as in London, is terrific in places. Most places of entertainment close early (about 6 o'clock), the shops close early, the cafés close early. Tramcars still run late, but only at half-hour intervals; before, they ran every few minutes. It is hard to find a place where one can get a good meal. Woolworths, one of the places undamaged, is about the only shop serving reasonably-priced hot meals.

Last night I discovered a dance-hall, not in the centre of the city, where they have dances every night. It was crowded out (99 per cent civilians), but I enjoyed myself. Admission is

1/6d., so I shall not be able to afford to go there often and buy meals as well. Reading will be my chief pastime, I think. Of course, there are the pubs, but these I am not in the habit of frequenting.

Jan. 7th   Listened to a discussion among some soldiers in a Salvation Army canteen. These were some of the remarks of the two with the most to say: 'Italy won't stick it much longer ... But the war will go on a long while yet ... I don't think the Italians have much heart in this war ... They can't have, or they wouldn't surrender so easily ... If Germany wins the war the average German won't benefit, but the ruling classes will. Come to that, the average Englishman won't benefit if this country wins. The ruling classes will, but people like you and me will still have to work hard for our £3 or £4 a week. Still, I shouldn't wonder if the working man doesn't stick up for himself a bit more after the war, when he sees all the money that's been spent ... Oh, I don't know. There'll be greyhound races and football matches again to help him forget. It's only while all those things are closed down that he has to sit at home and either mope or think. When the war's over it'll be back to the good old days of Greta Garbo and Robert Taylor ... His little home and family are his world. He doesn't want to go fighting for something he knows b— all about and doesn't understand.' (One continually finds among soldiers the desire to discuss things rationally, without emotion, and to find out the truth, whether it be pleasant or unpleasant. Some, of course, are still swayed by their patriotic emotions.) One soldier read out part of Charlie Chaplin's final speech in *The Great Dictator* ('Soldiers of democracy, unite,' etc.).

Jan. 11th   Visited one of the two pantomimes running in Sheffield. Because of the blitz these have a morning and afternoon performance daily, instead of in the afternoon and evening. The theatre was packed out in the afternoon when I went, and I had to stand for half the performance. Jokes against the Italians were well received, e.g. 'Have you heard about the battle of Cascara?' 'No, I haven't.' 'We got the Italians on the run,' or again, 'Did you know the Italians have given up fish and chips?' 'Given up fish and chips? No, why?' 'Because they've run out of Greece.'

As far as I know, the two theatres I have mentioned are the only ones open. Another is closed, with a notice up: 'Closed until happier times'. All cinemas still standing in the centre of the city, as I have said, close early. I found another dance-hall tonight, some distance from the city. It is run by soldiers, the admission was only 3d., and there was a big crowd there and plenty of girls. There was a good band and refreshments, so you get better value for 3d. than for 1/6d. at the other place.

Jan. 13th   Food is the chief problem here and I, personally, spend more on it than on anything else. The food we get from the Army is poor and insufficient, and we all have to buy food elsewhere to supplement it. Hot meals are hard to get because the gas supply has been upset by air-raids. Woolworths is the best place to go – the cooking is done by electricity there. I went there today and had two sausages, an egg, and chips, bread and butter, tea, and a sweet for only 1/11d. – the best meal I have had since I have been here. Every day I buy snacks at the Salvation Army canteen.

As there are few entertainments, I do more reading now. At present I am reading Steinbeck's *The Grapes of Wrath*.

Jan. 19th   In the last few days the weather has become of equal importance with food in our daily lives. In a way the two things are connected. For several days we had to walk to our meals down the steep roads slippery as glass with frozen snow. Last night there was a heavy fall of snow and today we had to wade, in places, through thick drifts of it. Some do not bother to walk to breakfast any day, but today, because of the snow, hardly anyone went. Dinner, however, was the best we have had while I have been here. It was the first time I have really had enough, but only by virtue of having two helpings of each course. (Usually we get only one course, to everybody's discontent.) For a change the food was not badly cooked.

The desires for enough food, warmth, and entertainment are the dominating factors in our lives here, not the war (for we have had no air-raids lately). Entertainment is scarce, so that when there is anything on the weather is not such a deterrent as it might be. It did not stop me and about 200 others going to a dance last night. But almost every other night of the week I spend in the Salvation Army canteen, eating, reading, writing. Occasionally I go to the YMCA, but that is farther to go and you cannot get anything to eat after five. I have not been to the pictures since before I came here, a period of three weeks or more, the longest time in years I have been without going to the cinema.

Transport in the city is about the only service which has not been seriously disorganised. Trams and buses still run from early morning to late at night, except that they are not so frequent after about seven. Even the snow has not stopped them. The roads have been cleared and today services are more or less as usual

Jan. 20th   Talking about the African war, one chap said: 'Looks as though we're going to try and kick the Italians right out of Africa. We want to kick the Froggies out too. They wouldn't fight, the bastards.'

Expenditure on food today – 3/4¹/₂d., a record.

Jan. 22nd   Food – 1/9d.

Jan. 23rd   Army food now a little better, probably because of complaints, and we get a second course most days now. The meat is rather poor, though. Expenditure on foods today only 1d. for a cup of tea.

Talk among the men this afternoon developed into a long and complicated argument on Capitalism v. Socialism, which finally led nowhere. Socialists were in a slight minority, but put up a very good argument. One of them said that a man still retains his class status when he enters the Army, since his origin and outlook remain the same.

Jan. 24th   Food – 1/3¹/₂d. Total for five days – 6/10d. This works out at an average of 9/6d. a week, nearly half my wages.

I learned today that I shall not be going abroad after all, not being physically fit for service in tropical climates. This will please my family and they will not worry about me so much. I am not sorry either, and I certainly shan't be sorry to leave Sheffield as I know it. Tomorrow I go to Leeds.

Jan. 25th I arrived in Leeds late in the afternoon. Not knowing my way about, I could not go anywhere far from the tram-stop where I could catch a tram back to my billet. I went to a wine lodge, where it was warm and bright and there were plenty of people, and had a drink. The bar was circular and underground, so could be used as an air-raid shelter. I stayed down there and just looked at the people.

Jan. 26th Had a look round the town. Not much doing on a Sunday. It was snowing; not many people about. Noticed several cinemas, but none open. I looked about, as I always do in a town new to me, for canteens and clubs for the Forces. I found a YMCA and a church canteen.

Jan. 27th One of the first things I noticed here was that the Army food is a great improvement on that at Sheffield. It is adequate and well-prepared. Why can't it be the same everywhere?

Went to the pictures (the cinemas and theatres open in the evening here) for the first time in weeks. I missed the last tram back and spent the night at the YMCA, which is open all night.

Jan. 28th Went to the pantomime – Arthur Askey in *Jack and Jill*. Very good show, well-attended.

Jan. 31st The last three or four letters from my sister have shown that she is very busy preparing for her wedding tomorrow, but it is a big disappointment for both of us that I shall not be able to be there. She says, 'I wish more than anything else that you will be there.' Family events such as this seem more important to me than the progress of the war, etc. You cannot live your own life in the Army, you are one of a million machines. Your life is planned out in advance and you are forced to live it.

Feb. 1st Fellows on sick parade this morning were talking about the invasion. The general reaction was: 'Let Hitler come

66

and get what's waiting for him.' It is generally thought that any invaders will get a very hot reception.

Feb. 3rd   Saw a new (to me) poster today, the first one for a long time which seemed to have significance. It showed a picture of a tank in action and the slogan was: 'Lend to Attack'. The change-over from 'Lend to Defend', coming as it does at a time when Britain is attacking in Africa, represents a definite change in attitude and a skilful variation in propaganda. It opens up a whole field of differences between the Government which was responsible for the 'Lend to Defend' poster and the present Govt.

Feb. 4th   Am busy at the moment following up the discussion on 'God and the War' in the *News Chronicle*. Intend to send my own views on the subject shortly.

Went to see *The Great Dictator*, which is being shown at two cinemas here this week. As comedy it was excellent, but as a take-off of the dictators not up to my expectations. It certainly seized on many superficial features of dictatorship and ridiculed them, but it did not bite deep and show up the evil roots of Fascism, except slightly in the speech at the end. This confirms the opinion of a friend of mine, who wrote to me about it: 'We saw *The Great Dictator* on Monday, and I was as disappointed as I expected to be. It was a great deal less funny than his earlier films, while the way he takes off Hitler without in the least seeing (or showing) *why* Fascism exists and *how* to eliminate it in all its forms, is nothing short of tragic in a man of such one-time genius...'

Feb. 8th   The capture of Benghazi is big news, but is not being talked about much in this unit. In fact I have heard very little war-talk among soldiers just lately. Food is a much more important subject. Although it is much better than it was at Sheffield, there are a fair number here who grumble about it. Actually it is fairly good in quality, but hardly sufficient in quantity, and one still has to spend a good deal on extras.

Feb. 9th   Changes in the Government led an Irishman to express his opinion that they were all 'too old-fashioned. They all ought to be kicked out.' A sergeant was not so extreme, but said there must be changes. 'I'll tell you who *is* worth his salt – Anthony Eden,' he said. 'Of course, Churchill's a good man.' 'No, he isn't,' said the Irishman, 'he's no better than Chamberlain.' The sergeant strongly disagreed, but Chamberlain came in for a good deal of abuse from both. Both finished by saying they were fed-up with the war and wished it were over.

Some of us have been detailed for fire-watching at night in different parts of the town until further notice. This has caused resentment, as we feel that this is a civilian's job (there are posters everywhere: 'Fall in, the fire-bomb fighters'). 'What's the Home Guard for?' said one. Apart from this, Leeds has had only one alarm in several weeks, and all think it crazy and unnecessary to wander about the streets in the middle of the night looking for fires when there is not even a warning on. All the time one hears grumbles about the stupidity of the military authorities, the red tape, the habit of doing things in the most awkward and roundabout way, the silly trivial things we are made to do, the shortage of food (tea today: one piece of bread and jam, a piece of cake, and a cup of tea). If only people knew of the discontent which seethes behind the façade of unity!

As a soldier said to me tonight, 'It's not aeroplanes and guns and munitions that'll win this war. It's food. No-one can live without food.' And all the time, too, one hears soldiers saying that they're fed-up with the war, fed-up with the Army, fed-up with the petty tyranny, will be glad to get out of it. 'If I'd had any sense,' said the same one, 'I'd have been a conscientious objector, but I hadn't the guts. I was too soft.'

It was not until after I had written the preceding that I read a piece in the *News Chronicle* concerning a police check-up on fire-watching laggards among firms in Leeds.

Feb. 10th   My name down for posting again.

Feb. 11th   Moving to Peebles in Scotland on Thursday. I would much rather be nearer home, but it will be interesting to see something of Scotland for the first time.

Feb. 12th   I was tired after doing fire-watching for three nights previous, so I did not bother to get up to go to breakfast. I got up at about 7.30, dressed, rolled up my bed, and had a wash.

Today is my 21st birthday. At home it would have been something of an event, but here it is like any other day, and I forget for long periods that this is the day when one is said to have 'come of age' and assumes full adult status and responsibility. But to me it has no such importance.

After washing, I have to get ready for the adjutant's parade, as I am leaving tomorrow and all men leaving have to be inspected by the adjutant. Preparation includes polishing buttons and fixing up 'marching order' equipment. Putting this equipment on is a struggle and getting it comfortable a work of art of which not many are capable. Having managed the first part, but not the second, of this procedure, I walked up to the company office for the parade at 9.45. It *would* have to be raining, just because one wants to keep one's boots clean. At the company office we have to wait about for some time, so I went and bought a *News Chronicle* and read it while I waited. Not much news today, but was interested in the article on 'The Problem of Pain' in the 'God and the War' series. While I was reading it the sergeant-major came and asked us if we all had pay-books, identity discs, and money. Most of us said they hadn't any money, in the hope of getting paid before leaving. I said I had a little, as I had quite a lot. The sergeant-major was annoyed with those who hadn't any. Then we fell in and the sergeant in charge of the parade found fault with everybody's dress, though he admitted that the rolling of my gas-cape was not too bad, so we all fell out and adjusted our equipment, then fell in again, looking, in my opinion, no better than we did before. Then we were marched down to the stores to make up one or two deficiencies in kit. Then we were marched back to the company office for further re-adjustments. 'I want you all perfect for this parade,' said the sergeant. Having made ourselves as near 'perfect' as possible, we were marched to the medical inspection room for examination for freedom from infection (chiefly venereal) and had to take all our kit off again *before* the adjutant's parade! Then we had to rush it on again in a hurry. This is the sort of thing that maddens one. Then we went down

69

to the depôt orderly room and the RSM came out and said the adjutant wasn't there and told us to wait. We waited about ten minutes, with the pack getting more and more uncomfortable, and still the adjutant didn't come, so we went back to the company office and it was all trouble for nothing. At the company office we had to wait for an inspection by the company officer instead. At length he came and gave us a quick inspection and asked us all if we had any complaints. This was really the last straw, so we all said 'No'. The complaint I would have liked to make would have been about being in the Army at all. Then he said he might pay us before lunch, so we waited, but in the end he didn't, so we were told to parade again at two o'clock.

I went back to the billet and took off my pack. I found a birthday card from my sister and her husband. By now it was lunchtime, but I did not go to the company dining-hall, but to a little café along the road, and had a well-cooked meal of rabbit pie, Yorkshire pudding, peas and potatoes, a piece of tart, and a cake and a mug of tea, all for 1/1½d.

After that I went back to the billet and talked to two new arrivals about where each other had come from, what this unit was like, etc. I went on parade at 1.45, and at 2 o'clock the pay sergeant told us that owing to arrangements he had not known anything about we would not be paid until tomorrow at twelve. We went to see the orderly sergeant for further orders, but he didn't really know what to do with us, so sent myself and two others to the sergeant's mess for fatigues. As we were allowed to walk down on our own and there was no check-up at either end, I did not go and the others probably didn't either. Apart from the unattraction of fatigues, they might just as well have given us the afternoon off in the circumstances.

I caught a tram into the town instead. First I went to the YMCA and had a cup of coffee and some cake and finished reading the paper. Then, about 3.15, I went into a newsreel cinema, which was full. Six features were shown, among them a film depicting achievements in this country before the war (new roads, housing estates, holidays for all, television, better health

70

services), but finishing each description with the words 'We forgot Germany', spoken in a most sinister voice. The film ended with the commentator saying that we would not let our children's lives suffer because of Germany. I was impressed by the glowing account of the improvements which had taken place in pre-war Britain, but felt that a list of the things which still needed, not only improving, but also abolishing would have been still more impressive. There was also a short film about shoplifting and a particularly childish coloured cartoon. Then there was a news review of recent events, including Roosevelt's recent speech to Congress, Churchill's tour of two sea-ports, and Haile Selassie's return to Abyssinia. The last two were similar, being accounts of how Britain is carrying on in spite of air-raids, on the note that you can't beat a people with such a spirit of courage and determination. I came out at about 4.40 and had tea (sausages and beans) at a church canteen. Then I went back to the billet and found a letter and 10/- from an aunt and a birthday card from my father. My aunt says that butcher's meat is hard to get and they have had no cheese for three weeks.

As it was ten to eight and too late to go to the pictures or variety, I decided to go to a dance-hall in the town. Admission is only 6d. for the Forces, including refreshments. The dance, however, was not very enjoyable; there were too many difficult dances like rumbas, tangos, and slow foxtrots. I stayed for only a few dances. Bored, I came out at about a quarter to ten, took a tram, and reported in at the company office. Then I bought some fish and chips for supper (a frequent habit) and went back to the billet. There I wrote some of my journal, cleaned my boots and buttons ready for the morning, and got into bed about 11.15. What a dull, insignificant twenty-first birthday!

Feb. 14th Travelled by night and arrived in Peebles about 9 o'clock this morning. I had had no sleep as I had to sit in the corridor for most of the journey. I also had to carry four blankets, as well as my personal kit – another of the Army's crazy ideas; we could easily be issued with blankets on arrival – so was somewhat exhausted when I reached my destination.[1]

Feb. 15th Conditions here not so bad, but routine not so

71

good. Proper beds to sleep on, the first I have seen for six weeks, plenty of hot water, reasonably good food. The place is hardly a hospital, consisting of a collection of huts, only three or four of which contain patients. Most of us are just doing ordinary training – squad drill, stretcher drill, gas lectures, fatigues, etc., with which I thought I had finished. This afternoon, Saturday, we had fatigues, instead of having the afternoon off, as in other units. The feeling is that we are given fatigues just for the sake of not letting us have too much spare time. It is not as though we do anything *useful*.

Perhaps the best aspect of this place is the splendid scenery all round; but it is lonely and cheerless to one who likes towns, with their crowds of people, shops, and cinemas.

Feb. 22nd   An uneventful week. Not much news reaches us up here. One has to go into Peebles to see the newspapers, mostly Scottish publications.

Feb. 24th   One of the fellows, looking at yesterday's paper, noticed a paragraph saying that the 19 age group would be called up by the middle of next month. 'They're young to be called up,' he said. 'Too young,' said another. 'I was only twenty when I was called up.' 'And how old are you now?' 'Twenty-one.' 'I should have thought you were at least twenty-seven.' 'It's the Army. It's put years on me ... How old are you?' 'Twenty-one.' 'Oh, you look about thirty.' 'I know; I'm old and grey.' One man of 33, however, said he felt younger since being in the Army.

Mar. 1st   Another lean week for my diary. Life soon becomes boring up here. Although not remote, we are sufficiently out of the way to make entertainment and information inadequate. There is no radio and no papers. There is no canteen, only a little kiosk which opens at midday and teatime for half an hour, where we can buy cigarettes and chocolate. One person is allowed two pieces of chocolate.

There is little to do in the town. My evenings are spent chiefly in reading (T. E. Lawrence's *Seven Pillars of Wisdom*). The days are more or less the same, equally dull. The recruits do their training and the trained men have to join in, but I, being on the sick-list, waiting to go into hospital, avoid most of the drill. In peace-time, going into hospital would have filled me with anxiety, but now I look forward to it, to escape for a little while from the Army's tyranny, and hope for sick leave.

There is little talk about the war, as we get no news. The bad weather increases the sense of boredom in us all.

Mar. 4th   Boredom relieved a little by the first ENSA concert to be held here. As we have no concert-hall it was held in the dining-hall, admission free, and drew a large audience. Perhaps because it was the first entertainment of its kind to be given here it received a better reception than it might have done, but nevertheless it was a very bright and lively show, which we must consider ourselves lucky to get.

By far the majority of the jokes, about 80 per cent, dealt with sex, the idea being apparently that any allusion to sex, however 'blue', would draw a laugh from the troops (which it invariably did). Of the rest most were cracks at Mussolini and the Italians, some even working in a sex angle as well, e.g. An Italian comes home and says, 'Where is my Bianca?' His wife replies, 'In bed with tonsillitis.' The Italian says, 'Good heavens, these Greeks are everywhere.' Most of the programme consisted of this sort of thing, either in straight cross-talk, or worked into short sketches. There were also some popular songs, not very well sung by a soprano, or rendered on a piano-accordion, and a couple of tap-dances. At the end there was a little community singing; the most popular song was 'Bless 'em All'. Finally the colonel got up and thanked the concert-party and said their show was very much appreciated, as we were working and training very hard and this was the first concert we had had.

Mar. 8th   Of the little news read in the last few days the most interesting to me is the BBC's notice to performers whose political views differ from the Government's and the protests which this has aroused. I am glad that MPs and other prominent persons have voiced their strong disapproval of the BBC's action, for this is indeed the very thing we are supposed to be fighting against.

These days, however, I have lost all interest in the radio, not having listened to it for weeks. Sport, also, has ceased to hold any interest for me. Reading and the cinema are still my chief leisure interests and, to a lesser extent, the theatre (of any description) and dancing.

I danced at the drill-hall tonight, after a haircut for which I had to pay the excessive price of 9d. After being in Scotland for three weeks I can understand the Scottish reputation for thriftiness, though I think it is often exaggerated. Scottish people are not really mean, but very careful in money matters, and they are colder, more puritanical than, for instance, the people of Yorkshire. Yet, I should think, once one has made friends with a Scot he would be as sincere and generous a friend as could be found anywhere.

Mar. 9th   Snatch of conversation after dinner: 'They say this lot'll be over by June.' 'Who says so?' *Old Moore's Almanac*, and it's never been wrong yet.' 'Well, I don't think it can last through another winter. You don't know how bad it is in civilian life. They're having meatless days up North, and when I was working up there you couldn't get cheese and jam.' Talk then went on about where you can and where you can't buy cigarettes. I have been smoking more since being in Scotland. Others have said the same.

Mar. 11th   At last we have got a canteen of our own, a makeshift one it is true, but a canteen all the same, where we can buy tea and cakes, etc. This makes it better for those who have to stay in camp in the evening, but I don't think it will give much more incentive for others to stay in. It opens only from 7.30 to 9.30 p.m. and is one of many run by the Church of Scotland. The minister who said a few words about the canteen said it should not be only a place to get a cup of tea and a bun, but also a social centre. This may be true, but in my view a canteen can serve that purpose only to a limited extent.

Mar. 14th   Last night and tonight alarms have been sounded for the first time since I have been here. We were ordered to

74

sleep fully dressed, including boots – an order which everybody thought ridiculous and, needless to say, was not completely obeyed.

Mar. 16th   Sunday. Church parade. Sermon was on the 'Love your neighbour' theme. The padre said this didn't mean that we could feel friendly to everyone we happened to meet, or that we could look at a map of the world and say we were friendly to all the people living in all those countries, because we couldn't feel like that; there were too many, and we would never have the chance to be nice to many of them, even if we wanted to. This seemed to me a poor, half-hearted Christianity. Though we cannot come into contact personally with all the people in the world, we come into contact with them through our Government's dealings with their Governments and by our opinions we can sometimes influence our Government (even if it is not democratic). The preacher took the idea of loving one's neighbour in its most literal sense, saying that we should merely try to get on well with those with whom we lived and worked. Thus he showed complete lack of understanding of the size and interplay of human relationships in these days when the actions of even small groups of people may have repercussions on the other side of the world.

Mar. 21st   Soldier's opinion: 'Before June I reckon they'll have to have a smack at us. I reckon the whole South-East coast, from Dover to London, they'll blitz everything ... Some people say they'll be glad to hear the church-bells ring. Well, when they do we shall know it's the end for one or the other. And if it's the end for you, you haven't got anything to worry about, have you?'

Mar. 22nd   Looking at this week's *Picture Post*, with its articles on the German terror film, J B Priestley, and the BBC ban, set me to thinking about the principles at stake in this war. For a long time I have had a grave suspicion, rapidly becoming a conviction, that we are not fighting for freedom and democracy at all, but that we shall have to fight harder still against Fascism in this country when the war is over. We may defeat Germany, but we shall not defeat Fascism at this rate; instead we seem to be making its continuance ever more sure. The *Daily Worker* is banned; while some other papers become more Fascist in flavour. Pacifists and Communists are victimised by the BBC; an attack is made on the progressive voice of Priestley. Some MPs, including Sir Samuel Hoare and Malcolm Macdonald, are out of the country; the member for this (Peebles) constituency is in prison; many others are in the Forces; thus large numbers of people have been virtually disfranchised. Some of Mr Churchill's answers to questions in Parliament, when closely examined, are unsatisfactory. Yet his tremendous popularity (like Hitler's when he first came to power in Germany) leads many to have blind confidence in him; they regard him as infallible. All these things, and others, show that strong reactionary forces are at work in this country. Such forces are attacking Mr Priestley, simply because he has stated things so clearly that even the most lowly intelligence can begin to see the truth, making it more and more difficult for him to be deceived by pseudo-progressive propaganda. These Fascist forces do not want ordinary people to think for themselves. In the Army, too, we are not wanted to think critically. Thus it seems to me that freedom and democracy are on the decline. It is a good thing, however, that democratic forses are still fairly strong and were responsible for the removal of the BBC ban. But the situation remains perturbing.

Later in the evening I went to a dance, crowded out with young people, and forgot all about the war. It is surprisingly easy to escape from it at dances or in the cinema.

Mar. 25th   Went on a long route march today, over hills which may have been beautiful, but were heartbreaking to anyone with a pack on and other impedimenta to carry and few stops for rest. I almost collapsed on the way home – I was not the only one – and all cursed the Army.

Mar. 26th   Read in the paper that J B Priestley's talks have again been stopped. It is now obvious that the BBC – in other words, the Government – wants only one point of view to be expounded.

76

Mar. 28th   Received a parcel from home containing tobacco and cakes. I do not expect much in the way of parcels now, as letters from my sister show that many things are hard to get. In a previous letter she says: 'Everything is becoming very difficult to get this way and people seem to think things will be worse. I think we are in for a hard time. Thank goodness it is the Summer we have to face … It looks as though I shall be conscripted. I am 25. Still, if it will help us to win we must do it.' The last part of this distresses me beyond words. I never dreamed that my sister now married, might be called upon for war-work.

The news of revolt in Yugo-Slavia is great – and unexpected.

Mar. 30th   A patient in the ward I was working in today said, 'Sounds like a story out of a novel, this Yugo-Slav business, doesn't it?'

Also heard in the ward: 'Is that *The People* you're reading?' 'Yes.' 'What's the star man say?' 'Who's the star man?' 'Lyndoe – Edward Lyndoe.' 'Oh, yes, I read him last week. He was good last week, wasn't he?' It is a marvel to me that anyone even reads this nonsensical dope, let alone thinks it worth consideration.

Corporal, who had been home for the weekend: 'I put my civvies on and felt human again.'

Apr. 2nd   Went out to a dance, and when I got back to camp at about 10 o'clock found a note to say that I had to catch the 10.30 ambulance to hospital that same night. The ambulance was late and I didn't get to bed much before 12.00. As usual, the Army keeps you waiting (I had been waiting about five weeks for a hospital bed) and then acts without warning at the most inconvenient time.[2]

Apr. 3rd   Had my operation, not a very serious one, in the morning. Just before I went in to have it I heard a patient who was going on sick leave telling another that he had 13 bars of chocolate to take home!

After the operation I felt fairly comfortable and lazily thought how content I would be to remain in the luxury of a spring-bed with sheets, good food, being waited on, and having nothing in particular to do, and never go back to the boring, futile routine of Army life, which I hate. I look forward to having the most pleasant time I have had since being in the Army. It may be wrong to feel like this, when thousands of people have suffered much more terrible experiences from air-raids than I have ever had to put up with in the Army. Yet the feeling was inevitable, and sometimes I think I would rather share worse experiences and be free than be safe but imprisoned. (In my unit the camp is often referred to as a 'concentration camp' and ourselves as already being 'prisoners of war'.) I use the word 'free' only relatively speaking, of course.

Apr. 4th   Ward orderly's comment on the British evacuation of Benghazi: 'They made a hell of a headline when we took it, but not much of one today.'

Apr. 8th   Life goes on in hospital calmly, comfortably. We talk and think a lot about sick leave. I read the *Daily Express* every day, but news now seems unreliable, because uncertain. The events of the last few days leave me rather bewildered, I don't know why. The Budget hardly interests me. I started reading E. M. Forster's *A Passage to India* yesterday, finished it today. The other patients I have met seem to prefer cowboy stories and thrillers.

The air-raid warning went last night, but I didn't hear it. Bombs were supposed to have fallen near.

Apr. 10th   News very depressing this morning. It is not a question of who is going to win that worries me, although of course I do not want Germany to win, but a question of how much more misery and destruction there must be before it all comes to an end. When Churchill speaks of the war in 1942 I become utterly weary of the whole business.

'We ain't beaten yet,' was another patient's comment.

Later in the day the depression wore off, but after 6 o'clock I asked a sister what the news was; she said, 'Oh, I don't know. It's too depressing. I didn't listen.'

Later there was an ENSA concert in the dining-hall and this

dispelled all gloom. It was a really first-class show, with a conjuror, a violinist, two comedians, a soprano, a pianist, and two soubrettes. At the end we were promised a similar show every week.

Apr. 14th   'Germans invade Egypt'. This headline alarmed me when I saw it, but reading further I saw that somebody had said that the situation is not alarming! Surely it is alarming when all the gains of the last few weeks are being lost more quickly than they were won. Nevertheless the news does not seem so depressing as it did on Thursday.

Apr. 15th   Last night I dreamed that I had my hands splashed with mustard gas, causing red blisters. Yet no-one else had been splashed, no-one knew blister gas had been used. Why I should dream this I don't know, as I have not thought much about gas.

Apr. 18th   In hospital here the war has still not touched us directly, but letters from home reveal how it has affected life there. My sister, for instance, says in a letter: 'Things are very difficult to get this way and I get tired out when I go shopping, what with queuing up for this and that and then when you get it home have to scheme and think how to make it last a week. I suppose we ought not to grumble, but if we could see an end to the war we would not mind these small hardships.'

Today, too, I read about London's worst raid and it makes me realise what a comparatively easy time I have had so far in this war. I have not yet experienced a full-scale air-raid. But though I have not suffered bodily – at least, while I have known some physical discomfort, I have not received any injury – I have at the same time suffered mentally. Apart from my general views about the war, I have been more anxious lately about my family, who live near to London. In my imagination I see all the hardship and worry which people in the bombed towns, especially London, have to bear.

Apr. 26th   The last week has given nothing much to comment on, except that the news has been somewhat depressing all the time. My sister says the same in a letter: 'I think the news just lately has been very depressing and I hate to listen to it. I hope we soon have some successes.'

Apr. 27th   Listened to Churchill's speech on the radio – the first time I had listened to the radio for a very long time. His statement that morale was best in the worst-bombed areas took some swallowing. 'You — liar,' one of the other patients said. The news that Wavell had only two divisions at any one time to use in Libya was also a big surprise to me. I was under the impression that he had an army of about 300,000. On the whole, although he did seem a little gloomier than usual, Churchill's speech did give new hope.

Apr. 30th   Went to the weekly ENSA concert, which was good of its kind. It was nearly all songs and comedy; no political jokes. One song they sang was 'When this blinkin' war is over', a sort of unwritten theme song which has been in circulation wherever I have been, but which I have not heard on the stage before. Some of the words were altered tonight – 'blinkin'' for 'bloody' for example. It starts off:

'When this bloody war is over,
Oh, how happy I shall be.
When I get my civvy clothes on,
No more guards for you and me.'

Unfortunately they played the wrong tune – the right one happens to be that of a hymn – and while the soldiers were singing their tune they were playing another.

May 1st   The news that the whole US Atlantic fleet is out on patrol seems to bring America another step towards entering the war. I expect it any day now. As another patient said the other day, 'America and Japan will be in it soon. It will be a world war before it's finished.' I am not sure about Japan, though it would not surprise me if she did come in.

Another item of news which struck me as important, though not given much prominence (in the *Daily Express*), was about some Scottish Liberals who had criticised Sir Archibald Sinclair for approving Churchill's hope that the present Government would remain in office for three years after the war. One of them said in a speech: 'If democratic government is to be a reality, post-war problems will have to be dealt with by a new House of Commons elected on a thoroughly reformed system.' I fully agree with this.

One of the objects of our propaganda at present seems to be to split Germany and Russia, but I don't think it is being very well handled. How could it be, when our leaders probably dread Communism more than Fascism even now?

May 4th   Was reading the *News of the World* and saw for the first time the official advertisement on precautions to be taken by the civilian population in the event of a gas attack. As far as it goes I thought it quite a good poster, but it leaves out some very important points. It does not explain that if a person gets a breath or two of vapour gas before he has put on his gas mask, he *will* at first feel *worse* after he has put it on, but that this will wear off if he keeps it on. Some people may think the 'discomfort' refers to the ordinary discomfort caused by wearing a gas mask. It does not explain why collars should be turned up and hands kept in pockets, does not say how long clothes will give protection against blister gas (which would not be very long), and puts what is consequently the best precaution – 'Take cover' – in small letters, so that I did not see it until re-reading. Also it omits the most important warning not to look up at the sky, since a minute drop of blister gas in the eye would mean total blindness. Also I think it should stress that a properly-fitting gas-mask gives 100 per cent protection against all vapour gases, which are really the more dangerous, since only in extreme cases would blister gas prove fatal. In my opinion the anti-gas campaign, at least as conducted by the Press, has been more calculated to create a scare than to get people to do what is wanted.

May 5th   Roosevelt's speech confirms my thoughts about America, which I mentioned a few days ago. I remarked to the newspaper-man this morning that I expected America to come in any day. He said, 'Well, if she doesn't come in now, I think it'll be too late. We're getting desperate now.'

May 13th   Today's news has me rather puzzled. The arrival of Rudolf Hess and Russia's recognition of Rashid Ali's government in Iraq are the puzzling items.[3] Hess's flight to Scotland, especially, is news which makes one wonder, gives rise to all sorts of intriguing implications and guesses as to the reason for his flight. It is best, however, not to try to guess, or one would soon be indulging in the most fantastic wishful-thinking. It is best just to wait and see. But whatever the motives for it, it is surely an event of the greatest importance for one of Hitler's staunchest supporters and most important leaders to come over here.

Perhaps the most fascinating aspect of Hess's escape was put into words this afternoon by another patient (a Jew) who said, 'He knows all Germany's secrets; he knows everything about Germany. He's a man behind the scenes.'

In capable hands, this event can be used to great effect in our propaganda. But is our propaganda in capable hands?

May 14th   Apparently one can have a surfeit of sensationalism, since two other patients expressed the view that there was too much fuss being made about Hess – 'Hess, Hess, Hess – the paper's all bloody Hess this morning' – and I myself thought that too much space had been devoted to him without enough facts to work on.

May 15th   Same opinion expressed by same patient again this morning: 'It's all about Hess. It's Hess on the front page, Hess on the back page, and Hess in the middle.' To me Darlan's negotiations with Hitler seem more important.

In the afternoon there was a concert, of which the star turn was Sir Harry Lauder, who was in good form and was enthusiastically applauded. At the end Lord Elibank, in thanking him, began to talk about Rudolf Hess, whose plane had landed not far from Sir Harry Lauder's house. He defended the Duke of Hamilton, his old friend, against any suggestion that he was the right man to whom to bring peace proposals. Then he said, among other things, 'Do not forget that Hess was one of the gangster six. Do not let us make a hero of him. Don't let us think because he came over here to save his own skin, or to make proposals, or both, that he is a good man.' I agreed with this, but disliked his jingoist, Blimpish manner.

May 16th   Today I have been one year in the Army. It has been a year in which I have often felt depressed and unhappy, but it has also been a year of new experiences, new places seen, and moments of great pleasure. But on the whole I hope I do not have to spend another year of Army life.

May 17th   I spoke a little to a patient who came here from Germany a few months before the war. I asked him if he liked this country better than Germany. He said, 'I like it better in every respect.' He said that he was not happy under Hitler. About the Hess business he said that it was 'difficult to say'.

May 24th   Listened to some conversation on the situation in Crete. One patient said, 'Reading between he lines it looks as though – trying to break it gently, you know – as though they're preparing us for the loss of Crete.' (It seems like this to me, too.) But another was confident that the Germans could not hold out, without tanks and heavy artillery. Both criticised heavily our lack of air defence and both took a very gloomy view of our prospects if we did lose Crete. 'We'll be in a bad way if we do,' said one. 'We're always too slow,' said the other, 'we should have gone right into Syria at the first.' He thought that the Germans must be losing thousands of men in the attack on Crete. The other said we were losing a lot too. I have a feeling of impending disaster.

May 25th   News of the loss of *HMS Hood* increases this feeling, but the news from Crete is a little more cheerful, especially the fact that the RAF is again in action.

May 26th   Moved to a convalescent home for a month, and here the war seems farther away than ever.[4] The only recreation consists of a few games, some books, and a radio. It looks as though boredom will soon set in.

May 27th   'I shouldn't be surprised if America declared war today,' said another convalescent. Later one came in and said, 'Heard the latest news? The *Bismarck* has been done in. The Fleet Air Arm finished her off.'

May 27th   The sinking of the *Bismarck* is, of course, cheering news, but in my opinion is second in importance to the news from Crete, which again seems grave and outweighs the more heartening news about the *Bismarck*. The papers, of course, give more prominence to the latter.

May 29th   The entry of America into the war seems imminent, but it will be none too soon, for the news from Crete gets worse. It is strange that the British, who were already there, cannot hold out against the Germans, who have all the difficulties of getting there, and we even seem to have difficulty in sending reinforcements.

May 30th   It looks like another withdrawal for us, this time from Crete, though one must not give up hope yet.

Apart from the news there might very well be no war on, for all it affects us here. The house is very comfortable, there is nothing to do except amuse ourselves, the food is good and plentiful, and the country round about very peaceful. We talk a little about the news, of course, but more about other matters, such as getting one's 'ticket', in other words, being discharged from the Army, for which almost everyone, both here and at the hospital, hopes. How we envy those who are ordered to send home for their civvy clothes!

I have been reading Pepys' *Diary* since being here. I wonder what that famous diarist would have written today. Indeed, he has one or two passages appropriate to the present time... Altogether I have read 18 books in just over eight weeks while I have been in hospital.

June 1st   The rationing of clothes is certainly a big surprise to me, though as a member of the Forces I shall not have to worry about it personally. At first glance the rationing seems severe, but I don't know how it will work out in practice. It seems rather a confused scheme and I think there will be many difficulties, people not knowing exactly what is rationed and how to use their coupons to the best effect. Also, children will probably not need as many coupons as adults, so that people with children will be able to use some of their children's coupons on themselves, while people with no children will have only their own. The fact that margarine coupons are to be used at first (until proper clothing coupons are issued) makes it all seem a little ridiculous.

The rest of today's news is unexciting, the good news from Iraq neutralising the vague, and therefore disquieting, news from Crete.

(Later.) The withdrawal from Crete, though not unexpected, gives me a feeling of profound disappointment. Once again we shall be able to boast about our skill in withdrawal, and the way the papers will try to make excuses without seeming to is sickening. Hitler will perhaps fancy his invasion chances now.

June 5th   Received a letter from my brother and he mentions the fighting in Crete and goes on to say, 'Although the German losses must have been huge, I'm afraid that the final success will give them more confidence to try the same here, although I have no doubt that it would be beaten...'

June 6th   Letter from my sister; she says, 'I wonder what fresh trouble Hitler & Co. are hatching now that Crete is over. What a dreadful business that was. I do wish we could have a few successes.'

I had a talk with another patient about how much longer the war would last. He said, 'If Germany is going to win it might be over quickly, but if we are going to win it will take a long time.' He thought it might last another five or six years, or even longer, but I said I did not think economic circumstances would allow either side to hold out so long.

June 9th   My father mentions clothes rationing in his letter today: 'As regards rationing of clothes, I don't think I shall feel that as much as the food business. I miss the cheese more than anything...'

June 11th   I read Churchill's speech in the paper and, as has been the case before in his speeches to Parliament (but not in his broadcast speeches), I felt some dissatisfaction with his attitude. He drew attention to the fact that Hitler has not had to account for the loss of the *Bismarck*, nor Mussolini for his defeat in Libya, as much as to say that he should not have to account for our loss of Crete, ignoring the fact that in this matter of public debate lies the very difference between democracy and dictatorship. Again, Churchill concentrated on disposing of the argument that we should not have defended Crete, which was, I am sure, the opinion of a small minority, in order to distract attention from the question as to why Crete was not *better* defended. He seemed very vague on this point. And although he often says that he wants to give the public as much information as possible, he seems to find numerous excuses for not doing so.

June 15th   The march into Syria proves unexciting and slow, and causes hardly any comment. The papers are making a lot of fuss about relations between Germany and Russia, but I think it is mostly propaganda, designed partly to raise morale by giving hopes of a war between Russia and Germany, and partly to try and split the two countries. Personally, I do not think Hitler would be so stupid as to involve himself in a war with Russia and I do not think Russia wants to help us.

June 16th   'Hitler's had his chance and missed it,' remarked another patient, 'the same as they did in the last war, when they had the chance to go right through and held back.'

June 18th   The system of radio-location by which enemy aircraft are detected, revealed by Lord Beaverbrook, was no secret to me. I had heard of it some time ago, even before I was called up, although I only believed it in a half-hearted way.
    In a letter my sister says she thinks that 66 coupons will be sufficient for her clothing requirements.

June 20th   Two people, a man and a woman, gave the opinion that Germany might soon be at war with Russia. I still think it unlikely, though of course it is possible. Whatever happens, I shall not be surprised. It may be some trick to fool us, while Russia is preparing to fight us and not Germany. The Turco-German pact did not surprise me, though I do not think it has any more meaning than any other pact and may soon be quite worthless.

June 22nd   At breakfast someone said that Germany had declared war on Russia. One of the nurses said that Rumania was going to help us, though how that can be when Rumania is already occupied by Germany I don't know. 'The war will soon be over now,' said someone else. I still hardly know whether to believe it and shall not completely accept it until I hear it on the radio or read it in the papers. If it is true, then I think Germany has spoilt her chances.

Listened to the 1 o'clock bulletin and learned the news beyond doubt. Like several other things that have happened in this war, it is extremely difficult to understand the circumstances that have led up to it. There is nothing straightforward about this war. In the maze of lies and treachery it is almost impossible to find the truth. The only conclusion that one can come to is that it is favourable to us. 'The Russians will slaughter the Jerries,' was one opinion. The comments on the radio have noticeably showed no warmth to Russia, no welcome to her as a new ally. The announcer spoke of Germany's move as being directed really against the democracies, hinting that Russia is not a democracy and not really one of us. I suppose this is all one can expect from our Conservative leaders, but if our attitude to Russia continues to be distant the war may still take longer to finish than it need. Collaboration with Russia and America would give us a marked superiority over Germany.

Churchill's speech did not please me so much as usual. There were good things in it, but on the whole it was too violent and abusive, more on a level with one of Hitler's. He was, however, honest in his attitude to Russia. It would have been hypocritical for him to pretend to be a friend of Communism. But his speech did not promise much in the way of co-operation.

June 23rd   One hardly knows what attitude to take towards

Russia, when one remembers that not long ago we were prepared to send an expeditionary force to help Finland against Russia and that the latter stabbed Poland in the back. Finland is again fighting Russia – so what now? The *Daily Mail* is more or less anti-Russian, and this may have influenced me a little. But my main feeling is bewilderment, a kind of frustration. When France turns against her former ally, when Turkey allies herself with Britain, then signs a pact with Germany, when Germany makes an agreement with Russia and then attacks her, and when Finland fights Russia first with our help and then with our enemy's, one may be excused for feeling bewildered. We need only to turn round and fight ourselves to complete what is very nearly a farce.

June 24th   Returned to military hospital yesterday. Conditions not so good here, but there is more entertainment. The wireless is now installed in every room, but there is no choice of programme.

June 25th   Co-operation is promised with Russia, but I am inclined to think that it will consist more of words than deeds.

June 27th   Overheard this morning: 'I think it's right what it said in the paper the other day about Hess's mission. He came to offer peace terms and then Germany and us to start a war against Russia.' This is a very plausible theory, one which occurred to me at the time of Hess's arrival. But since no information has been given I keep an open mind. I think the Ministry of Information has blundered in not giving any information on the subject. If the above rumour is untrue, then it should be dispelled straight away. If it is true, it would do no harm to say so, as it reflects no discredit on us, because we refused to be deterred from our main object. In any case Churchill promised a further statement on Hess. Why hasn't he given it?

My sister does not agree with me about Churchill's speech. She says, 'I like his nice strong adjectives when he talks about Hitler and Musso – such as "guttersnipe".'

July 1st   An old soldier's opinions: 'They're rationing

88

secondhand clothes now, so they've got you both ways... Then they come cadging for your money, but they don't say nothing about giving it back to you after the war. What about these millionaires? They ought to take all their money away from 'em and make 'em soldier for their pay... It don't seem as if we want troops – only planes and tanks, planes and tanks... There'll be some happy homes broken up after this lot, with all these women in the ATS and the WAAFS and that. All the women ought to be put in munition factories, instead of soldiering with all these different soldiers. There'll be a lot of divorces after this war...'

July 3rd   Apparatus has now been installed in the hospital so that a person's voice can be relayed over the radio-relay system. This evening the padre 'broadcast' a lecture on why we are at war. It contained a lot of truths, but missed out a lot too. Much of it was Empire propaganda. Although I hate the Nazi regime as much as anybody, I cannot understand how any clergyman can fall for the notion that this 'is a fight of good against evil, of God against the Devil, a crusade' (his own words).

July 7th   One patient, an oldish man, said he didn't think Germany could stand up to the combined attack of Russia and Britain: 'I don't think Jerry will try to invade us, and what with Russia's little bit and the RAF bombing I think they'll begin to crack – you know, get fed up with it. I don't think we shall see any more of the war than we are now. All we've got to contend with is the 'air-raids.'

July 9th   The welcome given to the Russian mission – people giving the Communist salute, singing the Red Anthem, etc. – seems almost comical in view of the recent outcry against Communists and the banning of the *Daily Worker*. Of course, the Communists have changed their tune too. But everyone agrees that Russia is giving the Germans a lot of trouble and the general feeling seems much more confident than it was a little while ago. This is true for myself as well.

'The best thing Germany could do to finish the war would be

to invade us,' said a soldier today. 'We shall beat them easily,' said another. 'We shall beat them, but not easily,' said the first. 'Oh, yes, we shall. The German people are getting tired. They've been virtually at war for the last six years.' The conversation went on to survey the whole war situation: Turkey wouldn't fight, Japan couldn't conquer China, the Russians were doing well, we might invade Germany soon – these were some of the points made.

July 10th   Most important news for me today is that I am to be discharged from the Army on medical grounds.[5] Nothing could please me more than this. Civilian life may be harder than Army life, as I have known it – food rations will be less (but better prepared), clothes rationed, air-raids more disturbing, and there will be none of the soldier's privileges. But I shall have more personal freedom. I shall not have my life controlled for me to such a degree, I shall be with my own people, and I shall probably be able to do more useful work as a civilian than as a soldier. My service in the Army has seemed to me a sheer waste of time. Now, paradoxically, I am going to see what the war is like. Tomorrow I shall be on my way home.

Another man said he didn't want to get out of the Army, as he was sure of his food, his bed, and his bit of pay, but as a civilian you didn't set so much food and though you might get more pay you had half of it taken away from you. There is always the other point of view.

July 12th   Travelled overnight from Scotland and arrived home this morning. Outwardly everything seemed the same, and I was glad to be back among familiar things and people. I think it will be easy to slip back into civilian life; already the Army life is sliding rapidly into the past. The chief element to which I shall have to get accustomed is the rationing of so many articles. I have a month's leave during which I shall still be paid by the Army, so I shall have no need to hurry into a civilian job.

July 13th   When the radio announcer said there would be a special announcement at 2 o'clock, we all wondered what it would be and most of us thought it would be something to do with America. When it turned out to be a treaty with Russia it was rather a disappointment. 'They could easily have included it with the news,' said my brother-in-law.

The *Sunday Pictorial* ballot on who should be removed from the Government was of interest, and I agreed with the results. The paper emphasises the fact (as other papers have) that Churchill needs better men behind him if he is to conduct the war successfully. What the papers seem to overlook (deliberately, I expect) is that Churchill chooses his men and is really the one to blame.

Sampled some cheese which my brother-in-law makes out of sour milk to supplement the cheese ration.

July 14th   In my opinion the authorities are still acting stupidly over the question of playing the Russian 'Internationale' on the radio. I fail to see how it can have a subversive influence, and it helps to confirm my belief that there are many officials who would rather not co-operate with Russia.

July 17th   As I expected, the rationing is the most difficult thing to get used to. Besides the many articles which are rationed, there seem to be various others which are scarce, although unrationed. As I told my sister, 'I don't understand all this rationing.' One of the biggest surprises to me was to see a notice on the door of a pub, saying 'No beer', though this does not affect me personally.

A man on a bus this morning: 'The news seems to be good this morning. The Russians are holding the Germans and giving 'em some back.'

I think the papers are making too much fuss over the Victory V campaign. What good the campaign, if there really is one, will do, I don't know. I don't believe half the newspapers say about the extent of it. The way they write about it, it sounds like extracts from a cheap thriller.

July 18th   Spent the day in London. It still seems the same to me, in spite of all the damage done. Its streets were as busy as ever, and the cinemas and theatres seemed to be almost in full swing again. The theatre which I visited in the afternoon

(Victoria Palace) was packed. However much London is bombed it will always seem the same.

July 19th   A salvage drive was inaugurated in the town by a former Prime Minister of Canada. One of the things which has struck me very much since my return home is the number of organisations which have been set up either to deal with various problems of individuals or to help the war effort. One street in the town consists entirely of offices such as the Citizen's Advice Bureau, Kitchen Front Bureau, Women's Voluntary Service recruiting office, etc.

The town seems busier than it was, with more people about, though some may be evacuees. Entertainments have increased, I think. Cinemas now open on Sundays, there are three or four dances a week, and more concerts than there used to be.

July 22nd   Agreed with the *News Chronicle* editorial this morning, which said the 'V' campaign was being overdone. Vs have appeared all over the place. As the *News Chronicle* said, the effect of the campaign will be spoilt by running it amongst ourselves.

July 23rd–25th   Went for a short stay with my brother. His wife finds food the greatest difficulty, jam especially, as no fruit can be obtained to make any and the ration of 1lb a month is not enough. She said, 'The only way you can get anything is if you know someone.' The clothes rationing does not seem to bother most people as much as I thought it would. Everyone I have spoken to thinks the ration is adequate. Men are more affected than women, however, as a suit and overcoat would use up the greater part of a year's ration.

My sister-in-law asked me what I thought about the Hess affair and I said I thought he wanted to make peace and get us to help Germany fight Russia. I said I thought we had handled the affair badly from a propaganda point of view; Churchill had promised a statement, but had not given it. She said, 'Yes, he (Churchill) talks a lot, but doesn't tell us much.'

July 27th   The Japanese crisis brings the World War nearer. My cousin, who is in the RAF, mentioned the possibility of

Japan attacking Russia from the rear. 'Then Russia would be fighting on two fronts, as well as Germany,' he said. In my opinion Germany can hardly be said to be fighting on two fronts, since there is very little to engage her on her Western front. My father said, 'I don't think America is quite prepared for war, else she'd have been in before.'

July 30th   By far the greatest inconvenience of the war at present is the difficulty in obtaining food. The women-folk, especially, who have to do the shopping, find it a wearisome and trying business. Most food articles are virtually rationed, whether coupons are required or not. Customers at the local Co-op, for instance, have a special card with columns for tinned milk, biscuits, canned fish, preserved pastes, jellies, dried fruits, cereals, and canned fruits. The columns are cross-divided into weeks, and if a certain article is bought the card is initialled for that week. But supplies are not available of all these articles every week. Biscuits may be obtainable only one week in six, and then one has to go in on the day they happen to have the supplies to be sure of getting any and then there is a queue. In spite of this, however, I find food at home better than Army food, chiefly because it is much better prepared and, even with civilian rations, more varied. Fortunately we have a good supply of vegetables and some fruit from our own garden.

The tobacco shortage is very bad at present. Some of the shops close for short periods at a time.

July 31st   Went to the Labour Exchange about a job. I was told to come back tomorrow and they'd see what they could find me. I have not much idea of what I want to do, but I want a job that will last after the war.

News of the war in Russia is encouraging. Perhaps the die-hard Tories, who said Russia would not last more than a week or two, will not despise the 'Reds' so much now. At the cinema last night people clapped Stalin and news of how the Russians are resisting.

Aug. 1st   Was interviewed for a job at a factory, but as it would mean a lot of overtime I shall not accept it. Instead I went to see about a post as laboratory assistant in a hospital, which would mean more travelling, but more reasonable hours and more interesting work.

A lady in a bus remarked, 'I don't believe in the papers. I think they make the worst of things.'

Aug. 2nd   Succeeded in getting the job.[6]
In the market of this town, where I shall be working the biggest crush was at the sweet-stall, which had a very large supply of chocolate and other sweets. People were spending anything up to £1 on sweets (some were perhaps owners of shops themselves).

Aug. 3rd   Was very interested in Beverley Baxter's article in the *Sunday Graphic* on Churchill and his critics. I usually dislike his articles, but this time I was more or less in agreement with him. Churchill's attitude to critics who are only trying to help is most unsatisfactory. On one point, however, I disagree with Baxter: he says, '...the country at this moment would prefer Mr Churchill's absolute dictatorship to any possible government of which he was not the head.' This I do not believe and I, at any rate, would be definitely against it.

Visited an aunt and uncle in the afternoon. At the big house where my uncle works there are still a few evacuees. My aunt said, 'You should see the difference now from what they were when they came. And three of them have won scholarships.' Everyone (there were six of us) agreed that travel for pleasure over this Bank Holiday weekend was stupid and unpatriotic and a waste of coal and petrol.

There seemed to be a feeling of consolation that Germany would not have it all her own way with air-raids this winter (though neither would we). My uncle said, 'We're not out of the wood yet by a long way.' My father said there were 'dark days ahead'. This did not seem due so much to lack of confidence as to a desire to be prepared for anything.

Food was a main topic of conversation. My father said how difficult it was for men like himself who took their lunch to work with them. He used to be able to pack meat, ham, cheese, or egg sandwiches. Now only cheese is available, but 2oz of that is not enough. My uncle said, 'Food hasn't got the staying power it used to have.' My sister said, 'I always feel hungry; I'm always eating.' My father and uncle both said they had got thinner.

Asked about things in general, my uncle said, 'I think they're all a lot of rogues and liars, including some of our own people. I don't believe half what they say. They say things which are contradicted soon afterwards.'

Aug. 5th   Now that I have started work it seems that travel is going to be one of the biggest and most expensive inconveniences to me. Fares come to about 15/- a week if I stop where I am, but I may be moved elsewhere. Midday meals will cost a good bit, too.

Aug. 9th   Comments by two men on the Russian raid on Berlin: 'It seems as though the Russians are not so backward as we thought.' 'If we could arrange with the Russians to bomb Berlin together, or on alternate nights, we ought to be able to shake them up a bit.' 'Yes, they know which way our bombers come from and they've been able to concentrate their defences on that side. Now they won't know which side the bombers will come from.'

This weekend a contingent of tanks is to be on view in various parts of this district, to build up the tank campaign. Posters all over the town announce the coming of 'Waltzing Matilda and her family of tanks'. This propaganda campaign seems to have captured a good deal of attention.

Although I think the number of clothes coupons is sufficient, the idea of making 20 of them not available until next year is rather unsatisfactory, from my point of view at least. On discharge from the Army I was allowed 20 coupons. With some of these and some I borrowed from my father I have bought a shirt, two pairs of socks, two collars, and some underwear. If I buy another shirt I shall only just have enough, with the new issue of 20, to buy a suit this autumn. But apart from this there is almost nothing else which I shall need. If I had the use of the other coupons now I could manage much more easily.

In the evening I went out to go to a dance, but could not get in, as there had been a new order by the Chief Constable limiting the numbers to 250, which number were already inside.

Aug. 10th   The tank display this afternoon attracted a big crowd of people, but I did not consider it very impressive, there being only three small tanks which drove around and climbed a few bumps, sometimes slipping back or getting stuck.

Putting the clocks back has again made the black-out an unpleasant reality which we had almost forgotten in the past few months. My sister said, 'I dread the coming of winter,' and I think it safe to say that the majority of people do.

Aug. 14th   I did not hear Mr Attlee's broadcast this after-noon, but two of my superiors did and afterwards I heard them talking about it. 'Well, it wasn't half so drastic as I expected. I expected at least that America had declared war,' said one. 'Yes, it was rather an anti-climax. I thought it was something about America and Japan.' 'Of course, it's very idealistic, but...' 'It may seem more important later on.' 'Yes, it may not seem much now, but perhaps we shall look back and think it's more important. What we want *now* is more dramatic news.' On the question of territorial claims, one said, 'We piously say we don't want any more territory, but we don't say we've got too much to handle now, or that we're going to give any back that we have got.' Personally I think the announcement worth its advertisement; its idealism appeals to me. I do not approve the declaration without reserve, though, as the clause which says that only aggressor states must be disarmed smacks of insincerity.

If the resulting statement, as given out by Attlee, was not dramatic, the meeting itself (between Churchill and Roosevelt, at sea) was. I asked my sister if she was disappointed or not; she said she was. My father was too.

Aug. 18th   A friend of mine has met one problem of the black-out with an ingenious contrivance by which the light goes out automatically when the outer door is opened.

Aug. 21st   The news from the Russian front is disquieting, partly because the way in which the papers are giving what news there is has that quality which it had just before the final disaster in France, in Greece, in Crete. But this does not mean that this sense of foreboding will be fulfilled this time. I believe that the Russians are still quite capable of counter-attacking, but on the other hand the Germans seem to employ superior tactics. I do not think it wise to begin giving up hope yet, as when my father said the other day, 'I said all along the Russians couldn't keep it up.' The fortunes of war can easily swing in the other direction.

Aug. 24th   Of all Churchill's speeches I think tonight's was his best. I have criticised some of his previous speeches and there may have been points in this one which could have been criticised, but after listening to it one does not feel like giving it anything but praise. It was moving and inspiring, a magnificent message of hope. There seemed to be some change, difficult to define but nevertheless there, in Churchill's outlook, as though he were recognising new points of view. One wonders whether he has been influenced by his meeting with Roosevelt.

Aug. 25th   I asked a man I work with what he thought of Churchill's speech. 'Well,' he said, 'I've heard more fiery ones.' I said, 'I prefer them when they're not so fiery.' On the British invasion of Iran, he said he thought we were right in getting in there before Germany.

Two women on the bus were talking about the milk rationing, remarking on the smallness of it. 'Half-a-pint's bad enough,' said one. 'I thought half-a-pint *was* the least they were going to let us have,' said the other. 'If they increased the butter ration it wouldn't be so bad. I don't mind about the cheese, but I do like a bit o' butter ... And the beastly old marge is horrible, isn't it?'

Aug. 27th   Three subjects which I have heard most often as topics of general conversation lately are milk rationing, Quentin Reynolds*, and Iran.

---

* American reporter of the British wartime scene.

At home we are trying to improve our black-out by putting up thicker curtains.

Aug. 28th   The attempted assassination of Laval is welcome news. It shows that all is not quiet in France and it may rid the world of one of its evil influences.

Aug. 30th   Tried about ten shops before I was able to obtain some tobacco. For some time I believed the Government assertions that supplies were low because people were smoking much more than they used to, but now I have come to the conclusion that this is merely an excuse for their failure to maintain supplies. There has been a shortage now for many weeks, so it is impossible for anyone to smoke more than previously, yet there is still no improvement.

Aug. 31st   The continued newspaper assault on women to do war work is, I think, being overdone and being carried on in entirely the wrong way. The papers seem to want to tear away everybody from their normal life. But even in wartime I think some people, especially women, should be allowed to carry on their normal pursuits. Beneath the turmoil of war the natural current of human affairs must go on; I do not think it can be dammed up. In any case, if the Government and the Press want to persuade more women to do war work, they are not going the right way about it by abusing them, saying they are 'helping Hitler to win', and so on. I realise, of course, that there are still some idle rich who do practically nothing useful and should be made to work, but that is true just as much in peacetime as now.

Sept. 1st   Remarks overheard during the day: 'The Germans won't waste their men on trying to destroy the Russian army. All they want to do is to capture their industrial areas and put their army out of action.' 'Still, the Russians have done pretty well.' 'Yes, they're the only ones who have stood up to the Germans at all, the only ones who have given them a real fight. Everyone thought at first they (the Germans) would go through them like going through butter.'

'The more civilised a nation gets, the less it wants to fight' (referring to America).

'Why don't they use the Flying Fortresses more?

'I don't see how Hitler can try to invade us, with so many of his men in Russia.'

I listened to the news at a friend's. 'I wonder why we have to register for onions and not for other vegetables,' I said. 'I reckon that's what it will come to. We shall soon have to register for everything,' said my friend. His wife said, 'I don't think it'll affect us much.' 'No,' he said, 'it's not really for us. It's for the people in London and other big cities, who haven't got back gardens. There's thousands of 'em, who are feeling the pinch of this war. *We're not.*'

Sept. 3rd   My boss this morning: 'It looks as though the Russians are getting ready to lose Leningrad.' He also remarked on the fact that our total losses in fighter planes had been announced, but not our bomber losses, which are presumably much heavier.

Very interesting news was the attack on Moore-Brabazon. I am prepared to believe the allegations and I think there are several in Whitehall who are as much anti-Russian as anti-German. When Russia first became our ally I was doubtful whether our co-operation would be very enthusiastic, and it certainly looks as though those doubts were justified.

At a time when food is one of the biggest difficulties, it is rather surprising to find a restaurant where one can obtain extremely well-cooked and adequate meals at a price cheaper than one would expect in peace-time. Yet at the café where I have my lunch one can get meat and two vegetables, a sweet, and tea for 1/3½d. There are not many customers, so service is quick. At a Lyons in the same town one can wait half-an-hour for not such a good dinner at a higher price.

Sept. 4th   Was very interested in the article in *Picture Post* on astrology. It shows up the newspaper astrologists for the worthless impostors they really are. Pseudo-scientific, they exploit the credulity of the uneducated masses. There should be more articles like this until these misleaders of public opinion are driven from the pages of the Press. As I read the article my sister looked at it too. 'Oh, Lyndoe – that's the one W believes in,' she said. 'Does she believe in him?' I asked. 'Oh, yes, she's a great follower of Lyndoe.'

My sister has had to register for war work and has been offered a job with her old firm in the same department; this is secretarial work at a factory. Work will not be hard, she will not start until 10 o'clock and will have Saturday mornings free, so her position will not be so inconvenient as it would be if she had to do some other work assigned to her by the Ministry of Labour. In talking about it she mentioned the case of a girl who wanted to leave the factory to take a job nearer home, but the factory did not want to let her go, so protested to the Ministry of Labour, who forbade her to leave. Now she does very little work and makes as many mistakes as possible, and the firm would like her to leave, but now they cannot get rid of her.

Notices have been put up to say that there will be a reduction in the number of relief buses (the buses serve most of Essex). This will be a cause of annoyance to many, as travel is already a great difficulty. Most buses are overloaded at most periods of the day, cannot cope with the number of travellers.

Sept. 5th   Interesting piece of local news is the rejection by an urban council of a proposal to ban the works of P. G. Wodehouse from the local library. Most members took the broad view that they were works of art which had nothing to do with the writer's political activities. It was up to the public not to borrow his books if they didn't want to. The motion was defeated by 14 votes to 5.

Sept. 7th   My sister asked me if I would go to church with her, as it was a National Day of Prayer, but I said no. I think these prayers for victory are absolute hypocrisy. Carry on this war to the bitter end we must, but do not let us bring God into it. Why should God help us to kill more Germans than the Germans can kill Englishmen? – for that is what the prayers mean in plain language. God is on neither side, or both, and if every day were a day of prayer I do not think it would make the slightest difference to the outcome of the war. We have not been so righteous in the past that God should be on our side. People may get some comfort from praying to God, but it is a false comfort, and they are really blinding themselves to reality. I do not say this because I do not believe in God, but because I do not believe in prayer.

Sept. 9th   Left home at a day's notice to take up another post some distance away.[7] My stay at home was therefore short-lived, but after being in Army billets for over a year I do not mind living in billets (of a more congenial nature) once again, and as the job is to be permanent it is worth it. My work is that of pathological laboratory technician, for which the RAMC gave me training, so that however much I disliked the Army I have something to thank it for.

On the way there our bus was stopped by the police and all passengers had to produce their identity cards. One woman had not got hers, so the police inspector asked her whether she knew she could be detained for it and gave her a stern warning, but let her continue her journey. Said another woman, 'That's the law, that we've always got to carry them with us, and we can't break the law, whether we like it or not.'

The *World Review* put my view of the tobacco situation in a nutshell when it made a crack at the tobacco firms for 'telling us that the reason we are smoking less is that we are smoking more.'

Sept. 11th   I asked my landlady what she thought Roosevelt would say in his speech. She said, 'Oh, I don't suppose it'll be any different from what they usually say. About all they do is talk.' Talking about Socialism, she said she thought that there would have to be some sort of Socialist system in this country after the war. I agreed.

Sept. 12th   Overheard remarks by two men on Roosevelt's speech: 'I noticed he only mentioned German and Italian submarines – not Japan.' 'Yes, I think there's something fishy going on out there.' 'I think it's as good as a declaration of war.'

Churchill's statement on India is profoundly disappointing; it is almost unbelievable. The *News Chronicle* rightly condemns it; it will indeed make the Atlantic Charter, in that journal's words, 'a symbol of hypocrisy'

Sept. 15th 'They ought to have had Russia in this war at the start,' said my landlady's husband. 'Well, they had the chance,' I said. 'Yes, but they wouldn't accept it,' he said.

Sent. 16th Mrs H: 'It says in the paper the Americans think they'll soon be in the war.' Mr H: 'They must come in. I don't see how it can finish without them.'

Saw the captured German terror film at the local cinema, but was not very impressed by it, either as German or as British propaganda, except that it was a warning against over-optimism.

Sept. 18th Some of the papers are getting worried about our lack of aid to Russia. When Germany invaded Russia I thought that our co-operation with the latter would consist of more words than deeds and, up to now, so it has proved. I feel, like a good many others, that we must take a risk if we want to give Russia any substantial aid. The question is: do our leaders *want* to help Russia?

Sept. 19th Conversation this evening included some comment on the war in Russia. Two of the men thought that a British attack in the West was necessary and not unlikely; they discussed where a landing might be made. One of them said he didn't think the Germans would ever vanquish Russia; they could not even hold what they had won through the winter. I said if the Germans did win they wouldn't do it very quickly. He said he didn't think air-raids would be so bad this winter.

Sept. 20th Again the antipathy of certain members of the Government towards Russia is made apparent, this time by Capt. Margesson's article in the *Star*. Apart from his attitude to Russia, the man's fundamental insincerity and dishonesty are obvious from this article. Regarding invasion, I think it would require as big an effort for the Germans to invade us as they are putting into the invasion of Russia, and I am sure it would be impossible for them to carry on two such campaigns at once. Therefore our chance to strike is now. But Margesson apparently wants to keep the Army at home to help the farmers. The *Daily Mirror* rightly points out the absurdity of calling up the farm workers. Men like Margesson – a notorious diehard and party politician – should be removed from office before it is too late.

Sept. 21st   The capture of Kiev by the Germans comes as more of a shock because it was unexpected and carried out apparently without much struggle. It was almost too easy. If it had been Leningrad or Odessa, it would not have been such a blow. However, perhaps this will serve to speed up our help to Russia, which now becomes even more urgent.

Sept. 22nd   Talking about the Russian war this dinnertime, remarks were made on the way in which German claims are usually admitted by the Allies after being denied for about three days. 'It gets you down,' said one man, 'the way they deny it for three days, then admit it.' Someone else said he didn't like the way the radio announcer kept saying 'these reports are of course unconfirmed.' Another said if you wanted to know the truth about the land (but not the air) operations it was best to read the German communiqués. Then the conversation turned on to the newspaper military 'experts', whose articles were unanimously condemned as utter nonsense. One man said it was sometimes impossible to tell the difference between some of the military experts and *Beachcomber*, and we wondered why they got paid for it. With all this I am in complete agreement.

Sept. 23rd   Saw *Target for Tonight*, the much boosted RAF film, but did not think it deserved all the praise it received in the papers. It was certainly interesting and quite soundly made, but it was not half so spectacular or thought-influencing as one was led to suppose. Two other people said it was not up to their expectations and someone else said she had heard several people express disappointment. I can hardly regard it as a propaganda film at all, at least not in this country, though it might be in some other countries.

Sept. 24th   I have still not got my new issue of clothing coupons. I have been trying to get them for about a month, have applied at different offices, and just when I could have got them I changed my address and it seems that I must unravel some more red tape at the new place before I can get them. It is exasperating that at each place one goes to nobody knows anything about the procedure for persons discharged from the Forces.

Sept. 28th   Home for the weekend. Travel a great difficulty, my journey requiring six or seven changes (by bus).

My sister is back at work again, but does not like it much, as it does not give her much time to do housework.

My father and I agreed that the radio programmes are very poor nowadays. I think the *Brains Trust* is about the best programme at present.

We all agreed, also, on the ridiculousness of all the newspaper blurb about Mary Churchill, who, apparently, has joined the ATS. The effusive and unreal accounts of what she has been doing, together with the innumerable photographs, nauseate me. 'The papers don't half print some bilge nowadays,' I said. Indeed, the real news and sane comment contained in most papers could be got into half the space.

Sept. 29th   The two papers I have read today both give a good deal of space to H. G. Wells' speech to the British Association. One recognises the need for planning a better future, but now I am getting rather fed-up with all the new World Plans, World Brains, World Encyclopaedias, charters, declarations, etc., etc., when in reality there is no worldwide feeling in favour of any one of them. What good are all the rules and regulations if the spirit is not there? There must be a change of heart first. Besides, all the talk of 'working out a framework,' 'studying trends and problems', 'setting up committees to make proposals' (to somebody else), making declarations 'with certain reservations in respect of existing obligations', etc. – this is all very well, but doesn't seem to get us anywhere much.

I have at length obtained my clothing coupons. I wrote a letter yesterday and received the coupons today, probably the quickest piece of work ever achieved by the Food Office in question. But it took five or six of preliminary negotiations, at two Food Offices, before this result could be attained!

Oct. 2nd   One of the nurses at the hospital said she didn't think this Government was any better than any other Government we had had. It's suffering from the neglect of its predecessors,' said one of my colleagues. 'It's suffering from capitalism,' was the reply. She thought the Government was content to sit back and fight to the last Russian.

Oct. 3rd   I agree with A. J. Cummings' criticism of Churchill's statement that Germany, 'while standing on the defensive in Russia', could launch three full-scale simultaneous attacks in three different directions. The key-phrase is 'while... Russia'. Germany could not stand on the defensive in Russia without keeping as many men there as she has now; if she withdrew men she would be overwhelmed by the Russians, would have lost the war.

I drew attention to the ludicrousness of the Anglo-German agreement to cease hostilities over the Channel for two days while sick and wounded men are exchanged. My landlady's daughter said, 'Isn't it daft? What do they keep on fighting for, then? That's what they send the bombers out for, to kill each other.' Perhaps we are too simple-minded; war is a complicated business.

Then we began to talk about the manifold injustices of this war. Mrs H's daughter did not see why rich society women should be able to dodge war work. 'If they do get called up they won't have to work in factories and get all dirty. They'll get nice cushy jobs,' she said. (She herself has just been interviewed for war work, has been given six weeks in which to get married, but will have to do factory work all the same.) Mrs H said she thought that kind of thing would always go on. I said they had put a stop to it in Russia. She said she would like to go to Russia and 'see how they work things'.

The monstrous evils – the known, deliberate, condoned evils – of war sometimes appall me.

Oct. 4th   Having got my clothing coupons, today I used 18 of them, with ten emergency coupons which I had, making 28 altogether. These were spent on a shirt and an order for a new suit (without waistcoat). The suit will cost more than I usually pay, but I can better afford it now.

At the pictures tonight, the audience had claps for Churchill in his RAF uniform, bigger claps for Russian troops.

Oct. 5th   In yesterday's *Daily Express* and today's *News of the World* the most important items, I think, were the appeals for a relaxation of the black-out, lights to be controlled by a master-switch. The black-out is undoubtedly a dominating factor in most people's lives. It weighs down tremendously on public morale. If the lights were to go up again I am sure people's spirits would soar enormously.

Mrs H said she reckoned the reason for the delay in the exchange of British and German sick and wounded was that the Germans wanted us to hand over Hess, but of course we shouldn't be such fools. I had forgotten all about Hess, so had not considered the possibility of this.

Oct. 7th   I cannot help quoting the following passage from the *News Chronicle*. First it says that it is still being questioned whether Hitler's announcement of a big new offensive is bluff or camouflage, then goes on: 'The odds still seem to be in favour of the first guess, with the reservation that bluff or camouflage might be intended as a mask for the preparation of a new offensive.' How long did it take the writer to work out this brilliant deduction? Passages like this are typical of most newspapers, as are vague statements which go something like this: 'Further news tends to show... if... he might... but...' with no end to the number of conditional clauses. What is the good of writing this stuff and what is the good of reading it?

At dinner today one man asked if anyone had read the *Daily Express* campaign for the lifting of the black-out. 'They always get what they want,' he said, 'so you can expect the black-out to be lifted before Christmas.' It doesn't look as though it will be, though.

Oct. 9th   Today's news is grave. Perhaps I have overrated the powers of the Russians, but I do not attach any blame to them; I feel rather sorry for them. But my main feeling is one of bitter, flaming anger at the inertia of our Government. I may be prejudiced in this respect, but I do not think I am far from the truth when I say I think that our help to Russia has been almost negligible. My landlady, however, said, 'Oh, I think we're sending help as fast as we can.' I simply do not agree. I feel as though I want to say, 'Kick out the whole present Government and let's have a new one.' Whether I should be justified in saying this I don't know. But our lack of action of any description is almost beyond belief. Are not our leaders sufficiently alarmed even now to take action? Complacently to condemn ourselves, and whoever else may still be in the war, to heaven knows how long a struggle, when some offensive action might prove decisive, is criminal.

Oct. 10th   The *News Chronicle* today says, rightly I think, that public anger is mounting higher than over the Norway fiasco. I have hardly any feeling of disappointment or despair, only anger. The public has had enough of this war; to let it drag on, always to our disadvantage, is maddening. The cry, Why don't we do something? epitomises all the ordinary person's feelings.

Comment at dinner today: 'I think they'll get to Moscow, but whether they capture it or not is another matter. It may hold out for months, like Leningrad or Odessa.' This is more or less my own view. I do not think the Russians will give in very easily. With our help we may yet save the day.

Oct. 11th   It makes one a little suspicious when one day the papers present the news in an extremely grave manner, as though preparing for the worst, then the next day, when Russian resistance has stiffened a little, present the news in quite a different light. The *News Chronicle* today, for instance, says it was impossible for Timoshenko to have been caught off his guard and ridiculous to say that Russia was finished as a military power. This may be true, but yesterday the same paper was as good as saying that Russia might soon be defeated. However, the news does seem slightly better today.

Saw the film called *A Day in Soviet Russia*, with commentary by Quentin Reynolds. A very interesting film. I don't suppose it tells the whole truth, but what it does show is impressive. The Russians do seem to be trying to use culture and science to build up a civilised life for everybody. That their achievements so far should be destroyed is one of the worst aspects of their struggle with Germany. Some Communists (presumably) were selling pamphlets about Russia in the lobby of the cinema. I bought one called 'Planning for Prosperity'. It was full of facts on the production of iron, how many children go to school, etc., which prove nothing.

Oct. 12th   The people with whom I live were talking this dinnertime about our help to Russia and seemed to agree that we were giving a good deal of aid. (I do not agree, neither do I think this is the general view.) 'Some people are too impatient,' said Mr H. 'I've got every faith in Churchill,' said Mrs H. Their son (home on leave) said that often things flatly contradicted by the Government have turned out to be true. This alone gives me hope that we may yet give Russia some substantial help. If I have been too impatient, so much the better, and I will take back all I have said if we do send help (not only supplies, but military action). All the same, the help will have been a long time forthcoming; it should have been evident by now.

Oct. 17th   Nothing that Beaverbrook or Churchill can say can allay my anxiety about our aid to Russia, until they can talk about some bold action already accomplished. But I am now almost resigned to be disappointed; I don't suppose we shall do much now. It is not good enough go say that we have promised Russia everything she asked for. Supplies can be sent only in instalments over a lengthy period; raw materials have to be made into weapons before they can make any difference to the struggle. Germany continues to press on, while our Navy and Army are more or less idle and the RAF operates only on a long-term policy. It is all very well to say that we are making plans for 1943, but is time on our side?

Oct. 18th   Mr H: 'It looks as though Japan will be in it in a week or so.' Myself: 'I expect that will bring America in too.' Mr H: 'Yes, I think America will have to come right in before it's finished. I don't think we can finish it on our own.' He did not think invasion likely, however, unless Germany conquers Russia, which also he did not think likely.

Oct. 19th   It does seem suspicious, as the *Sunday Pictorial* points out, that Lord Gort's dispatches should be published at a time when people are clamouring for military action to help Russia. It must be intended to create the feeling that we are not ready to carry out any action of this sort, which amounts to the trick of excusing faults by indirectly admitting others, employed more than once by Chamberlain and his followers. Otherwise there seems to be no point in publishing these dispatches.

Oct. 22nd   A man to whom I spoke said he thought the German thrust in the Donetz basin more dangerous than the threat to Moscow.

Oct. 23rd   My comment on the publication of Gort's dispatches seems to be justified. Lord Moyne yesterday said that 'the warning of Gort's dispatches and the lesson of Dunkirk should have gone home to everyone', and that it would be disastrous to send out another such expedition. Are we then no stronger than we were over a year ago? My confidence in the Government is rapidly dwindling. Someone seems to have drugged our leaders into a state of paralysis. Churchill himself seems to have adopted the stonewalling attitude.

Oct. 24th   At lunchtime today a man said, 'I'd like to read the Duke of Bedford's pamphlet, the one that's been causing all the fuss.' Another man: 'Who is the Duke of Bedford actually? Is he a Fascist?' First man: 'No, he's a pacifist.' Second man: 'Oh, perhaps he's been telling the truth, then.' Another man: 'Yes, that's very likely what it is. He's been spilling the beans.'

Oct. 25th   My first night fire-watching at the hospital. Actually the ordinary night staff are considered to be fire-watchers; eight other men form the stirrup-pump and trailer-pump parties. I have had stirrup-pump practice in the Army, but I wouldn't like to say whether all the others have. We can have supper and breakfast on duty, but this costs 2/6d., so the pay of 3/- for a 12-hour duty only just covers it. Fire-watchers at a factory near here, I am told, get 7/- a time. We do one turn every eight days.

Oct. 26th　　I had rather a heated argument with my landlady over our help to Russia. She thinks our leaders know what they are doing and we should leave it all to them. My point is that it is not wise to leave everything to a few experts who do not necessarily know what is the best thing to do every time. Criticism is essential. I would not mind so much if the Government would consider all reasonable criticism before rejecting it; it is their obstinate refusal to take any notice at all of what is being said and thought by other people which I dislike. At least that is the impression they give, and Government speakers have taken no trouble to remove that impression. This question of whether the opinion of a few experts is better than the opinion of a large number of clever, well-meaning, but only partly informed people is one of the most controversial of the moment.

Oct. 28th　　Opinion at the lunch-table today (four men besides myself) was that Roosevelt was doing his best to bring America into the war, but he could not do it too quickly as he had a lot of opposition to overcome, which he was doing subtly and as quickly as possible.

Oct. 29th　　Received a civilian duty gas mask and a steel helmet for my fire-guard duties. I have also been shown where all the fire equipment – stirrup-pumps, buckets, ladders, extinguishers, etc. – is kept. This will probably be all the instruction which I shall get in fire-fighting.

Nov. 2nd　　Mrs H said, 'You know what – I believe they do expect invasion. That's what they're holding all that tinned stuff back for.' It looks as though constant Government repetition of the likelihood of invasion is beginning to make people believe it.

Nov. 7th　　The last few days have been fairly uneventful. Today Stalin's speech shows beyond doubt that our help is not enough. It now remains to be seen how Government speakers will try to sidestep the question, this time direct from the horse's mouth, of what action we are going to take to divert German forces from the Russian front. Let us hope they will not try to sidestep it at all. Stalin's view on the Hess affair coincides with mine, which I have already recorded.

Nov. 8th   I have been reading Aldous Huxley's *Ends and Means* and my agreement with most of his ideas contrasts strangely with my desire for stronger assistance to Russia. For there is so much truth in Huxley's book that no-one with an honest mind can ignore it. One of the key passages of the book is this: 'The world sanctions two systems of morality – one for private individuals, another for national and other groups. Men who, in private, are consistently honest, humane, and considerate, believe that when they are acting as the representatives of a group they are justified in doing things which, as individuals, they know to be utterly disgraceful.' This is a great truth. Men condone cruelty and injustice and dishonesty when it is the policy of their country, but condemn it in the lives of individuals. Countries can commit crimes which are punishable by imprisonment or death when committed by one or a few persons. The punishment itself may be wrong in the latter case, but the crime is the same in both cases, all the same.

But one can support this war for two reasons which Huxley himself, though perhaps not consciously, admits. He says that reform must be carried out in desirable contexts, that is, it can be carried out better in a democracy than in a dictatorship. Even in a partial democracy there is more chance of carrying out reform than in no democracy at all. For this reason I want the democracies – even if only so-called – to be victorious in this war. Also Huxley says that the results of violence and injustice can sometimes be compensated for afterwards by acts of justice and peace. If Britain and her allies win this war there is more chance of this being done than if Germany does, though it is probable at first that public feeling will make it psychologically impossible for our leaders to do anything (even if they want to) except carry out a policy of revenge and punishment, as was the case at the end of the last war. But, unless this country becomes totalitarian, there will be more chance of pacifism becoming the means of attaining a real peace. Aldous Huxley rightly points out that the vast majority of people are pacifists in so far as they want peace, but that they are wrong in supposing that war is an appropriate means to that end. He goes on to point out many practical ways by which the world *could* be improved.

This book has had a more profound effect on me than any I have read for some time (he disillusions me about Russia too), but, for the reasons I have stated, I still want to see a British victory. Though I hardly know which of the two I am, I can see that a German victory would crush the hopes of pacifists and non-pacifists alike.

Last night we were talking about 'after the war'. I said that really nobody would 'win' the war, as all concerned would come out worse off than they were before. My landlady said that after the war would be the time when our troubles really would start. She did not think people would be content with things as they were before the war. 'Besides, they know too much about Russia now,' she said, a remark which I think highly significant. On another occasion she said she thought it quite possible that there would be revolution in this country after the war.

Nov. 10th   Man's comment on Churchill's statement that the RAF is now as big as the Luftwaffe: 'That's the best piece of news I've heard for a long time.' Regarding after the war, he said, 'When we have won this war there won't be any half-measures this time,' (meaning in connection with our treatment of Germany).

Nov. 11th   Armistice Day. This has never had much significance for me, and today it had less than ever. It is just a remembrance of futility and horror, but not as such – they call it heroism.

Nov. 14th   The first thought, or if not the first, the most serious, that comes to people when news such as the sinking of the *Ark Royal* is announced is of the number of lives involved. (It was the same when 37 of our bombers failed to return; people were reckoning up how many lives lost that meant.) When someone told us the news at lunchtime, the conversation of the men I was with dealt firstly with the embarrassment of the German propagandists through having 'sunk' the ship so many times before, then with the number of men on the ship, then with how it was sunk. When I got home to my lodgings Mr H said the ship was in tow at the time so that it was thought not many lives were lost – one of the most consoling features of the news.

Nov. 18th   I am sure that not many people do football pools nowadays, but a man who was on fire-watching with me tonight spent a considerable time filling in his coupon.

Nov. 19th   The replacement of Sir John Dill, aged 60, by Sir Alan Brooke, aged 58, drew forth some sarcastic remarks at lunchtime, such as 'Youth takes the helm.' Yet some papers are seriously treating the news from this angle!

The business over the Duke of Bedford is of interest. The *Daily Mirror*'s statement that 'we are all against the persecution of pacifists' is surprising, and I do not think it is true. Apparently Lord Simon is not against it, for one.

Nov. 20th   At last the Army is doing something. The advance into Libya, if big enough, may be a second front which will have important effects on the situation in Russia. A man's comment: 'I don't think they'll make the mistake of stopping halfway this time. They want to go right on to Tripoli.'

Nov. 21st   Referring to the Libyan campaign, a man said, 'I don't know which is the worst to endure, the huzzahs and hosannahs of the advance, or the glib excuses for the retreat.' Another man said, 'Oh, the retreat, I think.'

Nov. 22nd   My landlady said she soon ought to be making Christmas puddings, but she didn't know where the ingredients were coming from. My sister tells me in a letter that she has made hers already.

113

A copy of the *Worker's News* was delivered here today. This is the *Daily Worker* in disguise. They have even gone so far as to print the *Daily Worker* title as a cutting on the back page, so that at first glance one might think it was the genuine article, published in defiance of the ban. Although I am no Communist, I rather admire them for doing this; I thought they would sooner or later. To be consistent the Government ought to ban the *Worker's News* too, but they probably don't want to now that Russia is our ally, and if they did there would be a great fuss about it.

Mr H remarked to me on the Germans' huge capacity for replacing losses in men. But I said that could not go on indefinitely and he agreed. 'In fact,' he said, 'if they suffer a major defeat in Libya it may be the beginning of the end.'

Nov. 24th My landlady told me about the members of a local women's club who were given a lecture on Russia, which gave them the idea of having a nursery school for their children. The authorities said they would set up a nursery if at least 40 women would agree to do factory work. So far, only three women have put their names down.

Nov. 27th That the first triumphant fanfares of victory in Libya were premature is now evident. But although a warning note has been struck I am still pretty confident of a success for our troops. When one is fighting a strong and determined enemy like the Germans one cannot expect it to be easy going. The Russian situation is more disquieting.

The milk-rationing scheme, in the opinion of one man at least, is a farce. He said his ration had been cut down to one pint on the first day of the rationing, but since then he had been receiving his usual amount. Another man had had no cut in rations at all. My landlady, however, has had hers reduced to one pint a day, with an occasional extra half-pint. I said I couldn't see why there should be a shortage, but she said the yield was bound to go down in winter, owing to shortage of animal feeding-stuffs, and also a lot of milk was condensed to send to our troops abroad. I suppose this is quite true, but I still don't think milk should be officially rationed.

Nov. 28th   According to the British Institute of Public Opinion (in the *News Chronicle* today), a majority are in favour of the conscription of women. If that is the case, then I am one of the minority. Public opinion on this question may be somewhat different from private opinion, where it affects families directly.

'They ought to be able to do Benghazi and back before Christmas,' said a man jokingly, but with an undoubted belief in its possibility.

Nov. 29th   Three posters have attracted my attention today. The first was a Ministry of Health one which says 'Coughs and sneezes spread diseases' and then says 'Use your handkerchief'. The next one was issued by the Communist Party and says, as near as I can remember, 'Start an offensive in the West now'. The third was a National Savings one, a variation on an old one, 'Lend to defend *his* right to be free'. This shows a picture of a little boy and should appeal to parents. There is also an advertisement which has appeared in the Press frequently, on which Mr H remarked this morning: 'That's a good advert., "Britain's boys are all born fighters, Bovril builds the little blighters."' This, like two of the above-mentioned posters, contains a rhyme, which, though not essential, seems to be desirable in a good poster.

Home for the weekend. Milk rationing was one of the things which soon cropped up in conversation. Both my sister and my father have been cut down to the ration of two pints a week, with an occasional extra half-pint if the milkman can spare it.

Nov. 30th   The attitude of children to Christmas in wartime is interesting. I listened to two children, one about eight, the other a little younger, talking to their grandfather about it. The latter said that Father Christmas wouldn't be able to bring them much this year as he couldn't get the things, he couldn't go to Germany and get toys there. 'He can go to Russia,' said the older child, 'and America.' Their grandfather then tried to explain why this was not possible, but it took a lot of explaining to two children who really believed in Father Christmas, without

115

disillusioning them, why he couldn't go to America on his reindeer, since they wouldn't accept the fact that if he went on a ship he might be torpedoed.

Points rationing is another major topic of conversation. Today was the first time I had seen one of the pink ration books, and at first it looked very complicated. My aunt and a girl who keeps a shop also said they did not understand it.

A complaint about the new American foods is that they are very expensive. My sister had guarded against egg rationing before it started by buying about 100 from a poultry farm and preserving them.

When I got back to my lodgings tonight I asked my landlady if she understood the points rationing. She said she didn't know much about it, but 'expect the shopkeepers will do all that themselves.'

Dec. 1st　　'The position in Libya seems to have consolidated itself, favourably to us, I think,' said a man at lunchtime today. Someone mentioned Rostov. 'The retreat from Rostov's a big thing,' said another. 'One of the most amusing things is the German statement that they're retreating in order to punish the inhabitants.' 'I think that's one of the weak points about this German business – their propaganda,' said another, 'it's so stupid.' But the others did not agree with this, in view of past propaganda successes of the Germans. One man said British propaganda did not compare very favourably with it. The man who thought that German propaganda was stupid said that if America entered the war it would be as a direct result of German propaganda. He who thought our own propaganda not so good said he thought America would have a handful in the Pacific before the week was out.

The new BBC announcer, Wilfred Pickles, seems to have taken some people's fancy. When I was home for the weekend two people asked me if I had heard him. Tonight, as soon as he started to read the news, my landlady's husband said 'Pickles.' Perhaps it's only his name.

Dec. 2nd　　It looks as though we've got a tough nut to crack in Libya.

116

Dec. 5th   The general approval which the Press claims for the Government's conscription of women is something which I do not believe exists outside the newspapers. In fact most papers have for days been running a campaign, the purpose of which was not to *express* public opinion in favour of female conscription, but to *force* public opinion in that direction, by telling people what they ought to think. The *News Chronicle* today says that the girls concerned have accepted 'the call to arms in a quiet, philosophical manner'; my interpretation of that would be a 'half-hearted' manner. This is shown by the views of half-a-dozen girls interviewed, which are by no means enthusiastic. I am glad, however, that married women are not to be conscripted. I am sorry, on the other hand, that the military age has been lowered to 18½ and that children of 16 to 18 are to register. Why do the very youngest have to be brought so directly into contact with war? By this decision large numbers of the young and vigorous will be eliminated, there will be a majority of old people, and the young that are left will have been contaminated by the experience of militarism.

The regimentation of youth is one of the worst features of the dictatorships and it was to be hoped, for the sake of the future, that the youth of the professed democracies would have been spared this. What is this paradox which makes it impossible for a democracy to fight a dictatorship without becoming less democratic and more totalitarian?

It is quite probable, though, that there will be more enthusiasm amongst this youth group than among the women conscripts.

Dec. 7th   Mrs H, in spite of difficulties, has succeeded in making five Christmas puddings, although they contain no candied peel, less suet than usual, and are mixed with stout instead of milk!

The news tonight makes war with Japan inevitable, I think. (The news was of the Japanese attack upon the American fleet at Pearl Harbor.) 'I don't see how America can keep out of it now,' I said to Mr H. 'If she don't come in now, she never will come in,' was his reply.

Dec. 8th   One of my first thoughts on getting up this morning was to wonder whether we had declared war on Japan. (At 8.30 this evening, as I write this, I still don't know the answer.) At lunchtime today the men at my table were quite light-hearted about it. They made remarks about the kind of propaganda films Hollywood would now produce. 'I shudder to think of it,' said one. He also 'shuddered' to think what the cartoons would be like now, 'with all funny little men showing all their teeth.' Another dreaded the new heights of silliness to which the popular songs would probably rise. (Surely he meant to say 'depths ... sink'.)

My landlady this evening said it would have bad effects for us, as America would not be able to send us any more arms.

At least two papers have been trying, in the last week or two, to belittle Japan's strength and her chances if she should become involved in a war with Britain and America. I only hope they don't have to eat their words too soon!

9.30 p.m. Churchill's speech and the news already indicate that the Japanese attack is no laughing matter, that Japan's strength is not to be despised.

So now the whole world, with negligible exceptions, is at war, and the prospect, which had begun to look a little brighter, now seems darker. One feels that it would be pleasant to be an Eskimo or a member of some other uncivilised community which does not know war.

Dec. 9th   When I said 'negligible exceptions' I forgot Spain, whose entry into the war would be by no means negligible.

Dec. 10th   A man said he thought the Germans would renew their bombing of this country this winter; if they had to withdraw in Russia they would turn round on us. Another man said he didn't think the Russians would give the Germans much rest.

I was somewhat staggered when my landlady told me that two of our battleships had been sunk at Singapore. The Japanese have certainly made a good start from their point of view.

Discussing oratory at lunchtime, two or three of the men gave the opinion that Roosevelt is a better orator than Churchill. I think Roosevelt is at least as good as Churchill in this respect, but would not say better – their styles are quite different.

Dec. 12th   It is evident now that the *Prince of Wales* and *Repulse* were not sunk by suicide squads, human torpedoes, or secret weapons, but by a skilful attack by ordinary bombers and torpedo-bombers. It shows how much the Japanese were under-rated that the theory of 'human torpedoes', etc., should have been given so much credence in the Press. It is good that these theories have been squashed at the start and the true nature of what we are up against revealed.

Dec. 14th   Now that Japan has entered the war my sister-in-law said, 'I'm afraid it's going to drag on a long while yet,' which I think is the opinion of the majority. The bad news from the Far East, however, is just about balanced by the good news from Russia and Libya.

My sister-in-law's chief grievances seemed to concern prices and milk rationing; her chief worry about the possibility of being called up, as she does not want to go in the Forces or to do factory work.

Dec. 15th   Seditious remarks heard today: 'I think it would be better for us if we got rid of all this Empire.' 'Yes, it's no good to us.' 'Only to certain interests.' 'Malaya is one big ramp.' 'Let 'em all rule themselves.'

Dec. 16th   It has been almost funny the way all the countries have been declaring war on each other and the situation has now become so complicated that one cannot comprehend it all at once. Many people have remarked on this. One man said that one needs a table showing with which countries any particular country is at war and which not. Another said, 'The world's gone raving mad. They can do what they like as far as I'm concerned. I've lost all interest.' This is not so much bewilderment as a recognition of the craziness of the world. As far as I am concerned, too, the world is just one big madhouse.

Dec. 18th   I am afraid I shall ignore one official request this

Christmas, and that is the one asking people not to travel. I shall be having four days off, so am going home for the holiday. Since there are trains on any ordinary day for civilian travel (not necessarily on business) it is rather silly to ask people not to travel at all 'except for business purposes'.

A man told me he did not think that the Japanese would take Singapore; but it would not surprise me it they do.

Dec. 19th   The attack on Herbert Morrison seems to me to be justified. His record has been most disappointing and he deserves all the criticism handed out to him.

I came across a rare creature this evening: a man who always carries his gas mask (and steel helmet too).

Dec. 20th   Tried to do a little Christmas shopping, but it was hopeless – there were crowds of people everywhere. All I bought was a book for myself, but that was easy, as I knew what I wanted (*For Whom the Bell Tolls* by Ernest Hemingway). Most people seem to be making preparations of some sort for Christmas, though celebrations will of necessity not be so elaborate this year. The *Daily Mirror*, I notice, asks for the complete control of Father Christmas, so that we may be spared 'the hypocrisy of his blither about peace and goodwill'. The *Daily Mirror* is often too realistic, sometimes to the point of making itself absurd. The Christmas tradition is one of the oldest and strongest in this country; it will probably never die out. Personally, I think it is a good tradition which ought to be kept alive and Christmas is, in many respects, the time of year I like best. For a few days, at least, some people behave a little better to each other than they usually do and there is generally an atmosphere of warmth and friendliness. It may be rather hypocritical in these times, but it is the times which need changing, not Christmas.

Dec. 21st   Read a 2d. pamphlet on 'Health and Medicine in Soviet Russia'. It is an interesting pamphlet with a lot of facts, which, if they are correct, show that in the field of health Russia is far in advance of this country.

Dec. 22nd   The newspapers have made themselves look

120

rather silly today. For some days they have been suggesting that the Army chiefs were about to relieve Hitler of his position, when actually it was the other way about. In fact, the papers have altogether ridiculed themselves these last few months. Time and again they have had to contradict themselves over some piece of wishful-thinking, some vague rumour, or some ill-founded opinion. This has had such an effect in my case that when a newspaper says a certain thing is likely to happen I always half-expect the opposite. (I am half-afraid now that the Russian advance will turn into a retreat.) For some reason this usually only applies to good news (though occasionally bad news turns out to be not so bad), so the general effect is rather depressing, but if the balance was on the other side the effect would be complacency, and if good and bad news turned out to be bad and good with equal frequency, the papers would then be *absolutely* unreliable. I do not think it is good for morale for hopes to be raised high and then let down with a bang. The newspapers would do better to present the news more soberly and sensibly, instead of throwing themselves open to such wide margins of error. Papers like *The Times* and *Daily Telegraph* score over the more popular journals in this respect. The Press, of course, is not always to blame for the news it has to give (though it is for the way it presents it).

Lastly, one may say that an intelligent person can discover some of the truth by 'reading between the lines', substituting the opposite, converting the sickening euphemisms into plain language, and sorting out the half-truths and downright lies, but it is obviously more desirable that the truth should be given in a straightforward manner, and in any case the majority are not capable of extracting the truth in this way. I often do not attempt to do so, but just wait for the news to be confirmed or contradicted and try not to let my feelings be led astray too soon.

Dec. 23rd   'We shall finish our war with Germany before they (the Americans) finish theirs with the Japs,' said an AFS* man tonight. Regarding Churchill's visit to America, he thought

* Auxiliary Fire Service.

he (Churchill) had already been and come back before the news was allowed to be released, but I doubt this myself.

There is some dissatisfaction about the fire-watching arrangements at the hospital. Instructions are very confused; a supper costs 1/6d. here against 1/- at some other hospitals; no arrangement is made for replacement if a man is sick; and if a man does a turn for someone else and so does more than his allotted period per month he gets no pay for it, as he is only obliged to do 48 hours a month; and many smaller details.

Dec. 24th   Made the journey home in the evening quite easily. The train was almost full, but I managed to find a seat. According to the *News Chronicle*, the official policy of no extra trains seems to have been ignored. The point is that if the railway companies are able to cope with the crowds by putting on extra trains, why place a ban on travelling at all? One supposed that the reason for the ban was that the Government needed the trains for other purposes. If not, the ban is apparently meaningless.

Dec. 25th   Got up about half-past nine. Spent the morning at my sister's and read some of *Poverty and Progress*, Rowntree's social survey of York. A relation came round and talked to my father about the war. Regarding the entry of Japan he said, 'I reckon it's put two years on the war.' My father agreed and said, 'Undoubtedly they wiped out practically the whole of the American Pacific fleet ... Still, I suppose we shall muddle through in the finish.'

Gifts this year were on the small scale. There seemed to be plenty of cigarettes about (I had 30 cigarettes and two ounces of tobacco). Those who could spare coupons used them on small articles, such as ties, socks, and handkerchiefs. The rest consisted chiefly of what are described as 'fancy goods' – bottles of scent, jewellery, etc.

We had our usual Christmas dinner, including roast chicken and Christmas pudding (with threepenny-bits in it). Everyone I know around here managed to get a chicken for dinner.

In the afternoon I read a little more of *Poverty and Progress* and then paid a visit to an aunt. Returned to my sister's for tea and we had an iced Christmas cake. 'Aren't we lucky to have all this?' said my sister, 'It's as good as peacetime.' 'If we don't do any worse than this for the rest of the war,' said my father, 'we shan't starve.' Yet according to Rowntree's survey there were many families in peacetime who were living below the minimum nutritional level required for health. How are they faring now?

(I almost forgot to mention that we listened to the King's speech in the afternoon. It wasn't really very noteworthy.)

About seven we went round to my brother-in-law's family's house, where there were several other people. We played games for the children until about half-past nine, then played a card game and darts until nearly midnight. Drinks were not so plentiful this year, but there was a little port and sherry. In fact the main items lacking this year were wine, nuts, sweets, and fruit. For supper we had sandwiches of 'Treet', the imported American food, which we all thought very tasty. Altogether, it was a very enjoyable Christmas, not much different from our usual peacetime celebration.

Dec. 26th   Enjoyed listening to Churchill's speech to Congress in Washington. It was a solemn speech, especially its reference to taking the initiative in 1943, but it was full of vigour and encouragement. 'One of the finest speeches I've heard him make for a long time,' said my father.

Dec. 27th   Comments on Churchill's speech: 'He's wonderful, isn't he? – speaking all that time.' 'It was nice the way he referred to his parents, wasn't it?' 'He seems to have taken America by storm.'

Dec. 28th   Some people, however, did not enjoy Christmas as much as I did. One man said, 'It's the worst Christmas I've experienced.' My landlady said, 'It's been a funny Christmas.' One of the main reasons for this, I think, was the shortage of Christmas extras.

Dec. 29th   Looking back on the past year, I must say that it has not been humdrum or uninteresting. War certainly brings movement and excitement into one's life, although at the same time it may make it less happy. The world scene, too, has changed its colours and proportions frequently and gives one much to conjecture on, though one may not approve of many happenings.

In the last year I have been both more happy and more unhappy at different times than ever before. I have read more and danced more, one a serious pastime, the other frivolous, but both things which give me the greatest pleasure. It has been a full year of experience and has left me individually in a better position mentally and physically (though I may not have thought so all the time) than this time last year. Some would say I have been lucky, but I do not believe in luck.

As a world-citizen, however, I despair more and more of the world situation. The main aim of the nations seems to be to plunge themselves into every possible crime and degradation. It is so tragic, it sometimes seems comic. The prospect for 1942 does not seem brighter, but gloomier if anything. I am reconciled to a long and weary war, but as far as I am concerned the world can carry on in its own sweet way. Any part which I shall play in the war effort will be passive, not active. As an onlooker I am greatly interested in world affairs; as a participator I am apathetic. It is impossible to remain outside this war, but I am not going actively to join in it. That is the only way to hold on to sanity.

Dec. 30th   As far as I can see, the Japanese aggression appears to be meeting almost no resistance, but the news of their successes is somehow not so disheartening as were the Russian reverses a few weeks ago. And now the Russian victories attract my chief attention; success is always more interesting than failure.

Dec. 31st   I notice that the *News Chronicle* hopes that the German people will 'be permitted to hope that the means of a decent existence will not be withheld from them.' So they are to be 'permitted to hope', but there is no guarantee that their hopes will be fulfilled. In this connection I disapprove of A. P. Herbert, whose piece of doggerel in last Sunday's *Sunday Graphic* throws all the blame on the Germans, Italians, and Japanese, abuses those who are not of a like opinion, and admits that his own attitude may be 'unchristian'. Yet among the things we are supposed to be fighting for are freedom of religion and freedom of expression. Men like A P Herbert should be locked up; their reactionary influence is harmful and insidious. They would have us back in the pre-war state of affairs, which we must avoid at all costs.

It shows how prejudiced I am that I should talk about freedom of expression and then say that A P Herbert should be locked up, so I retract that remark, but at any rate people with opposite views should be given the same freedom.

Notes

[1] Sheffield and Leeds were presumably just stages on the way up to Scotland. Peebles and the surrounding district were to be my location for the next five months. The camp was situated some distance out of the town at a spot named Glentress. In reality, the unit being formed there was a casualty clearing station. I never discovered their final destination, but if I had remained with them I would almost certainly have ended up in North Africa.

[2] Hospital at Peebles. The Hydro had been converted to a military hospital.

[3] Three days earlier Rudolf Hess had parachuted down at Eaglesham, just south of Glasgow, which was barely 40 miles as the crow flies from our camp just outside Peebles. I was a mere private and would not have been allowed anywhere near Hess, yet his peregrinations during this period covered remarkably similar ground to my own. From Scotland Hess was taken down to a safe house known as 'Camp Z', near Aldershot, where for a year or more he was looked after by medical staff and orderlies from Connaught and Cambridge military hospitals, both of which I knew and where I had finished my training about five months earlier. After my discharge from the Army I quite often passed the imposing entrance to Trent Park at Cockfosters, on my way to Cockfosters tube station, which I used a good ideal for travel into London or for visits home. I did not know that Trent Park was the HQ of the secret service, from where the

interrogation and assessment of Rudolf Hess was being conducted by Major Foley of MI6. It almost seemed that wherever I had been had at a later date some association with Hess.

The Hess flight to Scotland was a strange mission, and it is a strange flight of fancy on my part to think that I could have been in any way involved with him. As it happened, on the day of his landing I was on the sick list and was in the hospital at Peebles.
[4] The convalescent home was a requisitioned country house a few miles west of Peebles. Seen in perspective, this was really a blissful interlude. I spent a whole month there following a relatively minor operation, which today would hardly justify more than a few days in hospital. Perhaps the Army were hoping to make me fit for service. Whatever the reason, I spent a lovely summer month in the Scottish countryside, with little to do except eat and sleep, or wander round the grounds. I spent a lot of time reading library books. Sometimes I found a packet of cigarettes left on the bed. What was I complaining about?
[5] Manifestly, I was not cut out for Army life; I was of much more use as a civilian. In spite of this, however, I have been eternally grateful to the Army for two things – 1. My health was improved considerably – as a result of the operation on my sinuses, I was enabled to breathe properly, which due to the legacy of childhood illnesses I had not been able to do before. 2. They gave me valuable training in medical laboratory work, which proved very useful in my future career.
[6] This was a temporary post at a hospital in Romford.
[7] Started at Clare Hall Hospital at South Mimms, where I remained for the next seven years, except for a short but hectic period at the end of 1943. At this time I began to live in Potters Bar; my lodgings were about three miles from the hospital, so I travelled daily by bus. The area covered by the diary from now until the end of the war is normally the Potters Bar/Barnet/St Albans region, with fairly frequent diversions to London and occasional visits to Essex or elsewhere.

1942

Jan. 2nd   What a striking contrast to the usual run of news is Switzerland's decision to abolish the death penalty! It is strange how Switzerland always manages to remain neutral. She is probably too insignificant a country to matter in any military sense, but as an example of progress and humanity she puts the rest of the world to shame. She has no Empire, but are her people any the less happy for it?

Some other insignificant countries, on the other hand, have been so bold as to join the new Grand Alliance. We need not worry now: Guatemala and Nicaragua are on our side!

Jan. 3rd   Went to a cousin's wedding. He is in the RAF. There were some 70 guests and we had a reception breakfast which would have been excellent in peacetime, but was really sumptuous for wartime. The couple are not going to set up a home of their own until after the war.

Jan. 4th   What a fuss over two fiddling little raids on Norway! These may have been very well planned and carried out, but the publicity they have been given seems out of all proportion to their importance.

This passage from the *People* seems to me highly suspicious of a trumped-up atrocity story: 'Germans killed children and drained their blood for blood transfusion for their own wounded.' It just does not seem likely or feasible, or that it would meet the purpose for which intended. What mentality allows such stories to be printed?

The 'Coughs and sneezes spread diseases' poster has been

much improved by H M Bateman's drawings. The 'Billy Brown of London Town' posters are also worthy of mention; I heard someone quote from one of them yesterday.

Several homes now use wooden spills, which can be lit from the fire, in order to save matches.

Jan. 6th   My landlady said she was speaking to someone who thought there would not be any more blitz, but she quickly disillusioned her. Her husband said he thought we'd got it coming worse than we'd had it before. 'They're saving up for something,' he said. I also think we are likely to get heavier raids in the future and I do not exclude the possibility of gas being used.

Jan. 7th   Improvements have been made in the fire-guard arrangements at the hospital, as a result of complaints: a recreation room has been provided, the sleeping-room is to be cleaned out regularly and made more pleasant, suppers will cost 1/- instead of 1/6d., instructions to fire-guards have been clarified, and arrangements made about replacing men who are absent for any reason.

Overheard remark: 'It's obvious now that the Japs haven't been putting into the China affair all they could have done, else they wouldn't have been able to do all this... They've got all they want in China.' Another man thought that even if left alone, the Chinese would have beaten the Japanese. 'I don't see how a people of 100 million can possibly conquer a people of 400 million,' he said.

Jan. 10th   Noticed two more health posters, one on pre-cautions to take against influenza, the other on precautions against scabies. The great drawback of both was that they had about five minutes reading on them. I think pamphlets and radio talks would be more suitable for health propaganda. Posters cannot deal with the subject fully enough.

Jan. 11th   The cut in food rations comes as rather a surprise. 'I dread the fat rationing,' said my landlady.

Jan. 15th   I wonder where Churchill is,' said Mrs H, 'I wonder if he's on his way to Australia.'

Jan. 16th   The Government ought to know by now that to give no news at all is more disquieting than to give bad news. Yet hardly any official news, other than Japanese, has been given about the fighting in Malaya. Apparently the Japs are advancing without meeting any resistance to speak of. Someone promises British air superiority within three days, but the retreat continues just the same three days afterwards. Few people will be surprised if Singapore falls, yet this is our most important base in the Far East. Personally I don't care what happens to Malaya, Borneo, the Philippines, or Celebes. I care a little what happens to China.

Jan. 17th   Overheard in a barber's shop: 'But I think the Germans are having a rough time in Russia.' 'Oh, yes, but you must remember they are fighting a stubborn retreat.' 'They're butchering the people as they leave the places.' 'Yes, that's why you never hear of prisoners being taken nowadays. They (the Russians) stopped that when they entered Rostov. They found a school of children murdered by machine-gun.' 'I wonder why they (the Germans) always keep this barbarian spirit. You'd think they would lose that in evolution.' 'Well, this is an organised thing. In the last war some of our men did some funny things, and they have in this war, but that was only one or two here and there with the hooligan spirit. This is an organised thing.' 'It's horrible when you come to think of it, isn't it?' 'It's worse than the Boxer Rising, and that's the worst thing I remember in my life. This is ten thousand times worse.' Then the two men agreed that we should not make the mistake of letting Hitler escape punishment after the war. 'Still, there are not many places he could slope to,' said one, 'only Switzerland and Portugal and Spain.' 'Yes, I daresay old Franco would be glad to have him.' 'It's marvellous how Switzerland always manages to keep out of everything, isn't it?' 'No-one ever seems to take any notice of her.'

Jan. 20th   To a good many people the rationing of paper for book-publishing probably does not matter much. But to anyone like myself, who loves books of all kinds, it is of major importance. Without books – and I mean good books – life would be almost intolerable. The *News Chronicle* has done good service in emphasising this grievance. Authors and publishers are unanimous that it would not require much adjustment of the present scheme to make more paper available for books. Also, I think, restrictions could be made in several directions where they have not so far been made. Much redundant and worthless stuff is still being published. If this were restricted more paper could be allowed for high-class publications.

English literature, in my opinion, is the best in the world. If it is to continue to be so fresh talent must not be discouraged. It is part of the culture for which we are fighting. It would be more than a pity if there was not enough paper to meet the demand for informative books, new fiction, and classics. I believe there has been a great increase in reading during the war. I hope, therefore, that the Government will soon increase the paper ration.

Jan. 26th   This Libya business is getting rather tiresome, not to say farcical. It wouldn't be so bad if there wasn't such a lot of glorification written about it before the battle is won. Now if the Germans regain all their lost ground, which does not seem unlikely, we shall look silly, not for the first time. 'They'll be back in Egypt in a fortnight,' said Mr H. I wish that either the Germans or our own forces would occupy Libya and stop there, instead of chasing each other in and out.

'The Australians are getting the wind up,' (because of the Japanese advances) was an opinion I heard expressed today.

Jan. 27th   Remarks at lunch today: 'I think a lot depends on Russia.' 'I wonder what the Americans have landed in Northern Ireland for.' 'I reckon they'll use them to take over the Irish ports.' 'Did you hear Quentin Reynolds last night?' 'No, what did he say?' 'Oh, their Navy will be ready in 1945...' 'In ten years time I think nobody will be able to interfere with the Russians.' 'In ten years time there'll be nobody left to interfere with them.' 'Of course, they haven't beaten the Germans yet.' 'No, but they're the only ones to put up a good fight. With their vast territory they can keep up the fight. Holding up all those men – it's been our salvation.' 'It makes you wonder what would have happened if they'd attempted invasion.' 'I can't understand why they didn't.' 'It's a mystery to me.' 'They must have thought Russia would attack them in the rear.'

In the paper today I read that Benghazi would be useless to the Germans if they capture it. When we capture it, it is 'of great strategic importance'.

'Cheerful, isn't he?' said my landlady's husband when, in the report of Churchill's speech, it was said we should have to endure very heavy punishment in the Far East. 'Well, he always has been straight about it,' said his wife. 'That's what I like about him – there's no humbug about him.' I, also, think this one of his best characteristics, but it is no good being straight about blunders when to have listened to criticism would have been to avoid them. All criticism is not useful, but neither is it all useless. Because a thing is clamoured for it is not necessarily either right or wrong. But Churchill seems to think it is wrong. He wants to have it all his own way and, because he is human, he cannot always be right.

Jan. 28th   The banning of *Picture Post* in the Middle East, by the withdrawal of the subsidy, is disturbing. It is yet another instance of an intolerance on the part of the Government towards any revolutionary or critical ideas. It raises the possibility of the ban being extended, of further encroachments being made on the 'liberty of the Press', although I think the Press abuses its liberty. In principle I disapprove of newspapers being banned, but in practice I wouldn't care if certain papers were banned, as I consider their influence bad from a mental and moral point of view, pandering as they do to people's baser instincts.

Jan. 31st   Poster seen today: 'Millions (or 'thousands', I forget which) say, "Lift the ban on the Daily Worker."'

Feb. 1st   The weather is now a main topic of conversation. For the time being the snow is the first thing people talk about.

But talking about after the war my father said, 'There'll have to be a conscripted army for a few years after the war, however it turns out.' Also he said, 'There'll be a good many women doing men's jobs. Employers will take the cheaper labour.'

'Time seems to go more quickly in wartime,' said Mrs A. 'There doesn't seem to be any time,' said her husband. 'Time doesn't mean anything... It's just a waste of the years.' 'Everything's disorganised,' said my father. 'Where you used to do a thing automatically and everything seemed to fit in, things are disjointed now.' To me, time goes at a tremendous pace, yet, looking back on it, the war seems to have lasted an eternity. It seems to have blotted out all previous existence.

Feb. 2nd The *News Chronicle* makes a very pointed remark today, noting that, although we were supposed to have denied troops, etc. to the Far East in order to gain a victory in Libya, it looks very much as though all we shall get in Libya will be defeat. Churchill will have a job to answer this one!

Feb. 5th 'I see they won't have Sir Stafford Cripps in the Government,' said Mrs H this morning. 'Well, he refused,' said Mr H, 'because they wouldn't give him a seat in the Cabinet. Quite right, too. It's the same job Beaverbrook had, and he ought to have a Cabinet seat the same as Beaverbrook.' 'Churchill will be losing the faith of the country if he goes on like he is,' said Mrs H. 'It's no good fighting against social changes; they've got to come.' 'These Government changes make hardly any difference,' I said. 'Not a scrap of difference,' agreed Mr H. 'No, he's keeping his old cronies in,' said his wife. 'They'll be having him (Churchill) out of it, if he's not careful... There'll be a Labour Government after the war,' he said.

Feb. 7th Bought a new overcoat, costing me five guineas, (£5.5/-) and 16 coupons, which leaves me with six coupons. A much more expensive one, but a better one, than my old pre-war coat.

Heard a bus-conductor say he thought the war would last another two years at least.

Feb. 8th   My landlady said she thought this year would be the worst for rationing; after that we would be 'on the turn'. She hopes coal will not be rationed.

Feb. 9th   The soap rationing came as a surprise to me, as it did to everyone, I think. It is not a great inconvenience, however. What worries me most is the idea of the surfeit of atrocious jokes about it we shall have to put up with from the radio. My landlady said she had got some packets of soap-flakes put by.

Heard some good opinions of Sir Stafford Cripps' postscript last night. He is held in respect by many people, though this may be partly because of recent Russian successes, some of the prestige the Russians are gaining being reflected on our former Ambassador to that country. However, he is certainly a man of intelligence and socialist ideas and, in my view, is likely to become a figure of some importance in the future.

The membership of the local Communist party has increased by 50 per cent in the last three months. Membership is now nearly 60.

A man said at lunch today that a friend or a relation had received a letter to say that another relation had been killed in the disturbances when the American troops landed in Ireland, yet according to the papers the landing had taken place 'without incident'. Another man said the papers had told 'bare-faced lies' about the Libyan campaign. Another said, 'It's a wonder people continue to have confidence in them... Oh, but they'll put up with anything.' My opinion of the newspapers gets steadily lower.

One of the men quoted above thought that the Russian official news was an example we might copy. The Russians did not make wild claims, they were very cautious about what they said. This is so, and when the Russians claim anything one usually feels pretty sure it is true and not likely to be denied or altered in the next day or two.

Feb. 10th   The feeling is growing that we are having our present reverses in Libya and the Far East not merely because of inferiority in numbers and equipment, but also because the enemy are really too clever for us, or rather that we are too stupid for the enemy. This, of course, is the last thing that most people will admit. Most people will accept all kinds of excuses about our not having enough men or guns or planes or ships and so on, but if anyone suggests that the enemy is superior in tactics – oh, no! impossible! no foreigner could be cleverer than us! However, one man said that we had been outmanoeuvred in Libya, and others agreed with him. I suggested to my landlady that our enemies were too clever for us and she said, 'It seems very much like it.' The destruction of the Singapore Causeway is a case in point. Why on earth wasn't it blown up so that the Japs could not repair it? Here they are pouring men over it within a week of it being damaged! 'We never seem to do anything adequately,' said my landlady. She told me that a woman had said that her husband in the Army had told her that there would soon be an uproar over Churchill, as he was always drunk!

Feb. 13th   Fancy letting three German warships get through the Channel without sinking one of them! And then to lose 42 planes into the bargain! It is almost unbelievable. 'It's about the worst packet the Admiralty have had to face,' said one of my lunchtime companions, 'and they've had to face some.' 'Their ships must be better than ours,' said another, after someone else had said that our airmen had scored ten torpedo-hits. The first man said he was in a pub last night, at the time the German ships must have been making their getaway, and two naval officers were there who said those ships would be immobilised in Brest for the rest of the war. Turning to the war in the Far East, he said, 'This Singapore business is a very serious business.' Another man said, 'In three months we shall be using Darwin as our base.' In my opinion, the fighting in Burma is the most important at present and the loss of the Burma road would be an even worse disaster than the loss of Singapore. 'Except for the Battle of Britain and Russia, the war has been one long dreary tale,' said the second man. 'It doesn't seem as though we've been prepared anywhere, even feebly,' said a third. The first speaker said that if we didn't boast so much the disappointments wouldn't be so bad. Then one of the men remarked on a wireless statement that some of our troops in Burma had driven the Japs back 'at the point of the bayonet'. He said he felt like throwing something at the receiver every time he heard that phrase. This brings one to the question of pikes and bows and arrows for the Home Guard, about which everyone is joking now. What further humiliation and ridicule are we to bear? We are making ourselves a laughing stock.

The tone of all the talk I have heard lately shows not only a deep dissatisfaction and lack of confidence, but also alarm. Here are some more examples: 'It's a damned sight harder to push them (the enemy) out of these places, once they get them, than it is for them to push us out.' 'We advance half an inch and retreat six miles.' 'If they'd been our three ships they'd have been put down.' 'We don't seem to be able to do anything.'

Said my landlady tonight: 'I wonder if we shall win this war. Sometimes I feel doubtful.'

Feb. 15th   Dissatisfaction is now being shown not only with the Government, but also with the Prime Minister. I have often said things against him, but not until the last week or so has a voice been raised against him in public. The *Daily Mirror* says: 'Is it any longer true to say that we trust the Prime Minister, but do not trust his Government?' The *News Chronicle* says: 'Have we not been hypnotised by Mr Churchill's personality ... into acquiescence in an inefficient war direction.' By his refusal to listen to the demands of Press and Parliament Churchill has brought their anger on himself, and if he does not soon alter his Government they will put him out of office, if only to get rid of his Government, though our recent reverses have lowered his own prestige considerably.

Feb. 18th   I had a feeling that someone would say that it was better for the German battleships to be in Heligoland than in Brest. Now Churchill has said it himself. But it is a feeble and ridiculous excuse. Why waste 42 planes in trying to prevent an action supposed to be advantageous to us? The whole of Churchill's speech to Parliament struck me as feeble and dishonest. He had no excuse, and he merely degraded himself by making such an absurd one.

Feb. 19th   According to the barber who cut my hair, the war in Europe will definitely be over this year, the Germans meeting defeat in Russia. This is the favourite theme of a good many people, including newspaper writers, just now, namely, that Russia will crush Germany this year. It is a form of wishful-thinking which is just as likely to go by the board as the many other examples we have had in the past. I do not think the Germans will defeat the Russians, but I think the Russians will also have considerable difficulty in defeating the Germans. In fact, I think they will meet with some serious reverses when the Germans launch their almost certain Spring offensive. Eventually, however, I think the Germans will have to admit defeat, but it may not be this year. It is dangerous to think that we have just got to wait for the Russians to finish the war for us, though this idea is very tempting when the Russians are the only ones to have any success against the Germans.

Feb. 20th   The new Cabinet changes seem to be welcomed by the Press, and it is certainly good to see Cripps in the Cabinet, but I do not think the changes are by any means adequate. Kingsley Wood, Attlee, Greenwood, Anderson, Margesson, Morrison, Bracken, and several others all ought to be removed from office. By this slight concession, however, Churchill has probably avoided a political defeat.

Feb. 21st   Went to see Epstein's new sculpture, *Jacob and the Angel,* and was considerably impressed by it and chiefly by the physical strength which must be required to shape such an immense piece of stone. To make a recognisable shape at all, out of a huge slab of rock, let alone a work of beauty and meaning (which I think it is) is a great achievement worthy of praise.

Feb. 24th   I was glad to read Stalin's statement that the Russians were not fighting the Germans simply because they were Germans, but because they were invaders of their country, and that the Russians did not aim to exterminate the German people, but only the Nazi clique at their head. This is good propaganda and, if Stalin means what he says, good ethics. If we are to have a real peace after the war there must be none of this racial hatred. Some of our newspapers, however, adopting what they call a 'realistic' policy, have scorned the idea that we have no grudge against the German people. Their attitude has been the opposite of Stalin's professed one. Personally, I bear no malice towards the Germans as a race, or towards any other race. To talk of destroying a whole race is ludicrous, and to carry it out would be virtually impossible.

Feb. 25th   Have just seen an official pamphlet, dated 1941, called ARP (Air Raid Precautions) at Home'. I am fairly sure that not one in 50 of those who receive it will bother to do more than glance through it. To read this wordy, 28-page booklet would bore anyone to tears.

Feb. 26th   I read Sir Stafford Cripps' speech with approval. It sounded as though something might be done to make the sacrifice more uniform for everybody, to make the news more honest, to stamp out profiteering. And I especially liked his deprecation of dog-racing and boxing. Of course, we need recreation, but these so-called sports (also horse-racing) are not really recreation. I cannot feel that those who patronise them get any real pleasure out of them, but only a temporary excitement and an opportunity for gambling. They refresh neither the body nor the spirit and, as Cripps said, are out of accord with the times we live in. Even in peacetime they are in opposition to culture and a sensible way of recreation. Cripps struck me as the first of our leaders, not excluding Churchill, to have a sincere intention to improve things on the home front, to smooth out injustices, to back up the ordinary man. It needed a Socialist to do this.

Feb. 27th   My remarks three days ago on racial hatred were voiced again by two men today. Speaking about correspondence in the *Daily Telegraph* one said, 'For people who call themselves Christians, some of their opinions are disgusting. To talk of assassinating every German, it's—' and he expressed contempt. Another man mentioned Sir Robert Vansittart as a man who had always been anti-German and 'one of those people who think that if there were no German nation there would be no more war.' Indeed, if our aim was to exterminate the German race the battle would not be worth winning.

Mar. 1st   At home for the weekend and learned that there was a shortage of coal, some homes being without any coal whatever. My landlady says it is the same in this district.

Mar. 2nd   All the signs are that Java will not be held very long. We leave the command to the Dutch, the Dutch start 'scorching the earth', and talk is of fighting to the end, which means that an end is expected, if not certain. They don't say what end, of course, but when they talk like that it means defeat, because it is the end for us.

Mar. 4th   This is the sort of thing, often printed in the Press, which annoys me intensely: 'Even up to the end every Digger considered himself worth any ten Japs.' This is only the opinion of the Diggers – if one accepts the statement as true – but if in fact it was not the case (as it couldn't have been, or the Japs would not now be in possession of Malaya), why bother to make the statement at all?

Almost the most disturbing piece of news for me today was that, among the new clothing restrictions, there are to be no more double-breasted jackets or trouser turn-ups.

Mar. 5th   At first glance, the new comb-out of officers above the age of 45 seems a bold and constructive move. But when one reads that it applies only up to the rank of lieutenant-colonel it takes all the sting out of it. If it included the rank of general, it would be something to talk about.

Men have been round today taking down all the ornamental chains in front of the houses in this locality. But in doing so they left behind a row of iron staples all along the paths. Not very important, perhaps, but showing a typical English lack of thoroughness.

Mar. 6th   If one can judge by the newspapers (which is very doubtful), our Indian policy is likely to prove disastrous if it doesn't soon alter, for the Indians seem likely to offer more hindrance than help if the Japanese start invading India. The result of our capitalist, Imperialist policy has already been seen in Malaya, and the papers are no doubt right in this case in demanding better treatment for India. Obviously we should let the Indians govern themselves.

Mar. 8th   Java is as good as lost, and today I see quoted in the *News of the World* this message from the Dominions Office to Australia: 'At the moment the Empire team is batting on a sticky wicket, and the Axis fast bowlers have had some success. Our best bats are still to go in and the score will, in time, show that we can give, as well as take, punishment.' My God, what a sublimely complacent attitude! What a gorgeous example of the sporting mentality which is running this war as some sort of glorified Test Match! Heaven help us if we don't soon rid ourselves of the kind of people responsible for this sort of thing. And when I read further and learned that the Dominions Office regarded it as a good joke, I nearly went up in smoke! I fail to see what we have to joke about, and when responsible officials talk like this one becomes seriously alarmed as to their mental health.

Mar. 11th   Have heard no comments on the story of Japanese atrocities in Hong Kong. But cries of horror and indignation are hardly justified when the code of morality has been discarded, as it has been by all the nations at the present time. War itself is an atrocity, and the events which make up war vary only in their degree of savagery. Each side is bound to attribute to the other the most brutal qualities imaginable. No sane person would condone atrocities such as those described by Mr Eden, but when the condemnations come from a country itself at war and thus committed to carrying out acts of war only slightly less evil and less obvious, they have very little meaning.* It is a case of the pot calling the kettle black.

---

* Only three years or so later the Allies were to commit, against Japan, what might be considered the most hideous atrocity of all – the use of atomic bombs.

It is good news that Cripps is to go to India. He seems the best man for the job.

Mar. 12th   What has puzzled me somewhat lately is that the Russians keep on advancing, but never seem to get anywhere!

Brown bread (now that white is unobtainable for the duration) will take a little getting used to as a staple part of our diet, but, for my part, cakes, etc. made with wholemeal flour will be still more dislikeable. Chocolate I shall not miss, as having had scarcely any for several months I no longer have any desire for it. This is a luxury we can easily do without.

Mar. 13th   My landlady told me about some members of a local women's club who went to see what sort of meals their children were getting at school. The headmaster tried to prevent them from going in (suggested getting a letter of authority, which would have given him warning), but the women more or less forced their way in and saw the food the children were having. The meal consisted of a little soup with one under-cooked potato, which most children did not eat, followed by no more than a spoonful of some milk pudding, an obviously inadequate meal. The headmaster then complained that there were no proper facilities for providing meals. The leader of the women said that was what they wanted to rectify. The point is that the mothers would not feel disposed to go out to war work (and volunteers have been asked for in this district) if they knew that their children were not receiving adequate meals at school.

Mar. 14th   The loss of 13 Allied ships in the battle for Java is another great blow to our sea power. But the mood of the *Sunday Pictorial* seems to me the wrong mood altogether; its nauseating heroics leave me cold. There is no room for this sickening sob-stuff. What is needed now is a more purposeful mood, a cool and calculating, rational outlook. We cannot see clearly through this smoke-screen of emotion. It will not matter much if we are to get fewer newspapers if this is the stuff they are going to befog us with. The cold, scientific planning of our enemies is more than a match for our deathless heroism and skill in withdrawal.

Mar. 18th   A man's comment on MacArthur's appointment as commander in Australia: 'That's all we seem to do – change generals.'

Mar. 19th   I am glad American officers are being given positions of importance. They may bring a new vigour to our strategy.

Although the latest Allied air-attack is claimed as a great success, a careful reading of the report shows that only two sinkings seem to be at all definite. The official report says, 'These operations are *believed* to have resulted in … the probable sinking of one destroyer and the possible sinking of two destroyers.' How hopeful, but how vague!

Today's paper also gives an account of another outburst by Lord Vansittart, which I read with the contempt it deserves. He says, 'We shall not achieve victory by reliance on anti-Nazism.' Well, if Britain is not anti-Nazi, what is it? It shows that Vansittart thinks that we should not be fighting Nazism, but only the German nation, which means we are fighting a feudal war, with no ideals at stake. It also shows what was before apparent, that Vansittart is fundamentally a Nazi himself. He further deplores 'subtle distinctions between "good" and "bad" Germans, between "Nazis" and "anti-Nazis."' What is so subtle about these distinctions? Vansittart would try to paint the Germans all black and ourselves all white, which is not merely unsubtle, but plain stupid. He implies that we should meet German and Jap atrocities by committing atrocities ourselves, but of course, in our case, they wouldn't be atrocities. His whole speech is, in fact, utter nonsense.

Although as a matter of principle Morrison's threat to suppress the *Daily Mirror* is bad, in this particular case I would not mind much if it was suppressed, since if ever a paper abused its freedom this one did. No paper has been more hysterical and sensational than the *Daily Mirror*, more irresponsible and misrepresenting, more regardless of truth. It is a horrible combination of a children's comic, a twopenny 'blood', and a magazine for women. In peacetime it was just as bad, and its suppression could be justified on other than political grounds.

Mar. 20th   My comments of yesterday about the *Daily Mirror* were reiterated by four other men today. 'Something ought to be done to curb the newspapers. There's too much power in irresponsible hands.' 'Of course, there'll be an uproar if they do ban it,' said another. 'Yes, the sort of people who read the *Daily Mirror* are the sort of people who believe every word it says.' 'Morrison is doing a very courageous thing to attack the papers like he is.'

Incidentally, as a result of the new cut in the number of newspapers issued, my landlady now gets only one paper instead of two. I'm glad they have stopped the *Daily Mirror* and not the *News Chronicle*.

Mar. 21st   Eggs are rationed and egg dishes are cut out of most restaurant menus, but I went into a restaurant in St Albans today and found a plentiful supply of eggs. Yet it could not be said that they were only available to the well-off, since it was only a cheap restaurant and egg on toast, bread and butter, and tea cost me only 1/1d.

Mar. 22nd   Further thought on the *Daily Mirror* affair has caused me to modify my opinion a little. Although I don't withdraw anything I said about the paper (it would have been better if there had never been a *Daily Mirror*) the principle involved is perhaps more important than one's personal views about the paper. The Government have too much power in their hands; they should have to prove their case against a publication, instead of being able to suppress it without trial. Any newspaper is liable to be banned at the discretion of the Home Secretary. There is so much akin to Fascism in this that it cannot be condoned. If they want to ban the *Daily Mirror*, let them put its publishers on trial. Well-handled, the Government's argument could be easily proved.

Mar. 24th   Vansittart's speech has had its inevitable effect in Germany, the reverse effect to what is wanted from our point of view. Goebbels has put the same interpretation on the speech as I did, the only interpretation possible. Says the Berlin radio: 'The Allies never thought of fighting National Socialism, in which they are not interested. Their true aim is to fight this war as a war of annihilation against the German people.' By his exaggerated patriotism Vansittart is doing a great disservice to our cause. The kind of propaganda he supplies is the opposite to what is wanted. The Russians are supplying the need in a much more sensible and effective way.

Mar. 26th   Bus-conductor's remark this morning: 'The Jews are the only ones who are making money out of this war. A Jews' war, that's what it is.' It is rare to hear anti-Semitic views nowadays.

Mar. 27th   Although Morrison's threat to suppress the *Daily Mirror* may be defensible, his hint that the Government might attack the Press in general is much more alarming, and it is because the attack on one paper must not be allowed to spread to all papers that the attempt must be resisted at the start. Although I would not object very strongly to the suppression of the *Daily Mirror*, I hold no brief for Herbert Morrison. His tone is too autocratic for my liking. But he is obviously not the only one. As a man said today, 'Churchill's behind it, but Morrison's got to do the shouting.'

Mar. 28th   The Anderson shelter which has stood at the bottom of my landlady's back garden and which was used a few times at the time of the blitz has now been taken out by my landlord to make more garden space.

Mar. 30th   The Government's proposals for India seem to have much to commend them, but, as Mrs H said, 'They put off dealing with the problem for years and years and now they want to get it all settled in a hurry ... It now remains to be seen how far the Germans have got hold of them (the Indians).'

Apr. 1st   Although our promise of self-government to India is very belated, I think the Indians would be very foolish not to take the opportunity of accepting the proposals. It may be that they do not trust us to keep our promise, but this is hardly conceivable, as no government which made such a promise could survive if it did not keep it. The consequences will be very serious if the Indians reject our plan.

Reading a summary in *Picture Post* of what other papers said about the threat to ban the *Daily Mirror*, it is obvious that the latter is regarded as an outlaw by the rest of the Press, and it is only because they are afraid that the threat might suddenly be applied to themselves that they take the trouble to support it (except the *Daily Telegraph*, which frankly supports the Government). The present state of alarm in the Press is due, in fact, not to the *Daily Mirror* being the paper concerned, but to the fact that Morrison invoked Regulation 2D instead of the less dictatorial 2C.

Apr. 4th   Went home for Easter, and in response to Government appeals there were comparatively few people travelling.

Apr. 5th   Comment by my father: 'I'm afraid we're going to lose India.' He cannot see that times must change.

The air-raid warning sounded tonight, a sound now quite unfamiliar to me. But in spite of the recent lull my sister asked me if I had brought my gas mask, which I had forgotten to do though I had intended to bring it.

Apr. 6th   In spite of claims about the number of Germans they have killed and the number of places they have occupied, the Russians do not seem to be getting anywhere much. They are meeting very stubborn resistance and strong counter-attacks. Everything points to a big German offensive before very long, and I think the Russians will find it difficult to hold them. My landlady's husband said, 'I shouldn't be surprised if the Russians are driven back a long way.'

Apr. 10th   The apparent ease with which the Japanese airmen sink our warships has become an alarming matter. The news of the sinking of the *Hermes* is all the more grievous when, as in tonight's radio bulletin, it is immediately followed by an account of how some of our bombers attacked a German ship and 'probably damaged it with near misses'.

The bogey of black-out has now almost vanished again into the light nights of double summer time.

Apr. 11th   The failure of Sir Stafford Cripps' mission to

India, which has for some days dominated all other news, is a great disappointment. Especially must it be so for the *News Chronicle*, which printed a headline the day before saying, 'Congress Accepts British Proposals'.

Talking about after the war, a man said it depended on which way the country turned whether there would be an economic slump. If, as was quite probable he thought, it turned Socialist, money would be found for necessary reconstruction. If it remained under capitalist control, there would be a waiting period while the capitalists decided which were the most profitable interests in which to invest their money. He and another man agreed that this country would never turn Fascist.

Apr. 15th   The most staggering part of the new Budget is, of course, the big increase on tobacco and after that, probably, the increase on entertainment tax. The latter was the main cause of comment at lunchtime today. My own expenditure on tobacco is so small that even another 7½d. an ounce would not make it prohibitive, but 2/- seems such an excessive price for an ounce of tobacco that, all the same, I may feel compelled to give up smoking and spend what I save in this way on entertainments, which are much more important to me. Even so, it will mean having to be content with inferior seats at the theatre.

Apr. 17th   Feeling among some of my colleagues at lunchtime seemed to be that the award of the George Cross to Malta is an absurd thing to do. And indeed it is, for the only reason for the award is that Malta has had more air-raids than any other place. It may be argued that the people of Malta have withstood the ordeal bravely, but all they have done is to stay where they are and be bombed, and it is difficult to see what else they could have done. It is obviously an unsound idea to attribute certain qualities to a whole community indiscriminately. This award to Malta simply has no meaning; it would be just as sensible to award the George Cross to England.

Apr. 19th   The Sunday newspapers are full of a lot of rubbish

145

about two air-raids today, one on Augsburg and the other on Tokio. About the first the *Sunday Pictorial* says 'give all the pilots the VC', 'twelve of the bravest men Britain has ever bred', 'such a feat has never been even remotely attempted by the Germans ... doubtful if a single plane would reach its target', etc., etc. About the raid on Tokio the *News of the World* quotes other people as saying 'the beginning of the Allied offensive' and 'it is the end of Japan', and about both raids it says, 'the most formidable air offensive the world has ever known.' It makes one tired to read how any trivial little thing (though I do not suggest that these particular raids were trivial) done by the Allies has colossal implications, whereas anything the enemy does is belittled. The newspapers have no sense of proportion.

Two of the men on fire-watching duty with me said they thought they were doing more for the war effort by continuing to smoke than they would be by not smoking and putting the money thus saved into war savings, because the man who does the latter gets his money back with interest, while the smoker gives his money to the Government in tax without any chance of getting it back.

Later, one of them who was living in Jarrow at the time of its most acute distress, told how this 'murder of a town' was brought about. During the last war it was declared that Germany would be made to repay every ton of shipping sunk by her and under the Treaty of Versailles this was carried out. Germany had to build reparation ships, and as these ships were cheaper per ton than any that could be built in Jarrow the shipping companies preferred to buy German ships and thus the shipyards in Jarrow were thrown idle. This was one of the main causes of Jarrow's poverty.

Apr. 21st   The fuel rationing scheme is bound to meet with a good deal of opposition, if only because of perplexity over how it can be accomplished, and rationing is complicated enough already. One can understand how coal and paraffin can be rationed, but the rationing of invisible fuels like gas and electricity is difficult to conceive. It will certainly make things

146

more difficult for the housewife, already over-burdened with rationing details, shopping worries, and money considerations.

Apr. 26th The last few days have provided little to note in this diary, except perhaps a certain atmosphere of confidence due to a lot of paper talk about a coming offensive, to people calling for a second front in the West, to some heavy raids by the RAF, and to an occasional operation by the Commandos, who, with the RAF, are in the limelight these days. According to the papers we are taking the offensive and the enemy is being kept guessing, but it seems to me we should wait until the offensive has well and truly begun before crowing about it and in case our complacency is again rudely shattered by some unexpected and unpleasant enemy move. Big Air Force raids do not necessarily mean that we are going to invade Europe, nor do small raids on the enemy-occupied coastline; neither because people demand a second front does it mean that we are going to get it, though this seems a natural deduction by some sections of Press and public. My landlady's husband remarked: 'I reckon it's giving Hitler something to think about, these Air Force raids, but I expect he'll give *us* something to think about before long.'

Apr. 27th Two men thought gas would not be used in this war. One said, 'If it hasn't been used after two and a half years of war, it seems pretty obvious it never will be used.' The other said, 'I never have thought they'd use it; the danger of getting it back is too great.' The certainty of being repaid in kind is a strong reason against any belligerent deciding to use poison gas.

Apr. 28th Discussion at lunchtime today was on the possibilities of opening a second front in Europe. One man didn't think it was possible, but another said, 'I think we shall have to do something soon, even at a risk.' Two others thought we should attack when Germany is heavily engaged in Russia, but not before.

Apr. 30th To my landlady and her husband one of the most significant facts about the recent German air-raids on Bath,

Exeter, York, and Norwich is that they are all cathedral towns. I said I didn't think they picked those towns just because they had cathedrals; there would not be much point in it. But Mrs H said, 'We set store by our historical buildings.' Yet I wonder whether we really do set great store by them, or whether we only think we do because we have been told we do so often. After all, it is our dwelling-houses and places of work we care about most; I doubt whether any but a very few are terribly upset if a church is destroyed. Only a minority go to church and only a slightly larger minority have any feeling for the beauty or antiquity of a church. There are only a few exceptions, like Canterbury Cathedral, St Paul's, or Westminster Abbey, for which there is any sort of general regard.

May 3rd   Conversation between two men:
'Well, what do you think of this war?'
'I think things are looking pretty good. I think we've reached a turning point now.'
Later – 'Do you think the Germans are cracking? The papers say they are.'
'You can't go by the papers.'

May 4th   Occasionally a newspaper prints something worth printing and today the *News Chronicle* excels itself and prints two pieces I am glad to read. One is another exposure of the furniture racket, one of the worst examples of profiteering in this war. The other is an editorial attack on methods used at Army Battle Schools, where attempts are made to instil 'synthetic hatred' into the minds of soldiers. Not much need be said about this. It is so obviously a characteristic of Nazism that one can hardly credit it happening in this country. Deliberately to try to breed hatred among men and nations, as if there were not enough already, is contrary to our supposed war aims and to all civilised ideas, and it would make the establishment of a real peace after the war far more difficult.

May 7th   The British descent on Madagascar comes as a pleasant surprise to most, though one can't help thinking of German methods of 'protection'. The newspapers, too, seem a little premature in speaking of our 'occupation' of Madagascar, when so far our forces have occupied only a tiny piece of territory. But I heard a man say today, 'I bet the major part of the resistance is over by tonight. Once they capture Diego Suarez it's as good as over.' And a little later we heard that Diego Suarez had been taken.

This news is somewhat offset, however, by the sorry news from Burma, where British resistance is almost at an end, and where communication with China is cut off and India is menaced.

May 10th   I recently remarked that the fear of being given tit for tat is the strongest deterrent against any country using gas in war, and I think Churchill said the best thing he could have said, in his speech tonight (when he warned Germany clearly that she would be the victim of large-scale gas warfare if she used it first), to prevent it being used. All the same, how horrible it is that this threat should have to be given and still more so if we should have to carry it out.

May 12th   Churchill's broadcast seems to have met with fairly general approval, but my boss[1], who happens to be a Czech refugee, although strongly anti-Nazi, deplored the passage in which Churchill said the German people could stand outside their cities and 'watch the home fires burning'. 'We're fighting for better things,' he said and spoke of 'all this nonsense of hating your enemies'. He thought it would be better propaganda if Churchill distinguished between the Nazis and the German people. The man to whom he was talking thought this 'hate' campaign was designed merely with the immediate view of breaking down German civilian morale.

May 17th   There is no doubt good reason for confidence at the present time, but the newspapers, as usual, are somewhat overdoing it, going wild with prophecy and explanations of strategy, the only basis for which is in the imagination of the writer. Seeing the headline, 'Hitler will be defeated in 1942', my landlady said, 'I do wish they'd stop prophesying.'

149

May 18th   It is noticeable how much easier it is to obtain cigarettes and tobacco now. Either supplies have increased or consumption has decreased.

May 20th   Mr H commented, 'I wouldn't be surprised if the Japs do invade Australia.' His wife replied, 'I wouldn't be surprised at anything that happens in this war.'

May 21st   Although stockings are one of the major clothing problems of women in wartime, the matron at our hospital has insisted that nurses wear them in uniform, as stockingless legs are 'not in keeping with the dignity of the profession'.

May 23rd   Went home for Whitsun, found travelling quite easy.
    There was an exhibition of women's war jobs in the town. A large shop showroom had been turned into a factory machine-shop. Factory girls were there working their machines, turning out parts and fitting them together. Quite large crowds visited the exhibition and took much interest in the different processes.

May 24th   It is good to see that the system of 'hate' training at Army Battle Schools is to be stopped, but not content with making a simple statement about it, newspapers are going to the other extreme in their efforts to explain that men are now being taught to kill without any nasty feelings for their victims. What damnable hypocrisy! If the 'hate' system had been allowed to go on, some papers would have praised it as a 'realistic' method of training.

May 28th   At lunchtime today a man mentioned a speech made some days ago by Vice-President Henry Wallace of the United States. None of the English papers printed it in full, except *Reynolds' News*.[2] It was 'rank Socialism' he said.
    Apropos the Labour Party Conference, another man said, 'I don't see the point of the electoral truce now.' In my opinion, the political truce is an absurdity. If this is a democracy the people should be allowed to choose their own candidates, war or no war.

June 1st   Much talk today about Saturday night's terrific RAF raid by over 1,000 bombers on Cologne. Why was Cologne chosen? Why was the raid concentrated into one and a half hours? were two of the most interesting questions.

June 2nd   Raids by over 1,000 aircraft are very awe-inspiring and exciting, but on examining them rationally they lose something of their glamour. One man, after another had told him of the second mass raid, said, 'Isn't it disgusting?' 'Do you know how many were killed in the first one? ... twenty thousand,' said the other. 'Yes, it's horrible, but the Germans have asked for it – there is that about it.' 'I know war is war, but they shouldn't glorify twenty thousand killed.'

The *News Chronicle* today says that justice must be done 'in no gloating spirit', but 'gloating' is exactly what the papers are doing, with their detailed descriptions and eulogies of praise for those who planned and executed the raid. It is difficult to know what attitude to take, as a civilised person, towards air-raids which are nothing less than massacre, but which, on the other hand, may shorten the war. And raids on industrial targets, which are thickly populated, must inevitably involve great loss of life. This 'we-must-be-cruel-to-be-kind' point of view sounds like hypocrisy, yet it is the only point of view which can reconcile wanting to win the war and not wanting to hate our enemies. Yet what cries of horror and rage would go up if the Germans made a series of similar raids on our big cities! (Indeed, such cries did go up when they made raids on a much smaller scale than we are doing now.) We know from our own experience that air-raids are utter barbarity, yet we go on making raids and point with pride to their ever-increasing savagery. If one accepts war one must accept air-raids; if one accepts air-raids one must accept them on any scale; if one accepts them on any scale one must accept death on any scale. I repeat: what, as a civilised person, is one to think? I, personally, do not want to accept war, but neither do I want to accept the rule of Nazism – so I am caught between two stools.

June 3rd   There is rather a curious silence over what has happened in Madagascar. For about three weeks we have heard no official news of the operation, and today there is just a brief statement of the capture of some place only 25 miles from Diego Suarez, which was captured on the second day. We still do not know how much of Madagascar we have occupied, whether fighting is still going on, or anything about it. Why?

June 4th   In a letter my sister expresses what is perhaps a widespread opinion on the mass-bombing of Germany. She says, 'What dreadful raids we have made on Germany. I hope they are not in a position to retaliate in the same way. I wish aeroplanes had never been invented.'

June 11th   My landlady's comment on the Government's coal scheme: 'They daren't start coal rationing; it would hit the toffs too hard.'

June 13th   My opinion on the Anglo-Russian treaty may strike a note of disillusionment in the midst of so much eulogy, but I think it is the only honest view to take. Admittedly the treaty expresses good intentions, but mankind has never lacked good intentions, but has almost always lacked the ability to put them into practice. During the last 20 years treaties have meant next to nothing, and the League of Nations has been a tragic failure. There seems to be no promise, at the present time, of any high ideals being realised and it is absurd to pretend, as the newspapers are doing, that the mere signing of the pact is a guarantee of peace and prosperity after the war. Indeed, the treaty does not express any very high aims. It need only last for 20 years; after that time Britain and Russia can repudiate it with a clear conscience. Is this sincerity? The treaty also recognises the possibility of another war with Germany or associated States after this war. Does this show confidence in our ability to build a lasting peace? And what could be more vague than Article III: 'The High Contracting Parties declare their desire to unite with other like-minded States in adopting proposals for common action to preserve peace and resist aggression in the post-war period'? In fact, the treaty seems to me a very half-hearted affair. One shouldn't take any notice of the newspapers; they are duty-bound to make a song about it and to count the chickens before the eggs are even laid. A man said yesterday that in the photograph of the signing of the treaty Churchill's expression was as though to say, 'Sour grapes – but I've got to eat them.' It is certainly difficult to imagine Churchill collaborating with Russia in peacetime economic and political measures. I shall be very much surprised if, as a result of this treaty, the world becomes happy, peaceful, and prosperous for everyone; it would be naïve to expect that it should. The High Contracting Parties will, I think, be mainly concerned with Article V, which provides for the security of their own interests. All other lofty motives will be subordinated to this.

June 16th   There has been so much talk about a second front just lately and so many speeches by public figures saying that there is going to be one this year that, though I think there ought to be one, I'm beginning to feel that it's all a bluff. For it seems silly to go telling the enemy what we are going to do and when and where. I don't think our leaders are quite as stupid as that. Probably we are not strong enough to invade the Continent this year, so the next best thing is to try to make the enemy think we are. If we were really going to open a second front, surely it would be kept as a surprise. On the other hand we may want the enemy to think it is a bluff when actually it isn't.

June 18th   Once again the newspapers have made nonsense out of the Libyan fighting. One would have thought that they had learnt their lesson by now. But no – up to the last two or three days our forces were 'smashing through', had 'superiority in the air', etc., etc., and now here we are back again on the Egyptian frontier. (A man I know prophesied this two days ago.) Even the most gullible person must now be aware that we have been handed nothing but lies and half-truths during the battle in Libya. And it is no longer a joking matter, if it ever was. These continual reverses in Libya are lengthening the war. It's about time that campaign was finished.

June 22nd   Once again people are showing dissatisfaction

over the Libyan disaster, as well they might. I can remember
only a few out of many critical remarks heard today: 'I can
see them taking Suez before long.' 'So can I.' 'We don't seem
to get anything but setbacks.' 'We haven't any leaders, that's
why. There isn't a good man in the whole bunch, not even
Churchill. He never has done anything outstanding.' (bus-
conductor). 'I don't know where we should have been without
Russia. If he'd launched against us what he's launched against
Russia, we shouldn't have stood an earthly chance. Still, I
don't think he'll invade us now.' 'I don't know, he's mad
enough.' 'What it amounts to is that they had a better general
than we did. If Rommel had been on our side, we should have
won.' Thus it goes on. Can we go on like this? Periodically
we have to go through a stage of reverses and disappointment,
and all we get to offset it is the signing of a treaty, an
occasional 1,000-bomber raid, shouts about our second front
that's coming some time perhaps, and newspaper victories
which amazingly turn out to be either a defeat or some trifling
success which has been magnified into something more. The
last is the hardest to bear.

June 23rd   For weeks the papers have been talking about 'a
second front this year', 'victory this year', and so on, always
stressing 'this year'. This seems to me a very dangerous piece of
wishful-thinking; too many high hopes will be built up on it. I
shall be very surprised if the war is over this year.

We were talking of the second front at lunchtime, and one
man said that he had read in a paper that one result of the
Churchill-Roosevelt talks would be 'The setting up at least of a
psychological second front'. The laughter that followed wasn't
very polite.

On Libya another man said, derisively, 'Do you know what
the next move will be? They'll send Wavell back to Egypt
again. You see if they don't.'

June 30th   I am amazed that Churchill and Roosevelt can
declare that 'the overall outlook is more favourable now than it
was last year.' In spite of this, Churchill will have to face a
pretty critical House of Commons in the debate on Libya.

Someone has even had the nerve to move a vote of censure. One would have thought there was no limit to the disasters into which the present Government could lead us without losing the confidence of the House. Even now there is only a remote chance of the censure motion being carried – Churchill's personality is still too strong. Still, we are getting on – one disaster more and we might get a new Government. But it is astonishing that Parliament can be so hypnotised by one man that the Government of which he is the leader can survive defeat after defeat. Surely results should be the criterion of judgement? The result of the by-election at Maldon, where the Independent candidate won the seat although the Tory candidate had as his main slogan 'Churchill asks you to vote for—', gives some inkling of what the public thinks.

July 3rd   Tomorrow I start a week's holiday. I have been very busy at work just lately, especially for the last ten days while another member of our staff has been on holiday, so a break will be very welcome. This year I am splitting my holiday and shall be having another week in September. Normally I would be entitled to three weeks, but everyone is being cut down to two-thirds of their normal entitlement this year.

July 4th   Spent the day in London. I just strolled round in the morning, had lunch in a milk-bar, and in the afternoon went to see Somerset Maugham's play, *Rain*, at the St Martin's Theatre. A small audience, but a very interesting and well-acted play. Afterwards I would have gone to the Albert Hall to hear the Promenade concert, but there would not have been time to catch the last train home, so I had to give it a miss.

July 7th   Had an easy day; lazed about all the morning and part of the afternoon. I had nothing to read, so went out and bought a Penguin book, *Beyond The Headlines* by Timothy Shy, the *News Chronicle*'s witty columnist – an ideal holiday book.
    I visited some friends in the evening. Mrs A said someone had been round to ask her what she could do in the event

of a blitz. She said she could provide hot-water bottles and drinks.

My aunt agreed with me that the prices of clothes were much too exorbitant now. Dealers in every commodity seem to take advantage of the war to put prices up as high as possible. They must be making fortunes, but they are rendering a great disservice to the community. The fact that so many articles have to be price-controlled is a sufficient comment on the morality of producers, middle-men, and retailers, though there are exceptions. One small example of profiteering on clothes, which I have seen in at least two shops, is neckties marked at 10/6d. – a preposterous price.

July 8th   Went to London with my sister and brother-in-law. We did a little shopping in the morning and in the afternoon went to Kew Gardens, a very pleasant refuge from war worries. We had a very good tea there: lobster mayonnaise salad, tea and cakes, at a reasonable price. We left there about 6.30 and took the rest of the evening travelling home, including an hour's wait for a train.

July 9th   Paid a visit to my brother and his wife. Like other gardeners, he has put a lot of work into his garden, but has had to watch some of it come to nothing because of the continued dry weather.

July 10th   Got up late and found it raining steadily. Never, perhaps, was rain more welcome. Even I'm not grumbling, although I am on holiday.

Went into town in the afternoon and bought a sports shirt, which leaves me with only five coupons, as I have already used my three remaining old coupons and ten of my new ones on a sports jacket.

July 11th   My father gave me three of his old coupons to buy a pair of socks. The last five of my own will go on another shirt. What with the coupons and the prices of clothes, clothes rationing has turned out to be one of the biggest inconveniences of the war to me. I still need shoes, pyjamas, underclothes, and at least one more pair of socks, which soon wear out. On coming out of the Army a year ago, I did not have many clothes that were serviceable or that would not soon need replacing. The idea that it is patriotic to look shabby simply does not appeal to me. I must say also that women seem to get much more than men for their coupons and find it easier to keep up a smart personal appearance.

As on last Saturday, I could not go to the Albert Hall because of travelling difficulties, so I listened to the broadcast of the second half of the Prom, which was the next best thing. I have taken much more interest in serious orchestral music during the past year or two. But I like jazz too, and after listening to the London Philharmonic I went to a dance.

July 12th   Last day of holiday, which I have enjoyed in spite of wartime limitations. The only disappointment was that we could not go to see some relations at Clacton, as the police would not give us a permit. A glimpse of the sea again is what I look forward to as much as anything.

I haven't entirely forgotten the war during my holiday, but for the last week or so, while battles in Egypt and Russia are hanging in the balance, we have been waiting in suspense for something definite to think and talk about.

In nearly all the homes I have been in this last week there has been a great deal of jam-making and fruit-bottling; the crop of gooseberries and currants has been good, and now that it has rained there will be at least a few raspberries. These things will doubtless be scarcer than ever this winter, so everyone who has any fruit is preserving it somehow or other.

July 13th   Work again. A fairly busy day. In a few days my holiday will be forgotten.

July 15th   Comment heard today: 'The next thing – well, within three months – will be that Japan will attack Russia.'

Picture Post today has an article on the increasing popularity of serious music (I noted my own greater interest in it only the other day). There must be some reason for this increase in the number of lovers of good music, but what it is is not apparent to me, unless it is that the better class of music is more inspiring and heartening in these troubled times.

My landlady had an airgraph from her son in Libya. In it he says the British retreat was 'a great disappointment for us, when we thought we had him cold.'

July 16th   Poster seen today: 'The British Labour Party says "Lift the ban on the *Daily Worker*" – Morrison must act now.'

July 18th   The weather today so wet and so cold that we have had to light a fire. English weather is not very conducive to fuel economy.

July 22nd   A man said he knew a girl who was taken out of munitions and put in the Land Army. She was sent to an Earl's estate, and her job there was to look after the Earl's orchids!

The BBC's new policy on dance music – to exclude 'slushy' sentiment and to substitute more 'virile' songs – is not going to be liked by those who listen to dance music. The BBC has taken no account of what songs are the most popular in making their decision; if they had, they would have found that the songs they call 'sugary' are the very songs which are most popular. I am quite willing to admit that the words of some of these songs are painful and that 'anaemic performances by male singers' are to be deplored, but, on the other hand, some of the most virile and robust songs are also absolutely senseless. It is deplorable that, because somebody at the BBC doesn't like a certain kind of music and thinks nobody else should, we should be deprived of hearing some of the best songs. I only hope that the public and the dance-band leaders won't let the BBC get away with it.

July 26th   The other day a man said, 'I don't think we can fight Fascism without becoming Fascist ourselves.' Yesterday the Earl of Clanwilliam said, 'No democracy can ever wage war. In war-time you want an autocracy...' There is unfortunately a great deal of truth in this, and the process of this country becoming more and more totalitarian I have watched with ever-increasing misgiving all through the war. It is being brought about without the vast majority of people realising it – at least, without realising that in the long run it is harmful to their interests. However much of a democracy we were before the war, we are certainly much less of one now.

July 29th   The news from Russia is black indeed. The stubborn Russian resistance seems to be of no avail against the German onslaught. And still our policy seems to be one, from a military point of view, of almost complete inertia.

Have just finished reading *Out of the Night*, by Jan Valtin. This book is a detailed – so detailed that it can hardly be anything but authentic – account of the activities of an agent of the Comintern from 1918 to 1938. It throws a glaring light on Communist methods, which are shown to be as unscrupulous and brutal as the methods of the Nazis. The chief aim of the Communists is to gain power and, once it has been gained, to retain it by every means of treachery and oppression at their disposal. In these days of Russian resistance to German aggression we are inclined to forget that Stalin is as much a dictator as Hitler, that the Russian masses labour under as great a tyranny as the German people. Any system of government which depends on a secret police and acts of terrorism for its existence is a bad system, and Russia is ruled by such a system. I am not easily swayed, but *Out of the Night* is as impartial an account of Communist activities as it could be from the pen of a former ardent revolutionist, and the fact that he does not try to idealise every Communist idea or everything that is done in Russia gives greater conviction to his words. And these words have greatly disillusioned me about Russia and Communism.[3] The principles of Communism may be commendable, but I hope that we do not have a Communist government in this country, at least not on the Russian model, for principles are worthless when the methods are those of ruthless suppression of all those who hold different ideas and cynical disregard, in practice, of the professed principles. Give me democracy every time, whatever its faults and failings!

159

July 31st   The new Government announcement that gas masks need no longer be carried is somewhat absurd in view of the fact that hardly anyone has been carrying them, and also somewhat confusing in view of the fact that the reason given for the order to 'carry your gas mask everywhere' was that a gas attack might come at any time without warning. Is a gas attack any less likely now? Of course, the Government order is merely an acceptance of what has been an established fact for a long time. Speaking for myself, I have not looked at my gas mask for months and months.

Aug. 1st   Went to the Promenade Concert at the Albert Hall. How uplifting is the mighty surge of sound from a full symphony orchestra, what a tonic to a war-weary spirit. I feel sure this must be the reason for the ever-increasing popularity of orchestral music. Modern dance-music can excite; it can never inspire or satisfy in the way that great classical music can.

Aug. 3rd   (Bank Holiday) Had the day off from work, so stopped an hour longer in bed. After breakfast I wrote a letter, then went out on a short errand, and after that read a light novel, *Cheerfulness Breaks In* by Angela Thirkell, till lunchtime. After lunch I wrote another letter and, as it came on to rain, waited about until four o'clock before going to the local fete, which was in aid of the Aid to Russia fund. It was like all other fetes – after you have been there half an hour you are bored stiff. I stuck it for about two hours, in which time I spent 4d. on a hoopla stall (without success) and 8d. on some tea. Then, as the weather had turned almost wintry, I went to the pictures and saw a mediocre ice-skating film called *Ice-capades* and a film with Elsie and Doris Waters, called *Gert & Daisy's Weekend*, which was half comedy and half Government propaganda. I came out soon after nine, went home to my digs and had some supper, then went to do my turn of fire-watching at the hospital, getting there at ten o'clock. At half-past ten I went to bed, thus ending a very dull day.

Aug. 5th   More trouble in India has been threatening for

160

some time, but all the same the revelation that Gandhi would be prepared to negotiate with Japan came as something of a shock. Of course, the truth is not very easy to get at, both sides indulging in a good deal of mud-slinging and exaggeration, but it seems to be true that Gandhi had adopted an attitude of appeasement towards Japan, similar to Chamberlain's attitude to Germany before the war. I, personally, can understand Gandhi's pacifist ideas of 'non-violent non-co-operation', but what I cannot understand is why his attitude is more conciliatory, apparently, towards Japan, who is also an Imperialist power and a much more cruel one, whose intentions are nothing if not malignant, than towards Britain, who has at least offered India her independence after the war. If he is going to negotiate with anybody, surely it should be with us. To attempt to negotiate with Japan would be to invite invasion; merely to offer passive resistance to invasion would be to place independence more than ever out of India's reach. To have Japan in control of India would, of course, be disastrous for us.

Aug. 6th   Used my first four sweet coupons, half a month's ration. Not having been able to buy many sweets for a long time, I have lost much of the desire I used to have for them, and it is strange to be allowed more than one really wants. But the sweet-eating habit is not easily got rid of, and it is one which has always given me more pleasure than the smoking habit, so I think I shall give up smoking temporarily and buy sweets instead, which will also be less expensive.

Aug. 9th   Gandhi's protests of his love for the British may be genuine – probably are – but one can't help thinking them hypocritical, for Gandhi must know that he has chosen the worst possible time, for us, to start a civil disobedience campaign. My landlady is dead against Gandhi, says he is a Nazi agent, in league with the Axis. Whatever he is, it is difficult to see what the Indian Government could have done except to arrest Gandhi and the other Congress leaders. But this has not prevented rioting and already people have been killed. The *News Chronicle* rightly describes the sequence of events as 'tragic'.

161

Two men I heard talking were of the opinion that Churchill was out of the country, as nothing has been heard of him lately. 'In Moscow, I reckon,' said one.

Aug. 16th   Poster seen at the top of an escalator in a London underground station says: 'Must you travel?' This seems a feeble way of trying to get people not to travel. The poster is simply a meek appeal; it does nothing to persuade the traveller that his journey isn't necessary after all. As it is, everyone's immediate answer to the appeal is 'Yes, I must', for each feels that his or her journey *is* necessary, and the traveller goes on his way with a clear conscience.

Aug. 18th   The prophet of nine days ago was a bit previous, but his guess was not far out. Even then Churchill must have been on his way to Moscow. But how eager the newspapers are to seize on the event and to magnify it tenfold. Churchill's visit may have been important, but not perhaps in the way they think it was. Churchill said he went because he felt it his duty to speak his mind. This sounds suspiciously as though he found it necessary to tell Stalin that we could not give Russia any more help at present and that the Russians must carry on without a second front for a while longer. I may be wrong; I hope I am.

Aug. 20th   There doesn't seem to be much to say about the Dieppe raid except that for a brief period many people thought that the Second Front had begun, but these hopes were quickly dashed. There was pleasure that we had at last done something, but disappointment that we had not done more and hope that it is a promise of bigger things to come.

Aug. 24th   I worked out my landlady's 'fuel target' for her, calculating the average yearly consumption of gas and electricity and, from that, how many fuel units would be left for coal. Economising on gas and electricity, she can allow herself about two tons of coal a year (to keep within the target), which is about half her normal figure. This self-imposed rationing is pretty drastic, but I think the voluntary method is better than the compulsory.

Aug. 26th   I hope they won't make too much fuss over the death of the Duke of Kent. It may be a sad event for his family, but to other people it is of little interest. I am no more moved by his death than by the death of any other complete stranger.

Aug. 30th   There have been so many events in the last week or two – Churchill's visits to the Middle East and Moscow, the Dieppe raid, the entry of Brazil into the war, the American success in the Solomon Isles, the Japanese withdrawals in China – all of them of considerable importance, that the general picture of the war is rather confusing and difficult to keep in clear perspective. The picture, however, seems definitely brighter, for all the events I have mentioned have been in our favour.

There is one other part of this ever-changing picture, though, which is perhaps dominant and attracts most attention, and that is Russia's terrific struggle with the main enemy of the Allies, Germany. The ability of the Russians to withstand the massive German onslaughts and to launch powerful counter-attacks excites the admiration of all. The battle for Stalingrad, especially, is being watched with suspense, for on this depends whether the picture remains bright or again becomes dark. The fate of this battle is perhaps the fate of the whole German campaign in Russia, the fate of the campaigns in the Middle and Far East.

Sept. 3rd   The war is three years old today. I must say that three years ago I never thought the war would last as long as it has done. Now – the end still seems a long way off.

To mark the third anniversary today has been a National Day of Prayer – why, I can never understand. It seems to me just a waste of time, as well as rank hypocrisy. For God does not seem to me to come into this war at all. It is entirely man's doing and man's responsibility. Praying to God can serve no purpose, for this war, whatever label is attached to it, is a violation of all Christian ideas. It is an insult to God to ask him for his support.

Sept. 5th   The biography of Stalin I am reading now is not very complimentary to him. The author spent six years in Russia and, allowing for private bias, there should be a good deal of truth in what he says. He shows Stalin to be a cruel and unscrupulous tyrant and Communism to be just a name. This confirms the opinion I formed of Russia, Communism, and Stalin when I read *Out of the Night* a short time ago. But Stalin is very popular now, and when he appears on cinema screens he usually gets a special clap to himself, while Churchill himself may not get one. No doubt Stalin is a cunning military leader, but as a political idealist and a just ruler he simply doesn't exist.

Sept. 6th   A little while ago some newspapers were busy blaming the official spokesmen for the false optimism of the communiqués on the Libyan fighting. That some papers will exaggerate the news whatever the official version is shown by this passage from the *News of the World*: 'Although official reports from Cairo on the progress of the battle of Egypt have been distinguished by none of the extravagant optimism of the early days of the campaign ... the success of the Eighth Army is far greater in fact and implication than guarded and cautious communiqués suggest.' So in one breath the paper gets in a dig at the 'extravagant optimism' of previous official reports and then goes on to say that the now 'guarded and cautious' communiqués really hide a much more optimistic story!

Sept. 8th   The opening address of the president of the Trade Union Congress, Mr Wolstencroft, doesn't read much like the words of a Socialist. It sounds more like the speech of a narrow Imperialist and, as the *News Chronicle* says, 'should gladden the heart of Lord Vansittart', who is my pet abomination. How I abhor this racial hatred! And why do our socialists, with few exceptions, have to be such a poor lot? Their political colouring is nothing redder than purple.

Sept. 10th   Finished reading Stalin's biography, which leaves one with a very unfavourable impression of him, although I think the author (Eugene Lyons) is more than a little prejudiced against him. On many points this book corroborates to a remarkable degree what the author of *Out of the Night* has to say of Russia under Stalin. Two facts especially show that Russia was not a little to blame for this war. Firstly, at the time when Hitler and his party were planning to seize power, the German Communists (who were then the third largest party in Germany) actually co-operated with the Nazis against the Social Democrats, whom the Communists were told to believe were the main enemy. They rejected all offers by the Social Democrats to join forces against Hitler and his Nazis, who, of course, were really the deadly enemies of the Communists. If the Communists *had* joined forces with the Democrats Hitler would never have been the ruler of Germany. Secondly, the signing of the Russo-German pact in August 1939 undoubtedly precipitated this war. The fact that Russia is now at war with Germany cannot alter these two realities.

Sept. 11th   Churchill's statement on India is all that one could expect of him, and it certainly doesn't help to solve the problem. If anything, it will tend to make the situation worse.

Sept. 13th   Went to one of the *Daily Express* Centres of Public Opinion, held in Chelmsford, and spent a very interesting and enjoyable afternoon. The two platform speakers were Beverley Baxter, MP and Tom Driberg, MP. Before they spoke there was some community singing, finishing up with 'Land of Hope and Glory'. Driberg, a recently-elected Independent candidate, spoke first and said that he was sorry to hear 'Land of Hope and Glory' being sung, because he objected to the words 'Wider still and wider shall thy bounds be set', which were too imperialistic for his liking. Then he dealt with India and said he was dismayed at Churchill's statement, criticised the 'strong-arm' policy, and suggested that China, Russia, and USA should be called upon to give their help and advice. Then he went on to the controversial subject of whether we are fighting the whole German people, or only the Nazis. In this matter he declared he was an anti-Vansittartite (which I was very glad to hear) and that the idea of all Germans being irredeemably wicked and of wanting to exterminate them was as bad as Dr. Goebbels' racial ideas. For the idea that the Germans were a very special race on their own and had evil in their blood was simply Nazism inverted – the super-race theory in reverse. Also it was bad political warfare, as the Germans could use it against us in their propaganda. Driberg finished by saying that the leaflets we dropped over Germany should be made public.

Beverley Baxter then spoke and first answered Driberg's criticism of 'Land of Hope and Glory' by trying to distinguish between 'bounds' and 'boundaries' not very convincingly. He then defended the Government's India policy, which he thought we ought to be able to handle ourselves without outside help, and this developed into a defence of Empire. Then he said that we ought to have followed the advice of 'Colonel Blimp' (Low's cartoon character) in the pre-war years and we would not have been where we were today. Finally, speaking of the future, he said we must certainly see that this was indeed the last war and this could be done if men of goodwill would co-operate to disarm those who were not men of goodwill.

Driberg's speech was in every way more rational than Baxter's, whose speech was blandly hypocritical and cleverly abusive towards Driberg. I agreed with almost everything that Driberg said and disagreed with nearly all that Baxter said.

After these two speeches members of the audience, which was a fairly large one, were invited to speak. Quite a number did so. The second speaker (a man of about 35) said, 'I think we should become more and more pro-Vansittart. Every German is a Nazi and a killer... I look forward to the time when we are fighting in the streets of Berlin and when our bombers are smashing it to dust... That's the only way to treat the Germans.' This emotional outburst was loudly clapped. The next speaker, a very young man, said some of the views he had heard expressed were very serious and alarming (meaning the views of Baxter and his supporters). He said we must have the support of the people of India in this war. We lost Burma because we did not have the support of the people. Our refusal to co-operate had led to this war, he said (rather vaguely); after the war we must co-operate with every nation (but supposing they will not co-operate with us?). He also was well applauded.

A woman's point of view was that one of our most important tasks after the war was 'the future education of the youth of Germany'. This was very well received as being a constructive proposal. (Driberg pointed out in his summing-up that this task would be impossible if we were going to exterminate the German race.) An old man then spoke and said he thought 'co-operation' would be the keynote of the future. A young woman said that the most controversial question of the day was not whom we are fighting – though she pointed out that Stalin himself had said they bore no hatred for the German people – but how are we a going to win this war as quickly as possible? In other words, when are we going to open a second front? Another young man, who said he was a Catholic deacon, gave the Christian point of view: 'If you hate someone you become more and more like the one you hate, and I think a large body of people in this country are becoming Nazi-minded.' Another man supported Driberg because 'he is a fresh wind in politics. The present government has had seven years in office and its India policy has led almost to revolution in that country. I think that we should give Driberg's ideas a trial, whether we like him or not.' He thought the extermination of 80 million Germans was not possible, even if desirable.

There were 12 speakers from the audience altogether, and I was surprised at the high standard of speaking and at the clear thinking which some of the speeches revealed. At first it seemed as though the feeling of the audience was going in favour of Baxter, but on the whole I think Driberg's supporters won the day.

Baxter in his summing-up said, among other things, that he admitted our pre-war relations with Russia had been badly mishandled and that he did not think Germany would always be without goodwill, but that we should disarm her for 50 years just to make sure. Driberg concluded by picturing Baxter going down to defeat waving the Union Jack only, whilst he, Driberg, marched forward with the flags of the free united nations in company.

Such a meeting as this, no doubt, does not give a truly representative picture of public opinion, but it certainly gives people an opportunity to air their views and as an example of democratic free speech is really quite remarkable.

Just before the end I happened to glance at the community song-sheet and read the last four lines of the National Anthem, which so struck me that I must write them down here. I had never read them before and I am sure few people know them:

> May peace her power extend,
> Foe be transformed to friend,
> And Britain's rights depend
> On war no more.

Sept. 14th   Paid my first visit to a British Restaurant and had a very good lunch: stuffed lamb, potatoes and cabbage, date roll and custard, and a cup of tea, at the very modest price of 11d.[4] Thinking of the food situation as a whole, I think, and have thought for a long while, that Lord Woolton is one of the ablest Ministers in the present Government.

Went to see *Gone With The Wind* in the evening. Boosted perhaps more than any other film, it is certainly an extraordinarily fine film and I did not begrudge the 4/- I paid for a seat, though in principle I fail to see why such excessive prices should be charged for a programme only a little longer than a normal programme.

Sept. 15th   A good deal of play is being made around the fact that Russia will soon be facing winter again and that the Germans will have to spend another winter in Russia. But it is dangerous to take it for granted that this year the Germans won't be prepared for a winter campaign. Last year they weren't, but we ought to know by now how quickly the Germans overcome fresh obstacles, and the complacency of some commentators, official and otherwise, may receive a rude jolt.

Some comments passed on US soldiers by two other members of my family and myself: 'Some of them don't half look dopey.' 'They don't seem to have much to do.' 'Always mooching about the streets – even when I go to work in the morning.' 'They look a slovenly lot.' 'If anything happened, I don't reckon they'd be much good.' 'I expect a lot of them only joined up to come and see England.' Appearances may be very deceptive, but the US troops I have seen certainly have not looked very promising.

Sept. 20th   It is good news that our naval losses in the last two and a quarter years have been replaced. It is somewhat surprising, too, since we have lost four battleships, four aircraft-carriers, a score or more of cruisers, and a large number of destroyers.

Sept. 21st   In contrast, a piece of recent news which is deeply disturbing is the report of a Conservative sub-committee on the education of youth and the control of young people's leisure. More than once in this journal I have felt compelled to mention the gradual whittling away of democracy in this country. This Conservative report, which advocates compulsory leisure-time training for boys and girls aged 14–18, is unquestionably Fascist in essence. The conscription of youth is one of the foundations of the German Nazi regime, and if the report becomes Government policy it would mean the end of democracy here, too. That the youth organisations would be used to instil into young people Conservative propaganda, and Conservative propaganda only, goes without saying. The thin end of the wedge has already been driven in by the system of youth registration and the 'voluntary' enrollment – with a little gentle persuasion – in some youth organisation. How easy now to change over to a compulsory system!

Sept. 25th   The new order making fire-watching compulsory for women has caused a good deal of discussion at the hospital where I am employed, where the sisters and nurses have been called on to fire-watch. There is some objection among the men, not because they don't think women should do fire-watching, but because the old system, which was running quite smoothly, has been upset. The men will not have to do duty so often and the number of hours they do may not come up to the required minimum. It is thought that there are enough men and that it is not necessary to call on the women.

Sept. 26th   Talked to a man about the coal shortage. We agreed that it was somewhat astonishing that we had enough coal in this country to supply all our needs, without having to bring it over water, and yet there was not enough for everybody to keep warm this winter. The other man said, 'I don't propose to go cold this winter, if I can help it, just because of the Government's fiddling and fuddling during the last ten years.' I certainly think the Government is to blame, but nevertheless we have got to accept the fact that there is a shortage and try to be more sparing in the use of coal, although it may be very difficult to do. The weather, having turned cold already, doesn't give people much chance, so to speak, to prepare themselves to meet the full onslaught of winter. Neither have we been fortified by a hot, sunny summer; our 'fuel morale' has already been undermined. If it remains cold, the combined effect of a poor summer, quickly followed by a hard winter, may prove too much for people to restrain themselves from having fires. There is also the health question to be considered. If there is to be an increase in all kinds of illnesses through lack of warmth, then it is very questionable if the fuel saving will be worth it.

Sept. 28th   The meeting at the Albert Hall, convened by the Archbishop of Canterbury to define the part the Church must play in the post-war world, was very interesting and not a little encouraging. For some time now I have felt that the Church was a lifeless thing and, as such, not worth bothering about. Its teaching did not seem to be really Christian, and I had no use for a religion which was out of touch with the society in which it existed. But if, as seems likely from recent utterances by the Archbishop, the Church is going to give a lead to all those who want a progressive Christian society, I am prepared to follow it. It is a new social morality in everyday life which is needed more than anything else in world affairs.

Oct. 1st   Heard some men talking about Hitler's latest speech, which I had not read. One of them thought it 'very much to the point' and 'one of the most brilliant speeches of the war'. Another appreciated his remarks about Churchill and said, 'You can't expect to wear funny hats and not be laughed at by the enemy.' The first man said that most of Hitler's speeches had been fulfilled, whereas we had had 'three years of speeches and nothing for them'. The general opinion seemed to be that most of Hitler's statements were fully justified, and one man wondered why the papers had been allowed to publish it.

When I got home I read the speech and told my landlady I thought there was much truth in it. She agreed. It was a very confident speech and some of the remarks struck me as rather witty. It was much more matter-of-fact and coherent than usual, in fact quite different from Hitler's previous speeches. But it was not all truth and it did not show any lessening in Hitler's ruthless and malevolent outlook.

In the same paper I read a statement by Churchill on the Dieppe raid, which was thus robbed of much of its success and Hitler's speech was given added emphasis. I also noted that the life of the present Parliament is to be prolonged by another year, a fact which I view with much disappointment. If ever a Parliament needed reinvigorating, this one did. It is like a very old man, gradually decaying into complete helplessness and uselessness, but refusing to die a natural death.

Oct. 4th   The other day a man said of the Press comment on Hitler's speech, 'They read into it exactly what they want to.' This is amply borne out by what I have read in the papers during the last two or three days. They have made the speech seem to mean almost the exact opposite from what it seems to mean to any ordinary person. They have tried to prove that it shows lack of confidence and presence of fear. Perhaps they are right. Perhaps Hitler's psychological make-up is so abnormal that, when his armies have advanced over the greater part of Europe and a huge part of Russia and to within striking distance of Alexandria, and when the Allies have still to make a serious offensive against German positions anywhere, he is frightened and lacking in confidence. More likely, however, it is the psychology of people who write in the papers which is at fault. I only hope that future events will prove Hitler to have been *too* confident.

Talking of the Egyptian battle a man said, 'I shouldn't be surprised if they (the Germans) break through again. I think there's too much of this "wait and see" business with our people.'

Oct. 7th   In an editorial today, on Stalin's recent statement that he regards a second front to be of first-rate importance and that, in comparison with Russia's aid to the Allies, the Allies' aid to Russia has been little effective, the *News Chronicle* hits a big nail bang on the head. It makes clear that the chief point arising from Stalin's remarks is not whether or not we are capable of opening a second front, nor whether or not a second front is desirable, but that 'Stalin, who ought to be in full possession of such military facts as are relevant, is now backing the popular demand.' Stalin's words in themselves prove that there is little co-operation between the Allies and Russia. Of course, there is the possibility that we are trying to hoodwink the enemy, but in the light of past events and the present military situation, there is not much suggestion that we are in fact co-operating as we should with the Russians. The facts speak for themselves.

As I was writing the above a speaker on the radio said, 'Hitler's speeches should no more be taken seriously than his little black moustache.' What an amazing, and at the same time idiotic, statement for a radio commentator to make! The pronouncements of the supreme leader of our chief enemy – not to be taken seriously?

Oct. 11th   Mankind's goodness and desire for progress, and mankind's stupidity and capacity for evil, are both brought out in this week's news. First, there is the attack which is to be made on tuberculosis in this country. The methods to be used: mass radiography of supposedly healthy, as well as of suspect, people and maintenance allowances for the dependents of those undergoing treatment, are a great step forward in the fight against tuberculosis, which has increased enormously since the outbreak of war. This is one of the best pieces of news I have read for some time. On the other hand there is this ridiculous fuss about tying the hands of prisoners-of-war. Bombs may be dropped on each other's cities, every kind of weapon used to kill each other's men in the fighting line, ships sunk and the people on them drowned, but prisoners may not have their hands tied! The governments concerned rail at each other like children – 'You tie the hands of our men and we'll tie the hands of yours.' 'You do that and we'll tie up three times the number we did at first.' The British Government admits that five prisoners captured in the raid on Sark had their hands tied, but the fact that four of them were shot in trying to escape doesn't seem to worry anybody.

Oct. 13th   Churchill's speech at Edinburgh was, to me, almost boring. Apart from a few interesting remarks on Hitler's speech, it was the same old stuff all over again. I am getting a little tired of his rhetoric and metaphorical allusions, with never a really solid and encouraging fact, except in some minor field, to hang on to. Always Churchill speaks of the growing power of the Allies, never fully grown, of the offensive that is to come, of German atrocities that will one day be atoned for, of the 'ring of doom' that is closing in on Hitler (though from where he doesn't say), of the dark days we must pass through, and invariably finishing up with a reference to the light that is broadening and brightening and coming nearer, but never shines fully on us. If he can quote a piece of poetry, all the better. All this can be inspiring, but after a time it wears a bit thin, if there is no real accomplishment or important success to point to in the military field.

Oct. 18th   Home for the weekend and heard two remarks worth recording. One was made by my father: 'I shouldn't be surprised if we do see some fighting around Dakar.' The other by my sister: 'I think Stalingrad will fall now.'

Oct. 21st   Field-Marshal Smuts' speech did not thrill me very much. It was merely a long account of what has happened during the war, ending up with a very cautious and vague outline of what the post-war world may be like.

Oct. 24th   Went to the Piccadilly Theatre to see Fay Compton in *The Little Foxes*. It was a well-constructed play, and Fay Compton played the leading role extremely well.

Oct. 25th   It has been a poor week for my diary. Of the war news two items are worthy of mention. The battle of Stalingrad, indeed, has dominated the news for weeks past, and still it is undecided. It is amazing how consistently it has held the front-page headlines of the newspapers. I shall certainly remember the battle for Stalingrad long after other events have been forgotten.

The Egyptian battle has flared up again, but this time I am not believing anything until it has not been disproved by later events. The *Sunday Pictorial* has started off well with a big headline: 'The 8th Army Smashes Through in Egypt', when actually it has not smashed through anything yet.

On the home front it is mainly a story of restrictions and shortages in all kinds of commodities.

Oct. 27th   The forthcoming report by Sir William Beveridge on social insurance is receiving a good deal of attention in the Press. The report that one of its proposals is a minimum of £2 a week for every home after the war does not sound very promising however. £2 a week is inadequate to keep a family, even if it is only husband and wife, at a reasonable level of existence. 'You can't live on three pounds a week, let alone two pounds,' said my landlady. It is possible, though, that the newspaper report was not fully informed, so it is too early to judge yet.

Oct. 29th   American news seems to be more reticent than our own. Events of some magnitude are not revealed until weeks after they have happened, and then they are no longer of much interest. The Allied handling of news and propaganda has been, I think, deplorable and still is. Still we find that the interpretation of events is grossly distorted. Minor successes are magnified enormously; setbacks are slurred over. In the papers one reads a lot of drivel which is a vain, involved attempt to make any position whatever seem favourable, and if one bothers to read to the end one may find a brief sentence which is almost contradictory of what has gone before, but probably contains the truth of the matter. The most important and factual part is thus often tucked away where it is hoped that nobody will notice it. I can feel a little sympathy for the Press, though. They have had no big success to write about, so they have had to build up

174

minor achievements and even defeats into great and glorious victories. Our military leaders, in their failure to do anything impressive, are partly to blame for the deceit and exaggeration which have been handed out to us. All the same, the papers could present things in a truer perspective.

Oct. 30th 'What has happened in Egypt?' said a man at lunchtime today. 'The silence is ominous,' said another.

I have been reading *The Good Soldier Schweik*, Jaroslav Hasek's hilarious tales of the private soldier who is so stupid that nobody can get the better of him. Such comic creations, besides providing light relief, help us to see ourselves in a saner light.

Oct. 31st One of the latest restrictions, curtailing late bus services, will make the winter evenings drearier than ever now that one will not be able to go so far afield for entertainment. For me it will rule out visits to West End theatres and cinemas on a Saturday evening and musical concerts in North London on Sunday evenings. I suppose the restriction is necessary and, fortunately, I can usually find plenty to occupy my time indoors, but I like to go out one or two evenings a week.

Nov. 1st Saw a silly picture in the *Sunday Pictorial*, the sort of thing which makes me see red. It was a photo of the King and his two daughters 'practising' with a stirrup-pump. Part of the caption says: 'The King – just like you – has made a careful study of fighting incendiary bombs and is insistent on regular practice by his family.' What sheer humbug! 'Just like you', it says with oily flattery, knowing full well that the majority of people know little or nothing about fighting incendiary bombs. And if the King has made a careful study of the subject he should know better than to pump without his foot on the stirrup (as he is doing in the picture) and better than to have two people holding the hose, instead of one to hold the hose and one to fetch another bucket of water to be ready to use when the first is empty. If, for journalistic purposes, all three have to be in the picture, why have the stirrup-pump in it at all? If the stirrup-pump has to be in it, why not show it being used properly? We see so many pictures of the royal family and I expect that as individuals they are quite harmless, but I do object to the continual efforts of the papers to put them over as just an ordinary family, doing ordinary jobs of work. They only succeed in doing the exact opposite, in showing them as highly privileged persons – which is what we expect them to be.

Nov. 5th   This morning my landlady said, 'Rommel's been routed.' Looking at the paper, I said, 'They've destroyed a lot of tanks.' Mrs H: 'Yes, it's a proper rout.' 'I hope they keep it up,' I said.

At lunchtime comment on the Egyptian success was as follows: 'Good news, isn't it?' 'You wait a bit.' 'It sounds different this time, though – they've blasted their way through.' 'There's nothing to crow about yet, but they've smashed a stalemate, which is something in these times.' 'They're not out of Egypt yet.' 'They might not get 'em out of Egypt even now.'

Thus, although the news was accepted with caution, it was felt that this time it really was something to get excited about.*

The news had a different ring about it. This time it was no half-and-half affair, but a genuine victory. It promises to be the first really big victory on land that we have had.

Nov. 7th   The newspapers are in ecstasies. There are more maps than ever, showing arrows pointing in all directions, arrows inside arrows, arrows straight and arrows coiled and curving like snakes, and various other wonderful symbols. It is a military map-maker's paradise. As Mr H said, 'You'd think the war was over from the *Daily Express* headline.'

Nov. 8th   The continued success of our Army in Egypt, followed by the news today of the landing of American troops in French North Africa, suggests, as my landlady said, that 'this is the beginning of something really big in North Africa'.

Nov. 9th   Everyone is greatly heartened by the latest news. At lunchtime a man remarked what a shock it would be for Rommel if he got to El Ageila and found some of our troops

* This was the beginning of the Battle of El Alamein.

there waiting for him. There is also some surprise, as well as pleasure, that our forces should have broken through so completely, instead of having a long, hard struggle to drive the enemy back, especially as it is not so long since the 8th Army was on the retreat.

Nov. 11th   Bought a poppy this morning, but begrudged giving sixpence for the scrap of cloth and wire you get for a poppy now. A man I know refused to buy one, saying he refused to buy all flags, etc., on principle. As for keeping the two minutes silence, I was busy at the time and forgot all about it.

Events in the various theatres of war are now moving so rapidly that some people find it difficult to keep up with the pace of them. One just takes in the news items and wonders what is going to happen next. After lunch Dr R came back and said: 'Did you hear the news? The Germans have marched into unoccupied France and occupied Tunisia. I think they'll get beaten up, though. But it's amazing how swiftly they move ... Another thing they might try, if desperate, is to invade this country. I hope we haven't depleted our forces here too much.'

Hearing the statement on the 6 o'clock news that the church bells will be rung next Sunday to celebrate the victory in Egypt, my landlady said: 'That's daft. They should wait till it's all over.'

Nov. 13th   Churchill's speech in Parliament two days ago was one of the most interesting he has made, I think. It was more sober and more factual than usual, a pleasant change from his other florid, metaphorical manner and a marked contrast to his speech at Edinburgh a month ago. And this time he had something worth-while to talk about.

Mrs H remarked how difficult it was to manage with the milk now. It is worse than last winter, as then you could buy as much dried milk as you liked, whereas now you can obtain only one tin per person every eight weeks. It is impossible now, also, to make the points coupons cover everything for which they are required.

Nov. 15th   Remarking on the German retreat in Libya, my landlady said: 'There's something about this running away business that doesn't seem quite square to me.' Indeed, the German retreat is so rapid, so lacking in resistance, that one wonders whether there is not more in it than meets the eye. It is too good to be true; and one never knows what tricks the Germans have up their sleeves.

Nov. 16th I liked Sir Stafford Cripps' weekend speech on post-war policy. It gave no definite proposals, but it showed a clear realisation of what was wanted and a sane attitude towards post-war problems. I was glad that he wanted no vindictive approach to Germany after the war, as when he said that a policy of splitting Germany up into small states would only give rise to a movement for national unity in Germany, and that the problem of Germany cannot be dealt with separately from the problem of Europe as a whole. At present, I think Cripps is the most capable and progressive man to lead us after the war.

Nov. 17th Herbert Morrison, however, is one I would prefer to see out of politics, although he is a member of the same party as Cripps. Power has gone to his head, and I regard him as a traitor to the Socialist movement. Five other men with whom I conversed at lunchtime today had more or less the same opinion. Some comments they made on him were: 'Bumptious twirp,' 'Hypocrite,' 'I always switch off the radio when he's on,' 'I switched off and reached for the health salts,' 'I don't like his face – he looks a prig.'

About Darlan and the political situation in French North Africa opinion is somewhat mystified, but there is certainly something very fishy about it and it looks as though all sides concerned have acted more or less dishonourably.

Nov. 21st Bought a pair of new shoes which cost more than twice as much as the last pair I bought. However, I thought they were good wartime value. The Utility* shoes, though cheap, do not look very hard-wearing, their soles are thin, and their designs are not very attractive. These I would not buy.

---

* 'Utility' was the Government wartime standard for a variety of products.

icture Post, November 11, 1939

WHAT ARE OUR WAR AIMS?

"What are we fighting this war for?" The Government says it is "to destroy Hitlerism." But we need
*me more constructive aim than that if the whole world is to be with us. Each week for three weeks,
leaders of public opinion have written their War Aims to us. Now readers are writing theirs, too.

A YOUNG MAN'S AIMS:

"We are fighting this war as much for the
liberation of the German people as for that of
the Poles and Czechs, and for the preservation of
our own liberty. We must see that a sane system
of government is established in Germany. Then,
when Europe is free from the fear of aggression,
we can begin to construct a United States of
Europe and, eventually, a United States of the
World.

"If we want to achieve this end, we must not
let it be obscured by hatred, whatever atrocities
may be committed. War cannot be humanised,
but it is the fact that most of us want it to be that
gives hope for a new, Christian civilisation."

*E. A. Stebbing (age 19), Maidon Road, Great
Baddow, Essex.*

he house in Ormesby Drive, Potters Bar, where I had lodgings from 1941 to 1948. Mine
as the small room over the door (though the window has been altered).

Staff of Clare Hall Hospital at a New Year Dinner on January 12th 1943. We paid 7s. 6d (37½p) for what was considered a sumptuous repast in those days of rationing. The author is seated four from the far end on the right-hand side of the right-hand table.

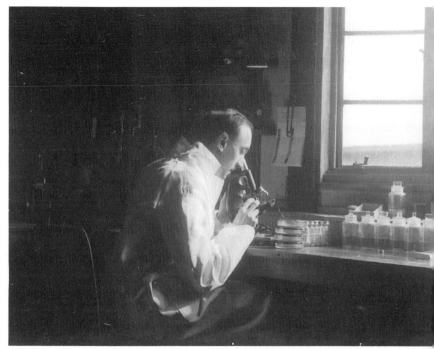

The author working in the laboratory at Clare Hall Hospital in April 1947.

Rotterdam, 15 March

Dear Mr. Stebbing,

One evening when, I was looking in some
Picture Posts, I read your article about:
"What are our war aims?" and was very interested.

Now war is over, but what has ~~removed~~ remained of all our nice and good thoughts?
Nothing!

If we want to achive this end, we must not
let it be obscured by hatred, whatever
atrocities may be committed. That is not possible, while the Germans have tormented
our poor people in the concentration camps.
Beasts were treated better.

Yes, a United States of the World has
constructed, but that is not what we meant.
Europe is not free from the fear of aggression. There are troubles everywhere.

And now the young generation has to choose
their way. Very difficult in this chaos. So
I want to know your opinion, what you are
now thinking about this world after 6 years?

I am a girl of 22 years. Febr. 1945 my dear
father and brother were executed by
shooting by the Germans. I call the Ger-
mahs "bloodhounds". Possibly you cannot
imagine what it means to losse your father
and brother in such a way. Please, try it and
tell me what has happened with you during
the war.

I hope, you will not be astonished about
this letter and write me soon back. Kindest
regards from

                                    Nelly.

My address is: Nelly Visser
                Borgens 10
                Rotterdam
                Holland

Nelly Visser and Ted Stebbing, somewhere near Oud-Leusden, Holland – July 1947.

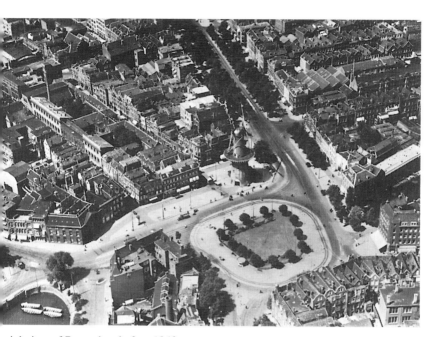

erial view of Rotterdam before 1940.

tterdam – the same view in 1946.

The two Visser gravestones at Rusthof cemetery, Oud-Leusden.

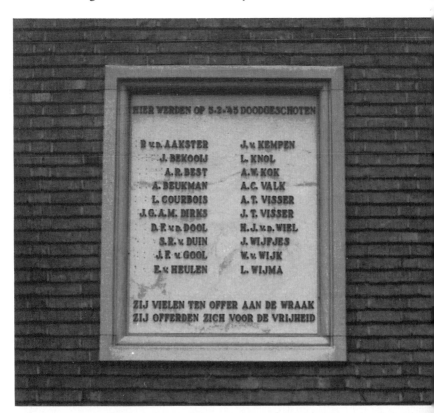

HIER WERDEN OP 5-2-45 DOODGESCHOTEN

R v.d. AAKSTER	J. v. KEMPEN
J. BEKOOIJ	L. KNOL
A. R. BEST	A. W. KOK
A. BEUKMAN	A. C. VALK
L. COURBOIS	A. T. VISSER
J. G. A. M. DIRKS	J. T. VISSER
D. F. v.d. DOOL	H. J. v.d. WIEL
S. R. v. DUIN	J. WIJFJES
J. F. v. GOOL	W. v. WIJK
E. v. HEULEN	L. WIJMA

ZIJ VIELEN TEN OFFER AAN DE WRAAK
ZIJ OFFERDEN ZICH VOOR DE VRIJHEID

The wall memorial in honour of 20 men, including the Visser father and son, who we executed at that spot on 5-2-45.

...e author (top L.) at Bad Pyrmont, Germany, in August 1950, with Mary and Leonhard ...iedrich, Stella Johnson and Muriel Lester (centre at front).

...onhard and Mary Friedrich, at Bad Pyrmont, 1950.

The Quakerhaus, Bad Pyrmont, 1950.

In normal times at this time of year the shops would be full of Christmas fare, gifts, etc., but this year, apart from Christmas cards and calendars, there is very little of a Christmassy nature in the shops. As a young woman said, 'It gets worse every year.' My chief anxiety is to change my fire-watching turn, which falls on Christmas night, so that I can go home for Christmas.

Nov. 22nd   The new Cabinet changes are very disappointing. One of the best men in the Cabinet, Cripps, is taken out and given an inferior job, while a much inferior man, Morrison, replaces him in the Cabinet. Whatever they may say about it in letters to each other, I have the idea that Cripps was too progressive for Churchill. Morrison, with his leanings to the Right, is more Churchill's man.

Nov. 23rd   Even if, as the *News Chronicle* suggests today, Cripps wanted to be relieved of his position in the Cabinet, it makes little difference to my remarks of yesterday. Whatever the details, the fact remains that Cripps is a man of much greater idealism, sincerity, and brilliance than Morrison, and the deplacement of the former by the latter is to be deplored. I can't understand why the Press have accepted Morrison's promotion without a murmur – in view of his past record regarding censorship of the Press – and glibly declare that it meets with general public approval.

Nov. 26th   'This time next year will see the war over,' said a bus-conductor.

Nov. 28th   The strongest impression which the scuttling of the French fleet at Toulon gives me is one of tragedy, a tragedy which is at the same time puzzling. It is tragic that a great fleet should be sent to the bottom without a battle, because there was nothing else it could do. And what can one make of a series of events in which German forces, who usually grab all they can, occupy all France except the port where the fleet is, then a former collaborator with the Germans (Darlan) calls on the fleet to join the Allies, then the French head of state orders the fleet not to obey Darlan's call, then the Germans march into Toulon, then the French resist, blowing up oil-dumps and arsenal and scuttling the fleet, plus several other complicating details? At all events, many Frenchmen are hostile to the Germans and the Germans have been deprived of the use of a formidable fleet.

Nov. 29th   Home for the weekend and travelling, both going there yesterday and coming back today, was an ordeal. I spent several hours waiting about for trams and buses. This travel business, especially at night, more than any other war restriction, makes me feel really venomous.

At home I found barrage balloons all over the town, erected since I was last there, everybody saying it won't be much of a Christmas this year, and the last buses leaving the garage at nine o'clock.

Nov. 30th   Two men said what they thought of Churchill's speech. 'The main idea,' said one, 'seemed to be to stop us thinking we're getting on too well.' The other said, 'Evidently he expects the collapse of Italy.'

Regarding the scuttling of the French fleet, a third man said: 'The truth of the matter is that the Germans have sunk the French fleet.'

About Russia the second man declared, 'That's the country that will finish the war.' Everyone says how marvellous the Russians are to be able to take so much punishment and yet survive to take the offensive on a large scale.

My landlady said the milk shortage was to be expected because of the number of cattle which had been destroyed because of foot-and-mouth disease.

Dec. 2nd   The Beveridge Report merited all the fuss that has been made about it, after all. It is something to look forward to after the war, if it is achieved, something worth fighting for. It is one of the most encouraging signs so far that the world after the war will perhaps be a little happier to live in. Hitherto there has been hardly anything to give one to suppose that the post-war world will be any better than the pre-war world. The Beveridge plan is a step forward, both practical and idealistic, and the enthusiasm with which it has been greeted in many quarters is also a welcome sign. Some of this enthusiasm may be feigned, and there is bound to be some opposition from the reactionary forces. However, a man said to me today, and I agree, 'I wouldn't mind betting the bulk of it is adopted within two years after the war.'

Dec. 6th   My landlady says she is going to put marmalade in her Christmas pudding instead of candied peel, which is unobtainable. 'I'll make one out of something,' she said.

Dec. 7th   Heard the first carol-singers tonight, but they seem quite incongruous now and it took me some little time to realise what was going on. They seem to belong to a separate part of our existence, or some previous incarnation that I had almost forgotten.

Dec. 9th   Mrs H said she went into a shop to buy some black-out material, but it was 10/11d. a yard, so she didn't even look at it. 'It's all a racket,' said her husband. In spite of price controls, profiteering is still rampant in many commodities.

In the evening I went to a meeting of the local Communist party, which was advertised as a 'Salute to the Bolsheviks'. It was the first Communist meeting I had been to, and I was not very impressed. I had expected a large audience, but there were not more than 30 people there and the rows of empty chairs were rather depressing. When I got there two men were still pinning up photos of Stalin, Molotov, and Voroshilov, and diagrammatic posters showing what has been accomplished in the Soviet Union, which hardly anyone looked at. The meeting started half-an-hour late. The chairman was dressed in black coat and pin-stripe trousers, looking as little like a Communist as possible. The first speaker was a young woman who dwelt for about half-an-hour on the glorious achievements of Russia. Her speech was quite well delivered, but smacked too much of having been got from textbooks. After that there was a collection; I didn't give anything, and I doubt whether they received more than half-a-crown. Then there was an appeal for new recruits to party membership, but nobody responded. After that there were questions and discussion. I was somewhat sceptical about most of the first speech, except when she said we must get rid of Halifax, Hoare, and Amery, and that we must distinguish between the Nazis and the German people. I had never spoken at a public meeting before, so I was surprised to find myself asking three or four questions and arguing with the speaker, and I was pleased that she could find no answer to one of my questions. She and another Communist member also found it difficult to answer a point raised by another member of the audience, who asked them to explain the sudden change in the policy of the Communist party when Russia entered the war, from opposition to support of the Government. I also asked why only about six out of an alleged membership of 120 were present. I did not believe the reply that they were all engaged in other duties.

I think one of the greatest mistakes of the Communist Party is to try to justify everything Russia has done and every line of party policy. Russia, they would have us believe, can do no wrong, and Communism is the ideal and perfect system of government. This, of course, is completely unacceptable to any thinking person.

Dec. 10th   I have heard several derogatory remarks about the radio 'Fuel flashes' and the latest idea – to have it in the form of a silly song sung in a silly way by some silly girls – is ludicrous and bound to be fruitless. People will simply laugh at it.

Dec. 12th   The London theatres, I should think, are doing more business now than they have ever done. Almost every available theatre is being used for some kind of theatrical production and almost all of them are playing to capacity, especially at weekends, when the West End is thronged with people in search of entertainment. People are probably not so particular about the quality of the entertainment they get now and many members of the Forces, perhaps with only a few hours' leave, are glad to get in where they can, which is why many inferior shows, which would not run more than a few weeks in peacetime, are now running for months. This (Saturday) afternoon I tried four theatres, with little hope of getting a seat and with less success. Two of them had no seats left at all, one had a £2/10/- box left, and the other had a few at 12/6d. In the end I got in for 10/6d. at a play I did not really want to see. This was *Murder Without Crime* at the Comedy Theatre.

Dec. 14th   Abyssinia's declaration of war on the Axis is merely funny, pure comic opera. As one man said today, 'That'll make Hitler laugh.'

Dec. 17th   Bought a few Christmas cards, which is all I am going to do in the way of Christmas shopping this year, not for reasons of economy, but because there are few gifts obtainable, either because of rationing or because of a general shortage.

Dec. 19th   In a speech yesterday Mr Arthur Greenwood said that in order to prevent Germany plunging the world into war again her war industries should be banned or internationally controlled and her army disbanded. With this I agree, but what about doing the same thing in all other countries? Why not prevent Japan and Great Britain and America and Italy and Russia and all the rest from making war by abolishing their war industries and disbanding their armies, navies, and air forces? Total disarmament seems to me to be an unavoidable condition of ensuring peace. I am afraid, however, that the majority of people will not admit the logic of this. Besides, the world of business and finance would never stand for it.

Dec. 21st   Heard the first performance in this country of the 'Ode to Stalin' by a Russian composer, on the radio, and wondered whether it was a spontaneous piece of musical inspiration or whether it was produced to order to eulogise Stalin. 'Stalin's got a nice face,' said my landlady. I think many people are deceived by that smiling, fatherly face with large moustache, which is in reality the face of a cruel and implacable dictator.

Dec. 23rd   Comment by an Army sergeant: 'Russia will have a lot to say after this war. I reckon they'll just about exterminate the Germans. I think they're entitled to, too.'
    He said that he and his wife had spent two hours looking round for toys for their children, without success. If there were

any available they were at 'impossible prices'. Some people, however, are earning so much money now that they don't care what they pay and people who do not earn so much have to suffer for it. 'There aren't many patriotic people in the country – only as far as their pockets are concerned,' said my landlady. This is perhaps a sweeping statement, but not altogether wide of the mark.

Dec. 24th   Having found someone to do my fire-watching for me tomorrow, I left off work early and made the journey home. There were not great numbers of people travelling.

Dec. 25th   Christmas is always a time of good things to eat and drink, so here are the meals we had today: Breakfast: egg and bacon (instead of the usual boiled ham); dinner: roast duck with vegetables, Christmas pudding; tea: trifle, iced cake, mince pies, etc.; supper: cold tongue and pickles.

Gifts were fewer this year. Mine consisted of two handker-chiefs, a few cigars (by smoking which I broke an abstinence of four or five months), and 15/- in money. Things scarce or missing this year were drinks (except soft drinks), nuts, figs and dates, Stilton or Gorgonzola cheese, and fruit; but sweets, as far as I remember, were more plentiful than last year.

We spent the day quietly until teatime, when we went to a family party at my sister's mother-in-law's house. There were eight of us altogether. After tea we played various games and tricks and did the 'Hokey Cokey', all of which caused much amusement, until about twelve o'clock.

The news of Darlan's assassination came as a surprise, but everybody to whom I spoke thought it was no loss to us.

Dec. 31st   The past year, like the year before, is one I can look back on with satisfaction from a personal point of view. I have enjoyed both work and leisure hours, have been in as good health as to be expected, put £25 in the Savings Bank, increased my knowledge and widened my tastes.

From an impersonal point of view, the first nine months of 1942 were perhaps the most depressing of the war, but in the last three months the position has improved beyond belief. On the home front some restrictions have proved irksome, but I think we are better off than most other countries at war and that we could put up with much more inconvenience before we could be said to know what real hardship is. (There are individual exceptions, of course.)

1943 promises well.

Notes

[1] Dr Konrad Rosenberg, a Jewish refugee from Czechoslovakia, was a pathologist at Clare Hall for a time, though only on a part-time basis.

[2] *Reynolds News* was a Left-inclined Sunday newspaper, now defunct.

[3] *Out of the Night* lifted the lid on Russia as far as I was concerned; in future I would not be deceived by extravagant claims for the Communist system. Yet I have sometimes been surprised never to have seen mention of this book from that day to this. Was it because it was published at an inauspicious moment in the progress of the war, when criticism of Russia may not have met with approval?

[4] This British Restaurant, where a good lunch could be obtained for 1/- (5p), was in St Albans. These restaurants were a boon for poorer people.

1943

Jan. 1st   It is good that we are to have a Ministry of Town and Country Planning, but why on earth do they choose Mr W S Morrison, of all people, to be the head of it? For a job that requires foresight, boldness, expert knowledge, and creative ideas, they have chosen one of the most insignificant, least imaginative, least informed, and least revolutionary of men! Let us hope the new Ministry will soon be placed under the control of someone more suitable.

Jan. 6th   Saw Noel Coward's much-boosted film (said to be the greatest British film ever made), *In Which We Serve*. It is indeed a fine film, realistic yet restrained, free from the blatant propaganda which spoils so many films of this type, extremely well-acted, technically brilliant. But I do not think it is the greatest British film. Although the story is good, it is not a really great and moving one.

Jan. 7th   I have refrained lately from mentioning the Russian exploits, but admiring remarks about their wonderful deeds have now become a commonplace.

Jan. 12th   Went to a New Year dinner for those of our staff who cared to pay 7/6d. There were about 70 of us and we had soup, goose, chicken, potatoes and Brussels sprouts, Christmas pudding, mince pies, and beer, which, in these days of rationing, must be reckoned a sumptuous repast. After the dinner there was dancing until one o'clock; we did the Conga and the Hokey-Cokey, which latter seems to have become more popular lately.

Jan. 15th   This year, so far, has been lacking in diary material. Conversation about the war has decreased considerably. The war in Russia has developed into a slow, remorseless struggle, with few outstanding events (although in itself it may be as far-reaching in effect as the most exciting victories); the Eighth Army is at a standstill; nothing much is happening in the Far East; while in French North Africa the position, both military and political, is so obscure that it is impossible to form an opinion about it. On the home front only the possibility of bread rationing has provoked some comment of a mild nature.

Jan. 17th   The calm has been broken unpleasantly by the return of German bombers over London. The air-raid siren went for the first time in months in this district (extreme North London). 'That's because we raided Berlin,' said Mr H. 'I thought they'd be over,' said his wife. However, no bombs fell near. The guns fired almost continuously, sounding like distant thunder. Some of us stood at the back door looking out, but there was nothing to see. Mr H said he liked to see what was going on rather than to sit indoors wondering what was happening and imagining all sorts of things.[1]

Jan. 18th   Sending reporters with the bombers which raided Berlin struck me as a refinement of horror, a kind of ghoulish gloating. Do we have to turn something which ought to be distasteful to normal people into a sensational newspaper story with all its lurid details, so that newspaper readers may be able to enjoy a vicarious thrill in bombing Berlin? It is a perversion of what is anyway inhuman.

There was a good deal of talk today about last night's raid. 'We're going to have that game again – Berlin, London; Berlin, London,' said one man. 'And what good does it do?'

Jan. 21st   There has been some unfavourable comment on the air-raid warning system after the two recent raids. In the night raid on Sunday and the daylight raid on Monday, the guns started firing immediately the 'All clear' went. It is reported that the warning had not gone when a bomb fell on a London school, killing many children.

187

There is some speculation, too, about where Churchill is, since Attlee gave the war review in the House of Commons. North Africa has been mentioned as a likely place. 'If he doesn't get a picture of himself wearing a fez in the papers,' joked one man, 'he's missed the chance of a lifetime.'

Jan. 27th   The above surmise was full on the mark, then. But it was rather disappointing, after the momentous news we were led to expect, to find that it was only another meeting about which we cannot be told anything concrete.

Of Stalin's non-acceptance of the invitation to be present, three or four men thought that it was rather because he didn't want to be there than because he couldn't be there.

Jan. 28th   For the first time since the war began, we are getting used to good news. For about four months we have had a continuous run of favourable news, from Russia, from North Africa, from the Far East, and the tone of German and Italian news has been such as to give us increased hope. The capture of Tripoli seemed to follow in the natural course of events, rather than as a climax to a period of suspense and uncertainty. We are in danger of falling into complacency again.

A new word has come into our language, or at least it has only just come into fashionable usage. The word is 'global'. Newspaper commentators now talk wisely about 'the whole global conception of war' and 'a global offensive', though what such phrases mean heaven only knows.

Jan. 31st   The daylight raids on Berlin yesterday were a piece of daring which appeals to one's sense of humour as well. The thought of Goering and Goebbels being forced to run for cover as they were about to make their speeches (whether that was actually the case or not) is a comic one, which reinforces the present public mood of confidence. The fact that the speeches of the German leaders were lacking in their usual arrogance was another encouraging point.

Feb. 1st   Further to the speeches of Goering and Goebbels – the papers make much of the admission that the Germans were deceived by the Russian camouflage of their military strength in the Finnish war, but they omit to mention that we were equally deceived. A man said to me: 'What would have happened if we'd sent an expeditionary force to Finland?' It would be embarrassing for us to recall what was said about Russia at that time!

It is just possible that the purpose of the recent gloomy German propaganda is to lull us into a false sense of security, but it is most unlikely, since it must at the same time have a depressing effect on the German people, and the German leaders would not risk this unless they were in a serious position.

The reason for Hitler's silence provokes considerable speculation. The possibilities are intriguing.

A young woman's attitude to her work in a factory is interesting. She described the operations of making a screw, performing the gestures of pulling down levers and saying what the machine did, so that it really sounded interesting. She said that one of the men came and asked her riddles, but she kept on working. Some of the others said, 'Oo, look at her, working for victory!' Her view is that as she is only part-time she'd better make the most of her time. Besides, there is not much to show for her work – 100 screws don't look much, and it takes a morning to make 100. 'I'd like to spend two months in every factory to get an insight into everything,' she said.

Feb. 2nd   I'm not exceptionally cynical, but it seems fairly obvious that Turkey's friendship towards the Allies is only a matter of expediency. The *News Chronicle* says that the meeting between Churchill and Inonu 'would not have taken place unless either the Turks had become absolutely convinced of Germany's forthcoming defeat or the United Nations had been able to send them war material on an impressive scale.' The writer (Vernon Bartlett) refers to what was really sitting on the fence on the part of the Turks as 'keeping the Germans guessing'.

German attempts to represent their defeat at Stalingrad as

something heroic are being belittled by various commentators, but there is no doubt that if we had been in the same position we should have tried to do exactly the same thing.

Listening to some records of Kreisler this evening, I wonder again at the strange kink in human nature which makes men able to create such beautiful music and at the same time to wage the most bestial war.

Feb. 4th   I think the Government are initiating these debates on post-war reconstruction to take Parliament's mind off present times,' said a man at work today. 'Yes, a smoke-screen,' said another. These are two youngish men of the sort that likes to make an impression by saying cynical and pessimistic things. The cynicism of one seems to stem from disillusionment, while the other's seems to come from a desire to emulate him, without necessarily expressing his real private opinion. They merely try to outdo each other in making witty and, as a rule, destructive remarks. Thus I doubt whether the first comment noted above was the real opinion of the speaker. And I expect if the Government were to start debates on present-day events, they would say that it was in order to avoid thinking about post-war problems. In any case, the assumption is false, since Parliament has plenty of opportunity to discuss both war and post-war matters.

Feb. 6th   Heard some careless talk in a barber's shop. A man was telling how many guns were manned at a local anti-aircraft site, how many more would be manned in how long a time, and other details. There is still much of this kind of talk.

Feb. 7th   Sir Stafford Cripps' weekend speech was a timely one and reaffirms my confidence in him. We must not be deprived of a better life after the war through lack of resistance to the activities of anti-progressive forces.

Feb. 8th   'Spectacular, but—' was how I heard Churchill's recent 'tour' described by one of the men I mentioned four days ago. Churchill certainly has a flair for the sensational, but these meetings may have important consequences.

I have heard several people express the belief that the war will be over with Germany this year, if not with Japan. I'm inclined to think so myself.

Feb. 14th   Some people think otherwise, however. 'They keep on talking about the war going on into 1944,' said my landlady rather regretfully. 'I think it will, myself,' said her husband.

The *Sunday Pictorial*'s latest 'campaign' is against the BBC for 'brighter Forces programmes'. Personally, I think the BBC does a very good job in trying to cater for all tastes. There are bad programmes, of course, but on the whole programmes have improved considerably. The *Sunday Pictorial* is very much mistaken if it thinks the BBC ought to be like itself – cheap, glaring, superficial.

Feb. 17th   I did not expect the present Government to accept all the proposals of the Beveridge Report without reservation, but I did expect a little more enthusiasm for it than was shown by the speeches of Sir John Anderson and Sir Kingsley Wood in the Parliamentary debate. They followed the age-old formula of praising and accepting the main general principles, then nibbling and gnawing at the separate specific parts with excuses, modifications, postponements, and uncertainties until nothing is left. The effect was disappointing, but I can understand the Government's point about the difficulties of implementing the report now. There are many problems to be considered; but what worries me is that it seems very doubtful whether the Government wants to do anything *after* the war. It is not to be expected from a Government under strong Tory influence, unresisted by a tame Labour party.

The Americans do not seem to be doing very well in Tunisia. 'I thought the Americans were going to walk in and swipe everything,' said my landlady. On the other hand it does one's heart good to read of the continued Russian successes and of the gloomy German comments on them.

Feb. 18th   The weather this winter has favoured fuel economy. In fact, I think we have had more sunshine this winter than last summer. Today is almost like a day in June; it makes you feel good to be alive, war or no war.

Feb. 19th   Some talk at lunchtime today about the debate on the Beveridge Report. One man said they ought to have shelved the whole thing until after the war, as we could not afford it now. We ought to wait until we were prosperous. Also, he said, the Report presupposed a long era of peace, whereas, he thought, we were in for a long period of war, perhaps for the next one hundred or two hundred years (!). Another man disagreed entirely – he thought the Beveridge proposals were a necessity. (The first man is only about 30, the second is over 50. One might have expected their views to be the reverse.) He did not think economics came into it; if we wanted a thing we just had it. After a few years of the Beveridge plan we should probably find ourselves prosperous. Neither did he think we were going to have a long era of war. A third man said that if they didn't carry it out now they wouldn't after the war. Myself, I think it would be better not to have it at all than to have only a half-hearted attempt at it.

Feb. 21st   The Ministry of Health's Press advertisement, 'Ten Plain Facts about Venereal Disease', is a useful first step in its campaign against VD. A lot more is needed yet. These plain facts must be followed up by more detailed facts and by arguments as well as facts. The propaganda must be long-term and persistent, because the prejudices and ignorance to be overcome are deep-rooted and not easily broken through. People must be gradually and persuasively re-educated. Fact No. 7 in the advert. seems bad psychology to me, with its rather disapproving talk about 'free-and-easy sex behaviour' and 'clean living is the only way to escape infection'. This merely serves to antagonise the people whom it most directly concerns, by making them feel socially undesirable, morally culpable. Whatever their morals, however, diseased persons must be sympathetically treated. The Ministry of Health would do far better to recognise the weaknesses of human nature than to make the puritanical remark that 'abstinence is not harmful', which is very much open to dispute.

192

Education in schools is being adversely affected by wartime circumstances, if my landlady's nephew, aged 12, is any judge. He says that at his school they have had several different maths. teachers and now they are at a less advanced stage than they were with a previous teacher. Some teachers, he adds, do not know their jobs.

Feb. 22nd   Some concern, though as yet not serious, is being shown at the position in Tunisia, judging by remarks I have heard in the last day or two. 'Anyway, we've "straightened our line",' said one man sarcastically. 'Then the Germans will make another kink in it.'

Feb. 23rd   There was some resentment among the men at our table today at Stalin's complaint about the absence of a Second Front, in his order of the day to the Red Army. One man said: 'Who held the front in 1940? Why didn't he open up a Second front then?... What about our convoys to Russia?' 'What about our North African campaign?' said another. A third said: 'What about Burma and Malaya?' The second speaker went on: 'We've got a big enough front to hold on the sea without another one on land. Why should we have to put up with these insults?' These remarks are, I think, quite justified, and it is not very helpful of Stalin to keep harping on the subject, but the fact remains that Russia has borne most of the weight of the German might while we have done comparatively little to relieve her.

Feb. 24th   It seems that the Government have made such a mess of the Indian problem that they cannot get out of it and, unwilling to admit their mistakes, are determined to go on with their present policy whatever happens. The situation is probably more serious than is allowed to appear. If Gandhi dies in prison, I think there is almost bound to be a bust-up, perhaps with disastrous consequences. If they released him the bust-up would not be quite so certain, but it is probably too late now to do anything except prepare for the worst.

The problem of clothes is becoming almost acute for me. I am going to work with darns in the knees of my trousers, which I have never done before. I am almost ashamed to be seen in them. I am badly in need of pyjamas and socks, but cannot buy them until the next 20 coupons come into use, which fortunately will not be long now. I shall have to reprieve an old suit which I had not intended to wear any more, but at least there are no holes in it.

Feb. 26th   I can't quite understand why sugar is to be used to make a new 'yeast food'. Sugar is a valuable food in itself, and if there is a surplus of it anywhere (I was much surprised to learn that there was), what about us having some of it? After all, it is not a luxury, but a vital necessity. All this scientific mucking about with it seems a waste of good sugar to me.

Feb. 27th   Was glad to read that the Minister of Health had 'announced an all-out attack ... on the deep-seated ignorance and prejudice of the public' (about venereal disease). But I was not so glad to read the Archbishop of Canterbury's remarks about 'the sacredness of sex' and 'the duty of chastity'. I didn't expect that kind of rubbish from him. What is sacred about a natural, biological process? One might as well call eating sacred! This attitude only emphasises the idea that VD is something sinful and shameful, and tends to inhibit openness on the subject. The Ministry of Health's campaign will lose much of its effectiveness if it adopts the Archbishop's line and tries to combine a policy of education and enlightenment with a doctrine of the sacredness of sex. The one will neutralise the other.

My landlady has no patience with Gandhi. 'I hope he does die,' she said. 'He's been bought by German money.' Her idea about Indians and all coloured foreigners is that 'they're nice to your face, but the minute your back's turned they'll have a knife in you.' And again, 'You can't treat them like white people.' In my view, our very mistake lies in trying to treat them like ourselves. Their totally different habits, beliefs, and traditions demand totally different treatment. As it is, we don't understand them and they don't understand us, except in individual cases – not as whole communities.

Notice seen in a restaurant: 'Is your roll really necessary?' I don't mind cutting down on bread, but I'm not inclined to eat more potatoes. Wartime diet is now becoming noticeably dull and monotonous.

Went this evening to see the Russian comic opera and ballet, *Sorotchintsi Fair*, a gay and colourful affair which well rewarded my curiosity. The singing and dancing were splendid.

Feb. 28th   Further thought on the Beveridge Report (which occupies quite a lot of my thoughts these days): it would help to remove the money incentive from life. The argument of opponents of the report, that it would destroy initiative and incentive to work, is nearly always put forward by people who are well-off, especially wealthy employers, and is really a blind to hide their fear of being robbed of their power over the worker – the power to give or withhold work and wages, to make the workers dependent on them for their livelihood. They want security for themselves, but not for others. Even if the argument were not a blind, it is not a valid one. No-one could live comfortably on the allowances made in the Beveridge plan for a long period – the allowances are not as generous as all that. It is an insult to most ordinary people to suggest that, given the Beveridge proposals, they would lack the incentive to work. What would life be without work?

Mar. 3rd   This district hopes to raise £120,000 in 'Wings for Victory' week. There are about six dances and three whist-drives to be held in aid of it. Personally, I never bother much with these tank, warship, and aeroplane weeks. I don't see the point of them. Having these campaigns will make no difference to the number of tanks, etc. produced, and they will be paid for anyway. They are merely ways of decreasing the spending power of the public, which may be a good thing, but in themselves contribute little or nothing towards victory and are mainly a waste of time.

I was glad to see a letter from A A Milne in the *News Chronicle* rebuking A J Cummings for saying that we must accept Russia's lukewarm attitude towards our war effort without demur. There seems to be quite a large 'Russia can do no wrong' school of thought. In spite of Russia's great military achievements it does not follow that everything that Russia says or does is unquestionable.

Mar. 4th   People still find it difficult to understand the Government's reticence about air-raids. It is ridiculous to suppose that the Germans do not know what town they have bombed. The communiqué about last night's raid on London, though it mentioned London casually, was most unsatisfying and gave no intimation of what really happened. 'So that's all we shall hear about that,' said my landlady. 'If that's all they give London,' said a man at the hospital, 'what do they say when a bomb hits a small village and almost wipes it out?' 'Oh, that's "A reconnaissance plane crossed the Channel" ... Unless it manages to get its school hit – it's big news then,' said another man.

Mar. 5th   The catastrophe at a London tube shelter during the air-raid two nights ago, when 178 people were suffocated in an accident at the entrance to the shelter, was a major topic of conversation today. I don't think anybody believes that, as the official statement says, 'there was no sign of panic'. There must have been panic. In a situation where panic would be expected it is stupid of the authorities to say there was none, when the accounts of some of the survivors make it clear that there was panic. One man said it was directly comparable to the first statement about the fire on the *Normandie* in New York, when it was said straight away, before any enquiry, that there was no evidence of sabotage. Again, there is the usual official reticence about where the incident occurred, one of the first things people want to know. I have already heard that it was Bethnal Green. This is the sort of occurrence which, if the facts are not given as soon as possible, will be grossly distorted by all kinds of rumours.

I noticed a slight alteration in the Press advertisement about venereal disease. In the final paragraph dealing with the first symptoms of syphilis and gonorrhoea, we are now told where the symptoms appear, a point hitherto omitted. I see by today's paper also that Church leaders are much concerned over the increase in sexual immorality. This is a very controversial subject, but I will say that it is not necessarily immoral to *have* VD; the method by which a person contracts it may or may not be immoral. Certainly the Church is right to condemn the spread of sexual immorality, but immorality is increasing in almost all other aspects of life. It is an immoral world we live in and war, the greatest immorality of all, is one of the main causes in the spread of VD. Yet the Church can condone our part in the war, can ignore economic and political immorality (though Dr Temple is giving a great lead in drawing attention to these other immoralities).

Mar. 6th   There was a huge crowd round the Lancaster bomber in Trafalgar Square this afternoon. This seems to be one of the main propaganda showpieces in London's 'Wings for Victory' week. One or two remarks I heard in the crowd were: 'It isn't really very well done. It doesn't look as big as it really is,' 'Isn't it a lovely one!'

Later I went and saw the play, *The Petrified Forest*, but was rather disappointed with it. The acting didn't seem to bring out the full dramatic quality of the story, made it seem just a gangster yarn plus sex interest.

As I walked towards Piccadilly tube station I noticed one of those magazine-stands which only come out after dark; a light is fixed so that it shines on the lurid covers of pornographic books. Then as I entered the tube station there was a policeman controlling the people, so that there should be no more accidents such as happened the other day, and suddenly I felt completely disgusted with our civilisation, in which people call bombers 'lovely', gangsters are heroes, vendors of pornography come out at night, and policemen have to prevent people from suffocating themselves in their panic. With the image of the play I had seen still in my mind, I thought how petrified our civilisation is, not free, natural, or happy, but cold and hard and cruel, like a stone, like a frozen corpse.

When I got home my landlady, talking about the shelter accident, said that nobody believed it was a woman falling which caused it, but the panic of the people, who pushed each other over.

Mar. 7th   One of the best pieces of news on the food front is that my landlady's pullets have started laying. Last week I had a fresh egg for breakfast on three days. Today we started having condensed milk in our tea to sweeten it, in order to save a little sugar for jam-making. It is quite a good substitute. Meat and fish are difficult problems in this district.

Re the shelter accident: the *Sunday Pictorial* says that a doctor says that it happened because there was only one door, the *News of the World* has it that a doctor (presumably the same one) had made several complaints about the lack of a hand-rail on the stairs, without mentioning that there was only one door. Mr H said that nothing they could say would make him believe there was not a stampede. That is my feeling, too.

Mar. 9th   Our hospital is trying to raise £250 in 'Wings for Victory' week. I believe they have already got about £200. One of the sisters gave £10.

The speech made yesterday by Henry Wallace, Vice-President of the USA, was one of the most significant of recent months. It brushes aside all pretence and gets down to hard facts. It crystallises the prospects for the post-war situation. When this war between 'democracy' and Fascism is over, then, if we are not careful, the conflict between capitalism and communism will lead to another war. This, I think, should be the overriding consideration in our post-war conduct (providing, of course, that we do win the military war).

Mar. 10th   Went to a dance in aid of 'Wings for Victory' week. The chairman of the local British Legion branch made a speech and said, among other things, that 'Hitler has as much chance of winning this war as a celluloid cat has of getting through hell chased by an asbestos dog.' He then went on to point out the danger of over-confidence! Another notable event of the evening was when a man who was auctioneering a pair of stockings fell over backwards into the band, broke a clarinet clean in two and damaged a saxophone, making a fearful fool of himself into the bargain.

Mar. 12th   The new VD poster is more or less on the right

198

lines, going into a little more detail about venereal disease, presenting the facts straightforwardly, hitting one or two fallacies on the head. So far I have not heard anyone talk about this Press campaign. There are probably a large number who read the posters, but don't say anything about it, curiosity on the subject being widespread, but mention of it in public still not done in polite society. I wonder how long it will be before people talk about VD as they do about illnesses like 'flu or rheumatism (although some folk still talk about complaints like TB or cancer in whispers).

Mar. 13th   I still don't quite know whether to believe there is any real mystery about Hitler or whether it is all a newspaper fabrication. There are certainly some grounds for wondering where Hitler is, but it is easy to make a mountain out of a molehill. The papers are making all sorts of wild guesses; it is quite an entertainment to read them. The majority of people seem to think that something has happened to Hitler.

Two comments made by men on 'Wings for Victory' week: 'These big concerns put their money in one week and take it out the next.' 'It's just to get the poor people's money.'

The German attempt to regain Kharkov was unexpected. It will be a disappointment if they recapture it, but not an overwhelming one, as the Russian successes on the central front will make up for it.

The fact that we are making terrific bombing raids on Germany doesn't make everybody happy. My sister said, 'I think we shall get some bad air-raids before long ... Don't you think all these air-raids are terrible?' Personally I abhor this gloating over the extent of our bombing. There can no longer be any pretence that our bombs are aimed at military targets only.

Mar. 16th   Conversation at lunchtime today:

1st man: 'I can't understand why they made Eisenhower commander-in-chief in North Africa.'
2nd man: 'Politics.'

199

3rd man: 'I don't think the Americans would have been in it
              if we hadn't dangled the carrot of their man being
              C-in-C in front of them.'
4th man: 'I think they expected to walk into an empty country.
              They didn't think they'd have to fight for it.'

Further derogatory remarks were made about the Americans.

I was very glad indeed to read of Sir Richard Acland's challenge to the issue of a writ for the Eddisbury by-election and his demand for a revision of the electoral register. It was a clever remark of his that if you can register for chocolate and fire-watching you can register for democracy. Attlee's whining reply, 'It is very inconvenient to have the matter raised like this,' re-emphasised the pitiful weakness and insincerity of the Labour leaders. I think it is high time that this stupid farce of an electoral truce was abolished. Thousands of young people like myself have no opportunity for making our political opinions felt in any effective way.

Mar. 18th   Another announcement about VD in the Press, putting previously stated facts in a new light. One point that has not been brought out yet is that there may be a period of years between the stages of syphilis, a fact which causes much complacency and neglect.

Mar. 20th   Bought two pairs of pyjamas, which used up 16 coupons and cost 12/6d. each, a very reasonable price and the quality quite good. As I still had five brown coupons left this means I have still got nine red coupons, but these won't last me until August. The clothes ration seems inadequate now; if it is reduced, still more those of us who never kept big stocks of clothes will have to go about looking like tramps. A suit I have pulled out of oblivion to wear for work is older than I can remember, and I also have an overcoat which is several years old. However, owing to careful use, they are still in fairly good condition. It is the smaller articles of clothing which are the bigger problem.

Mar. 21st   Churchill's speech tonight was about the most satisfying one he has given, though not completely so. It had at once a steadying and a heartening effect. He was right in making no promises, for we do not want promises, but at the same time he gave us something optimistic about 'after the war'. He showed that the Government has been thinking about post-war problems and intends to tackle them with some degree of imagination and boldness. Hitherto, it has been the lack of official explanation and reassurance about post-war policy which has caused much of the misgiving and dissatisfaction of recent months. Churchill's speech should act as something of a sedative. I was not, however, satisfied with his remarks about election prospects and one could make other criticisms about what he omitted to mention, but one can't expect everything and what he did say was very encouraging. My landlady said afterwards, 'That's to buck us up, that is.'

Mar. 24th   Further thought on Churchill's speech, together with some comment in the *News Chronicle*, have revealed some grounds for criticism. His remarks on private enterprise, for instance, were typically Tory. Although I do not want private enterprise to be organised out of existence, I do not think it should be allowed – as it has been in the past – to develop into purely selfish profit-making.

Churchill's attitude was one of 'Get on with the war and leave post-war problems until Hitler is beaten.' That was his personal attitude, but he realised that people will get on with the war much better if they have the stimulus of a post-war reward, so he gave us his Council of Europe and his Four-Year Plan. He offered us quite a cheerful prospect, but it sounded like a piece of subtle electioneering, since there is bound to be a general election after the war.

Mar. 27th   The Ministry of Health have adopted an imaginative and determined policy in issuing a new Press advert. on venereal disease every Friday. Yesterday's offering, in the form of a letter to a doctor and the latter's reply, struck a human note which is very desirable. I hope this technique will be continued and improved. There is still much ground to cover.

Mar. 29th   Tucked away in an inconspicuous corner of the paper today were three lines saying that over 1,000 tons of oranges, condemned as unfit for human consumption, had been dumped on the Tees-side. How did such a scandalous occurrence come about? Why was such a large quantity of a valuable food allowed to go to waste?

Apr. 4th   It is strange how, once in a while, there comes almost a complete lull in the war news. For several days now there has been nothing doing on the Russian front, nothing in the Far East, only slow progress in Tunisia, on the home front a few minor topics of varying interest (the chief of them, perhaps, being the commencement of double summer time). Of course, this lull is only relative. To those people living in Russia, in China (of whose struggle it seems to me we ought to hear a lot more), in Tunisia, many things may be happening, but to us, living comparatively comfortable lives, it requires some big event or something which immediately concerns us, such as an air-raid, to make us really sit up and take notice. But perhaps this is the lull before the storm.

Apr. 6th   According to the *News Chronicle* anti-Semitism is on the increase, and from various incidents which have been reported recently it would appear to be true, but I have not noticed any evidence of it in this district or among people with whom I have come into contact.

I was pleased to see my own opinion endorsed by the Bishop of Winchester, who deplored the present tendency to gloat over the RAF raids on Germany.

This evening my landlady, her daughter, and I spent a long time talking about the sweets which have gradually been vanishing from the shops since before the war. It made our mouths water to think of chocolate drops, liquorice sticks, slab toffee, coconut squares, peppermint bulls-eyes, coconut ice, sugared almonds, etc. Shall we ever be able to get them in any quantity again?

Apr. 10th   Went to see *Desert Victory*, the film of the 8th Army's advance from El Alamein to Tripoli. It is at once one of the most interesting, thrilling, and technically brilliant films I have seen, all the more impressive because it is authentic, a record of an actual event. Whatever one thinks about the horror of war, anyone with feelings cannot fail to be excited by the tremendous artillery barrage which begins the attack, or by the tanks rolling forward, or by the German dive-bombers diving vertically down. One cannot help feeling, too, how smooth and easy our lives here at home are by comparison. This film is great propaganda, should boost morale a lot. It enhances the glamour which has been built up round the 8th Army, the first of our land forces to give us victory over German land forces. Nothing succeeds like success!

Apr. 13th   'I think it's very fair,' was an elderly, working-class woman's comment on the Budget. There doesn't seem to be anything very upsetting about it; it again taxes the non-essential items, and it will be the heavy drinkers and smokers who will feel it most. If it causes them to reduce their smoking or drinking it will be beneficial, I think. As far as I am concerned what will affect me most will be the increase in entertainment tax, but as I don't smoke, rarely drink, I don't think I shall have to economise on entertainment.

Apr. 17th   I see by the paper that a doctor, who is an authority on the subject, has opposed the Archbishop of Canterbury's views on the use of prophylactics to prevent VD. I agree with him, for, as he says, to prevent the use of prophylactics is 'preventing prevention'. The Archbishop's views, on many things so enlightened, on this subject are unsound and prejudiced. The Ministry of Health's campaign against VD seems to be losing its vigour. Its first effort has not been followed up as it should have been; there has not been a new poster for some time. If the campaign is to do any good the attention of the public must be kept continually focussed on it. The radio should be used as well as the Press. And I think the Ministry should state clearly that prophylactics are one of the weapons against the disease and, as such, are not to be condemned. There are many other details which should be explained. Having started mass education on the subject it is no good being half-hearted about it. Incomplete knowledge may be as harmful as ignorance.

Apr. 18th   The weather is a very dominant topic at the moment. I don't think anyone remembers such hot weather in April. If it remains like this many people will take no notice of the Government warning not to travel at Easter. The gardens need rain, though.

The numbers of bombers lost in our raids on Germany are beginning to reach proportions where people feel somewhat concerned. My landlady's husband has remarked about it several times in the last month or so. When we lose 55 planes in a night one can only think that the Germans have much better methods of combating night-raiders than we have.

A good example of confusing Government statements was recently given us when we were told almost in one breath (a) that the coal deficiency had been made good, (b) that coal production was decreasing and the position might become serious.

Apr. 22nd   An alleged milk shortage has caused a spot of bother at work. All milk for morning and afternoon tea has been stopped, no tea is served to non-resident staff with the midday lunch. All the non-resident staff are grumbling about it, and nobody seems to believe there really is a shortage. One of the typists told me that the milkman takes away 20 gallons a day because a certain person in authority won't sign for it. We have been making our morning and afternoon tea with dried milk, but it doesn't taste very nice.

Thank goodness I have a holiday from tonight until next Tuesday morning. We've been up to our eyes in work just lately, and it is beginning to have a tiring effect.

Apr. 23rd   Referring to a remark by a radio commentator last night that 'there is no sign of war-weariness', my landlady said, 'Everyone I meet is war-weary, fed-up to the hilt with it.' The commentator probably meant that there has been no great lowering of spirits, but all the same, the way the war drags on and on is becoming more and more monotonous.

The train on which I travelled home for Easter this morning was packed, and I had to stand all the way.

Apr. 24th   In my home district much of the talk is about the recent air-raid on the nearby town, the worst it has had. A great cause for wonderment is the fact that nobody was killed although there was quite heavy damage.

Apr. 25th   Visited a friend. He had a holiday from work and Home Guard, so he was gardening. 'I don't see any sign of this war ending,' he said. His wife said that many lives were saved in the air-raid by the Morrison indoor shelters.

No hot cross buns or Easter eggs this year, but I don't think anybody misses them much.

After tea I went to have a look at a crater left by a land-mine which fell in a field during the air-raid. I did not expect to see such an enormous pit. It was about 20 or 30 feet deep and about 30 yards across, big enough to hold a couple of houses. The earth inside had been churned up, great clods of earth had been flung all round the crater, branches had snapped off trees, and the general impression was as though there had been an earth-quake. Several people stood looking at it – it has become one of the local sights, and it is really quite an experience to see it. One is conscious of the awful force which the mine must have had. It was indeed a blessing that it fell in open fields, and not among buildings. My Aunt N said that it was the biggest one that has fallen in England; a specialist had been to see the crater and said so.[2]

Apr. 26th   Went to see my aunt. 'When peace is declared,' she said, 'I shan't do anything that day. I shall have a lazy, lazy day. I might get hi-tiddley-hi-ti.' After a pause she went on, 'I wonder if we ever shall get them days back again.' 'What days?' I asked. 'Why, like they were before the war,' she said. 'I hope we shall get better days than that,' I said. 'Why? I was contented enough. What better do you want? They were better than it is now.' I didn't argue much. Obviously it is better to be at peace than at war, but I don't suppose anything will ever be the same again.

205

Apr. 28th   Some men were talking at lunchtime about the American troops in this country, and all agreed that they were untidy, slack, spoke a different language, were altogether different from us. This seems a pretty widespread opinion.

May 5th   In spite of the recent further increase in the milk ration, we are still not allowed any milk for morning or afternoon tea, nor a cup of tea at lunchtime. This is just ridiculous official perversity. Yet when the Public Health Committee came down yesterday they had the best of everything. That is the sort of thing which makes me feel like joining the Communist Party.

Some people now get too much milk. One married man, with two children, said: 'We have to stop the milkman leaving it, or the milk bottles pile up in the hall like a row of skittles.'

Yesterday the *News Chronicle* expressed its dissatisfaction with the Ministry of Town and Country Planning. When Mr W S Morrison was appointed as its Minister I knew immediately that we had been palmed off with another dud. While he remains at its head we cannot expect any more than a little beating around the bush.

Today the *News Chronicle* prints a brilliant cartoon, showing the Beveridge Report as the Sleeping Beauty, vested interests as the witch, and seven members of the Cabinet as the Seven Dwarfs, weak and timid, with the caption 'No Prince Charming'. In spite of Churchill's recent broadcast, the plans for post-war reconstruction leave much to be desired.

May 6th   Getting unhappy in my work. We are having more and more work piled on to us, expected to do it in the same length of time, lack of co-operation and consideration from some of the medical and nursing staff becoming more marked. The meals we get at lunchtime are gradually getting worse and worse, chiefly due to bad cooking. Sometimes accumulated circumstances make me feel as though my nerves will snap, but they never do and this seems to make the strain more acute. I feel the need of some emotional outlet.

May 8th   Went to the barber's. The barber said that the

Germans cut off the ears and take out the eyes of some British prisoners.

While waiting for my haircut I picked up a paper and made the discovery – I had not previously seen a paper for the day, or heard the radio news, or heard anyone speak of it – that Allied forces had taken Tunis and Bizerta. The news thus came as a complete surprise to me, since I wasn't expecting their capture so quickly in any case.

May 9th   'I wonder where the next front will be,' said Mr H. He thought it would be in the Balkans. He also thought that if things began to go wrong for Germany, the Japs would attack Russia in Siberia.

One point which surprises me is that none of the papers I have seen yesterday or today give any credit to General Eisenhower, the C-in-C, for the Tunisian victory. Alexander, Montgomery, Anderson, all get a share of the praise, but not once did I see Eisenhower's name mentioned. I think this is rather unfriendly to and unmerited by the American. I am glad the King sent his message of congratulations to him.

I noticed that some triumphal music was played after the one o'clock news today, a new departure I believe.

May 10th   For lunch at the hospital today we had fish and chips (we get this at least twice a week) followed by a pudding which consisted mainly of damp bread. Witty remarks absolutely sizzled across the table.

May 12th   Mr B: 'Who is it Churchill goes to see, Betty Grable or Rita Hayworth? I'm certain it's not Roosevelt – nor Mrs Roosevelt.'

May 14th   Saw four posters about venereal disease on official notice-boards. One showed the silhouette of a man walking past signs marked with the months of the year and with the words 'Delay is dangerous' and 'Free advice is available'. Another showed the silhouette of a woman walking along some parallel lines towards a clinic entrance, with the words 'Treatment must be continued'. The third showed the figure of a bride in wedding dress, captioned with the words 'Here comes the bride' and at the bottom words to the effect that the man who infects his wife commits a monstrous crime against her and against any child that may be born. The fourth poster was just a list of the nearest treatment and advice centres. My main criticism of these posters is that they were not large enough to attract much attention. One might also say that the use of silhouettes and geometrical backgrounds was a too impersonal approach, but probably both the personal and the impersonal approach are necessary. The lines running right across the second poster give an impression of continuation, and the use of silhouettes permits the idea that the person might be anybody and that his or her anonymity would be preserved.

May 15th   My Saturday morning off. I thought about spending the day in the country, but bus services being what they are I decided against it and went up to London instead. I tried to obtain seats at three theatres without success, and at the fourth could only get one for the matinée. Between lunch and theatre I sat in Leicester Square gardens and finished reading the poems of Oscar Wilde. Then I went to the theatre, where *Let's Face It* was showing. It was feeble even for an English musical revue, which is saying something. When I came out a prostitute said 'Hullo' to me near Piccadilly, but I ignored her. Even had she been young and good-looking, which she wasn't, I would not have risked it – I have no desire to contract VD.

After tea I looked round the Royal Academy for half an hour. Few good pictures, I thought; mostly pots of flowers and portraits of uninteresting people. One of the best was Laura Knight's picture of a factory-girl at work; it had life and meaning. I did not have time to look at them all properly, so perhaps I shall go again. Afterwards I wandered round Green Park, which really was green, then on to Hyde Park, where I listened for some time to a couple of orators who afforded me more laughs than *Let's Face It* had done. After that I went home.

May 18th   Comments (all made by men) on the RAF raid on Germany's two biggest dams: 'Wasn't it a fiendish trick, though!' 'Why haven't they done it before?' 'Do you think

208

Germany will pack up now?' 'I can't see it.' 'Considering the size of Germany, it's just a pin-prick. Because they fill a newspaper with it, it doesn't make it any more than that.' There was also some discussion as to whether there were any similar dams in this country.

I am in two minds about it. It was certainly a brilliant military exploit, skilfully carried out, and may do considerable damage to Germany's war industry, thus helping to shorten the war. But I can't help thinking of the people who will be flooded out of their homes or drowned.

May 19th   Listened to Churchill's speech to Congress. The usual stuff, I thought, nothing very outstanding. The most important point was his promise to give America full aid in the attack upon Japan. 'Very good speech,' said my land-lady.

Thought (after hearing more news about damage caused by mining the German dams): Is it a prelude, by disrupting the enemy's communications on a large scale, to invasion?

May 21st   Air-raid warnings have been pretty frequent recently, sometimes four or five a night, sometimes accompanied by quite heavy gunfire, but I have slept through nearly all of them, much to my pleasure, as I don't believe in losing sleep because of air-raid warnings. Only once have I heard the siren lately and that was because I had been up late to a dance, it was a hot night, and there was a storm with thunder and very vivid lightning, so I could not get to sleep. Once I was woken by gunfire, but not for long. Happily, no bombs have fallen in the vicinity. I feel sorry for those who spend sleepless nights simply because of sirens wailing and planes going over.

May 23rd   Saw another poster about VD. It had a picture of a woman taking a pill and gave this warning, 'Quack "cures" are useless'. In smaller letters it said, 'No self-treatment ever cured syphilis or gonorrhoea. Free advice, etc.' This again I thought was a quite well-designed poster, but not big enough. They should be big enough so that their message can be taken in almost at a glance as one passes by, as many people would probably be too embarrassed to be seen studying such a poster, especially those whom it directly concerns.

Another poster which attracted my attention was one advertising Volunteer Agricultural Camps, where one can go for a holiday and help on the land at the same time. The details looked so inviting (half-fares paid, good meals, work paid for, evenings free, entertainment facilities, etc.) that I decided to write for full particulars, as it would be a complete change for me to work on a farm and lead an open-air life.

May 24th   The dissolution of the Comintern, in my opinion, is an extremely significant event. It will certainly remove much distrust on the part of Britain and America and make their co-operation with Russia more firmly-knit. But at first, reading newspaper comment, I was afraid that it also meant that Russia was adopting a more nationalist policy (and I hate narrow nationalism). Thinking it over, however, I decided that it means just the opposite. For although the Comintern was internationally organised, it was only so organised to serve Russia's own interests. The disbanding of the Comintern means that Russia is more prepared to co-operate with other countries without trying to influence their political constitution and thus that her policy is more international. Of course, it does not make Communism any more attractive in itself, but it will be a test of the sincerity of Communists everywhere outside Russia. My opinion of the British Communist Party will go up if it does not change its tune just because Russia has let go the reins. My opinion of the Labour Party will go up if it allows the affiliation of the Communist Party, because the unity of the working classes is essential. My opinion of British and American statesmanship will go up if it makes a reciprocal move towards Moscow.

May 28th   I am not now so keen on going to an agricultural camp for my holiday. A girl I know who went to one last year said they had to sleep on the floor beneath a leaky roof and there wasn't much to do in the evening. Also, in the local paper today there is news of a complaint about lack of sanitary arrangements at a nearby camp. I have also received particulars of the camps for which I wrote and find that, instead of 26 camps to choose from, as advertised on the poster, there are only 11. Only the bare facts of what is expected of you and what you must take with you are given. There is no information about food, sleeping accommodation, or recreation facilities. So on the whole I feel less and less inclined to go.

May 30th   (At home for the weekend.) I had a dream last night, as follows: I was standing beside an Army officer at night. He lent me his binoculars and through them I saw a black shape in the sky. A searchlight revealed it to be an enemy bomber; I could see the black crosses on it. A fighter attacked it and seemed to ram it, ripping it from one end to the other. But the bomber flew on for a little while, the fighter crashed, and finally the bomber crashed too.

My sister's recently-acquired table-shelter looks quite well in the living-room. It is comfortable too, and B says she feels safe in it. It apparently satisfies the urge to get under the table in an air-raid and at the same time gives genuine protection. As one can have one's meals off it, it serves a double purpose.

June 4th   For the last few days the main war news has been confined to our bombing of this, that, and the other place. My landlady said, 'I see that somebody says that our bombing will finish the war this year. I wouldn't be surprised if it does, myself.' 'I would,' I said, 'I don't think bombing alone will win the war.'

June 5th   Woman in bus, to another woman, 'It's hard to hate everyone because they're German. I know I can't, anyway.'

Went to see *The Dancing Years*, the biggest theatrical success of the war, but was not remarkably impressed by it, though it seemed to get better and better as it went along and some fine music and dancing made it very enjoyable.

June 7th   Another important speech by Henry Wallace (US Vice-President) deals with our duty towards German youth after the war to educate them in the democratic view of things. Wallace strikes me as one of the few politicians of moral integrity. Stafford Cripps and Richard Acland are two others.

June 10th   My landlady finds that making the tea ration go round is one of her biggest problems. Having coffee instead of tea for supper does not help much. As a result of rationing, she says, 'I have never seen my cupboard so bare.'

June 11th   Mr H remarked on the quietness of the war-scene, but said, 'I think it's the lull before the storm.' Most of the talk at work yesterday and today was about whether Pantellaria would fall or not. General opinion was that it would be a tough nut to crack.

June 16th   A man's comment on the King's visit to N Africa: 'When they said on the wireless "The following important announcement has been made from Buckingham Palace" I thought the Second Front had started. When they said the King was in North Africa it was rather an anti-climax.'

June 17th   The Labour Party Conference this week has shown to what dismal depths that party has degenerated. Its deliberations have been utterly futile and negative and make one wonder what claim it can possibly have to represent the working-classes of this country. Today's main resolution was, to me, the most disappointing of all, when a majority of more than two to one rejected a motion deploring a policy of revenge towards Germany after the war. Apart from the morals of the matter, this shows complete lack of sympathy with the working-classes in Germany and a hasty, intolerant, and probably fallacious assessment of the position in Germany. We in this country, though by no means democratically ruled, do not know what it is like to live under a tyrannical dictatorship. Therefore it is not possible to appreciate what is going on in the minds of most Germans unless one is a German or has lived in Germany for some time recently. One cannot form an impartial judgment of the behaviour of the German masses. In any case, whatever the blame attached to them, it would be highly immoral to adopt a vengeful policy after the war. Also the idea of making the Germans 'pay for the war' would in reality be quite impracticable.

June 18th   Have now definitely decided not to go to a volunteer agricultural camp for my holiday. I noticed in the paper that the organiser of the camps has resigned for some unspecified reason, and this clinched the matter. Instead I have arranged to stay for one week with an aunt in Dorking.

June 20th   There is now a feeling of suspense about the military situation. We are waiting for big news, wondering when and where the Allies are going to invade Europe and when the war in Russia is going to flare up again. Any day now I expect to hear that the big offensive has begun.

June 22nd   The BBC news bulletins have become very monotonous just lately. Nothing but news of air-raids. I wish they would make some variation and give us more non-war news.

June 24th   Took the day off, as I worked on Whit Monday and had a day owing to me. In the afternoon I went to see Shaw's play, *Heartbreak House*, with Edith Evans, John Laurie, and Deborah Kerr, at the Cambridge Theatre. In the evening I went to the Promenade Concert. I am afraid I nearly went to sleep during Vaughan Williams' new symphony – it was so hot and the music was so quiet. Stravinsky's fantastic *Firebird Suite* and John Ireland's stirring *Epic March* were the two items which appealed to me most.

June 26th   Press and radio now openly gloat over the fearful air attacks being made on German and Italian towns. These terrific assaults may be an essential part of our strategy, but there is no need to be so pleased about it. One cannot think of the effect of these raids without a feeling of solemnity.

July 5th   Listened to J B Priestley's third talk in his new radio series. It is good to hear him back on the air again. Tonight's talk – on what our post-war conduct should be – was a tonic of sane thinking.

July 8th   Home propaganda has been at great pains just lately to prove that Cologne Cathedral was not destroyed, but only slightly damaged, in a recent air-raid. Why all this fuss is being made I cannot understand. Bombing is not so exact, except at very low levels, that a comparatively small target, such as a cathedral, can be deliberately hit or not hit with certainty. Cologne Cathedral might just as easily have been completely destroyed, but nobody in his senses would have thought that it had been a deliberate act of vandalism any more than the destruction of Coventry Cathedral was a deliberate act of vandalism. When bombs are falling by the hundred, a cathedral is just as likely to be hit as any other kind of building.

July 10th   At last the news we have been waiting for – the invasion of Sicily. It is great news, but lack of any details and its not complete unexpectedness rob it of some of its excitement. At any rate it has come at the right time, when the Germans have just started another offensive in Russia.

Went to the Army Exhibition in Oxford Street this afternoon. Excellent use had been made of the bombed site, the exhibits well adapted to the ruined structure of the building. It is a very interesting and exhaustive exhibition and gives one a good idea of the enormous amount of material required to equip an army and of the need for economy on the home front. But such slogans as the one which says that if everyone saved half a slice of bread a day it would save so much shipping seem rather badly worded to me.

In the evening I went with a friend to the Promenade Concert at the Albert Hall. It was a lively programme and a very large audience – we could only get seats in the gallery. A new work by Benjamin Britten received a great ovation.

Afterwards we went to a restaurant near Leicester Square and had some supper, which was alleged to be steak and chips, but we were very dubious about what kind of steak it was. We had grave suspicions that it was horse-meat.

July 13th   In their enthusiasm over the invasion of Sicily some newspapers have made the mistake of giving too much space to too little definite news. Today the *News Chronicle* devotes almost the whole of the front and back pages to reports from eight different correspondents. There is thus a great deal of overlapping and padding, and most of it is sheer imagination. Half a page could contain all the real news and the rest be given over to other items – there must be plenty of other things happening besides the invasion of Sicily.

July 19th Went to the Promenade Concert again, my third visit during the current series. This time it was a Russian programme, a very noisy and exciting affair.

July 21st Although the invasion of Sicily is perhaps our biggest offensive action of the war, it does not seem to have aroused so much enthusiasm as the Tunisian campaign. I think this is because enemy resistance has been comparatively weak and the fighting has not been on a big enough scale to make it exciting. As it has gone in our favour from the beginning and relatively few details have been made known, people have been inclined to take the whole business for granted.

The apparent fall from grace of Henry Wallace, USA Vice-President, is disturbing news, for he has seemed to be a man of great worth. Was he too radical for certain influential parties in American politics? There has been an alarming increase in isolationist, capitalist, and conservative views in America just lately.

July 24th There are surprising differences in food supplies even in limited areas. My landlady said, 'I don't know why it is, but C seems to be able to get anything. She's got a pound of sultanas and a half of currants put by for Christmas. There hasn't been any dried fruit up this way for over a month.' C lives in a town about four miles away.

July 25th Was talking to a girl at a dance tonight and I said, half-seriously, that the war would soon be over. She said, 'You're optimistic, aren't you?... I don't see any sign of it yet.' It seems to be the correct thing to say that you think the war will last a long while yet, whether you really think so or not.

July 26th Mussolini's resignation came as a big surprise, but a pleasant one. What was more surprising was the apparent total collapse of the Fascist system. I do not think that Italy will hold out much longer, although the new government will have to make a pretence of carrying on the war for the sake of prestige. The new government, however, is not one which I should like to see remaining in power, as it is still mainly a reactionary one, and a very makeshift one at that, with few, if any, really competent men in it. Nevertheless, the event must be a severe blow to Germany and opens up favourable prospects to us.

July 28th   Two men today said that they thought the events in Italy were planned by Germany and that Italy was by no means out of the war yet. 'It will pay Germany to fight in Italy,' said one man. It would, perhaps, if Italy was a strong strategic position, but it is such a vulnerable area that it is doubtful if the Germans themselves would try to defend it.

July 30th   There were some unfavourable comments at lunchtime today about the way the newspapers are reporting the Italian business. One man called it 'wild guessing' and said that 'the Germans are probably quietly occupying Italy.' If the Germans really are behind it all, I can't see why they have allowed the Fascist Party to be disbanded.

There was also some talk about Jews and refugees: 'Any nice house you see, it's owned by a Jew.' 'That's a fact.' 'It's amazing what these refugees will go out and spend on food ... and they go about in fur coats and jewellery.' 'There *are* some nice Jews.' 'Oh yes, especially professional Jews – but business Jews! And as long as they're real English Jews, they're all right. These Polish Jews, though, are about the worst.'

Aug. 3rd   There is something shocking about the raids on Hamburg. It is no good being soft-hearted about war, but one can't help imagining the terror of these awful assaults on an already much-bombed city. The raid on the Ploesti oilfields, however, is a good example of a daring and telling attack on a vital strategic target.

Aug. 6th   As A J Cummings points out in the *News Chronicle*, Hitler's silence in the face of so many German reverses is very strange. Lack of news about Hitler has been so marked for several months that I would not be a bit surprised if something queer has happened to him.

Aug. 8th   Comment by my father on the war situation: 'The tide is beginning to turn now.'

Aug. 9th   Comments by two men on the Hamburg raids: 'It's inhuman.' 'There won't be a city left standing in Europe if we go on like that.'

Aug. 10th   A man (aged about 40) said he thought the best way of dealing with Germany after the war would be to split it up into small states, each state governed by one of the Allied powers, with a combined central government. He admitted this was only one of many theories and said that the League of Nations was also a good idea. My landlady said you heard so many different theories you didn't know what to think.

C (age about 26) said she was afraid something would happen to Mr Churchill, 'dodging about like he does'. His latest trip seems to be the occasion for a family holiday.

Aug. 13th   The local 'Holidays at Home' programme is not likely to keep anyone at home for a holiday. Do the authorities really think that a few Punch-and-Judy shows, a miserable little fun-fair, a brass band, a garden fete, and the like, will keep anyone from going away? If they want to persuade people to stay at home they should provide a programme which would help to take the place of a holiday away (though what would serve this purpose I don't pretend to know). The local programme certainly won't keep me at home; tomorrow I am going to Dorking for a week.

Aug. 14th   Arrived in Dorking about 5.30 p.m. After tea I had a look round the town..Saw a new VD poster in a public lavatory. It depicted a small boy standing in a cone of light. 'Tomorrow's citizen' was the heading; in smaller letters, 'Do not let him be handicapped by venereal disease passed on by his parents. Make sure you're fit to be the parents of the citizens of tomorrow.' This is another telling poster like those I have mentioned before, but again the manner of display was not very good. The VD publicity campaign is being maintained fairly well, but there could be much more variation in methods.

Aug. 15th   Morning – climbed up one of the hills surrounding the town and had a magnificent view over the valley. Afternoon – listened to an outdoor concert by a ladies orchestra, who played a lively programme. Evening – went for another walk. Heard that Rome had been declared an open city.

Aug. 16th   Legs very stiff after yesterday's climb, but went and climbed about some more hilly ground in the morning. Went to Reigate in the afternoon and had a look round. As it was getting dark, we watched a stream of bombers going out. As they droned steadily over, with their navigation lights on, they had a deadly fascination. A lot of people were out looking at them. 'Italy again, I reckon,' said one.

Aug. 26th   Illness cut my holiday short, and I have not been able to make any notes until today. As the last ten days have been spent in the local hospital (and I may spend many more days in the hospital where I work, to which I am going tomorrow), I can give only a few brief comments on the outstanding pieces of news. Probably the dominant news has been the advance of the Russians, especially the capture of Kharkov. Unnecessary fuss has been made about the capture of Kiska from the Japanese, as it doesn't seem to be any good to anybody, being covered in fog most of the time. The Quebec Conference, of course, was one of great importance, but I got tired of the somewhat vague and rambling statements which were made about it, and one of Roosevelt's remarks in his speech to the Canadian Parliament was merely silly. He said that if the enemy could have heard what the Allied plans were, they would know it was better to surrender now than later. If that is the case, why not tell them our plans and let them surrender now and get the war over? Another interesting news item was the announcement of the Russian plans for reconstruction in recaptured areas. They certainly lose no time in making plans (how different from our Government!) and must have confidence that they will not lose these areas again. The heavy raid on Berlin was also big news, but the surprising thing was that everybody seemed to know it was coming, including the Germans, as the loss of 58 of our planes proves. The appointment of Himmler as Minister of the Interior in Germany seems to show that Hitler is getting worried about internal affairs. To sum up, the war news has been thoroughly satisfactory for us in all respects.

In spite of this, one of the other patients remarked on the recent scantiness of news. 'If it wasn't for the Russians there wouldn't be any news. They'd have to say, "Sorry, no news this morning."'

Aug. 29th   It is extraordinary, in view of the above comment, that the announcer this morning should say, 'No important news has come through during the night, and there are no headlines'!

The papers are creating a terrific mystery out of the death of King Boris of Bulgaria. Why can't they wait until they know the facts?

Aug. 31st   I was relieved yesterday to learn that I need not stay in hospital any longer and can have my holiday again as soon as one of the other men returns from his. But this morning I woke more tired than if I had done a hard day's work and then had no sleep, so I did not go into work. After breakfast I went back to bed and stayed there until 3 o'clock, when I got up feeling much better and went out and bought some Parrish's Food and some vitamin capsules, which I hope will buck me up.

Sept. 2nd   Black-out episode: I was just taking the black-out down before getting into bed and kept the light on to take part of it down. No sooner had I done so than there was a knock on the door and a lady warden told my landlord about a light showing. I had not noticed that there was a piece of cardboard missing from the small top window, which showed the light when I took the curtain down. But, as Mr H said, 'She must have been waiting on the doorstep.'

Sept. 3rd   I did not remember that this was the fourth anniversary of the outbreak of war until this evening, when Mr

219

H remarked about it being a National Day of Prayer, which he thought was 'all a farce'. Except that it is not funny enough to be a farce; it is just plain silly.

Good news about the invasion of Italy, but I heard very little comment about it today.

Sept. 4th   Mr H's opinion on our attack on Italy was, 'The Americans will land farther up the coast.'

Made another start to my holiday, which I shall spend chiefly at home this time. Plenty of room on the train.

Listened to the recording made in a bomber over Berlin. It seems rather a morbid curiosity to inspire such a thing, but I must admit that I wanted to listen to it, though it was less thrilling than I expected.

Sept. 8th   Spending a quiet holiday. Have not been out far.

The Russians still provide the most interesting news. The Italian campaign is slow and dull.

Later – Although I thought Italy would give in fairly soon, I did not expect it just yet. But Mr A had been expecting it all day – he takes the *Daily Mail*, which prophesied big news from Italy 'any second', whereas the *News Chronicle* had no mention of it. Of course, it was very cheering news. S said, 'A landing in the West now will help things on a bit ... I think it will come before the end of this month.' He expected much heavy fighting in Italy yet, to drive the Germans out. Also, he said, 'If the Russians get to Berlin first they'll want a lot to say in the peace conference ... they'll want a lot to say as it is.' My father said, 'Germany will crack up suddenly, like she did in the last war.' A factory-worker said that when they heard the news some of them danced round the shop and the women wouldn't do any work. 'It's silly to think the war's over,' said S.

Sept. 9th   My aunt said, re the Italian surrender, 'It'll soon be over now ... I felt twenty years younger.'

Went to Southend, my first visit during the war. It did not seem greatly altered, except for the barbed wire along the front. Part of the beach was open, and there were plenty of people on it.

Sept. 10th   Went down to Clacton to stay with relations for the weekend. It seemed much more altered than Southend had done – barbed wire all over the place, streets barricaded, most of the hotels occupied by soldiers, gardens allowed to go to waste, many shops shut, the pier closed, only a tiny bit of the beach open, and comparatively few people about. But I am told that it is better now than it was when the evacuation 'scare' was on.

Sept. 15th   A woman (age 50–60) in a train expressed this opinion: 'There may be another war in a few years time, I shouldn't be a bit surprised. I don't think this is a war to end war. They'll start making munitions again afterwards ... The Russians will have no mercy on the Germans, when they get into Germany. They (Russians) are a cruel race. They'll have a tooth for a tooth. You can understand it, after all they've suffered ... None of this slaughter need be. It could be a peaceful, lovely world with plenty for everybody.'

Sept. 19th   S (whom I quoted on September 8th) said, 'It doesn't seem as if the invasion plans are going to be carried out, now they've lifted the ban on the South Coast.' My father said he didn't know what to make out of the manoeuvres recently carried out in the Channel.

Sept. 20th   Mrs H said, 'I have my doubts about that Mussolini business.' I have my doubts, too. The *Sunday Pictorial* said that 'experts' were certain it was not Mussolini's voice which was broadcast by the German radio. A *News Chronicle* reporter was equally certain it was. The photograph published yesterday, alleged to be of Mussolini, was so blurred that it might have been anybody. There's something fishy somewhere.

Began work again, feeling much better for my holiday.

Sept. 25th   Although the Russian victories – and they undoubtedly are victories – make exciting reading, one fact which is liable to be overlooked is that the Germans are making an orderly withdrawal, taking with them the bulk of their men and material.

Sept. 26th   The new Government changes favour the Tory party and do not offer much prospect of social reform. Mr H said, 'I thought they'd have brought in another Labour man' (as Chancellor of the Exchequer). While keeping up the farce of a political truce, Churchill makes certain of keeping any progressive elements out of the Government.

Another disappointing piece of news was the resolution passed by the British Medical Association opposing a State medical service. I appreciate the view that medical science should not be made a political issue, but all the same reform is badly needed in this field. The panel system is often unsatisfactory, so is the outpatient system at hospitals, and there is much to be said for health centres possessing up-to-date methods of diagnosis and treatment, which everybody could go to. Last year the BMA was in favour of this idea, but apparently the thought of losing some of their fat fees has caused them to do a hasty about-turn, or else some reactionary influences have been at work. Whatever it is it throws a poor light on the medical profession, and I hope that the Government will introduce the idea of health centres even if the BMA doesn't like it.

One can't help feeling a little disillusioned at the above two items of news. During this war there has been a vast amount of talk about social reform, but not a sign of action.

Not long ago I saw a poster bearing a photograph of some starving Greek children. In today's *Sunday Pictorial* I saw a photograph of some starving Indian people and it made me think of the poster. True, the famine in Greece is a result of deliberate action by the Germans and the famine in Bengal is not, as far as we know, the result of any deliberate action by the British Government. Nevertheless, it is very ironic that what is happening in German-occupied Europe can also happen in the much-acclaimed British Empire.

Oct. 2nd   Shoe repairs are now becoming something of a problem. Shops about here cannot take more than a certain number of orders at a time, owing to shortage of leather. My landlady said, 'Everything is getting the same now. Life is one continual worry.'

Oct. 3rd   The military situation continues to be satisfactorily handled, but the handling of the home front leaves very much indeed to be desired. The recent outbreak of strikes are an instance of this. Much of the blame, as far as one can judge from newspaper reports, seems to lie with the miners, who are acting in an irresponsible way, but there must be something radically wrong for such widespread unrest (and the strikes have not been entirely confined to the mining industry). Some papers say that the real reason is the Government's failure to take any action towards social and economic improvement at home. This may be true, for the Government's failure in this respect has been marked. What a sorry show, for instance, came of the Minister of Health's plan for farm-workers' cottages! What a flop the Ministry of Town and Country Planning has been! How completely has nothing been done about the Beveridge Report! There are many other examples. All this has caused a lot of dissatisfaction just below the surface of everyday life, which only requires some small incident, such as has occurred in some of the coalfields and not in itself justifying a strike, to bring the discontent to a head. The record of the trade unions and Labour leaders has not been such as to gain the confidence of the workers. They have not attempted to tackle the root causes of the trouble. The attitude of the Government seems to be that because the military situation is well in hand they are safely entrenched and need not bother about domestic difficulties. If they continue to think like this they are heading for a fall.

Oct. 4th   My landlady stuffed up the ventilators, as they were showing light. I said I shouldn't have thought it mattered, as how were we supposed to get air into the rooms? She said we weren't supposed to have air during the black-out. This is one of the worst aspects of black-out, as rooms get so stuffy, and if you want to open your bedroom window you have to fumble about in the dark to remove the black-out. Then if you want to put the light on again for some reason, you cannot do so unless you put it all back again.

Oct. 6th   For the second night in succession the wireless

223

was cut off and shortly afterwards the siren sounded. Then we heard the barrage over London begin and we went into the non-blacked-out front room and watched the firework display.

Oct. 14th   Pressure of work, as I am studying for an examination I am taking next month, tiredness, and the fact that there has not been much of interest to observe just lately, have led to some neglect of this diary. Also I have had a large amount of correspondence to do, dealing with Income Tax, sickness benefit, taking the examination, obtaining a grant from my insurance society for eye-testing and glasses if necessary, and with family matters. The reason I am having my eyes tested is that I think the tiredness I often feel in the evenings may be due to eye-strain, as I do a lot of reading and writing and my work entails much use of the eyes. But maybe the strain of wartime life is having some effect.

Italy's declaration of war on Germany deserves some comment. My feeling of disgust is not so much because our former enemy may hope to escape punishment by coming over to our side, but because it shows the utter unscrupulousness of everybody concerned in this war. There are no limits of dishonesty, brutality, treachery, to which any country will not descend to serve the cause of 'expediency' or selfishness.

Oct. 20th   For the third or fourth successive night the air-raid warning sounded last night and our nerves were again kept on edge by the continuous thunder of the barrage. I asked a man today if he thought these small raids were preliminary tests of our defences before sending over heavier forces. He said no, he didn't think the Germans had sufficient aircraft to make big raids.

Mrs H said that, according to General Smuts, we could look forward to the war being over in six months. 'He didn't actually say so,' she said, 'but he suggested it.' I cannot see how she arrives at this conclusion, for if we were to invade in the West now the war might be over in six months, but if, as Smuts says, the main assault will not begin until next year it will be very surprising if it is over in such a short time. Mrs H thinks that once we do invade it will soon be over. This may be so, but is by no means certain. All this is just for the sake of argument, for Smuts' speech is nothing to go by. What do public speakers mean when they say 'in such and such a time the end will be in sight'? How near does the end have to be before it is in sight? How can you tell how near it is? Speakers have been using the phrase for the last year or more, but apparently the end is still not 'in sight'. Obviously it will not be in sight until it comes.

Oct. 22nd　　The air-raid warning was early tonight. Heavy gunfire close at hand and a plane buzzing around made us a little uneasy. We went and had a look outside, but there was nothing to see. There was silence for a while, then some more gunfire farther away, followed by a zooming noise and a bump, which put the wind up us. It sounded as though a plane had been brought down. Mrs H said, 'It sounds as though we're in for a night of it.' I said, 'Perhaps that's finished it now.' She went outside and spoke to a neighbour. She came back and said everybody was outside talking. Not long afterwards the 'All clear' went.

Oct. 23rd　　It seems fairly certain that the plane which came down last night was one of our Lancasters, as it crashed not far away and several people said it was. Some people saw it come down in flames and two parachutes bale out. Somebody else said eight men were killed, which would tally up, as there were ten in a crew. The burning question is: was our own plane shot down by our guns?

This afternoon I went and had my eyes tested. The optician said I had slight eye-strain and should have spectacles for reading.

Oct. 24th　　Newspapers are now preparing the ground for the possibility of an early German collapse. The Russian break-through on the Dnieper, our continuous heavy bombing of Germany, and German admissions that the position is very grave and appeals to the German people to stick it to the end, render such an event not unlikely. For some time now there have been indications that all is not well inside Germany, and I would not be surprised if there is a sudden complete collapse on their home front.

Heard Noel Coward's postscript tonight and disliked it intensely. His smug hypocrisy, his sneering manner, his misrepresentations, his sentimentality, nauseated me. He accused those who want to adopt a reasonable attitude towards the Germans after the war of being 'sentimentalists' and then went on to be sickeningly sentimental about wounded British soldiers. His type of emotionalism, in fact, is the sort that obscures the truth, hinders cool-headed thinking, and breeds war. He also accused the 'sentimentalists' 'not,' as he put it, 'of forgetting the dead, but of forgetting the living'. This was just one of his misrepresentations, for those of us who, whilst recognising their misdeeds, are tolerantly disposed to the Germans are usually those who are tolerantly disposed to all peoples, particularly living ones, and wish to see better standards of living for everyone, whereas cynics of Noel Coward's calibre are the least likely to do anything to improve the lot of the lower classes. Then, to make an impression I suppose, he used the word 'bloody', but said in his refined manner it sounded horribly unnatural and snobbish. My feeling about him was clinched later in the evening when somebody in a variety show sang his latest song, 'Don't let's be beastly to the Germans'. How clever it is, yet how stupid! How persuasive, yet how false!

Oct. 29th   A man at work said that Churchill, in an unguarded moment in his speech about the rebuilding of the House of Commons, revealed that he thought the war might be over by this time next year, when he said that we might be looking for jobs rather than men. I noticed that too, and certainly think that another year will see the end of the war. The German retreat in Russia is no longer planned or orderly.

Oct. 31st   Mrs H said, 'I don't think bread will be rationed.' The food situation is still being extraordinarily well handled by Lord Woolton. I did not realise, until the *Sunday Pictorial* pointed it out today, that he has been responsible for an important social reform. For although some articles of food are still highly priced, the essential elements of our diet are fairly distributed (with few exceptions) at a reasonable price, to all classes, and in the British Restaurants one can obtain an excellent meal very cheaply. Lord Woolton is not given to making political utterances, so I do not know what his politics are,* but he is obviously a very able and practical man and is the sort we want to see in charge of social reconstruction, instead of duds like W. S. Morrison and the Minister without Portfolio, whose name I forget.

Finished reading *The Trial of Mussolini*, a book which gives a merciless indictment of British pre-war politicians (some still in office). It did my heart good to read it.

Nov. 1st   Two comments heard at lunchtime: 'I hope we don't hear too much tripe about good Germans and bad Germans after this.' 'No, they're all painted with the same brush.' These remarks depress me somewhat, for they are examples of an all too prevalent intolerant and dishonest attitude.

I am beginning to revise my opinion of Herbert Morrison. Whatever his failings, he has some sound ideas on post-war industry and economics. He made another encouraging speech this week-end, attacking big financial combines.

Nov. 4th   Now that the results of the Moscow Conference have been published and the newspapers, etc. have had their say, I still cannot see what all the raving is about. It is a step in the right direction, but there is nothing really solid or constructive about it. The references to Austria and the treatment of 'war criminals' are definite enough, it is true, but they won't help much to establish a positive peace or to make people happier and better-off. I put 'war criminals' in inverted commas, because although I agree with the principle that the war criminals should be punished, the question arises as to who are

---

* Perhaps a surprising admission, but it is quite true that at that time I thought of Lord Woolton as being purely a businessman and not necessarily having any allegiance to any particular political party.

the war criminals. Are they confined to the Germans? Is there a given standard as to what is a crime in war? How does a war criminal differ from an ordinary criminal? Isn't war a crime? It seems to me that if we start picking out the war criminals the number will run into thousands, of many nationalities.

Returning to the Moscow agreement, there is nothing much in it that is not vague enough to be contradicted in the twinkling of an eye. Agreements are often broken; how can we be sure that this one will not be?

Nov. 9th   I think Churchill has overdone it this time; he has misjudged the mood of the people. In his speech today he once again reminds us that the worst part of the battle is yet to come, that we must redouble our efforts, that now is not the time to rejoice, etc., etc. This may be true, but it seems to me that his approach should have been 'The enemy is beginning to falter now. One more big effort and it will soon be over.' As it is, he asks for the effort, but fails to give the incentive. He continues to emphasise the strength of the enemy when it is obvious that he is weakening. Stalin struck the right note the other day when he spoke of Germany being on the verge of catastrophe and victory not far off. Churchill's reiterated warnings of the hardness of the fight are now merely boring. We know it will be hard, but let's get it over.

As regards fire-watching and Home Guard duties, which Sir Walter Citrine thinks should be relaxed, I do not think there should be any slackening of fire-watching duties, but Home Guard requirements could easily be lightened.

Nov. 12th   When I wrote about a fortnight ago what a good Minister of Reconstruction Lord Woolton would make, I had no idea that he was about to be appointed to that post. I am delighted that he has been. Perhaps we shall see some action now. But my landlady said, 'What did they want to move him from the Food Ministry for? He was doing all right there.'

Nov. 13th   Received notification that I had failed in my examination and was, of course, disappointed, though not very surprised. It means that I shall have to take it again in six

228

months time. I make no excuses for myself, but I do not feel deterred.

Nov. 15th   In this war, at different times, almost every country, big and small, has been the scene of some political or military crisis. In the last four years I have learnt at least as much geography (and history) as I did at school. Now it is the Lebanon, a tiny little country which I had known only vaguely as a name, not knowing that it was a separate country or where it was. The action of the French in arresting the whole Lebanese government is incredible. It shows a startlingly Nazi-like attitude, though I must say I have always had my suspicions of de Gaulle. As one man said today, 'It shows you what to expect after the war.'

Nov. 16th   My landlady said that she queued up for $1^3/_4$ hours for a rabbit today. On a freezing cold day like today this seems little short of insane. It should not be necessary for women to do this kind of thing. As Mrs H said, there is very little to be had off the ration nowadays, and only by having fish, rabbit, sausages, or something else which is not rationed, can the meat ration be supplemented. I said I would rather go without than queue up all that time.

Nov. 18th   'Listening to the news last night,' said a man at lunchtime, 'it sounded as though we were back in 1940 – the loss of Leros, the Germans pushing the Russians back, and ourselves giving ground in Italy.' There was particular criticism of our weak defence of Leros, especially as it is so near to Turkey, who would be sure to take a poor view of the affair. General Maitland Wilson was mentioned as being associated with past failures. One man said the Germans may have done it for home consumption, a small victory being more acceptable than a big stalemate. There is probably something in this view, but even so our 'half-baked way of doing things' (as another man put it) is deplorable.

The other day my landlady's husband said, 'There won't be any Second Front this year now.' I am afraid it is beginning to look as though this will be the case, now that the weather has changed.

Nov. 19th   Press propaganda in the fight against VD seems to be getting better. The 'Leaves from a Doctor's Notebook' have an authentic ring and an imaginative approach. But the Press is still the only medium of which adequate use is being made; film and radio are more or less neglected.

Nov. 20th   Herbert Morrison continues to neutralise the good effect of his speeches by his actions as Home Secretary. His latest false move is to release Sir Oswald Mosley, which has produced an uproar he probably never expected. A lot of explanation will be required.

Nov. 22nd   Some men were talking about the release of Sir Oswald Mosley. One said that Morrison must have some good reason for releasing him, probably that he is very ill and they do not want him to die in Holloway Prison ('the first Fascist martyr') and that it is silly to start protesting before the facts are known. This is a sensible point of view, and I retract what I said two days ago until Morrison has given his explanation.

Nov. 24th   Morrison's explanation seems pretty reasonable. If Mosley is in a state of health dangerous to life, it would be merely vindictive to keep him imprisoned just for the sake of it. If he had been a Communist, cries of 'persecution' would have gone up from the Left sections of the Press. Mosley is now harmless, anyway, and as he is to be kept under strict surveillance he is not likely to cause much trouble. Morrison's mistake was to release him while Parliament was not sitting, without a public explanation. Even so, his statement was not too convincing. It is difficult to understand why Mosley could not have had adequate medical treatment in hospital, but this point may perhaps be overlooked.* Morrison should have foreseen the fuss that has arisen and should have been prepared to meet it. As it is, a terrific volume of criticism, largely fomented by the Press and not really genuine, has been allowed to accumulate without any effective answer. It is not so much what Morrison has done as the way he has done it which is to be deprecated.

* Mosley, in fact died in 1980.

Nov. 26th   Spent the afternoon looking for digs near to where I shall be working next month, without much success. At one place the terms were £2/5/0 per week, at another only a double room was available. Finally, although it is not as near as I would like, I went to a lady who had been recommended to me and she said she would see what she could do for me.

Nov. 28th   The following opinion was expressed by Mr A (age about 60): 'There's bound to be unemployment after the first few months after the end of the war.' Also, he thought, this war 'is five years of your life wasted.' 'Yes,' said his son (age about 30), 'you can't make any plans or do anything.' This is a very real effect of the war. One feels fettered, like a patient in a hospital, forced to adopt an unfamiliar and unpleasant way of living, longing to get back to normal activities.

Nov. 29th   Saw the following advertisement in one of the local papers: 'Beveridge Report. Some clauses, which are not included in the official Report in Brief and have not been printed by any newspaper, might have an adverse effect upon England's religion, freedom, and culture. Residents in C— who are willing to oppose the plan are invited to write to —' I was annoyed by this advertisement, not because of its author's antagonism to the Beveridge Report – one does not expect the plan to please everyone – but because of his palpable dishonesty. He does not come out into the open and say he does not like the Report and does not want to see it implemented, but pins his argument on to some clauses which have not been published in the Press (and can therefore be of only minor importance), which 'might ... culture'. The 'might' is good. He is determined to oppose the Report, but the only premise on which he can base his argument is that such complex, variegated, and indefinable entities as England's religion, freedom, and culture 'might' be adversely affected. How this could be so, I fail to see. Still, no doubt he will get some replies, because there seem to be many who are only looking for some pretext to oppose the plan.

Dec 1st   My father annoyed me considerably by going out and saying, 'Don't forget the black-out if I'm not back.' The war has been on for over four years, and he tells me not to forget the black-out!

After hearing the report on the debate in the Commons on the release of Mosley, my opinion on the affair has further crystallised and is now almost the reverse of what it was when the release was first announced. As one speaker in the debate said, if nothing had been said after the announcement of his release, Mosley would have sunk into oblivion. The newspapers, in their indignation, have probably done Mosley a good turn by making him seem so important. In any case, Mosley is as entitled to his Fascist beliefs as Gallacher is to his Communist beliefs, provided that he does not try to force them on other people. To keep him imprisoned just because he is a Fascist is playing the Fascists at their own game. Morrison comes out of the affair rather well, although I still think he handled the announcement badly. At least he had the courage to make his decision knowing that it would be unpopular, and he deserves respect for this.

Dec. 7th   After going up to London one day last week to see a play (the comedy *Love for Love*, with Yvonne Arnaud and John Gielgud), I came home with a fearful cough and a sore throat and since then I have been laid up with flu. This is the second time I have been ill while on holiday this year, though my holiday finished two days ago and I have not yet returned to work. I managed to travel back to my digs yesterday, but I don't think it did me any good. It is even difficult to buy any decent throat tablets now.

As far as Christmas is concerned this year, I shall not bother much about it. I may send a few cards. There is nothing in the shops worth buying – nothing but rubbish at absurd prices. There is very little poultry to be had, and without this I don't think one can make a pretence of keeping Christmas.

Dec. 8th   Sensible people are beginning to realise that the idea of 'trying the war criminals' is nonsense. As a speaker in a debate in the House of Lords said, we should be shooting Germans for years after the war. I simply cannot understand why some people want to follow up this savage war with a further series of bloody deeds.

232

Mrs H told me of a story she had heard of a 'seven-ton bomb' which has only just been discovered three years after being dropped. I pointed out that seven tons is about 15,000 pounds and the biggest one the RAF has dropped on Germany is 4,000 pounds. She supposed it should have been seven hundredweight.

Dec. 11th   Again somebody, a woman this time, has declared that trying war criminals is 'bunkum'. I see also that somebody has demanded that Mosley be tried as a war criminal – as if enough idiocy has not already been manifested over that affair. So already, it would appear, war criminals have been found in a country other than Germany. Where does this lead? Not only Mosley, but his followers and many others besides, must be indicted. And if Britain's war criminals are to be prosecuted, so must those of other countries. Logically, vast numbers of people can be labelled 'war criminals'. As Lord Lytton said, wholesale massacres would result and lynch law be let loose. One also notices that the assumption that the 'criminals' would be found guilty is implicit in the demands – judgment is a foregone conclusion.

Managed to find some digs within reasonable distance of my new job.[3] After some haggling I fixed it for 35/- a week. Even this I can barely afford. The last week or so has increased my financial burden tremendously. First I had to begin paying Income Tax, and I expect another assessment. Then I became liable for superannuation, including about three months arrears. Now I have to change my lodgings on increased terms and it will mean double the amount of fares I used to pay and I shall also have to pay a reservation fee for my room in my old digs, to which I shall be going back. Even when I get my increment, which is due, I shall not be able to do more than make ends meet.

Dec. 14th   A choir of carol-singers came round this evening. They had good voices and for a short time conjured up a really Christmassy atmosphere. Carols and cards (the latter unreasonably expensive) are now almost the only readily available means of expressing the Christmas spirit.

At the risk of being boring, I must make further comment on the trial of war criminals. In the *News Chronicle* today, A J Cummings, quoting Lord Vansittart, says 'the list of names of those to be committed for trial should include ... who have been guilty of brutality to prisoners and slaves.' Now one of the great principles of British justice, we are told, is that all accused are presumed innocent until proved guilty. There is no point in having a trial if it is categorically stated beforehand that the prisoner is guilty. The whole idea is just a hypocritical farce to salve the consciences of those who want to have their revenge.

Dec. 16th　At lunchtime today, discussing Mr Churchill's illness, nearly all the men were agreed that Mr Eden was the best man to take his place, although one man thought he was too much of an old-school-tie man.

Dec. 18th　Bought some Christmas cards, but begrudged the money I paid for them. There was nothing worth having under 5d. Seven cards cost me 3/5d. and a small calendar I bought cost 2/9d.

I think everybody has been anxious about Mr Churchill for the last few days, but it seems as though he is past the danger stage now.

Today ends my first week in my new job, and what misgivings I had before I started have now practically vanished. I have had less work to do than at my other job, because although there is quite as much work to be done, if not more, there are more than twice as many people to do it. It has been interestingly different work, too, and I have learnt quite a lot in a week. My only concern is financial, but I should begin to get straightened out after Christmas. I want to get through my stay here without drawing on my savings, such as they are. It will be a strain, but I think I can manage it and it will be worth a little austerity for the experience I shall gain.

Dec. 29th　Once again I have had to neglect my diary because of illness, pleurisy this time. Since about August I have had a run of ill-health such as I have not had for several years. I

234

wonder how much of it is directly attributable to the war – quite a lot, I should imagine. For some time the health authorities have been trying to make out that the health of the nation is better than it was pre-war. I simply do not believe this. Figures of deaths from certain causes do not prove it, neither do figures of the incidence of certain diseases. There is a whole mass of data on the everyday health of people to take into account: how many people carry on working though not feeling really well, how many have odd days off for minor ailments more than they used to, etc. This would probably reveal a much lower level of health. In any case, tuberculosis and syphilis are definitely on the increase, and the former can be regarded as a rough pointer to the general state of health. When somebody went to get a prescription made up for me, the chemist said that prescriptions were taking longer to make up as there were so many people ill and requiring medicine.

I spent Christmas in bed, instead of going home, as planned. However, I had quite a pleasant time. I had about the same number of cards as usual, but fewer presents, though including an unexpected one from my landlady. We had a good Christmas dinner – roast chicken and vegetables, Christmas pudding and mince-pies. We also had a Christmas cake for tea, but without icing. All other luxuries were missing.

The most exciting news of the period has been the sinking of the *Scharnhorst*.

Dec. 31st   Looking back on 1943, I do not feel quite as satisfied as I did a year ago. There are two main reasons for this: firstly that my health for the last four months has not been good, and secondly that in the last two months I have had a greatly increased financial burden. But the first two-thirds of the year were good, except that work increased a good deal; I saved more than in the whole of last year. Prospects are pretty good, too, once I have finished paying out and provided my health does not let me down. The end of March should see me in good circumstances.

Of course, 1943 has been an excellent year in the war fortunes of the Allies. There has been some great news, and almost all news has been cheerful. On the home front, however, there has been little progress in social or political reform; conservative influences have been the most powerful.

Notes

[1] My landlady was a thin, grey-haired, middle-aged woman who wore spectacles. She was also hard-working and considerate, but was not physically strong. She had once been companion to a fairly well-off lady and had been abroad to Madeira with her. Although not well-educated, some of her comments about the conduct of the war and politics generally could be penetrating.

She was the second wife of Mr H, a rather short, stocky man, whose first wife had died. His peacetime occupation was that of a jobbing gardener, but he had to supplement his income from this with a factory job. He had two grown-up sons and a daughter from his first marriage, and they all married and had children of their own.

They were a steady, undemanding couple, perhaps not very ambitious, who were glad of a little extra income provided by lodgers. I stayed with them for seven years.

[2] Though not a major industrial target, Chelmsford had three factories vital to the war effort: Crompton Parkinson's, makers of electrical motors, etc.; Marconi's, much involved with radio-communications; and Hoffman's Engineering, who made ball-bearings. Several of my friends or relatives worked at one or other of them.

[3] I had been seconded to the North Middlesex Hospital in Edmonton for about three months, mainly to widen my experience. This entailed changing my lodgings to somewhere nearer my place of work. Eventually I found board and lodging .in Winchmore Hill, but even this meant a longer bus journey than previously.

1944

Jan. 1st   The doctor said I could go home for the weekend, so I went. Having received no wages for two weeks and having paid out nearly all I had, I had to draw £1 from my Post Office savings to pay my train fare, an unprecedented occurrence. When I got home my father wormed it out of me that I was hard-up, and he more or less forced £5 on me. This may sound funny, but I really was very reluctant to accept it, because it was the first time I had had to borrow money and I hate doing it.[1]

Jan. 2nd   A Christmassy kind of day. I received a belated Christmas present, a book from my cousin. Then I went up to my sister's and we had Christmas pudding for dinner and iced cake for tea. My sister's parents-in-law came to tea and the others played cards afterwards, though I felt too tired. The other men were smoking cheroots and, miraculously, a bottle of port had been obtained from somewhere.

Jan. 3rd   When I returned to my lodgings I found one week's wages and some sick pay waiting for me, so I need not really have borrowed the money.

I brought my landlady a lemon, one of about 20 which my father had sent him from my cousin in the RAF in North Africa. Lemons are a fabulous fruit now and oh, to see (and eat) a banana again!

Food is fairly good at my lodgings, though not quite so varied as at my previous ones. Breakfast usually consists of porridge, a rasher of bacon and a small piece of fried bread, and bread and butter and marmalade.

Jan. 6th   Bought two pairs of socks at 2/8$^1/_2$d. a pair. They were Utility, heavyweight, and of quite good quality. The thicker socks seem to be of much better value than the thinner ones, which are hardly worth buying. I still have seven coupons left, just enough for a shirt.

Jan. 7th   Bought the shirt – price 12/6d.

Two women in a bus were talking about salvage. One said, 'They tell you to put your bones out, but nobody comes and collects them.' This is quite a common complaint about salvage. My landlady has been complaining that the dustman hasn't been for a fortnight. People do not want their homes cluttered up with rubbish.

The shortage of crockery and good cooking utensils is also becoming acutely felt. The thick, plain crockery and the shoddy tin pots and pans, which are all that are now obtainable in most places, are so unattractive and highly-priced that a good many people would rather go without than buy them. One would think that such necessary articles could be cheaper and better-fashioned.

Jan. 10th   Started work again. At lunchtime there was some discussion among some men about the relationship between Russia and Poland. One said, 'The Russians will go up to the post-1939 frontier.' Another said, 'The Poles will just have to put up with it.' A third man: 'I think they'll do pretty well. I don't think the Russians will do the dirty on them, except to go as far as the post-1939 border.' The three agreed that mixed populations were one of the main causes of trouble between nations. The Sudeten Germans were one example, and the Russians and Poles in White Russia and the Ukraine were another. The solution, they thought, was to move the different nationalities into their respective countries – 'Russians go over there, Poles come over here.'

Jan. 12th   Went to see Ibsen's play, *Ghosts*, at the local repertory theatre.[2] It was an excellent production, but I found the play too morbid and tragic even for me.

Jan. 15th   My landlady objected strongly to an official

notice in the papers, which told parents not to let the children's milk get into their own cups. It was an insult to mothers, she said, and she didn't like the way we were being dictated to now. We had no freedom now; we were going the same way as Germany.

Jan. 18th   Overheard a man say he wondered what was the meaning of the report in the Russian paper *Pravda* that two English diplomats had negotiated with Ribbentrop for a separate peace and why the Russians had allowed it to be published. While I am quite willing to agree that the Russians deserve full praise for their military victories, I have never had any illusions about the unscrupulousness and dishonesty of the Russian leaders. Their uncompromising attitude over the Polish frontier question is further evidence of their selfishness. Theirs is not the spirit which is wanted if we are to have international co-operation and goodwill after the war.

Jan. 21st   About a quarter to nine the air-raid warning wailed. My landlady said, 'I thought that's what would happen. They always come over when they've been bombing Berlin like that. I wish they'd stop doing it.' Then the gunfire started, the heaviest London has heard for a long time.[3]

Jan. 22nd   Was up early this morning, but only by accident. The siren went again in the early morning (about 4.30, I think) and was followed by a tremendous barrage of gunfire, heavier than that earlier in the night. I was in two minds about getting up, but now and then the noise would die away and I thought I would stay where I was, when the guns would open up again with undiminished violence. However, I stayed in bed until the 'All clear' went an hour or so after the warning. Soon afterwards I heard somebody moving about and, not knowing what the time was, thought it must be about the usual time for getting up. But apparently somebody had got up during the raid and then came upstairs again, so causing me to rise nearly an hour too early. I did not mind, though, as I had been thoroughly woken up and was tired of just lying in bed. When I got to work everybody talked about the raid. One girl actually slept all through it, but all the others thought the guns sounded louder than they had done before. One man thought the raids would continue and was surprised we had not had them – on such a comparatively big scale – before.

Jan. 24th   The most cheering news tonight was that restrictions on turn-ups to men's trousers, double-breasted jackets, etc. are to be removed. I should think all men are jubilant at this news. As one man said, it was a useless restriction, as the majority of men either refrained from buying suits or else got round the restriction somehow. And I expect many members of the Government disliked it as much as anybody, which may be one of the reasons for the removal of the ban.

Jan. 25th   The new Allied landing south of Rome has rekindled a little public interest in the Italian campaign, but chiefly in the hope that it is the forerunner of bigger events.

A somewhat alarming piece of news is the spread of Fascist influence in South America. Our achievement will be much lessened if we find that we have wrenched the Fascists from power in Europe only to see a new sanctuary for them and their like in South America. Fascist influence is already strong in Argentina and Bolivia.

Jan. 27th   There was much anti-Jewish talk at the lunch table today. Of ten people, including myself, six were definitely anti-Jewish, three expressed no opinion, and one was not definitely pro- but not anti-Jewish. One man mentioned that the only shops with radio valves were Jewish shops, who had bought up the stocks. 'The only way to stop that,' said another, 'is to put a brick through their window and every time they put a new one in to smash it again.' I was surprised to hear such talk; it was reminiscent of the German pogroms.

Several persons expressed satisfaction at Montague Norman's illness. 'I hope that — pegs out,' said one.

Jan. 29th   Went home for the weekend. Speaking about post-war credit my father said, 'That's all a farce ... We shan't ever get that.' He is not the first I have heard to express that view, but I disagree. No Government would dare to go back on that promise, because it would be flung out of office at the first attempt.

Another air-raid warning tonight, again after a heavy raid by the RAF on Berlin. We had over an hour of heavy gunfire. Twice we heard what we thought were bombs whizz down and ducked under the table (what good this is I don't know; I suppose it is just instinct), but we did not hear any explosions afterwards.

Jan. 30th   Going back to my digs tonight I noticed that there were more tube-shelterers than there have been for some time.

Jan. 31st   Fire-watching night. At suppertime there was some conjecture about the German 'secret weapon' – a radio-controlled bomber. Myself and another could see only a limited use for it; we would soon find an answer to it.[4]

Feb. 3rd   Received my Income-Tax coding notice for the 'Pay-as-you-earn' scheme today. It was incorrect, as it made no allowance for my superannuation, so I sent it back.

Feb. 5th   My landlady was able to buy some oranges. They will be most welcome, for if there is any criticism to be made of the food rationing it is that there is almost no fruit to be had. It is one of the most important things which is lacking in our diet and for which there is no real substitute.

Feb. 8th   Some opinions expressed during lunchtime conversation: 'Hitler will shoot himself, the other leaders will escape ... Himmler, Ribbentrop, and the rest should be tortured ... Remember Rotterdam and Warsaw ... It doesn't matter what territory we capture as long as we kill Germans ... The Italian campaign is doing good because we are killing Germans and making them draw on their reserves ... The Eighth Army has something up its sleeve ... Hitler is no coward.'

Feb. 10th   Although coke is supposed to be obtainable in any quantity, transport difficulties often limit the amount which can be delivered. Thus my landlady does not always get the amount she orders, so we have a gas fire instead of a coke fire most of the time. The gas fire is not so warm, and tonight it was quite cold sitting in the room.

Feb. 14th   One of the men where I work always takes a vitamin tablet at lunchtime to make up for present deficiencies in diet.

In the nine o'clock news it was announced that 'the Americans have advanced 200 yards in Cassino'. To measure advance in yards makes it sound ridiculous, and one wonders why it was considered worth mentioning. There has been a good deal of uneasiness and criticism about the Italian campaign, emphasised by the fact that it was necessary for the Prime Minister to make a statement about it. This statement and the fact that we have not yet had to withdraw from the Anzio beach-head are reassuring.

Feb. 15th   I feel rather bored with the war news at present except for a moderate interest in the Russian fighting and the Finnish crisis. Home news is more interesting, particularly the West Derbyshire by-election (where I hope that Lord Hartington will be resoundingly beaten), proposals for electoral reform, etc.

Feb. 16th   There was some particularly virulent anti-German talk at lunchtime today, mainly confined to two men. They tried to outdo each other in ferocious suggestions of what should be done to the Germans, including sterilisation, ingenious methods of massacre, and atrocities which troops should be allowed to commit without the public knowing about them (involving the banning of all newspapers!). There was also some heavy irony about not gloating over last night's big raid on Berlin. I was frankly surprised to hear such extreme views, but I wondered whether they were really sincere. I think a lot of it was an effort to make an impression; but if they really believe those things, then in their efforts to hate the Germans they become identical with their own images of what the Germans are. Their counterparts in Germany made Germany what it is.

Another man said, 'I think the big push (invasion) will come before the end of March.'

Feb. 17th I do not know why there has been so much fuss about the bombing of the Cassino monastery. I share what seems to be the general view that if it was necessary to bomb the Germans in the monastery they should have done it without raising the question of its morality. For if we have made up our minds to bomb the enemy it makes no difference whether the enemy is in a factory, a monastery, or in his home. The morality of bombing itself is another matter altogether. It is equally true that human lives are more important than buildings, only in this case, presumably, German lives don't count. The *Daily Mirror* says: 'In a living world it is life that matters.' This would be an admirable principle if it were not related to the question of bombing historic buildings, since one of the chief results of bombing is death.

Feb. 18th I am really delighted that the Independent candidate has won the West Derbyshire by-election by quite a large majority. How could a man like Lord Hartington know how to represent ordinary working-class people? It was obvious that he did not put himself up for election because he was interested in politics, but was put up merely to maintain the family tradition. That is the last type of person we want in Parliament. I have heard the theory that the other candidate, Goodall, was put up by the Hartington crowd in order to split the Opposition vote. I am quite prepared to believe this theory, and it is all the more satisfying that the presence of the third candidate had no effect on the result.

Feb. 19th I have not been through many really bad air-raids, but last night's was the worst that I have experienced. I was woken up in the middle of the night by explosions and then followed over an hour of terrifying tumult. I thought the gunfire would bring the house down; it was one continuous bedlam of noise and the whole house shuddered with it. Even more frightening than the demented drumming of the guns was the buzzing of the enemy bombers low overhead; they seemed to be circling over our house, and any minute I expected a bomb to come crashing down, but only occasionally did I hear the thud of one some distance away. Round the edges of the black-out curtains I could see brilliant flashes of light. I did not get up partly because I was too lazy, partly because I was too scared, and partly because it was too cold.

This evening I saw about 20 people queuing up for evening papers. The headlines were about last night's raid.

Feb. 20th   Took some of my belongings back to my old lodgings, where I shall be returning in a week's time. Buses were not running all the way owing to some delayed-action bombs, from Friday night's raid, being in the vicinity along a short stretch of the route. We had to get off the bus, make a détour by Tube, and get on another bus.

Feb. 21st   Another hectic three-quarters of an hour last night, though fortunately before we had gone to bed. Always after such a raid people the next morning are full of what they saw and heard, where bombs fell, what sort of bombs, flares etc. fell, how many planes there were, etc., etc. One man I know plots out the approximate position of fires with a map and compass. My landlady, somewhat opposed to bombing whichever side does it, made some tentative suggestions that there should be a bombing truce.

At lunchtime today the subject of the Second Front was brought up. One man said, '*We* shan't start the Second Front, Jerry will – if we're not slick.'

Feb. 22nd   The Bury St Edmunds by-election promises to be as exciting as the West Derbyshire one. It will be disconcerting for the Government if the Independent candidate wins and will prove beyond a doubt that the public are fed-up with the electoral truce.

Several people have remarked that in spite of the terrific anti-aircraft barrages which are put up over London, very few planes are brought down. One man said it was because the gunfire was not co-ordinated.

Feb. 23rd   Fire-watching again last night, and for the first

244

time had to get out of bed and go on patrol. Standing outside, steel-helmeted, we watched a vivid display as the heaviest barrage of the war (described as such today) roared up. It lasted about an hour, but no bombs were dropped in our neighbour-hood.

Previously we had had pancakes with lemons for supper.

While writing the above the guns have been firing again, though not as much as last night, but once a piece of shrapnel crashed against the door. Now the 'All clear' has gone.

Feb. 24th   Went to the local cinema to see *San Demetrio, London*, a splendid presentation of a true story of this war, in which the characters and incidents are vividly lifelike. It struck me as a human and truly heroic film. While watching it the air-raid siren shrieked and several people went out. Again there was heavy gunfire and at the end many people waited in the vestibule until it was over, but some drifted away during lulls in the firing.

Feb. 25th   Afterthought on Churchill's speech – his warning cuts both ways: while it may help to sober those who were becoming over-confident, on the other hand it is rather depress-ing to keep on being told that the war might not be over this year.

Feb. 27th   Returned to my old lodgings; returning to my old job tomorrow. As far as I am concerned, the exchange of jobs has been a very successful experiment. In some respects I shall be sorry to go back, in others pleased.

Feb. 28th   Reading newspaper reports of Lady Violet Bonham-Carter's speech and of the Labour Party's decision to keep up the electoral truce, I have come to the conclusion that the Liberal Party and Common Wealth are the only parties worthy of support. The Conservative and Labour parties now seem to be almost indistinguishable, and my sympathies have always been with the Left. It is about time that the younger generation had a chance to express its opinion; in the electoral truce and the dishonest arguments used in favour of it by Conservative and

Labour people, we can see the beginnings of Fascism. The Liberal Party and Common Wealth seem to hold out the most hope for ordinary people.

Rather surprisingly to many people, but a great relief too, the last three nights have been raid-free and we have been able to sleep in comfort.

Mar. 4th   Went home for the weekend. In the evening I visited my aunt and had quite a long discussion with my uncle and cousin about the 'Pay as you earn' tax, the mathematics of which is very complex and very interesting.

Talking about the metal-painted strips of paper which the German raiders are dropping to interfere with radiolocation, my cousin said that the metallic substance is poisonous – if you rub your hand on it and then rub your eye it sets up inflammation. I did not believe this.

Mar. 7th   My landlady said she did not think that Churchill was a man for the common people. 'I don't think he'll reign long after this war,' she said. This has long been my view. Only today I was thinking that really Churchill resembles Hitler in several ways – in his pugnaciousness, his flair for leadership, his nationalism, his cunning in maintaining the domination of his own political party, but he is more subtle than Hitler, less extreme, less brutal. I would not call him a Fascist in temperament, but then British Fascism would not be the same as German Fascism.

Mar. 9th   Nothing seems to satisfy the coal-miners. I don't know much about their working conditions, though I feel certain that they could be much improved and the miners doubtless have a legitimate grievance, but all the same they must be lacking in a sense of responsibility to be continually going on strike, especially when they had agreed to previous arrangements. Theirs is such a vital industry that we cannot do without them; they know this and take advantage of it. In few other industries would they dare to strike so frequently, knowing it is sabotage to our war effort. But obviously there will be no peace in the coal industry until some radical change is made.

Having now had a chance to listen to the new General Forces radio programme several times, I do not think it much better or much worse than the old programme. There is too much news, bells, chimes, and 'Lillibulero' for my liking, but some programmes are a slight improvement on the old ones, so this makes things even. I have heard several people say, however, that they do not like the new programme.

Mar. 10th   In spite of the continued talk about and preparation for the Allied invasion, the massive air assaults on Germany, the most important news still comes from Russia, where the German armies are slowly but surely being torn to pieces. Said Mrs H tonight: 'They've got some jolly good generals over there' (in Russia). The names of the Russian generals are becoming quite well-known.

Mar. 13th   My landlady has got hold of some story that all buses will be taken off the roads. Her daughter and I both pointed out that life must go on even when the invasion starts, though it is conceivable that in some areas buses will be taken off temporarily. She was also rather perturbed about the rocket-guns which the Germans are supposed to have. 'They reckon they'll reach to the east side of London at least,' she said. I said that it was no good looking for trouble before it comes.[5]

Mar. 14th   Had the afternoon off. In St Albans I bought some vitamin A & D capsules and an anthology of poetry, compiled by Lord Wavell, called *Other Men's Flowers*. Afterwards I went to the pictures and saw *The Lodger*, an excellent thriller about Jack the Ripper.[6]

One of my landlady's not uncommon exaggerations irritated me a little this evening. She often jumps to wild conclusions from trivial facts and gives credence to all sorts of unlikely stories, irking my precise and fastidious mind. After the warning tonight, during which we heard many planes going over, she said, 'There must have been hundreds of them', when it is very unlikely that there were as many as 200. After seeing three bomb craters in a field in Barnet, caused during the raids about three weeks ago, she said, 'If they had fallen on hard ground they'd have brought the whole of Barnet down', an absurd idea.

Mar. 16th   Quite a heated discussion at work about the Jews. Our secretary, Miss B, and I were pro-Jewish, another man anti-Jewish, and the third man did not make his position clear, but seemed to be more or less neutral. Miss B and I had the better of the argument. We pointed out several inconsistencies in the anti-Semite attitude: that objectors to the Jews' presence in this country failed to pursue this view by turning them out or by putting them in concentration camps; they condemned Hitler for persecuting the Jews and then refused the Jews the right to a decent life anywhere else (Hitler was at least consistent in his policy towards the Jews); they expressed dislike for the Jews' way of living – forced on them by centuries of having to fend for themselves in hostile communities – but put in the same position they would do exactly the same things themselves. We suggested that Palestine should be opened to the Jews. The answer was that if we did they wouldn't want to go, but this was met by saying that thousands of Jews had already been refused entry, in favour of the Arabs, a much less civilised race. But the main force of our argument was that those who hated the Jews failed to deal with the problem either way, but just allowed things to drift. I thought the best solution of the problem would be to ignore the Jews as such and admit them to the full rights and privileges of the country in which they happen to be living; eventually they would be absorbed and forgotten.

Mar. 18th   A man in the barber's shop said his brother, who had been a prisoner-of-war for two years, had just been sent his calling-up papers! Somebody said he hoped our organisation would be better when the Second Front started.

Mar. 20th   My landlady mentioned a cartoon in the *Sunday Express* yesterday, picturing some Japanese prisoners, and neither of us could understand why in cartoons Japanese are always represented as ugly little men with protruding teeth, because they are not all like that, and why in books and films

Chinese are usually shown as the sort that would stab you in the back. This is the type of disguised dishonesty which annoys me intensely.

Mar. 23rd   Although I said the other day that there was a slight improvement in some programmes in the Forces Programme, I still think there is room for much more improvement in both that and the Home Service. Good music is not lacking, though I think many members of the Forces would like a little more serious music. There are not enough good plays, and those that are produced are put on at bad listening times. I, personally, would like to hear more talks about books and literary subjects. There is too much second-rate variety and scrappy programmes of gramophone records. The Brains Trust has badly deteriorated; members seem to be chosen simply because they are well-known and not because they know a lot nor even because they can talk well. I listen to it only infrequently and half-heartedly now. On the whole I think that a more intelligent and mind-stimulating type of programme is required. Controversial subjects should be allowed to be discussed freely.

Mar. 25th   Another warning last night at 11.30. We, that is, myself and two others, stood outside the trailer-pump shed at the hospital (we were fire-watching) and watched the barrage over London, which was very heavy. At times it looked as if someone had thrown a handful of sparks into the sky, when two or three dozen shell-bursts would appear all at once in a cluster. The alert lasted over an hour; inside the ARP hut one of the fire-watchers went fast asleep. After the 'All clear' we went and had a cup of tea; when we went to bed it was a quarter to two.

I rose about 7.30. It was Saturday, and I had the whole day off. After I had had breakfast at the hospital (porridge, Spam and chips, bread and marmalade, tea) and had been back to my lodgings I went up to London, hoping to get a seat at the Albert Hall for the concert in celebration of Sir Henry Wood's 75th birthday. I went to the Albert Hall and found that there were no seats at less than a guinea left. I didn't feel like paying a guinea, so turned away, but outside I thought, Why not be extravagant for once? and in any case I almost certainly would not be able to get in at any theatre, so before I could change my mind I went back and bought a seat. Afterwards I was not sorry, as all the proceeds without deductions, about £8000, are going to a fund for building a new concert-hall in London. After lunch (salad, marmalade roll, coffee) at a snack-bar and having a little time to spare before the concert, I strolled in Kensington Gardens. There I saw some soldiers in football kit being marched to their game, and was glad that my leisure was not thus disciplined. Then I went into the hall, where there was a great crowd. There was loud applause when Sir Henry Wood came on to the rostrum. This had died down when there was renewed clapping for somebody in the audience. I could not see whom it was at first and turned to an airman next to me to ask who it was. He said, 'Montgomery, I think,' but then I turned again and saw that it was the Queen and the two Princesses. Then we settled to enjoy the concert, which was excellent, though I thought it might have been more varied. Except for Elgar, all the composers represented were German and the programme was rather on the heavy side. I thought that some Russian music, which Sir Henry has done so much to make known, should have been included. Afterwards I went by bus and tube to Piccadilly and had a snack (two dried-egg sandwiches and a cup of coffee). Then I made my way home, but had to wait an hour for a bus at Cockfosters, as there was a very long queue there, which made me irritable and spoiled an otherwise enjoyable day.

Mar. 26th   A perfect Spring day, sunny and cloudless. I went for a walk in the morning. Squadrons of bombers going over made me think of a similar day some time ago, when I had felt how unnecessary the war was, what contentment there could be.

In the afternoon I wrote a couple of letters, one an airgraph to my cousin in Italy, saying that I thought the war was approaching its climax.

During the evening my landlady said she wished she had kept cartoons since the beginning of the war. I often wish I had done this, particularly those of Vicky in the *News Chronicle*, which I consider to be as good as those of Low.

I interrupted writing this to listen to Churchill's speech, one of the most brilliant and clever he has made. He seemed rather over-sensitive to criticism, but answered that criticism very effectively, though not entirely satisfactorily.

Mar. 30th   The attitude of Churchill and his government towards their defeat yesterday in the Commons, on the question of equal pay for men and women teachers, surprised and angered me. The question had no relation to the prosecution of the war and could not possibly be regarded as indicating lack of confidence in the Government. All the good effect of Churchill's broadcast the other night is undone as far as I am concerned – he boasted about his Education Bill, but now we see how good it is (not forgetting Government dodging in respect of fixing a date for raising the school-leaving age). Talking to my landlady about Churchill's attitude, I said it was 'ridiculous'. She called it 'childish' and said, 'I sometimes think he's not sure how he stands.' What makes it so silly is that today's vote of confidence makes no difference to the issue at stake; those who thought that women teachers should be paid as much as men will still think it, though they support the Government on broader issues.

Apr. 5th   The continued mining strikes, recklessly and stupidly prolonged by the men in defiance of their leaders and the Government, have lost the miners much of the sympathy which the rest of the public had for them. But all the same I was rather ironically amused by the fact that Bevin, a Labour leader, while denouncing the miners, can go to a luncheon at the Dorchester to do it. In a Press photograph, fat and grinning, with a glass of wine or brandy in front of him, he looks more like a 'bloated capitalist' than an eminent trade unionist.

Apr. 8th   Went home for Easter. Travelling was comparatively easy, as my home is in a restricted area. At Chelmsford I was questioned by the police and asked to produce proof that my home was in the district. Although I could not give absolute proof, I was allowed to pass through. The ban will certainly make travelling much more comfortable for those who have a legitimate cause to travel.

In the evening I visited my aunt and uncle and, during some talk about the invasion, mentioned that I thought it likely that the Germans would drop paratroops to interfere with our communications, etc. My uncle disagreed, but I thought he was being over-optimistic, because he did not like to face up to the unpleasant possibility. I have no doubt that the enemy will do everything he can to upset our organisation.

My cousin's wife gave me some almonds which her husband had sent her from Italy. I forget when I last had any.

Apr. 11th   Started smoking (a pipe) again, for no particular reason. The tobacco I bought cost 2/5d. an ounce; it used to be 9d.

Apr. 14th   Air-raid alert last night, for the second consecutive night. There was some gunfire, but it did not last long.

Apr. 15th   All military leave is now cancelled, as I have heard from several sources, including a soldier himself. Surely this means that the fun will soon start. I hope so. We are tired of waiting for it.

Apr. 18th   We were talking about holidays at work. The chief said when the invasion started there would not be any holidays, so we had better squeeze a week in quickly. I have an invitation to spend a weekend with some friends, so decided to write and find out if I could get it extended to a week.

The word 'invasion' is on everybody's lips now. It crops up in every conversation.

Apr. 23rd   (Sunday) The day being so hot and summer-like, I took a bus-ride to Luton, had tea there, and looked round the town, where I had not been before. As always when seeing the peaceful beauty of the countryside, now at its best, I was almost overwhelmed by the feeling of the futility of war. (I inadvertently wrote 'as always', for the war seems to have been going on almost ever since I can remember.) I also felt how lucky I was to be able to enjoy the day as I did, when others were fighting and suffering.

Apr. 26th   Surprised at the no-change Budget and heard little comment about it. One young woman expressed some misgiving, however, about the possibility of an increase in the cost of living, which Sir John Anderson proposes to allow. This proposal certainly warrants some criticism. It will be adversely felt by the poorer classes and will ensure the continuance of the economic dominance of the well-to-do.

Apr. 28th   Read about Acland's protest that only Tory speakers were allowed to air their views on the radio. It was a timely protest. We never hear any but the tame, orthodox Government speakers. The Government may be safe now, but a whole mass of latent criticism is piling up against it and will be let loose when the war is over.

May 3rd   Read a sensible article on strikes in *Picture Post*. It clinches my previous suspicion that all this talk about the strikes being caused by 'Trotskyites' is all eye-wash. As the writer of the article points out, such people could be detained under Regulation 18B without trial. The new order obviously affects the liberty of any ordinary person openly to criticise the industrial policy of the Government.

May 4th   I see that Aneurin Bevan may be expelled from the Labour Party for attacking the trade unions over the new strike order. I agree with Bevan; the trade unions can hardly be said to represent their members now; they just tag along behind the Government, under the thumb of Ernest Bevin. Active and virile minds like Aneurin Bevan's are too dangerous for the tame and mediocre leaders of the Labour Party (with one or two exceptions), but by expelling their most able members that party is committing suicide. I was talking to a man who said it was ridiculous that a man, elected by the people, could not stand up in Parliament and express his sincere opinion. Indeed it is the sort of thing that might happen in Germany. It makes a mockery of our Parliamentary system. Men like Aneurin Bevan, alive to the dangers of Fascism in our own country, are the sort of men we want.

May 6th   I bought two more volumes of Proust's novel, *Remembrance of Things Past*, of which I had already read the final volume first and had been so fascinated by it that I had already bought another volume, which I am now reading.

May 8th   I am planning to have a week's holiday in about 11 days time. I intend to spend the first two or three days with some friends, who live not far away, and the rest of the time at home.

May 11th   Today has been dominated by my having one of my front teeth out. It started to ache yesterday, got worse during the night, so this morning I went and had it out. I had hoped to go to work in the afternoon, but felt so queer that I had to lie down. Now as I write this the pain has worn off and I feel myself again, but the gap in my teeth looks very unsightly and it will be over a fortnight before I can have a denture.

In the evening I had a visitor who said she had heard a rumour that holidays had been cancelled.

May 12th   The rumour about holidays confirmed – nobody to have more than two days at a time and that only provided that one can be easily contacted.

May 13th   Bought a pair of flannel trousers without turn-ups for six coupons, but am having turn-ups made for them, a good way of getting trousers with turn-ups at the reduced coupon-rate.

My landlady having spoken several times about food dumps which are being built round about, I looked out for them today and saw about a dozen in the process of construction (one group of six, and two of three each), long tunnel-like structures of corrugated iron on a concrete base. My landlady thinks the food will be for the occupied countries after the war.

May 18th   Mrs H said, 'I don't know why I still keep salvage. They never come and collect it.'

May 23rd   Last day of my brief holiday. Went to London with a friend. Looked round the. Royal Academy summer exhibition; nothing very original there. Later we went to see a splendid play, *This Was a Woman* with Sonia Dresdel, at the Comedy Theatre. Coming home I said to my companion, 'Was our journey really necessary?'

May 24th   Went to a dance at which some American soldiers, as well as some British soldiers and naval officers, were present. I asked three of my partners what they thought of the 'Yanks'. One said, 'As a whole they're not too bad, but individually they're awful.' The second said, 'The ones I've met have been very nice.' The third said, 'I danced with one; he was a very nice lad. But I've no time for them really.' A man I spoke to was rather more emphatic, 'I don't like 'em. They think they're It. This is our country and I'm an Englishman, etc...' There seems to be a good deal of prejudice against the Americans; it is more or less fashionable to make rude remarks about them. I must admit that they do not make a very good impression on me: they have a natural assertiveness and conceit which is rather unpleasant (they probably can't help it, but this does not alter the fact), but I refuse to share in a vague generalisation which makes all Americans (or all Germans) uniformly contemptible. At the dance tonight they were quite as well-behaved as our own troops, if not better.

May 26th   Two statements reported in yesterday's and today's paper respectively annoy me very much. First comes Mr Churchill's statement on foreign policy with regard to Spain. He declares a surprising friendliness towards General Franco. He also says that this is less of an ideological war than it was. The second statement obviously has to be made to justify the first. We have previously been given to understand that this is a war against Fascism; now we are told that a Fascist state, bolstered up by Germany in the past and helpful to Germany in this war,*

---

* In later years I married a Spanish wife, but this has not altered my opinion of Franco and Spanish politics and of Germany's part in the Spanish Civil War.

must not be interfered with. This is a piece of political expediency, but the reason given for it is really too much to swallow.

The second speech was by Lord Vansittart, who always does get my goat. Speaking about the shooting of 47 British prisoners-of-war, he calls it 'murder' and 'massacre', which must be avenged. I am not against the bombing of Germany, since war is war, though it is an abominable thing, but the fact remains that these airmen may have killed hundreds of helpless people with their bombs, and if they are captured can hardly expect not to run the risk of losing their own lives. It is hypocritical to wage total war and then to expect mercy from one's enemy.

May 27th   Went home for the weekend. Found travelling better than I expected. One train had been cancelled, but I queued for the next for about half an hour and got a seat. The only discomfort was the heat from the blazing sun.

I found everybody at home well, but heard less satisfactory news of my brother, who should have his appendix out, but cannot get it done at his local hospital, as it is being prepared for Second Front casualties and only urgent cases accepted. But it seems silly to wait until his case becomes urgent and perhaps dangerous before admitting him.

May 30th   Going to the dentist's, I saw some Italian soldiers. Some wore brown uniforms, others khaki. I was taken by surprise to see 'Italy' on their sleeves. I heard a man say they were prisoners-of-war who had been given the opportunity to join a non-combatant unit on the side of the Allies.

On my return I looked round my landlady's garden. She had been putting straw under the strawberry plants. In spite of the recent frosts, some of the apple trees looked as though they would yield a good crop of fruit. Tomatoes were coming on well in the greenhouse. I didn't pay much attention to the vegetables, for I know little about gardening, but I was more interested in the flowers – lilac, lupins, roses, irises, aquilegias, and some I did not know.

Later my landlady remarked, 'Well, it's nearly the end of May and the invasion hasn't started.'

June 4th   The Italian campaign takes an added interest now that Rome is almost in our grasp. Previously, because of the hard going and the relative insignificance of the territory involved, the campaign has seemed rather dull. Now we see that it has been a very skilfully conducted battle since we began our last offensive and that, over difficult ground and against strong opposition, the advance has been surprisingly rapid.

June 5th   The capture of Rome has come even sooner than I expected. It is perhaps the biggest triumph our troops have had, at least it seems so, because Rome is the largest and most famous city they have yet captured. Even if it had not been, the enemy's resistance has probably been the strongest they have had to face, so in any event it is a splendid victory.

June 6th   During a somewhat busy day at work I have done my best to keep a record of people's reactions to today's great news of the invasion of France.

Even before I got up this morning I thought something big was happening because of the number of aircraft going over, many more than usual. Going to work there seemed to be fewer people about and there was only one other person on the bus, which heightened my presentiment of a great event.

But it was not until after I arrived at the hospital that I heard the news, from a patient who has been coming to do a few jobs for us. I was not very surprised, for the above reasons and because for some time past I have been prepared to wake up and find that the invasion has started. One of the first things my boss said was 'We can expect a few air-raids now.'

What struck me particularly was that the invasion has come immediately after the fall of Rome. Were they waiting for this, to increase the element of surprise and to take advantage of a time when the enemy has suffered a bad blow to prestige and morale?

My boss and Mr W continued to talk of what Churchill had said about the organisation required for such a vast operation. My boss said, regarding Churchill's post-war position, 'He seems to be a man of action. I think he'll get things done.' Mr W: 'All I hope about the present Government is that they're in office long enough to see their post-war plans materialised.' His tone of voice seemed to indicate that he thought this might not happen.

A nurse came in and said, 'I wish it didn't have to happen. Still, it will soon be over now it's started – in a couple of weeks, do you think?' I said, 'Probably six months or more.'

At lunchtime the talk was rather perfunctory, as nobody knew many details. We told each other scraps of information. We all went and listened to the one o'clock news in one of the wards.

The afternoon was quiet. Sister L came in and said, 'Thank goodness it's started. It was the suspense that got you down.' I think everybody is excited. One or two have expressed the opinion that the Russians would now begin a new offensive.

Listened to the King's speech, but I have no patience for people who keep bringing God into the war on our side. As far as I am concerned war is a hideous and evil thing, in which God, if he exists, can have no part. All this prayer-giving, apart from being futile, is harmful in that it obscures the truth.

Listening to the news afterwards, I was impressed by the overwhelming strength of our attack and by the elaborate arrangements which the BBC had made to give the news at first-hand to the public. The weakness of the enemy resistance was also surprising, but no doubt the Germans have something up their sleeve. 'It seems too good to be true,' commented my landlady.

June 7th   A quiet night last night. A quiet day, too, for me. I did not come into contact with many people, but the main point arising in conversation was the expectation of a German counter-attack. One man brought a portable radio to work in order to hear the news.

I cannot help feeling a sense of wonderment that life goes on just the same here, while not so very far away one of the most momentous events in history is taking place.

June 9th   Rain nearly all day. Not much conversation about the invasion. At lunchtime one man said, 'I wonder how soon we'll see it on the pictures.'

Received an unexpected increase of two shillings per week in the cost-of-living bonus in my wages today. This applied to everybody; our cost-of-living bonus is now 19/- a week.

My landlady, her husband, and I talked about the invasion at news-time. Mrs H had at first had the impression that the securing of the beach-heads had been a 'cake-walk', but had now altered her opinion. I think the first announcements did give a wrong impression, but not to the extent of making it seem a 'cake-walk'. Losses were no doubt fewer than were expected, but the landings were not by any means easy. Mr H said that it would certainly be no cake-walk. He said, 'I don't think we shall do much there for a fortnight. We can't afford to move forward yet. We've got to get our supplies in.' He thought another landing was likely, perhaps in the south of France, near Marseilles.

June 10th   Saturday and my morning off. Feeling a little guilty at going out to enjoy myself with an invasion on, I spent the day in London. I soon rationalised the feeling of guilt out of existence, however. My job is not remotely connected with war work; as long as I was not actually impeding the invasion I saw no reason why I should not spend my leisure as I liked.[7] Anyway, in the afternoon I went to see the play, *There Shall Be No Night*, with the American pair, Alfred Lunt and Lynn Fontanne. This story of a Greek family at the time of the Axis invasion of Greece seemed rather appropriate to the present occasion. In the evening, with a forlorn hope of getting in at the Albert Hall, I joined on the end of an enormous queue and, much to my surprise, succeeded in gaining admittance. It was the first Promenade concert of the fiftieth season, but I did not enjoy it as much as I would have done in any other part of the hall, for I had to go right up to the top gallery and, not being one of the first in, could not find a position where I could see the orchestra.

June 12th   The new Russian offensive was not unexpected, but its direction, against the Finns, was rather a surprise. One man said he did not think the Finns would hold out for long. 'They only needed one more push when they asked for peace terms a little while ago.'

June 14th   Fire-watching last night. Got almost no sleep after about one o'clock. The noise of aeroplanes and of some mysterious explosions which occurred one or two at a time at regular intervals kept me awake. There was no air-raid warning and the regular intervals between the explosions, which were not very heavy, suggested that they had no enemy origin. This morning there was considerable speculation about the cause of the explosions, but nobody had any definite information, except one woman who said it was 'practice'.

June 15th   The explosions heard the night before last were only Home Guard practice after all.

The news from France tonight seemed a little evasive, as though things were not going quite as well as they should. However, the battle is only just beginning and it is too soon to be either optimistic or pessimistic.

June 16th   The air-raid warning went at about a quarter-to-twelve last night, and after a little while there was a big explosion, followed by some gunfire. After an interval there was some more gunfire, nearer this time, so I got up and came downstairs. By the time I had done this everything was quiet again and after about three-quarters of an hour in which nothing happened I went back to bed, although the 'All clear' had not gone. When I got up this morning the 'All clear' still had not gone. My landlady's husband came home from night duty and said he had heard a rumour that the Germans had made a landing at Dover. I was inclined to give some credence to this, because I thought that something queer must have happened for the warning to be so prolonged and because I thought it likely that the Germans would try some form of 'attack as the best form of defence'. My landlady said she had a premonition that something like that was happening.

Soon after I got to work the 'All clear' went. One man said he thought perhaps the Germans had been firing rocket-guns.

Another man, who had been fire-watching all night, mentioned radio-controlled bombs; somebody else spoke of radio-controlled planes. I had taken my portable radio to work, and at twelve o'clock we heard the news of the pilotless planes. Mr U said the Germans must be daft to use them. I was glad there was no truth in the rumour about a German landing.

At lunchtime there was much talk about the new weapon. One man remarked that people seemed to be pleased rather than depressed about the news, their attitude being, 'Hurrah! the Germans have got pilotless planes'. I suggested it was because they had expected something worse. I said I thought it would be fairly easy to find an answer to them. Opinion was more or less unanimous that the Germans would not be able to do much with them, because of the apparent impossibility of using them with any precision. 'Just a clever gadget,' was one remark.

When I got home my landlady had no such favourable opinion, thinking that the pilotless planes could be directed accurately and that it would not be easy to counter them, since we must have known about them for some time and had not found an answer yet.

There were several warnings during the day, but we did not see or hear any activity.

June 17th   Again much talk about the pilotless planes what they look like, where they have fallen, what value they have, etc. I do not think they will have any significant effect on the course of the war unless they can be used in very large numbers. Another man said he did not think they had any strategic value.

In the afternoon I bought some clothes, using nine coupons. I found I had more coupons than I thought I had, as I did not know the two token coupons were worth three each, so I have ten left.

While I was in the barber's shop, the siren went. 'Quite like old times,' a man said, referring to the daylight raids during the blitz.

In the evening I went to see *Gone With The Wind* for the second time and enjoyed it quite as much as I did the first time.

It is a completely satisfying and convincing film. There was also a newsreel showing the entry into Rome and some shots of the invasion, which I did not think very exciting. During the performance several warnings and 'All clears' were flashed on the screen, but I did not see anyone go out.

All day I have heard people talking about the pilotless planes.

June 18th   Another long alert last night. This morning my landlady said that relatives of some neighbours had come down from London, as they could not stand it any longer, it was worse than during the blitz. Interest in the P-planes outweighs all other news, even the fighting in Normandy.

June 19th   Talk about the pilotless planes is almost endless, and I simply cannot remember nor have I had time to make notes of everything that people have said about them today. Already I have heard of many places where they have fallen and listened to a detailed description of them from a person who has seen one. It seems that they travel at a great speed and at a low height – too low both for radiolocation and for the anti-aircraft guns. One man said, 'They must have a terrific store of them,' and said someone had told him that they were sent over at a rate of one every three minutes. Another person, a woman, said they came over 50 at a time and the trouble was 'they can't do anything to deal with them.' Another man said, 'People seem astonishingly windy over them. I can't see that they're any worse than an ordinary air-raid.' I asked another man, who had seen the damage done by one, how great the damage was and he thought 'about as much as a land-mine'. My landlady said, 'I suppose everyone has different experiences and they judge it according to their own experience.' The question uppermost in people's minds is probably: will we be able to find an answer to the P-plane (or 'Bumble-bomb' as one man called it)?* I think we shall, but it seems more difficult than I at first thought, because they are not apparently radio-controlled, as I had

---

* It was not until somewhat later that the P-planes, or flying bombs, became popularly known as 'doodlebugs'.

imagined. Yet I must admit that these things have put my nerves on edge more than ordinary raids. I suppose the novelty of them, the devilish ingenuity, has something to do with it. It is with a mixture of fear and curiosity that we look up at almost every plane that goes over, half-expecting it to be a pilotless one. Everybody seems to want to be able to say that they have seen one.

I spoke to a friend over the phone and she said, 'It's a worrying time, isn't it? We are sleeping downstairs now.' I heard of some other people who were going to sleep with their clothes on until these attacks are over. These are sure signs of nerviness.

June 20th   Heard a girl say, 'When they sent over five or six hundred bombers, each of which could drop several bombs, nobody bothered much.' A debatable point, but it has some truth in it. I expect the increased anxiety over the P-planes is because they can appear more or less as a bolt from the blue.

June 21st   I do not think I have ever heard so much discussion over anything as over the P-plane. Everywhere it is the dominant topic of conversation. Most people now know what it looks like and how it works; the talk is now mainly about where they have fallen, what damage they cause, and how they can be combated.

June 22nd   Received a letter from my sister. Regarding the pilotless planes she says, 'I think they are uncanny, as there is no human element.'

I went to have a look at the destruction caused by a P-plane which fell in Tottenham Court Road three days ago. I was surprised by the small extent of the main damage. I could not get a close view as the area was roped off, but the really bad damage seemed to be confined to quite a small area, with damage due to blast (windows out, smashed woodwork, etc.) extending for a good way around. Another man who was looking at it said to me, 'If it wasn't for the loss of life, we could thank 'em for that,' and, looking at the squalid buildings which had been ruined, I agreed. But damage varies greatly in different circumstances.

Later I went to the Promenade Concert at the Albert Hall. The thought of the flying bombs did not deter me from going, for the chances of one falling in any particular place are more or less the same anywhere. Just before the concert began the warning sounded and soon afterwards there was an explosion, but there was no further interruption.

When I got home I found my landlady feeling disappointed because she had missed the opportunity of buying an enamel saucepan this afternoon, not having heard about them until they had all gone.

June 23rd   Mrs H said she got 'really panicky' last night because of planes going over and explosions, and in the end she got up and dressed, so she had almost no sleep. But I slept all night and didn't hear a thing.

June 26th   Saying that he had heard that an anti-aircraft battery on the South coast had shot down 1400 flying bombs, a man estimated that so far the Germans must have sent over 5-6000 of them.

My landlady said that the baker told her he had not got enough bread to finish his round, as those who worked in the bakery had to stop work continually for the flying bombs.

June 27th   I heard one of the flying bombs for the first time last night – and I hope it is the last. It seemed to come low over the houses and the noise made the house vibrate, then abruptly the engine stopped and I thought our last hour had come. I put my head under the bedclothes and waited, but nothing happened for about a minute and a half, when there was a faint thud in the distance, miles away. I had expected a deafening roar. I lay awake for some time afterwards, listening to others exploding some way off. When I came down in the morning my landlady said she had still not recovered from the shock.

At work, a girl who lives nearer London said it had been London's worst night. A man with whom I work said, 'I shall not be sorry when the invasion army reaches the Pas de Calais area.' Burning questions at the moment are: Are the flying bombs ndiscriminate, or are they aimed at definite targets? (I think they serve the enemy's purpose, which is simply to do as much damage as possible, upsetting civilian morale at the same time.) Can they turn, or do they have to fly on a straight course? Does the engine always cut out before it falls? There is so much discussion on them that I am getting a little tired of not hearing anything else, except for a few references to the capture of Cherbourg, though the Russian capture of Vitebsk is probably as important and the Italian campaign is going very well.

June 29th   When I arrived at the hospital I was surprised to learn that a flying bomb had fallen just at the back of it, for I had not heard it explode, though my landlady said she had heard a terrific bang in the night. It had fallen in a field about 20 yards from the nearest building and the blast had done a considerable amount of damage, but fortunately only one person was slightly injured. Four wards have been made unsafe and this has entailed much moving of patients about today; some of them have had to be evacuated. One man, who was sleeping in the wooden hut nearest the site of the explosion and had a miraculous escape from injury, went back into the wreckage after a half-bottle of whisky, which he found upside-down, but intact, and which he and another promptly consumed.

Thanks to the dislocation of routine we have had rather less work today.

July 1st   There are two main attitudes to the flying bombs, from the point of view of personal safety – those who think it safer to sleep downstairs or in a shelter and those who think the chances of being killed or injured are the same either way and prefer not to sacrifice comfort for the doubtful advantage of sleeping downstairs. I am one of the more fatalistic ones; if a bomb is going to get me, it will get me, it is no good trying to dodge them. It is better to lose as little sleep as possible than to wear oneself out in the effort, perhaps futile, to avoid extinction. I admit that those who shelter in the Underground are fairly sure of survival (though there is the risk of death from pneumonia or some other illness), but we have no shelter near us, so I continue to sleep upstairs.

I went home for the weekend, standing all the way in a packed train. This time there were no police to question passengers getting off the train. At home, as everywhere, the P-planes were much talked about. My sister said, 'They don't seem to be getting the better of them.' My aunt said, 'I think it's a coward's trick.' Mrs S said, 'I get up as soon as the warning goes.'

The strain seems to be telling on many people.

July 2nd   Returning to my lodgings tonight, found the train so crowded that I had to get in the guard's van. In the tube stations the shelterers had returned in force.

July 3rd   One of the men I work with has got to find fresh lodgings, as his present landlady is so upset by the flying bombs that she is evacuating to some safer place.

July 6th   My landlady has offered to put up my colleague as well, so tonight I helped him to move in.

July 7th   Churchill's statement on the flying bombs must have modified the ideas both of those who were inclined to exaggerate and of those who were inclined to belittle their importance. For while I thought that more bombs had been sent over (a few days ago I mentioned the figure 5000 – nearly twice as many as have actually been launched), the casualty figures (one killed and about four injured per bomb) were higher than I expected. At first I did not think the flying bombs would be much more than a nuisance, but now I think they have had a considerable effect: doing quite a lot of damage, causing many casualties, and fraying people's nerves tremendously. 'There has been quite an exodus from London,' said someone at work today. This, and the working hours lost, and the sleepless nights must have dislocated London life appreciably. But all the same I think many people still exaggerate the effect. They talk and think about them too much, believe too much of what they hear about them, magnify each detail by the attention they give it.

Because of the flying bomb which fell at our hospital,

entailing extra work for many people, the restriction on holidays has been relaxed to allow a week to be taken. Our department has had less work, because many patients have been sent home, but we receive the benefit of the concession and I am going to have a week the week after next. It's an ill wind that blows nobody any good!

I had an argument with my friend, K, about the wisdom of the Germans in making flying bombs instead of ordinary bombers. I thought that bombers would have been of much more military value to the Germans; with them they might have prevented or seriously hindered our invasion of France. He thought that due to our bombing they could not produce enough bombers quickly enough and they did the best they could in the circumstances; in fact, 'they knew they were beat.' The latter statement may be true now, but I do not think it was when they first began to work on the flying bomb idea. In any case, I think even a small number of bombers would have been of more use to them than the flying bombs. I really cannot understand the German policy.

July 8th   I had a ticket for the Promenade Concert this evening, but as these have been cancelled I went and got my money back and went to a play instead. There were plenty of people about London still, but the fact that I was able to get a theatre ticket late in the afternoon proved that the flying bombs were keeping many away from the theatres. Several theatres are closing down. The play I saw was *Uncle Harry*, a finely acted drama of the psychological thriller type, but I thought the acting was rather wasted on a not very elevating theme.

July 10th   Waiting for a bus tonight I saw a woman, obviously of poor means, staggering through the rain carrying a big bundle of bedding towards a surface shelter, followed by a little girl who could not keep up with her. This struck me forcibly as one of the most moving sights I have seen during this war.

July 12th   It seems somewhat silly to me to remove the ban on certain coastal areas at the same time as evacuation from

London is taking place. Now the places where evacuees might have gone will be filled with holiday-makers.

July 13th   Went to see a new British film, *The Way Ahead*, depicting Army life from the arrival of some new recruits at a training depot to the time when they go into battle This film, in my opinion, is a masterpiece. Perhaps because I have been in the Army I appreciated it more, but it was so vividly real that I felt that I was living the same life as the soldiers in the film. The last scenes were as thrilling as anything I have seen on the screen. British films have undoubtedly reached a very high level since the war. Films like *Desert Victory*, *San Demetrio, London*, *In Which We Serve*, *The Way Ahead*, and others, make Hollywood attempts at depicting the war seem pitifully unreal and childish. These British films have original treatment, inspiring themes, acting of the highest quality, gripping realism, superb technical skill in the making of them. I only hope the good work continues after the war.

July 14th   Talk about the flying bombs has died down a little at last, partly because things have been quieter during the last two or three days, in this district at least.

July 15th   Started my holiday by standing up all the way home in a packed train. Travelling is no fun these days.

July 16th   One of the sunniest days we have had since March. Spent most of the day at my sister's, playing with my nephew (now about 16 months old), reading Proust, and gathering mushrooms in the nearby fields.

July 17th   Went to get my emergency ration card and was sent to the police station to get a form signed to say that I was permitted to stay in the area. This I was granted with surprisingly little difficulty.

Hearing that one could visit certain seaside towns in the banned area without much trouble, I risked going to Maldon this afternoon and found this to be a fact. The place looked pretty dull, but it was nice to smell the sea breeze again.

July 19th   Bought a copy of the official account of the battle

268

or Tunis. The account is clear and concise and the maps are good, but the photographs – with a few exceptions – are only fair in quality and choice of subject. However, as a whole, it gives the reader an excellent picture of the Tunisian campaign.

I bought this book to read on the train going to Clacton, where again I got in without being questioned. I sat on the beach for an hour before and an hour after lunch, enjoying the sunshine, then went to visit some relations. One of my cousins, who had been very nervous during air-raids, was much better since two incendiary bombs fell on the house in which she was living. I said I did not think the war would last much longer. A friend of my relations voiced the same opinion: he said it would be over in August. Certainly the war is going well on all fronts. In Normandy, though progress is slow, we are still on the offensive; in Italy the capture of Leghorn and Ancona are two further highlights in a swift advance; on the Russian front several Russian offensives are throwing the Germans into confusion; and we must not forget the Far East, where, if nothing spectacular is happening, the Japanese are gradually being forced on the defensive. I do not see how Germany can hold three or more offensives much longer.

July 20th The siren sounded just after midnight and, as several flying bombs had come over the previous night, I decided to get up this time, mainly out of curiosity, but also out of fear. My curiosity was rewarded, for I came as near to seeing a flying bomb as I have yet done, seeing one like a moving light caught in the searchlights.

Today I went to see some friends and saw a church which had been twice hit by flying bombs. We were having tea when we heard the exciting news of the attempt on Hitler's life. 'Pity he wasn't killed,' was the universal opinion.

July 21st Mrs S asked me this morning if I had heard that civil war had broken out in Germany. Someone had told her that it had been announced on the wireless.

I went to London later in the morning. In the café where I had my lunch two men were talking about the attempted assassination of Hitler. 'Germany has cracked,' said one.

269

In the afternoon I went to the Zoo, where I had not been since I was a child. Some animals and reptiles have been removed for the duration, but there are still plenty of interesting exhibits. The Giant Panda (which we may never see again in this country) thought a little disappointing; a smaller and less publicised variety of panda seemed a more attractive animal.

July 22nd   Up again last night because of the flying bombs. One exploded fairly near. The loss of an hour or two's sleep can be very tiring after only one or two nights of it. What those people who get up at every warning must feel like I cannot imagine.

In the absence of any detailed news about the anti-Hitler conspiracy, the papers are guessing and elaborating on what little evidence they have. I abhor this tendency on the part of newspapers, when they do not know the facts, to invent the facts for themselves. But whatever the details, I think there can be no doubt that there is something seriously wrong at the top in Germany and it strengthens my opinion that Germany can't hold out much longer.

July 24th   Back at work. At lunchtime one of the men said, 'There's one thing about this Hitler business; it will help to cover up the Caen episode.' There were some further derogatory remarks, not so much about the progress of the battle, but about the way it has been reported. At first it was described as a 'terrific breakthrough', but after three days the advance has been insignificant. I have no doubt that we shall eventually get the Germans on the run, but, as too often the case, the newspapers are too eager to count their chickens before they're hatched.

July 26th   My landlady afforded a good example of how some piece of news can be wildly exaggerated by an unthinking remark. She said, 'They dropped 27,000 tons of bombs on Stuttgart last night.' Knowing this figure (almost ten times the biggest load yet dropped in a single raid) to be impossible and knowing how hopelessly inaccurate some women are with figures, I said, 'You mean 2,700 tons.' But she insisted that it was 27,000. Then I realised that she meant 27,000 incendiaries, which proved to be the case.

July 28th   One of the men who was fire-watching with me last night said it was the first decent night's sleep he had had this week. Flying bombs had kept him awake the other nights.

Now that there are no musical concerts in London I really begin to miss them. A young woman to whom I mentioned the lack of concerts felt the same. A film I saw this evening was a good substitute for a concert however. Called *Battle for Music*, it told the story of the London Philharmonic Orchestra's struggle to avoid disbanding at the outbreak of war, and how well it succeeded. Great music does indeed have an uplifting and refreshing effect on drooping spirits.

July 31st   Flying bombs are still a major topic of con-versation. The other day someone said that in certain pubs anyone who mentions them has to stand drinks all round. At lunchtime today there was a good deal of discussion on the effectiveness of the balloon barrage. Nobody seemed to think that it was of much use.

Aug. 2nd   When we heard that Turkey had severed diplo-matic relations with Germany I said, 'She's been sitting on the fence long enough. I suppose now that she knows Germany is done for she thinks she'll come in on our side.'

Churchill's speech was pretty optimistic. His reference to the possibility of long-range rockets being used by the Germans and his advice to Londoners to evacuate if possible was rather disquieting, however. My landlady seemed quite alarmed. Certainly the flying bombs are ordeal enough; a worse one might have serious effects on a much larger number of people.

Aug. 3rd   At last we are making the progress we have been waiting for in France. This, combined with the spectacular Russian successes, makes one feel that the end is drawing near.

Morrison came in for some derogatory remarks today. Appar-ently he said that he could think of more horrible things than the long-range rockets. The man who mentioned this said it was silly to talk like that and inclined to make people panicky. I agree, but I do not think the Germans will have much time to use their rockets, if they use them at all, before their complete military collapse.

Aug. 6th A marvellous batch of news today: the whole Brittany peninsula cut off, the Russians fighting in Prussia, Florence captured. If it wasn't for the 'doodlebugs' there would not be much to worry about.

Later. Although all this morning's news was not strictly true – the Russians being not yet in Prussia and Florence not fully in our hands – these events are probably so near as makes no difference. I and two other men were talking about the general situation. One of them said, 'I don't think the end is far off.' He thought the Normandy front was the most important. The other man said, 'Well, I hope old Joe Stalin gets to Berlin first. Our people would be too soft with 'em.' But whoever got there first, he thought, the Russians would want – and should have – a big say in the matter.

Aug. 7th 'What's the betting Hitler won't use gas?' my friend K said to me this morning. I said I doubted whether he would use it over here, but he might use it against our troops. Somebody else remarked on the possibility of gas-containing rockets being sent over.

All the pubs round here were shut this evening, having sold out. My landlady said, 'There's a rumour they're holding the beer back for the peace celebrations.' K said he thought the war would be over in about three months.

Aug. 11th Have heard of several men recently who have evacuated, or are trying to evacuate, their wives from London, partly because of the 'doodlebugs', but also because of the threat of long-range rockets. A doctor had the idea of getting a caravan and living out in the country, but the difficulty is to get a caravan. My boss, in spite of the fact that he has sent his wife to Wales, said one might just as well stay in London, as there was just as much chance of being hit by a bomb anywhere else. This is true for a large part of Southern England, but I think if one can get well to the North or West one is safe there.

Went to see *This Happy Breed* in the evening. This is another extremely good British film, which shows pretty clearly that what causes wars, or quarrels of any sort, is not so much a difference of opinions as the violence with which the opinions are held. The film was produced by Noel Coward, however, and was full of his touches. There is something about all his work, something too bright and plausible, too superficial, which irritates me.

Aug. 15th   The news of the Allied landing in the South of France took me by surprise, but, looking back, I realise that the South of France has been the focus of a good deal of attention during the last few days (heavy air attacks on the Riviera, reports via Spain that the enemy has been withdrawing troops from SW France, etc.), and subconsciously I have been aware that there was something unusual about this attention, but without suspecting that we were going to land there. Now the Germans will have another front to fight on. If the new offensive goes as well as that in Normandy, German resistance in France may soon be broken.

Aug. 16th   One man's opinion today was that all the talk of the war being over next week was silly optimism. He also thought that the Germans would get out of the Falaise gap. Another man said that the longer the war lasted the better (!), as then the war would be sure to move on to German territory and they would be sure to get 'a good bashing'.

Aug. 19th   'Best news we've had. I think this *is* the beginning of the end,' said one man today, regarding the merciless destruction of the German army in Normandy.
This evening I saw my first flying bomb by daylight. I had a good view of it, as it passed almost overhead. Seeing it, I felt almost the same as I imagine a savage must feel on seeing an aeroplane for the first time, a kind of awe and fascination, but no fear, because I could see it was going over (and, in fact, it flew out of hearing). With its cross-shaped body and flames coming out of its tail it seemed like something supernatural and malevolent, a strange fiery symbol, an evil apparition.

Aug. 23rd The liberation of Paris gives one a kind of exaltation. I am rather surprised that the French people managed to get rid of the Germans themselves, but the fact that they did makes it more pleasing still, for the Germans must have been weak to give in to the citizens of Paris. This act is in the greatest French tradition; surely it will rank with the barricading of Paris and the storming of the Bastille. One feels that events are moving swiftly; our armies will race through France and will soon menace Germany itself. We, who have had to bear the ordeal of the flying bombs, hope that the territory from which they are launched will soon be overrun. Early this morning there was a concentrated attack by flying bombs, and tonight it is said that German bombers have been over again.

Aug. 24th At work today I and two other men were talking about the progress of the battle in France. One said the Germans would put up a stiffer resistance when they reached the Maginot Line. I said I didn't think it would prove so very formidable. He said that undoubtedly the Germans would have made it stronger since they took it in 1940. I said we should overcome it somehow, by going round it, sending masses of airborne troops over it, landing in Belgium, or by breaking through it by sheer force.

There were some derogatory remarks about Rumania for 'swopping sides' now that she could see the game was up. At breakfast I had laughed at King Michael's statement that 'We march by the Allies', but my landlady had said she did not think these small countries could help themselves. I pointed out that Greece and Yugoslavia had not collaborated with Germany. I thought there was some truth in her remark, however, but when I used it at work my own counter-statement was turned against me. While Rumania's actions are not very honourable, her people are probably not basically any different from the Greeks or Yugo-Slavs.

Aug. 25th It was interesting to note a little paragraph in the paper stating that the Germans have lost 3,600 planes since D-Day, yet we have had the impression that the enemy has had almost no air-cover.

Aug. 26th Events are moving apace. Now, Bulgaria is out of the war, the French are rising, the Germans will soon be fighting on their own soil in the East and in the West. The jubilation of the people of Paris is beginning to enter our own hearts.

Aug. 28th Miss B, our secretary, did not think our troops would be in Berlin this year. 'They (the Germans) will get behind the Siegfried Line and dig in for the winter.'

Aug. 30th Talked to two men about the war. One said, 'I think we shall be fighting on German soil in a fortnight.' We discussed the extent of the Maginot and Siegfried lines. They, too, thought we should 'skip round' the Maginot Line somehow. 'Sedan is a weak spot,' said the second man.

Opinion seems to be inclining towards the idea that we have not much more to fear from the flying bombs, although last night was apparently very noisy. I say 'apparently' because I did not wake all night and am only going on what people have said. I heard one explosion before I went to sleep, however.

Aug. 31st Had another chat with the two men mentioned yesterday. One said, 'Do you still think the war will be over this year?' I replied, 'Yes – the first week in December.' The other said, 'I'll go one better than you and say the first week in November.'

Sept. 1st The terrifically swift British advance to Amiens and the promotion of General Montgomery to Field-Marshal are the two most exciting items of news today. 'You can't keep pace with it,' a man said of the advance.

Sept. 3rd The fifth anniversary of the outbreak of war. Looking back, my main feeling is one of awe at the huge panorama of events which we have lived through. What a lot of things have happened, to me personally and to people in general. In the comparative safety of what I feel to be the last weeks of the war, I can say that I would not have missed it for anything. (No doubt, if I had been in the battle-line I would not say that.) During these five years we have run the whole gamut

275

of emotions, have seen human nature at its most naked. We have
had to put up with many unpleasant things and now we feel that
our patience and fortitude have been rewarded. Today the news
is better than ever – Finland out of the war, Allied armies on
Germany's doorstep, a new offensive begun in Italy, the Red
Army preparing for its final attack. Victory is in the air.

Sept. 5th   My landlady said victory must be near because
several products are being sold in red, white, and blue packets.
She had a packet of starch substitute with a Union Jack on it and
the admonition to 'Buy British Goods', a slogan which has been
missing through the war, because it has been unnecessary, and
now seems premature. The other day my landlady had a large
rib of beef from the butcher's, a joint which she had not had
since the beginning of the war and which, she said, was a sign
that the war was nearly over.

It is a great relief that we have almost had the last of the
flying bombs. Now that the Allies are in Holland and the
Channel coast almost all in our hands, the enemy will not have
anywhere from which to send the bombs.

Sept. 6th   Numerous planes towing gliders have been going
over this afternoon and, of course, there has been some speculation about where they were going, Norway and behind the
Siegfried Line being two conjectures.

Heard a woman say, 'The gas-man said it will be over in ten
days.'

Sept. 7th   The lifting of the black-out is as though the chains
of imprisonment have been thrown off. For so long we have
been forced to grope about in darkness at night that at first the
lights will seem strange and unnatural. One man said, half-
jokingly, 'For years afterwards we shall have a feeling of fear
when we switch on a light, a feeling of being haunted.' The
black-out has been such an integral part of the background of
war that now it is ended one feels that the war itself must be on
the verge of ending.

Sept. 8th   'If we do have any more raids I think they'll be the
old-fashioned sort – you know, with ordinary bombers – none of

hese new-fangled things,' said one of my lunchtime colleagues oday.*

Sept. 9th   We have not heard a siren for some days now, and we are beginning to feel safe from them.

Saw a shop window full of flags of the Allied nations. They were only small ones, 1 yard or 1½ yards long, costing 10/11d. and 15/11d. respectively.

Went to the pictures in the evening and, among other things, saw some newsreel pictures of British flame-throwers as used in France. They are truly fearsome weapons. The main film was *Cover Girl*, a gaudy Technicolor musical, but very unoriginal.

Sept. 10th   Went to a concert given by a symphony orchestra formed by employees of a local aircraft factory. It was a very laudable performance, though they attempted some works which are too difficult for a young orchestra and there was a very poor audience, which must have been discouraging for the orchestra.[8] Being at the concert, I did not hear the gunfire which other people had heard and which, we learned later, was coming from the French side of the Channel.

Sept. 12th   About four days ago there was a big explosion in the evening which shook our house and was heard at several widely-scattered places. Since then I have heard various rumours about its cause, the most popular ones being that a munitions factory or a gasworks blew up. Several agree, however, that it took place at Chiswick. Early this morning there was another explosion, which I didn't hear, but which has set everybody talking. People are beginning to think that these explosions were due to the German V2 weapons, probably rocket-bombs. It seems quite likely, but if so, why have they not been more frequent?

Sept. 13th   Miss B had some fresh information about V2s.

* This prophecy, as was to be demonstrated in only too short a time, could hardly have been more wrong! Almost within hours the rockets began to fall, as later diary entries show.

They are rockets which travel at 800 mph, she said.[9] One left a crater 17 feet deep. Five came over last night. Stories are spreading, all somewhat vague, but one thing is certain: there have been several unexplained explosions, too frequent to be gasworks or munitions dumps blowing up.

This evening I saw the film, *The Song of Bernadette*, and with it a newsreel showing how the flying bombs were fought. The pictures showing the things being shot down were thrilling, and it almost made me feel ashamed to see the gunners working like Trojans and sometimes losing their lives, when a bomb they had shot down crashed onto their camp, so that we could feel more safe.

Sept. 14th　　More talk about rockets today. One man suggested that the rockets may be falling all over the country. Another man was supposed to have heard ten explode last night. Another story was that where one had fallen everything was covered with ice. I heard two other men agree that it was 'definitely enemy action'. Someone else thought they might be shells from long-range guns. In the absence of any official reference to the matter rumours are inevitable, and one would think the Government would give some statement, if only to prevent evacuees from returning to London, as they are doing in spite of the Government's general warning to stay away.

Sept. 16th　　Warning just before daylight. We learn from the news later that more flying bombs have been sent over, launched from aircraft. So we are not finished with the wretched things yet.

Sept. 17th　　First night without black-out. The effect was a little disappointing in our neighbourhood, but not so much as to be insignificant. Coming home at about 10.45 I saw only a few scattered lights, but even these gave some relief to the darkness, hinted at better things to come. When I got home I found that my landlady, though dispensing with the boards that used to black-out my bedroom, had put up the thick curtain as well as drawing the thinner ones, because, she said, 'The thin curtains don't come right across.' I found, however, that they could just be made to cover the windows and took the thick curtain down.

Sept. 18th   Mr B talking about the dim-out, as it now is, said he saw only one or two bright lights last night. 'I don't think it will make much difference. People haven't got alternative curtains,' he said. Another man said, 'I felt a bit guilty with the light on.'

My landlady put the thick curtain up in my bedroom again tonight. I think she still feels a little uneasy about it, but I took it down again. I spent part of the evening packing for my holiday in Cornwall, which starts tomorrow.

Yesterday we saw scores of gliders going over and guessed that something was up. The landing in Holland was great news. It shows how we can jump the Siegfried Line if necessary, though it looks as though we have already broken through.

I looked out of the window as I was going to bed, but could not see a single light in our road.

Sept. 19th   Had a good journey to Newquay. The train was not too crowded and I had a seat as far as Plymouth, where we had to move up to the front of the train, which was already full. It was 6.15 by the time I arrived at Newquay, and after I had found the house where I was to stay and had some supper I was too tired and it was too dark to go out again, as I did not know my way about.

Sept. 20th   Spent most of the day exploring the cliffs and beaches of Newquay. Weather excellent, sunny all day.

I have struck lucky with my hotel. The food is splendid, almost more than I can eat and of the best quality. The room is comfortable and well-furnished, the people are pleasant, and the house is only about three minutes from the sea. But it is a pity that the black-out is not lifted here.

Sept. 21st   The description of the Germans' V2 weapon, as given in the *News Chronicle* today, corresponds very well with rumours I have heard about them falling on London, mentioned a few days ago. The paper says that some are reported to have fallen in the North Sea, so it is an even bet that some have actually fallen in this country, but the authorities have not said anything about them because the Germans are still experimenting with them and are not sure what results they have had. The Government have been complaining about evacuees returning to London, but really they have only themselves to blame for giving people a false sense of security.

Sept. 23rd   Some of the other guests were talking about the American troops at breakfast-time, generally deploring their lack of civility, and I was rather surprised to hear one woman say, and the others agree, that the black Americans are much nicer than the white ones.

Newquay is not very crowded now, partly because it is late in the season, partly because many of the evacuees have left, partly because of other wartime difficulties. There are plenty of wounded soldiers about in their hospital blues, the Ministry of Pensions having taken over two or three of the larger hotels as hospitals.

Sept. 25th   At a little village near Newquay I saw a notice calling a public meeting to appoint a committee 'to raise funds for the Welcome Home and the Peace Celebrations', which I thought a little premature.

A strange shortage of sweets about here; there are none to be had anywhere.

Sept. 26th   The Government's social insurance plan comes at a rather unexpected time, catching us off our guard as it were. At first sight it seems a bold and far-reaching scheme, going far along the lines of the Beveridge Report. The trouble with the Government's reform schemes, however, is that some snag arises when it comes to putting them into practice.

This news. overshadows some that is of more immediate importance: that the Germans have cut the main road of our corridor in Holland. I heard a man in a restaurant say, 'It's a nasty business in Holland.'

Went to Truro today, saw the Cathedral, and thought what a lot of skill and expense man puts into making shrines for his superstitions.

Sept. 27th   One rather obscure point about the Government's social insurance plan is how it affects medical treatment. If everybody is to be included in the insurance scheme, then everybody will be entitled to free medical treatment. Yet previously the Government stated that doctors can still keep their private practice under a State medical service. The new plan seems to be inserting the thin end of the wedge of State control behind the doctors' backs. I think it is a good thing, but what will the doctors have to say? No doubt the big insurance companies will put up a lot of opposition, too.

Sept. 30th   Last day of my holiday, probably the best I have ever spent. This was largely because it is the first visit I have ever made to Cornwall, and Newquay stands in what must be one of the loveliest stretches of coast in Britain. There was an abundance of places to see and marvel at. But also it was because I escaped from the war to a great extent. Here there was plenty of good food (in spite of rationing), no sirens, no doodlebugs, pleasant company, little talk about the war, no fire-watching to do. Only the presence of a few English and American troops and wounded soldiers, the newspapers and the black-out reminded me of the war. Of course, there were other signs, as everywhere, such as fantastic prices in the shops (25/- for sunglasses, for instance), poor travel facilities, stretches of barbed wire, etc., but we are now so used to these relatively minor, or less conspicuous, signs that they no longer seem special to wartime conditions.

Oct. 2nd   Heard some talk of the Press accounts of the unconfirmed German attempt to invade us in 1940 and how it was defeated by a sea of burning oil. Looking up my diary, I find that at the time the rumour I heard was that the invasion had been beaten off by electrified wire defences.

Oct. 3rd   The remarkable fact seems to be that, temporarily at least, the Germans have stabilised both the Eastern and Western fronts. How much longer must we wait for the final collapse?

Oct. 5th   At lunchtime today several anti-Semitic remarks were passed, or rather, anti-foreigner remarks. 'What fools we were to have them (refugees),' said one man, who later asked what were Capt. Ramsay's activities before he was imprisoned. Another man said he (Ramsay) had a club whose slogan was 'Britain for the British'. 'Well, can't we join?' was the rejoinder. This kind of feeling is undoubtedly growing, as is the desire for harsh treatment of Germany after the war. I, too, am more in favour of stern measures in dealing with Germany than I was, but my chief motto is still 'Live and let live'.

Oct. 7th   Bought a new pair of shoes, quite a nice soft leather, price 35/-. The shopman said he had had them in stock for over a year, otherwise they might not have been of such good quality.

Oct. 8th   My landlady had a party for her grand-daughter's christening. Among other eatables there was a delicious iced cake with real marzipan icing.

Oct. 9th   The stiff German resistance on all fronts is tending to disillusion those, like myself, who thought the war would be over this year. Miss D said she had hoped her brother, a prisoner-of-war, would be home by Christmas, but 'It doesn't look as though he will be now.'

Heard some disgusted remarks about accommodation being provided for Italian prisoners, but not for bombed-out English people.

Oct. 10th   At lunchtime I mentioned that there was to be a radio discussion on what to do with Germany. One of the other men said, 'What to do with Germany? I could tell 'em in two words.' Another said, 'Wipe the lot out. Exterminate the whole race. That's the only thing to do.'

A flying bomb fell about a mile away last night, but I did not hear it. Fortunately it fell in a field and did no harm. This evening my landlady said, 'We shall be darn lucky if we come out of this war alive.'

Oct. 14th   Went home for the weekend. Between Liverpool Street and Stratford I noticed, from the train, fresh destruction among the grimy houses which line the railway, probably due to flying bombs, possibly to rockets. Always an ugly part of London, it looked even uglier now, but somehow those rooftops, church spires, and factory chimneys seem so friendly that I could not help feeling sorry for the humble families who had been deprived of their homes.

In Chelmsford I had a haircut and tried to buy a copy of Somerset Maugham's latest novel, *The Razor's Edge*, which I had already tried to get, without success, in St Albans, but with an equal lack of success. New books go out of print very quickly now. I am now reading *Kilvert's Diary*, which I had bought as an alternative to Maugham's book. This is a delightful diary and I am very pleased to have it.

Oct. 15th   Heard a terrific bang in the night, but must have gone to sleep again directly I heard it, for when I woke up in the morning I thought I had dreamt it. Later, however, my aunt asked me if I had heard it and said someone had told her it was a rocket. Apparently you can tell a rocket by its double bang.

The war news, having been comparatively dull for the last few days, has now become more exciting again. The capture of Riga and Athens, the imminent fall of Aachen, and the colossal air-raids on towns on the Rhine (which may be the prelude to a big offensive on the Western front), and Hungary's desire to get out of the war, are mighty blows at Germany's resistance.

Oct. 18th   Hearing the news that the Germans had begun to wipe out the Poles in their concentration camps, Mrs H said, 'They (the Germans) want exterminating. That's the only way to deal with them: do the same to them as they're doing to others.'

Rabbits (for eating) seem to be fairly plentiful now. I have had three or four meals of rabbit recently. We were having a supper of delicious stewed rabbit, potatoes, turnips and carrots tonight as the radio news-reader was telling us about the starvation in Greece. Mrs H said, 'It makes you feel ashamed to sit down to a dinner like this, doesn't it?'

Oct. 19th   The formation of a German Home Guard and the obstinate defence of Aachen make it apparent that the Germans will fight every yard, that we shall have to shatter every German town. Well, if they refuse to have any sense knocked into their heads it serves them right.

Oct. 20th   Riga, Athens, and now Belgrade – one by one the capitals of Europe are returning to their rightful owners. Budapest will probably be the next.

Listened to the Dutch Prime Minister describing the plight of Holland, beset by flood and famine, threatened with epidemics, its people massacred and deported by the Germans. I felt overwhelmed with pity. Why do such things have to be? Poor suffering world, filled with misery and destruction when there is no need for it.

Oct. 22nd   Went to a concert at the Albert Hall. I was late getting there and there were only 10/- and 2/- seats left. I went in the 2/- ones, up in the gallery. Pouishnoff was the soloist in the popular Tchaikovsky 1st Piano Concerto.

Had tea afterwards at the Pop Inn in Charing Cross Road. A salad, bread and butter, and tea cost me 3/2d., a somewhat exorbitant price I thought. Leicester Square and Piccadilly were crowded with girls and British and American troops.

Oct. 25th   My landlady said, 'It's a job to get anything for breakfast now.' Today we had Shredded Wheat, sardines, bread and butter and marmalade.

The *News Chronicle* made a very pointed comment yesterday, when it remarked that while a port as big as Gibraltar could be prefabricated and towed over to France to supply the invasion armies (truly a marvellous achievement), accommodation could not be provided for the bombed-out. One realises the difficulties of the problem, but surely this is a need demanding the utmost priority and urgency of treatment, and the Government are not tackling it half boldly enough.

Oct. 28th   Spent an hour or so this afternoon looking round bookshops in Charing Cross Road. As usual, I saw about a dozen books I would have liked to buy, but had to be content with a cheap copy of Evelyn Waugh's novel, *Put Out More Flags*. About 6.15, as I was going down the convenience in Leicester Square, there was a loud explosion. When I came out a man said that it (whatever it was) had exploded in mid-air. Presumably it was a rocket, as there was no warning. After that I queued up for the gallery at the Princes Theatre, where ballet was being performed, but was unable to get in, so I went home. In the Underground I saw a poster, quoting, in large letters, Nurse Edith Cavell's words, 'I must bear no hatred in my heart', and I wondered who, in these days when it is thought rather unpatriotic not to hate the Germans, had caused the poster to be exhibited.

Oct. 30th We were listening to *Monday Night at Eight* when there was a fearful explosion, followed after a few seconds by another a little less loud. We were all pretty scared, but there were no more bangs, so we went outside and had a look. Mr and Mrs H thought it had been an enemy plane dropping bombs, but I thought, from the distinct double bang, that it was a rocket. A young man who lives next door said it was a rocket. He said that the two explosions were due to the fact that the rocket first exploded in the air and this explosion threw the warhead to the ground, which caused the second explosion.

A point which rather puzzles me is, why have the Germans themselves not said anything about these rockets?

Nov. 1st Rockets are now a common topic of conversation. More of them seem to be coming over now. A man was saying today that he thought they were worse than the doodlebugs. Many people can see no point in the official silence on the subject when everybody knows about them and the Germans must know within a little the capabilities of their own weapons.

I read a revealing account in the *News Chronicle* of the state of affairs in China. If true, it shows that we are supporting a very undesirable form of government in China, a dictatorship of the most restrictive kind, whose censorship allows almost nothing to reach the ears of the outside world. My suspicions were aroused some time ago, when the *News Chronicle* printed some articles on the difficulty of getting news out of China and on the conflict between the Kuomintang Government and the Chinese Communists. Now these suspicions are still further strengthened. Of course, we must continue to support China, if only because every country should have its freedom and because Japan is our own enemy, but let us hope that when Japan is beaten we will not tolerate in China a government which is essentially as tyrannous as that of Germany.

With a good deal of speculation going on about when the next general election will be, I have been thinking about how I should vote and have tentatively decided that the Liberal Party holds the most attraction at the moment. Strictly speaking, I would prefer a more Socialist government, but both the Labour and Communist parties seem to me too weak and insincere to deserve support, while the Liberal Party has a vigorous and practical policy. Not long ago the Common Wealth Party appealed to me strongly, but it does not seem as if it will survive as a separate party, whereas the Liberal Party is firmly established and previous Liberal Governments have a good record. I would not dream of voting Conservative. Probably Sir William Beveridge's entry into Parliament as a Liberal has helped to crystallise my ideas, but it only brought to the surface an already strong underlying inclination.

Nov. 3rd   Went to see *The Seventh Cross*, a film emphasising that (at least, in 1936) good Germans do (or did) exist. It was a very sincere and moving film.

Rabbit again for supper tonight.

Nov. 7th   I said to Mrs H today, 'It's difficult to imagine anyone besides Roosevelt as President of America.' The coming election there is one of the dominant pieces of news at the moment.

Nov. 8th   Tasted the best fish I have had during the war – filleted plaice, quite fresh and perfectly cooked by my landlady. It almost melted in one's mouth.

I was at a dance tonight when the siren sounded, but nobody took much notice. I asked a girl I was dancing with if she came there often. She replied, in a matter-of-fact tone of voice, 'Monday, Wednesday, and Saturday, every week,' as though stating her hours of business (which perhaps she was).

Nov. 9th   I am glad that Roosevelt has been elected for a fourth term as US President. This will ensure active American cooperation in post-war measures to preserve peace.

At last the Germans have let out a few comments about the rockets and the papers have been able to print some conjectures on the nature of the weapon. I heard a good deal of talk about them today. One that hit a factory at Luton is said to have killed 180 people. I heard of a woman who has only a kitchen and an air-raid shelter to live in, but refuses to leave.

It is an appreciable pleasure now to wake up in the morning and find oneself still alive. One never knows when a bolt will come out of the blue and put an end to one's earthly activities.

My landlady and I listened to Churchill's speech broadcast from the Mansion House. We both thought he sounded a little tipsy.

Nov. 15th   A tiresome day at work, full of hindrances and irritations.

Nov. 16th   Our fire-guard duties have now been relaxed to one turn in 27 days, a welcome relief.

Nov. 17th   My landlady said that one of my shirts was in such a sorry state that it was hardly worth mending. I said I didn't mind what it was like as long as the holes didn't show when I was wearing it, so, as I have not enough coupons to buy a new one, unless I can cadge some off my father, she said she would see what she could do with it. The trouble is that nearly all my shirts are going the same way. Apart from two sports shirts, I have only one really decent shirt and four others in various stages of disintegration, two of which are pre-war.

Nov. 18th   Went out this morning with the intention of doing some Christmas shopping. I spent some time in the 'bargain' basement of Selfridge's and bought a padded coat-hanger, a calendar, and some Christmas cards, all grossly over-charged.

That was all the shopping I did. It seems to me that certain people collect all the rubbish they can, such as wood-shavings, old tin cans, bits of paper and string, make something out of them, and then charge fantastic prices for them. I saw some table-mats, made by mixing wood-shavings with some sort of glue and pressing them into flat squares, priced at 1/- each. This is just brazen robbery.

In the evening I went to the Adelphi and saw *Anglo-Russian Merry-Go-Round*, a pot-pourri of singing, ballet, and comedy, representing English and Russian characteristics and designed to promote Anglo-Russian friendship. George Lacy was superbly funny as a female impersonator; Nina Tarakonova's dancing was of an equal high standard. Altogether it was a very pleasing show. Coming out into the Strand, I found that the new street lighting enabled one to walk without the aid of a torch.

Nov. 23rd　　The new Allied offensive on Germany has made exciting progress. One man said he still thought it possible for the war to be over by Christmas. I think it possible too, but not very probable.

Nov. 25th　　Went to St Albans in the afternoon, hoping to do a little Christmas shopping. But it is the same everywhere – scandalous prices for goods which are not worth having. Still, there were plenty of people out shopping, so I suppose some of the rubbish gets sold. I bought some more cards (a really nice card costs 10d., but I refuse to pay more than 6d.) and two small presents, but I could not see anything suitable for my young nephew. Toys are the biggest racket of all.

Nov. 26th　　About nine o'clock a fairly loud explosion shook the house, though it was a good way off. 'What a blessing it will be,' said my landlady, 'when we are free from all bangs.'

Nov. 28th　　It is strange that no sooner is a European country liberated than its natives start quarrelling among themselves. The French, the Belgians, the Italians, and even – or rather, especially – the Poles, whose country is not yet freed, are all bickering over who shall rule. The more I read about their squabbles the more glad I am that I am an Englishman. We are so much more sensible about our differences of opinion.

Nov. 30th   The *News Chronicle* complains today because Churchill said that Parliament would not be able to deal with many of the proposed measures for social reform this session. Churchill's statement may have seemed rather unenthusiastic, but I certainly did not expect that such a big scheme as the social insurance plan, for instance, could be got working for a year or two. The reconstruction of our cities is one of the most urgent problems and should have priority in Parliament.

Dec. 1st   Did a little more Christmas shopping. I bought a small blackboard and easel, made out of rough wood, and some coloured crayons for my nephew, costing 4/6d. I also bought two 1/6d. cigars for my father and a book called *Flowers in Britain*, to be a joint gift from K and myself to our landlady.

Dec. 7th   It is very difficult to be sure of the rights and wrongs of the situations existing in several liberated countries. On one hand it would appear that reactionary governments, supported by the British Government, are trying to keep down all anti-Fascist elements. On the other hand it would seem that the lawful governments are opposing extremist forces who are seeking to gain sole power by means of violence. There is a fairly sharp division between the protagonists of both ideas. Most likely there is some truth in both arguments; what is true for one country is not necessarily true for another. In Greece and Belgium the constitutional governments seem to be doing their best for their countries in the face of extreme Left opposition, while in Poland and Italy the British Government seems to be backing anti-progressive forces. I can certainly see no excuse for the British Government's disapproval (amounting to a ban) of the proposal to appoint Count Sforza as the Italian Foreign Secretary. We should allow the countries concerned to *choose* their own governments, while discouraging tyrannies *imposed* by either the Right or the Left. The tragic thing is that all this dissension suits Germany's game perfectly, especially if it causes disagreement between the major Allies, as it already has between Britain and America over the Sforza affair.

Dec. 8th   Three men, to whom I spoke at lunchtime about the Greek civil war, expressed the opinion that 'We should clear out and let them get on with it. The Germans won't bother to come back.'

Dec. 9th   Mr H said that he would like to see a strong Liberal government after the war. This remark arose out of some conversation about yesterday's debate on British policy in Greece and other 'liberated' countries. Mrs H said Churchill had made a fighting speech and she thought he was losing his hold. This may be true, and some of his critics made very telling points yesterday, but oddly enough I am inclined to agree with Churchill, at least as far as Greece is concerned. His was a masterly speech, in which he showed his true greatness. But there is something to be said for both arguments and I wouldn't like to give a definite opinion on the matter.

I notice that glycerine, almost unobtainable for a long time, is now on sale again without restriction.

Dec. 10th   A wretched day, cold and wet. Stayed indoors all day (it being Sunday).

Dec. 14th   I came home feeling somewhat depressed. This afternoon at work everybody seemed to annoy me. I suppose it was really myself who was to blame.

My opinion on the Greek affair sways from one side to the other. Since Churchill spoke last week I have become more and more inclined to disagree with him and to think that our policy in Greece may well prove disastrous. It is a waste of our fighting strength, it is contrary to the principles which we are supposed to uphold, it will make the Greeks hostile to us, it may antagonise America and Russia, it is the sort of thing one might expect from Germany. How close is the resemblance to German intervention in the Spanish Civil War! After Aneurin Bevan's speech to the Labour Party conference I am more than ever inclined to hold this view. Incidentally, I am glad that Bevan has been elected to the executive of the Labour Party; he may infuse new life into that characterless organisation. The coalition of the three political parties in the Government is obviously almost at breaking point. The Greek struggle may in fact have a tremendous influence on world politics.

Dec. 16th The Labour Party conference has given me a little more confidence in its general membership, if not in its leaders. On more than one issue the rank-and-file rebuffed the council, and many of the speeches struck a bold and challenging note.

Bought a shirt, costing 21/-, using my last two coupons and five borrowed ones. I also bought a few cigars. I don't often smoke now, but I like to indulge in a cigar or two at Christmas.

Visited some friends, one of whom said that Churchill is going out of favour with the Forces. One of her brothers had written unfavourably of him. I think Churchill has little appeal to the majority of young people.

Dec. 17th Political affairs are like a leaden weight on the trend of the war. A little while ago everything was going fine for us and we were looking forward to a speedy victory. Now what Germany has been hoping for – political dissension within and amongst the Allies and the liberated countries – has happened, threatening to split the coalition in this country and the unity of the Allies and thus to prolong the war of which everyone must be sick and tired. Although I do not say that we are the only ones to blame – far from it – it does seem that the British Government's policy on the liberated countries and those still to be liberated is too rigid and high-handed. As regards Greece I am now almost completely anti-Government. Churchill seems to have misrepresented the situation.

Dec. 18th A rather noisy night last night. I did not hear the siren, but was awakened by the noise of a doodlebug going almost directly overhead. Shortly afterwards the engine shut off and then there was a frightening bang, though actually it must have been some way off. At intervals there were three more explosions, one too near for comfort.

Dec. 19th I am not very worried about the German counter-attack into Belgium. With our greatly superior strength we should be able to smash it. Still, one must not be too complacent.

Dec. 21st   Some people are frankly worried about the German offensive, its speed and strength. Others think it is the best thing that could have happened, as it may give us the chance to inflict a decisive defeat on the enemy.

Dec. 22nd   My landlady said, 'I've never heard so much grumbling as I've heard this year.'

Her husband: 'You can't wonder at it.'

Mrs H: 'No, this is the worst Christmas we've had ... I think so many people were counting on the war being over by Christmas that it has fallen flat now. People are thoroughly sick of the war. You can stand so much for so long, but there comes a time when you can't stand any more.'

Didn't do much work today; most people were celebrating in a restricted fashion. I went to a dance in the evening with P. It was crowded with Yanks and silly little girls and unfaithful married women, jitterbugging for all they were worth and generally misbehaving. Two Yanks started fighting. The atmosphere was distinctly rowdy and unpleasant, but it was instructive to watch. There was a good band and we did our best to dance, but were continually obstructed by the jitterbugs. When we came out P said, 'I should think our men must wonder what they're fighting for, when they come home and see the women prostituting themselves like that.'

Dec. 23rd   Another doodlebug went over early this morning.

My landlady said Mrs C was very depressed by the news of the need for another 250,000 fighting men for the Army.

Dec. 24th   Went home for the Christmas holiday. The train was very crowded; I had to stand all the way home.

A rocket had fallen on a factory in the town the previous week, ruining many people's Christmas. About 40 people were killed and many more injured.

Dec. 25th   A very sharp frosty day, everything covered in white.

We spent a quiet Christmas day at my sister's. The two downstairs rooms were decorated with a little holly and one or two paper chains. For dinner we had chicken, followed by Christmas pudding. (In spite of the shortage, everybody I know had some kind of poultry. Many of the birds were very small, however.) In the afternoon some relatives came round for a short time and small gifts were taken off the Christmas tree. In the evening we played a card game and had a glass of port. There were a few nuts and some dates and sweets. Considering that this is the sixth year of war, I think we did very well for Christmas fare.

For presents I had seven clothing coupons and some money for a shirt, another sum of 10/-, a coloured handkerchief, a bar of shaving soap, a book, a cigar, and two packets of cigarettes. My nephew had a large number of toys, some home-made, which were good, some bought, which were mostly shoddy. He also had several picture-books.

Dec. 26th   Another very frosty day. Got up late and did little all day.

Dec. 27th   One of the hardest frosts I can remember. The trees looked marvellous.

Dramatic news about Churchill going to Athens. I hope he settles the trouble. The news from the Western Front is rather more encouraging.

Dec. 31st   Heard several rockets go down this morning.

My landlady had a small party today. Earlier we had had a dinner of chicken and Christmas pudding. It was a rather quiet party, however. Apart from K showing us a card trick and the handing out of gifts from a small Christmas tree, we just sat round and talked. There was some beer and soft drinks, dates, etc. We did not wait to see the New Year in.

Well, another year of war has passed. I think everyone is more than a little tired of the war, a little disillusioned about the prospects of the peace. For, though the coming year should almost certainly see the end of the European war, the hopes of international co-operation and progress after the war are rapidly fading. From one end of the world to the other one sees nothing but trouble and disorder. The peace, as I see it, will be a turmoil of quarrelling. Here in Britain the Government's policy – both foreign and domestic – is becoming more and more disappointing.

Personally, I have enjoyed life this year. The latter part of the year has seen an appreciable improvement in my health. I have not saved so much money as last year, but on the whole do not regret it. When I think how much many people have suffered I feel rather ashamed to be in such good circumstances.

Notes

[1] In those days we still received our somewhat diminutive salaries in cash in a weekly pay packet. It seems incredible that I could barely afford the 35/- (£1.75) a week for my lodgings. However, it should be borne in mind that the previous year I had been quite pleased at being able to save £25! Another useful comparison might be the fact that I thought the price I paid to see *Gone With The Wind* on 14-9-42, the equivalent of 20p. rather excessive. Or again, £1 was enough to cover my rail fare home on 1-1-44.

[2] At that time there was a small repertory theatre at Palmers Green, known as the Intimate Theatre.

[3] It was my misfortune that my move to Winchmore Hill coincided with a renewal of heavy air-raids on London. These were some of the heaviest raids since the Blitz. It happened that there was an anti-aircraft battery stationed in the nearby park at Winchmore Hill, and the almost continuous gunfire was nearly as frightening as the bombs. The hospital at Edmonton was even closer to the action.

[4] Strange that we had some prior knowledge of the German 'secret weapons' (V-1s), which did not begin operating until six months later.

[5] As before with the V-1s, intelligence about the V2 rockets must have leaked out somehow.

[6] During the 1939–45 war, of course, there was no television, but cinemagoers were well provided for. At this time there were

hree cinemas in Barnet, three in St Albans, and one named the Ritz in Potters Bar. Only one of these cinemas (at Barnet) has survived to the present day. Likewise, in my home town of Chelmsford there had once been five cinemas.

[7] On Saturdays we usually worked in the mornings until lunchtime, but once a month we had the morning off. Perhaps I was being a little hard on myself, for indirectly I was helping the war effort by involvement in the battle for health.

[8] The orchestra was the De Havilland Symphony Orchestra and the concert was at the Odeon Cinema, Barnet. Frederick Grinke was the solo violinist.

[9] In fact the rockets were travelling at supersonic speed. The only way to counter them was to bomb the launching sites, if known.

1945

Jan. 2nd   What we thought were rockets the other morning were actually, according to one story, American troops trying out a new gun.

Jan. 7th   All the newspapers are now playing up Montgomery for all they are worth. Now it is known that he has been given a bigger command they are trying to give him most of the credit for checking the German counter-offensive. Doubtless he played a great part in turning back the northward drive, but the American drive from the southern flank was equally important.

Jan. 8th   Conversation at lunchtime was largely about rockets. One man said, 'These things are getting me down more than the doodlebugs... Whatever will the next war be like?' 'It doesn't bear thinking about,' said another.

Jan. 9th   Snow on the ground. Mr B, one of the men mentioned yesterday, said today, 'I prayed last night, as I've never prayed before, for the people who were bombed-out yesterday.' He said that 21 rockets fell on London the day before yesterday. 'Still, when we're pouring phosphorus on German towns what can you expect?' he asked. In this wintry weather it is certainly dreadful for those who are bombed out of their homes.

Jan. 11th   The bread we are getting now is markedly different from the brownish-coloured bread we used to get in the early days of wholemeal bread. Now, while not officially white, it looks white and tastes as nice as pre-war bread.

Jan. 14th   Two heavy explosions shook our house this morning. Rockets are coming over much more frequently now. Will this bombardment never end?

Jan. 17th   How exhilarating is the news of the sweeping Russian offensive. The swift capture of Warsaw was a marvellous surprise. At our lunch-table today we were making guesses on how long it would take the Red Army to reach Berlin. One man said two months, another three months, I said six months.

The German salient in France seems almost to have disappeared. Although the German offensive was a sharp rebuff for us, no-one can deny that it has been most effectively squashed. Now perhaps we can join with the Russians in the final rout of the German forces.

Jan. 19th   After reading Churchill's survey of the war I am inclined to think that perhaps the Government's policy in Greece was right after all, or at least the best and fairest policy that could be carried out in the circumstances. Although one cannot always agree with Churchill, one cannot help respecting his honesty and in this speech especially his sincerity – in his remarks on Greece and other liberated countries, on our attitude to Germany, on the 'famous American victory' in the Ardennes salient – as unquestionable. This ranks as one of his finest speeches. Although I also admire Aneurin Bevan (Churchill's bitterest critic), I think in this case he is barking up the wrong tree when he accuses Churchill of misrepresenting the facts about Greece.

Jan. 20th   About 11 this morning, while I was at work, we heard a rocket go down, which sounded a good distance away, but the cloud of smoke which went up seemed quite near. Later I discovered that it had fallen about a mile and a half from my landlady's house. It had fallen near the main road and buses were being diverted round the scene. Smoke was still rising when I went by about three hours after it had fallen.[1]

I went home for the weekend, snow falling thickly when I arrived. Talking about the rocket to my father, he said that the nearer you are to them the less you hear of them. Some people living near a factory in the town which was hit by a rocket recently heard nothing until the ceilings started falling in.

Jan. 22nd   If the Russians go on at the rate they are going, they will soon be in Berlin and the war will soon be over. I do not see how the Germans can possibly stand up against such an avalanche.

I heard that 20 people were killed when the rocket fell the day before yesterday.

Jan. 23rd   I now hear that 28 people were killed by the rocket. Considerable damage was done, too.

I cannot help marvelling at the brilliance of the Russian strategy. The Germans are being outmanoeuvred all along the line. If only we could get going in the West, I think German resistance would collapse very quickly.

Jan. 24th   I have been battling for the last week or so against various aches and pains and gastric disturbance, suggestive of flu, so tonight I decided to make a real attack and have a day or two in bed.

Jan. 25th   It seems I have chosen a good time to stay in bed, as the weather has turned extremely cold.

Jan. 26th   Weather colder still, colder than I ever remember, I believe. It is an unfortunate coincidence that this cold spell has come when the fuel shortage is most acute. We had our electricity cut off for about 20 minutes the other morning. I feel especially sorry for the bombed-out, or rather, for those who are not quite bombed-out, but have to live in houses with windows or doors missing and with cracks in the walls and holes in the roof and sometimes without coal for the fire.

Jan. 27th   Got up this afternoon, feeling much better, but still with a shocking cold in the head. The paper says that some parts of the country have had the coldest weather for 70 years.

Jan. 29th   My cold not much better, so went to the doctor, who advised me to have a few more days at home. Before returning home I went to see where the rocket fell. The devastation was appalling.

In spite of the appeal to save on electricity, my landlady said she just had to have the electric fire in the kitchen while she did the washing.

Jan. 30th   Rain this morning, but it was so cold that the rain froze on the windows, covering them with a film of ice.

I spent most of the afternoon browsing through the *Oxford Book of English Verse*.

Jan. 31st   It rained most of the night, and nearly all the snow had gone this morning and it was much milder – a disconcerting change in temperature. I went for a walk in the afternoon.

Hitler's speech last night was defiant, but it was the defiance of defeat. Why don't the Germans admit defeat and save much needless bloodshed?'

Feb. 1st   I had intended going to the doctor to obtain a certificate to return to work, but I did not feel so well, so stayed in bed.

Feb. 2nd   After reading the paper I don't think the Russians will reach Berlin as soon as some people thought. The Germans will probably make a strong stand along the Oder and in any case will fight fiercely for the capital. But the German people must now see that the struggle is hopeless and that it is only a question of time before either the Russians or the Western Allies put the finishing touch to German military resistance.

Feb. 9th   At last our own offensive has begun. If only we did not have to keep slogging at the Siegfried Line and over flooded country we could, no doubt, advance as swiftly as the Russians. However, this advance is probably only the beginning of a general offensive all along the line. I don't think it can be long before the German front cracks somewhere.

Feb. 10th   My landlady said that her son had written from

France to say that it was quite true that many of the French people were on the verge of starvation and conditions generally were shocking.

Feb. 11th   My landlady's grand-daughter, aged two or three, was busy this afternoon building a house out of dominoes and draughts on the table, knocking it down, and saying – as well as she could in her unformed speech – 'Bombed-out'.

Feb. 13th   I could not help laughing at the picture of Churchill, Roosevelt, and Stalin, taken while they were conferring together in the Crimea. Churchill, especially, with his Russian fur cap and cigar, cuts a comic figure. I said to my landlady, 'They look like three music-hall comedians.' She replied, 'That's a fact. There's nothing inspiring about them.' However, the declaration which 'The Big Three' have signed sounds very promising.

The British offensive in the West seems to have faded out, probably because of terribly difficult ground conditions.

Feb. 17th   I heard a rocket go off in the early morning; it sounded quite loud and there was a long rumble afterwards. My boss could not be sure whether he had heard it or dreamt it.

Went up to town in the afternoon and managed to get a copy of Somerset Maugham's novel, *The Razor's Edge*, which I had been trying to get for some months and had been informed was out of print for the duration.

In the evening I went to the Saville Theatre to see *Three's a Family*, an extremely amusing comedy.

Feb. 18th   We all had a fresh egg for breakfast, my landlady's hens having started laying again.

Feb. 19th   Went to another show, '*Sweeter and Lower* at the Ambassadors – quite a clever revue, but not up to the standard I had expected.

Feb. 20th   Went to a play-reading at the local library. It was my first attendance, but I would have gone before if I had known about it. I found that the library circle, as they call themselves, have been meeting fortnightly since last November. There were 17 of us – 12 women, 5 men – and we had a most enjoyable evening reading Shaw's *Major Barbara*.

Feb. 21st   Potatoes are getting scarce.

Feb. 24th   Went home for the weekend. In the train a soldier was bemoaning the fact that his wife had left him for another man and wondering what he could do about it. A good many problems like this are arising now, and it is no good turning round and saying that the woman or the man is to blame for being unfaithful. It goes deeper than that. Prolonged separation is bound to have a disturbing psychological effect, and even where neither party has been unfaithful it will often be difficult, especially for young couples, to regain their old relationship.

Feb. 25th   Heard a story that some rockets are being exploded before they reach the ground by Mustangs carrying radio-location apparatus. As the rockets are (supposedly) radio-controlled, if the Mustangs can get within four miles of them they can send out a radio beam and destroy them. My landlady heard a similar rumour the other day. I am rather dubious about it, but I have noticed several times when a rocket has fallen that an aeroplane has gone over immediately afterwards, heading in the direction of the explosion.

Returned to my digs and Mrs H asked me how my nephew was. I told her that he was extremely active and self-willed, though very intelligent. We began to discuss why so many modern children are restless and uncontrollable. We put it down to the times we live in. I thought much of it was because parents were neurotic due to the war and this was bound to affect their children's behaviour. For the same reason parents could not stand the further strain of controlling their children and were inclined to let them drift.

Feb. 26th   The new offensive in the West goes well. It is obviously the real thing, intended to bring about the final collapse of the German Army.

Mar. 1st   A rocket fell on a golf course about three mile
away early this morning.

Mar. 2nd   Food shortages have been more of a problem
than ever recently. Meat has been in short supply this week. My
landlady said this morning, 'If I can't get any fish, I don't know
what I shall give you to eat tonight.' However, she managed to
get some fish.

Mar. 3rd   The air-raid siren sounded for the first time for
many weeks this afternoon. The Germans are sending over their
accursed flying bombs again. We heard one explode not very far
away.

Mar. 4th   The Germans apparently are going to have a
final fling at us before they yield. Piloted planes were over last
night and dropped a few bombs. I do not think it can last long.
With the defeat of the German armies west of the Rhine, news
of which is exciting us today, the end cannot be far off. I
wonder why the British Second Army is not mentioned in the
news about the Rhine battle, It is a little disappointing to think
that the Canadians and the Americans are getting all the
honours.

Mar. 5th   My landlady said, regarding the Germans' new
air attacks, 'It must be their last desperate throw.' At lunchtime
Mr W also expressed the opinion that it was a 'last fling'.

Mar. 6th   We had haddock for breakfast, the first for a
long time.

Mar. 7th   Cologne captured. Somehow the news doesn't
seem so exciting as it should. It will be really exciting when the
Allies are over the Rhine and, with the Russians in the East,
hastening the final rout of the German armies.

Mar. 9th   The exciting news (the crossing of the Rhine)
has come more quickly than I expected. Almost everyone
expects the war to be over soon; one or two are still cautious. I
cannot think that it will last more than a few weeks longer.

I was much struck by the pictures of Cologne in today's papers. Our bombing has left it a desolate shambles.

Yesterday I was discussing with two other men how the war would end. We more or less agreed that there would be no formal peace-making, for there was nobody we could make peace with. We would just go on until we had beaten the German armies, then set up a military government until we could form a suitable civil government.

Mar. 15th   Looking at the paper at breakfast today, I remarked that there was a possibility of a cut in the meat ration. This started some discussion among K, myself, and our landlady about the food situation. Mrs H finds the food problem more difficult now than at any previous period of the war. Among other things, there is a scarcity of rice, potatoes, and meat. Although the milk ration is increased, the cheese ration is reduced to compensate for it. The paper also reported that there was no prospect of an increase in the clothes ration for a long time.

I think most people accept the fact that the people of Europe are, on the whole, much worse off than we are and need food more than we do. At the same time, of course, everybody thinks we have had more than enough of rationing. They are also beginning to realise that though this will be the year of victory, it will probably be the worst year for rationing.

Mar. 17th   Went to see *Madame Louise* at the Garrick Theatre, a wildly funny farce, with Robertson Hare and Alfred Drayton in their best form.

Mar. 20th   Read Karel Capek's *RUR* at the play-reading circle tonight. We all enjoyed it, and it seemed particularly topical when the air-raid warning sounded while we were reading it.

Mar. 21st   The Germans are being battered everywhere, suffering great losses, but they stupidly prolong the struggle. Mrs H said, 'I can't understand why they don't give in.' At least, by the time it is finished the Germans will have had the meaning of war brought home to them with a vengeance, as it was not in the last war.

Mar. 23rd   There's a sense of expectancy in the air. The fine weather, the preparations which Montgomery is making behind a smoke-screen along the west bank of the Rhine, are pointers to something big. The Russians, too, seem to be poised for their final blow.

Mar. 24th   Bought an evening paper, something I very rarely do, for I had seen the headline 'Monty Over' and wanted to read the good news. It gave me a feeling as awesome as did the news on D-Day.

My landlady said she had used up her last points for the present period on a pound of rice, since after the present stocks are used up there will be no more for some time. She went to one shop, but there was no rice, so she went to another which had it already weighed and packed in bags, 'Ready for the onslaught'.

Mar. 26th   The announcement of the death of Earl Lloyd George must have given everyone who heard it a fright. That slow voice, beginning with 'It is with great regret..., gave me for one awful moment the idea that Churchill was dead. Mrs H said, 'I thought he was going to say "the Prime Minister".' It is rather strange that the man who led us to victory in the last war should die on the eve of victory in this.

Mar. 27th   Heard a man in the bus say, 'Patton's in Nuremberg ... 200 miles from Koniev. Have you seen the *Standard* headlines? They're printed like the American papers ... letters that big... Cracking – Breaking – Collapsing – Wide Open.' Later I discovered that Patton was not in Nuremberg. General Patton's rapid thrusts have attracted much attention, however.

Mar. 28th   Discussed when the war would end with Mr and Mrs H. The latter said she was speaking to another woman who said, 'If it doesn't end soon we shall all collapse. We're all keyed up to expect the end.' We all wrote down on a piece of paper the date we thought the war would end. Mr H put June 10th, Mrs H put April 25th, and I put April 9th. 'I'm waiting for

304

Zhukov to move,' said Mr H. Mrs H was concerned to know how long it would be before the rockets were stopped. I think the Germans will put up a stiff fight in Holland, also those in Norway.

Mar. 30th   Went home for the Easter holiday. My brother and sister-in-law, whose house is being repaired of rocket damage, were at home.

Mar. 31st   Too cold and windy to go walking far, but I went to look at the place where the rocket fell last December. It was a desolate scene: a few jagged walls standing amid heaps of rubble where several houses had been, on either side the battered hulks of several others, and behind them the gutted roofs of a factory. There were one or two rusty Morrison table-shelters standing by the side of the road, and one had been left partly buried in the ruins with its top caved in, and another was upside down on a pile of débris. And here and there amongst the ruins were still to be seen an occasional household article and even a china ornament; on the pavement was a trampled book called *Dulcie King*, a school prize for 1904. These objects had a terrible poignancy. This was the scene three months after the rocket had fallen, and I wondered how many years would pass before all signs of war have been obliterated from England. These areas of destruction will serve as reminders for many years to come.

Afterwards I went and wandered round the outside of my old school, which I had not seen for years.[2] It was much altered; new buildings had been erected where none had been before.

Apr. 1st   We had grapefruit for breakfast, the first of the war for me, as far as I remember.

Apr. 2nd   There have been no rockets or flying bombs over Easter and people who have been sleeping downstairs are speaking of going upstairs again. It is a great relief not to have the continual fear of sudden destruction nagging at us.

Apr. 3rd   I was speaking to P, who got married a few days ago. She asked me to look out for a house, or even half a house, if possible with a piece of land. Her husband, a farmer before the war, now in the Army, may take up farming again after the war. I'm afraid they have not much chance of getting a house at present. Housing promises to be the most acute domestic problem post-war. She said they were about 1200th on the waiting list for furniture permits.

Our troops are making splendid advances into Germany, but they cannot go too fast for me. How maddeningly the Germans persist in draining the war to its last bitter dregs. It is the more stupid because they will suffer more than we will.

Apr. 4th   I and two other men were talking about German propaganda. Even in their defeat the Germans make brilliantly clever propaganda out of it. C was listening to Haw-Haw last night. His line of talk was to the effect that though things were serious for the Germans, they would be much worse for us; the Russians would not stop when they met our armies, they would come on and occupy all Europe, eventually including Britain; in fact, the Germans were doing their best to let us in and hold the Russians back; they weren't really fighting us. Together with this were some more threats about V-weapons. This sort of thing makes you stop and think, for, as C said, 'There's a grain of truth in it.' No doubt the Germans would prefer us to occupy Germany rather than the Russians.

The BBC news bulletins are sometimes exasperating. Tonight. for instance, the 9 o'clock news was almost word for word the same as the 6 o'clock. Even if there is no fresh news at the later time, surely some variation could be made in the wording. Even the most exciting news can become boring if it is repeated two or three times in the same words.

Apr. 7th   Noticed a poster issued by the National Peace Council, whoever they may be, saying 'Hitler brought war. But what brought Hitlerism?'

Apr. 9th   I wish the Government would do something to stop the rampant profiteering in the sale of houses. Fantastic prices are being asked for the poorest class of dwelling. The

eople who make excessive profits out of the homeless do not
eserve to have the war won for them.

The *News Chronicle* today prints some photos of Dutch
lave-workers being forced to kneel before some German sol-
iers. A radio commentator tonight says that the worst atrocities
f which Germans have been accused are true, as he has seen
hem at firsthand. I am a confirmed sceptic, but there is no
efuting the mass of evidence that has piled up against the
Germans during the war. I still find it difficult to believe,
hough, that the majority of the German people are inherently
adistic.[3]

The subject of 'test-tube' babies is also prominent in the
aper today. I have not made up my mind about it, but on the
vhole, if all other methods have failed and both the parents are
villing, there seems to be nothing against artificial insemina-
ion. The question has moral aspects, of course, but it is silly to
ring religious dogma into it, as the Archbishop of Westminster
s trying to do.

Apr. 13th   The death of President Roosevelt is a sad loss,
oth to America and to the world. I was talking to two men
bout it today. One said it was a pity that he did not live to
njoy the final fruits of his efforts. The other said that perhaps
is name would be more highly honoured because he had died
luring the war and not after it. He even suggested that it
night have been better for Churchill's fame had he been killed
vhen he visited the Rhine recently. If he had died then he
vould have been a national hero; after the war he might not be
o well thought of. I said I thought Roosevelt had looked very
ll in his photo taken with Stalin and Churchill at the Yalta
Conference.

Apr. 14th   Saw *Peer Gynt* at the New Theatre. An impres-
ive and unusual play, impressively produced and acted by the
Old Vic company.

Apr. 15th   Further confirmation of Nazi bestiality was given
onight by an American commentator's first-hand account of
vhat he saw at the concentration camp of Buchenwald. How

degraded men must be to do the things which were done to the prisoners at this and other camps!

Apr. 17th   My landlady has now more or less completely done away with the black-out. We only draw curtains sufficient to satisfy the dim-out regulations. The house looks much brighter with the pieces of cardboard taken down from the hall windows and the thick curtain removed from the landing window.

It looks as though the Germans might hold for some little while to various pockets of resistance. However, the Russian offensive may alter things.

Apr. 18th   The Russians still refuse to let Allied newspaper correspondents visit the Eastern Front. This is strange behaviour on their part.

Bertrand Russell, writing in *Picture Post* today, points out the futility of the proposals for the new world security organisation to be discussed at San Francisco. The means of preventing aggression will be applicable only to those countries which are too weak to be likely to make war; the big powers will be free to aggress as much as they like. This would prevent small wars but not another world war. I think it is really useless to talk of world organisation in the present world-wide mood of cynicism and disillusionment.

Apr. 20th   Now we can really imagine what the German concentration camps were like. The sickening pictures which have now been published prove that they were veritable slaughterhouses. Two men I was speaking to about it were agreed that the only way to prevent such things happening again would be to exterminate the Germans. 'They're certainly not fit to live,' said one.

What a relief it will be not to have to bother about the black-out any more. But there are still a few reservations which mean that we have not finally got rid of it.

Apr. 23rd   We did not celebrate the end of the black-out but it was nice to go into my bedroom and switch on the light without bothering whether the curtains were drawn. I looked out, but there were no more lights than usual to be seen.

Apr. 24th   Had a letter from my sister. About the Belsen concentration camp she wrote, 'What a dreadful place that must have been at Belsen. I just can't forget it. It doesn't seem possible that such things could happen in a civilised world.'

Apr. 30th   Was home for the weekend yesterday and the day before. On Saturday we were excited by the news of Himmler's peace offer to Britain and America; but we knew that such an offer would not be accepted unless also made to Russia. But now that a definite desire for peace has been shown, everyone is naturally thinking that it cannot be many days before an acceptable offer is made. The American-Russian link-up, the gradual reduction of Berlin, the final stages in Italy, all point to an end very soon. Yet people are relatively calm about it, because the end has been expected for some time. The war has gone full cycle to a logical and fitting conclusion. What excites interest as much as anything is the fate of Hitler. Is he in Berlin? Is he dead? Yesterday's papers were only guessing. The capture and swift execution of Mussolini by Italian patriots was a well-deserved reward. Events in Europe are coming thick and fast, obscuring news of the San Francisco Conference, where the Polish question threatens to split Britain and America on one hand and Russia on the other.

The phenomenon of our weather is an almost equally common topic of conversation. Such a cold spell, including snow, after the recent heatwave, is simply amazing and extremely irritating, especially as it may do much damage to the crops.

May 1st   Still no sign of the final surrender.

Went to the play-reading circle. We read Shaw's *Man and Superman*, which was very good fun.

When I came home Mrs H said there was no fresh news. She thought perhaps we were waiting for Hitler to die before declaring peace. I said I didn't think it likely and I thought it quite possible that Hitler's death might be announced as a

subterfuge to give him a chance to escape. Shortly afterward,
Mr H came home and told us that Hitler had been reported dead,
so I stayed up to hear the midnight news, which repeated the
German announcement. I was surprised that Admiral Doenitz
had been appointed as Hitler's successor and that the Germans
were determined to fight on.

May 2nd   I have heard a good deal of scepticism about
whether Hitler really is dead.

May 3rd   The surrender in Italy seems to have led people
to expect a general surrender within the next day or two.
took my portable radio to work so that we should not miss the
announcement if it came. Mr L said that peace would probably
be declared tomorrow morning, as some of the local police
had received orders to report in London by 10.30 tomorrow
morning.

I went to the pictures straight from work. The newsreel of the
German concentration camps was being shown. It was horribly
gruesome; our feelings were not spared. Still, I think everybody
should see it, fully to appreciate the sickening and shameful
reality. I find it more than ever difficult to understand, however,
how such human degradation could come about.

When I came out of the cinema it was snowing and raining
and by the time I reached home it was snowing hard. This
weather is unbelievable.

When I got home I noticed that my landlady had put up four
small Union Jacks on the wall. She said she had heard two
women talking about Hitler. One of them said he might have
had his face altered by plastic surgery so that he wouldn't be
recognised. The other said no, he would escape in a coffin. I said
they must have been reading thrillers. I said that if Hitler was in
Berlin. surely the Russians would have found him, unless
perhaps, he had been cremated. F, my co-lodger, also thought it
possible that he had been cremated.

I asked Mrs H what she would do when peace was declared.
She answered, 'I shan't do anything. Some will go mad; others
will just heave a sigh of relief, like myself. I don't think there is
much sense in celebrating while we're still at war with Japan.

310

There has been too much tragedy in this war, for civilians as well; there's not much to celebrate ... I might have a drink.'

May 4th   Listened to the news several times, but nothing very exciting.

May 5th   A miserable wet day.
    I had written yesterday's note before hearing the news of the surrender to Montgomery, which was exciting enough. I am glad Monty has had his final triumph. The Germans seem to be determined to go on fighting the Russians, but they might just as well save themselves further bloodshed.
    I went up to town in the afternoon. Walking from Charing Cross Road to Leicester Square and Piccadilly Circus and along Regent Street, I saw hardly any signs of preparations for celebrations. The shelter at the entrance to Piccadilly Tube station was being taken down. In Regent Street I joined a long queue for the *Daily Express* exhibition of photographs of the German concentration camps. The pictures were as revolting as I expected. Those naked, writhing (though lifeless) figures make one think of Dante's *Inferno*; this must have been purgatory for those pitiable creatures. I think I have now seen enough of this horrifying evidence.

May 6th   'The Russians are an awkward lot,' said Mrs H regarding the Russian arrest of the members of the Polish mission sent from London to Moscow. 'That kind of spirit makes people suspicious when there is probably no need for it.'
    I stayed indoors during the morning and afternoon, reading and writing. At 6 o'clock came the announcement that V-Day would probably be before next Thursday. Mr H remarked that they had not surrendered in Norway yet and that the Russians were still fighting hard.
    Later I went to a dance at a dance-club.[4] They were selling delicious ice-cream there. One girl I danced with was not sure whether it was V-Day or D-Day we were waiting for!

May 7th   We have been in suspense all day, waiting for the official victory proclamation.

On our way home F said to me, 'If it's V-Day tomorrow, shall we go on the spree tomorrow night?' 'Where?' I asked. 'Go and see the floodlighting,' he replied. 'That's an idea,' I said. When we got home two neighbours were putting up flags outside their houses. One of them called out, 'We're not too optimistic, are we?'

Previously, at work, we had drawn lots to see who should work on V-Day and who on V+1 day. It fell out that F and I work on V-Day and have the next day off. I asked J, our junior, aged about 17, what she was going to do on V-Day. She said, 'I want to go up to town and go mad.'

At 9 o'clock it was announced that it would be V-Day tomorrow.

May 8th. VE day   When I awoke the first sound I heard was a cuckoo calling. It was a fine sunny morning, but there had been a heavy thunderstorm in the night. The church bell was ringing – the local church has only one bell with a rather mournful note. I got up at about 7.30, washed and went down to breakfast. There was a shortage of newspapers; all we could get was a *Daily Herald*, which we had to share with our next-door neighbour.

F and I went out to work just before 9 o'clock. Several houses had flags out, mostly Union Jacks. Buses were running a Sunday service, but we were fortunate in getting a lift in Dr S's car, an unprecedented occurrence – usually he goes by without offering us a lift. At the hospital a few flags had been put up.

We got down to work straight away, with the idea of clearing everything up and going off early. Nurse M came in and said she had been in London last night and there had been crowds in the streets then. I went out for some milk to make tea and saw some of the male patients wearing red, white, and blue caps which they had made themselves. Many nurses were wearing red, white, and blue ribbons and rosettes.

After lunch we went along to the local pub and had a drink or two, or, to be exact, three. F played the piano and the rest of us, including three or four nurses, sang songs, among them 'She'll Be Coming Round the Mountain', 'Bless 'em All', 'There'll

Always be an England', and a somewhat improper one called 'Roll Me Over in the Clover'.

After this we went back to work to finish off a few jobs that remained. At 3 o'clock I switched on my radio to hear Churchill's formal announcement of the end of the European war. I thought his 'Advance, Britannia' a bit melodramatic.

Soon after this we packed up and we had some tea at a lorry driver's pull-up in the village. There were plenty of flags flying in the village, including some from the last Coronation and even one from the Coronation of Edward VII.

We took a bus to the nearest Tube station and then went by tube to Leicester Square. At Leicester Square there was a great throng of people coming out of the station, and the street outside was swarming. In a side-street at the back of the Hippodrome was a crowd watching some soldiers and girls dancing to a street-band. A little farther on I met an acquaintance whom I had not seen during the war and spoke to him for a minute. Then we walked into the square and up to Piccadilly. There were crowds everywhere, but there was room to move comfortably. Here and there were ice-cream barrows and vendors of flags and other favours. In Piccadilly Circus the people were jammed together more. One man was seated comfortably on top of a lamp-post. A sailor was climbing up the side of a tall building next to the London Pavilion, while men on the roofs were throwing fireworks into the crowds below and emptying buckets of water over them. After several fireworks, which exploded with terrific noise, had gone off a soldier leaned out of a window and waved a white handkerchief of surrender. The crowd laughed. We made our way across to Regent St, down Waterloo Place and the steps to the Mall, and under Admiralty Arch to Trafalgar Square. One crowd was going in one direction and another in the opposite direction, but all were more or less orderly, just walking along calmly and looking around, though there was an unmistakeable air of gaiety. Now and again a little group would do 'Knees Up, Mother Brown', some were singing, others blowing whistles or waving rattles. We stopped and watched the people in Trafalgar Square for a while, then went down North-umberland Avenue to the Embankment; it was less crowded here. We turned up Parliament Street and went into the Abbey which was packed with people for the service. We walked round, then came out and continued up Whitehall. There was a crowd outside the entrance to Downing Street, hoping to see Mr Churchill. We saw some mounted police come out of Scotland Yard and go up towards Trafalgar Square. Outside Whitehall Theatre F said, 'Perhaps Phyllis Dixey will have too much to drink tonight and drop her fan.' We reached Trafalgar Square again and listened to some people singing to a banjo played by a man seated on one of the lions. F suggested that we should go to Hammersmith and come back to the West End later, so we walked up to Leicester Square Tube station again and went to Hammersmith.

We went to the Brook Green Hotel, which possesses an organ. F plays the organ and knew the organist there, who let him play for a little while. Two request numbers were 'There'll Always Be an England' and 'The White Cliffs of Dover'. There was a merry crowd there. We had two beers and an alleged cocktail each, came out about 9 o'clock and passed some people gathered round a loudspeaker listening to the King's speech, but we didn't stop. We went by tube back to Piccadilly, where fireworks were still going off, including rockets and coloured flares. A little group started a bonfire, but a policeman put a stop to it. We stayed there a while, jostled here and there, then decided to go down to Trafalgar Square again. In Regent St some servicemen and women were dancing on top of an air-raid shelter.

It was getting dark now and some torches were burning on the balcony of a building in Waterloo Place. A column of people marched by singing, and a WAAF girl brushed me in the face with something fluffy on the end of a stick. Across Trafalgar Square the National Gallery was floodlit. In the square some brilliant lights were playing on the people crowded round Nelson's Column and two searchlights were trained on Nelson from high buildings on either side. We wended our way up the Strand. On the front of the Tivoli a big red neon sign said, 'Gaumont-British Pays Tribute to the Soldiers and Workers of the Allied Nations'. The entrance to the Savoy was lit up with

314

green and white neon lights. There were no street lights – or if there were, none noticeable – but one little side-street had all its lights full on and stood out on its own like a showpiece. It was barricaded off, and the only people in it were an old lady talking to a policeman. It was like a brightly lit shop-window on a dark background, with the stationary figures of the woman and the policeman like dummies. (Looking back, this, strangely enough, is my most vivid impression of the day.) We turned into Aldwych, where Bush House was lit up. Buses were still running along Kingsway; there were few people here. We stopped to look at a little group of people round a bonfire in a bombed area; one was playing a guitar and the others were singing. We decided to walk to King's Cross. Euston Road, when we reached it, was dazzlingly lit as far as the eye could see and St Pancras Church was floodlit. We caught the 11.50 train and when it got out of the station we saw many searchlights feathering the sky, sweeping rapidly to and fro in a victory signal. Near the station where we got off the train there was a bonfire outside a pub and some girls were dancing round it.

We walked homewards; my legs and feet were aching. One or two houses had illuminated V-signs in their windows, another had a small floodlight in the front garden lighting up a tree with white blossom, lilac I think – it shone with a simple, yet symbolic, beauty. We arrived home just before 1 a.m. I sat down and read the evening paper, then went to bed. On taking my socks off I found that I had a blister on each foot.

I was too weary to consider my feelings now that the war is over, but I had no very marked ones, relief being possibly the strongest.

May 9th   This morning I had my breakfast in bed and got up at about 10.30, still somewhat tired after yesterday. Mrs H said they were getting ready for the children's party. I looked out of the window and saw some trees and a lamp-post or two decorated and flags across the road. I asked Mrs H what she had done last night. She said she had just listened to the radio, her husband being at work all day and not wanting to go out in the evening. 'The King spoke very well,' she said.

After lunch I decided to go up to the West End again and see what was going on. Coming out of Leicester Square Tube station I saw a girl kissing an American soldier in the middle of the road. There were thinner crowds and more traffic than yesterday, but in Piccadilly there were denser crowds and many were going along the Mall towards Buckingham Palace. In St James' Park the grass made a welcome resting-place. Near the lake was a little crowd singing to an accordion played by an American sailor. I stopped and listened for a while until it came on to rain, then made my way to Trafalgar Square and up St Martin's Lane. It was still raining, and on the spur of the moment I went to the ballet at the New Theatre.[5] There was only standing-room in the gallery, but I enjoyed the performance of *Coppelia*. When I came out, in Charing Cross Road a group of people were watching soldiers and civilians dancing to the sound of bagpipes.

I caught a train home, and again there was a bonfire outside the pub near the station where I alighted. Walking home I saw more V-lights than last night. In one place there was a bonfire on the grass verge by the roadside, a radio was blaring music, and people were dancing on the pavement. The little church was flood-lit. Again the searchlights were interlacing in a marvellous moving pattern of light.

I felt rather thrilled. We had come through. We had endured a great ordeal and now we could make a fresh start. We had won a great victory, but we were celebrating in a sane and disciplined manner. Surely we are the most civilised people on earth.

May 10th   C, my landlady's daughter, came over for part of the day. 'You can't realise the war's over, can you?' she said. She said they had kept up celebrations until the early hours of the morning in their road.

May 12th   After listening to the 9 o'clock news tonight, Mr H said, 'The news seems flat now.' I said, 'Things aren't half so exciting now there aren't any flying-bombs, rockets, or anything.' Indeed, the news, although full of significance, comes as an anti-climax after the excitement at the beginning of the week.

May 14th   Spoke to two or three people who were rather resentful about Russia's attitude. One man said, 'I don't like – I never have liked – the Soviet system. I don't like the people.' I said, 'It's just as much a totalitarian system as the German one was.' He said that he had heard that the Russian concentration camps were worse than the German ones.[6] Later in the day another man said, 'The Russians have as good as walked out of the San Francisco conference. I think Britain and America will co-operate regardless of Russia.'

May 15th   Play-reading night. We read Galsworthy's *Strife*.

Strife is an apt word for the state of Europe now that the war is over. One would have thought that everybody had had enough of conflict, but no, innumerable petty quarrels are springing up everywhere, countries are divided among themselves and against each other. Will this inflammation soon pass, I wonder? Is it only an aftermath, or is it the beginning of years of chaos?

May 16th   Life is rapidly returning to what it was before V-Day. There are differences, of course, but they are hardly noticeable. The atmosphere of celebration has almost vanished. People realise that we shall not get back to normal for a long time.

May 18th   Someone came round collecting in advance for the celebration of the end of the Japanese war. I believe this is being done in other streets. A few street-celebrations are still planned for this weekend.

May 19th   One of the roads adjoining ours was having its victory celebration this evening. When I went along it after lunch I saw about 15 Morrison table-shelters lined up along a short section of the road, which was beflagged. A bonfire with an effigy (presumably Hitler) was stacked ready in the middle of the road.

I went to St Albans and did some shopping, had tea there, then went to Barnet and saw *Blithe Spirit*, a delightfully funny film of Coward's play.

When I came home, at about a quarter to eleven, the celebration was going strong. A powerful floodlight, fixed on a tree, lit up the road. Fireworks were being let off. A man was playing a piano on the path and people were dancing in the road. Many others were watching. On two of the table-shelters were some plates of sandwiches, cakes, etc. The bonfire was a deserted heap of embers.[7]

May 21st   Whit Monday. Went to Lord's to see the England v. Australia cricket match. The ground was packed to capacity. Morning's play rather dull, but some bright batting by the Australians in the afternoon against rather weak bowling. Rain fell heavily after the close of play and kept on all the evening, spoiling an otherwise pleasurable day.

May 22nd   Saw the *Daily Express* headline: 'Attlee Launches Violent Attack on Churchill'. What an utter misrepresentation! Attlee's quite reasonable letter to Churchill could not possibly be called a violent attack. 'They don't half wrap it up,' said Mr H.

The new ration cuts – less meat, fats, milk, soap – though not entirely unexpected, are no less unpleasant for that. Mrs H said, 'I don't know what we are going to do. It looks as though we shall have to live mainly on fish.'

May 24th   At lunchtime we had some discussion about the forthcoming general election. The three of us thought it would be a pretty close struggle between Labour and the Tories. The other two seemed inclined to think the latter would win by a small margin, but none of us thought the result certain. Mr C said he thought the Tories would just get in on the strength of Churchill's popularity, but, he said, 'Churchill's popularity will wane.' He thought Bevin was a great man and also Morrison, though he didn't personally like him. The Labour Party have taken a strong Socialist line now that the coalition is ended, and I fancy their chances at the election more than I would have done a few weeks ago.

Himmler's suicide, like that of Goebbels, Hitler, and others, seems to me a confession of guilt and possibly of cowardice. They had nothing to say on behalf of themselves or of Germany; at the final crisis their pose collapsed and they made an

318

ignominious exit. They knew they had nothing worthy to show for themselves and had not even the courage of defiance (though they were obstinate enough not to surrender, this may well have been due to fear). Hitler's death still seems uncertain. My landlady suggested the other day that de Valera may be hiding him in Eire.

May 30th   I went to have a look at the German U-boat in London dock. I did not go inside it, as there was too long a queue waiting; it is a pity they do not have more than one on view.

In the afternoon I went to a performance of *The Skin of our Teeth*, the new play by Thornton Wilder at the Phoenix Theatre. The author calls it 'a history of the world in comic strip'. The theme of the play appears to be that, no matter what disaster befalls Man, he will always recover to start afresh. This is a great theme, but the author uses so many theatrical tricks – which are sometimes amusing – that the audience is merely confused and the play leaves no lasting impression. Vivien Leigh was good in the main part.

The orators in Hyde Park attracted my attention for some time. There seem to be two main types of speaker – the freak, who may be sincere, but merely affords amusement, and the trained speaker, who is out to make a definite influence on his audience. Three of the latter type I found extremely interesting. One, a most brilliant speaker, had a large crowd listening attentively, with hardly any heckling. He had for his subject the idea that morality, rather than rationality, should be the basis of human conduct. There are no real problems in the world, he said; we make our own problems by trying to rationalise our actions, which we know in our hearts to be wrong. The right action needs no justification. The so-called problems of economics, sociology, and politics are merely wool over our eyes. Everything boils down to right and wrong; we are all individually responsible for our actions. All this I agree with.

Another speaker, proclaiming himself a pacifist, said he had come from an overflow meeting at Central Hall, organised by the National Peace Council, where the speakers were Dr C E

M Joad, Vera Brittain, and several others. I did not hear all his speech, but he answered one question on whether we should forego more of our rations to feed Germany in the affirmative, on the basis of one common humanity of which the Germans are part. I wanted to agree with this, too, but the vision of the German concentration camps kept springing up before me, with all their inhumanity, for which the Germans must be responsible.

A third speaker was making an electioneering speech, raking out the dirty linen of the Tory members of the Government, but doing it humourously and with telling effect.

June 1st   Went to Southend for the day. The weather was showery, which was probably why there were not very many people there. Things did not seem to have altered much, but the atmosphere was quieter. I wondered how they would remove the big blocks of concrete all along the front; perhaps they will just leave them there, though they greatly obstruct the view of the beach and the sea.

In a local paper at home I read an article by the newly nominated Conservative candidate for the district. He has played cricket for Essex and tries to appeal to the electors like this: 'You don't change the bowling when the bowler is doing well … The game we are still playing is the war game, and the enemy is still batting, though two-thirds of his team are out. Who took all those wickets? Principally a man called Churchill…' So, incredibly, there are still people who think of war as a game. When does our side go in to bat?

June 2nd   I asked Mrs S about a pre-war friend of mine who had been a prisoner-of-war for two years or more and has recently come home. She said he looked very brown and very well and was to be married next week.

June 3rd   This afternoon I went to Hyde Park again to listen to the speakers there. I listened to two or three political speakers and observed that Labour and Liberal were running each other down, but the Communist speaker advised his listeners to vote Labour. But I really went to hear the speaker who so impressed me the other day. Eventually I found him addressing a large crowd. His speech had a profound influence on me, no doubt because – after thinking, watching, reading, and listening all through the war, trying to analyse what was going on – I had already arrived at much the same conclusions, though I regret that at times I have been swayed by the feeling of the day.

The speaker distinguished between people as individuals and as social communities. As the former they may be good, but as the latter are heading for catastrophe. Germans alone were not responsible for the war; we all had responsibility. The continual perversion of values by people and nations to suit their own ends was a major cause of our troubles; they said 'freedom' when they meant 'slavery', 'honour' when they meant 'degradation', and so forth. He said that he thought people were most free in this country and least free in Russia. Russia, he said, was under the rule of a monstrous tyranny, and the last thing it was was a Socialist state.

After his address a few of us gathered round the speaker and he admitted that his efforts were hopeless. For one thing, philosophically everything was arguable. He could only hope to reach a few individuals. He thought we needed spiritual enlightenment and took a catastrophic view of our civilisation. Several listeners seemed sympathetic with him.

And, looking at our world today, I take the same view. France's attitude over Syria, Yugo-Slavia's over Trieste, Russia's over almost everything, that of the Allies over the treatment of Germany, the attitude of party towards party and of class towards class, do not show a sign of goodwill anywhere. The San Francisco conference seems doomed to failure. It is a hopeless situation. Yes, it was a very satirical cuckoo I heard on VE-Day!

Notes

[1] This happened on a Saturday morning, while I was at work at Clare Hall. The rocket fell on some houses in the Southgate Road about 200 yards from the crossroads on the eastern side of Potters Bar.

[2] Chelmsford Grammar School.

[3] I was greatly affected by the 'photos of Dutch slave workers'. The coastal area of Holland was one of the last to be liberated; it had been stubbornly defended by the Germans because the missile launching sites were there.

[4] The 'dance club' was a Sunday dance venue at The Spot Café, London Colney. This café, which had a small dance-hall attached, has long since vanished.

[5] The Sadlers Wells Ballet had been bombed out of their usual home, but found temporary accommodation at the New Theatre.

[6] Comparison of Russian and German concentration camps. It was hardly possible for anything to be worse than the German ones. See first-hand accounts in 'Aftermath'.

[7] The street party referred to was in Oulton Crescent, Potters Bar.

AFTERMATH I

The end of the war in Europe seemed to be a convenient moment to end my diary. For nearly six years, with only one gap of three months or so, I had recorded what people had said and thought about the war, about Hitler and the Germans, about Churchill, about the black-out, rationing, and shortages, about radio and cinema, about official propaganda, about air-raids, about the newspapers, about transport and travel, about all the trials and tribulations of wartime. I had reported events, comments, and opinions as truthfully as possible; in some cases conversations were given virtually verbatim. Quite often I expressed my own views, which were genuine at the time, but perhaps 'in the heat of battle' sometimes rather thoughtless. Many opinions, if uttered in public today, would probably invite severe penalty, but I tried to be impartial and simply wrote down what people said. However, for reasons of wartime security no names of people or places could be mentioned, which perhaps is just as well – no names, no pack-drill.

As a family, we had come through the war relatively unscathed. We were never a large family. My father, brother, and sister, and myself, all survived without physical injury, and all my aunts and uncles and cousins came through safely, though we endured the same dangers and hardships as the rest of the population. Some of the diary entries indicate what might have been a different outcome.

I certainly considered myself fortunate to be still alive. At the end of the war I was 25 years old, single and unattached, and I had to get on with my own life. I was still studying to obtain my final qualifications in medical laboratory science, and I had little time or money to spare. From an old Post Office Savings Book I discover that at the end of the war I had £160 in my account – this was the result of about eight years' saving! I did not have a bank account at that time and I was probably earning £5 or £6 a week. I have no detailed accounts from the immediate post-war years, but can verify from a copy of a letter which I wrote applying for a mortgage in 1955, when I eventually married, that ten years after the war my salary was £13 a week.

These figures seem pitifully small by today's standards, yet I do not remember that I consciously felt deprived. In fact, my wages were slightly above the average, though I never expected to become wealthy in the Health Service. Later in the summer of 1945 I was able to spend a fortnight's holiday in Torquay, and though food rationing was even worse than it had been during the war, prospects seemed much brighter, though the war in the Far East was not concluded for another three months, with the dropping of atomic bombs on Hiroshima and Nagasaki.

We had lived through tragic times, and it was not going to be easy to adjust to the peace. The war had posed many moral dilemmas, as the diary often reveals, but to my way of thinking the atomic bombs had added a new and terrifying dimension to military power. For I was beginning to go through what I call 'a religious phase'; I was also becoming wrapped up in music and poetry, perhaps a natural reflex response after all the horrors of the war years.

It was time, then, to discontinue the diary and to turn to other matters. In the immediate aftermath, however, I was to experience two episodes in my personal life which were closely linked to the war years and came to signify, ultimately, why the war had been necessary. It may be wondered why, after such a long period of time, I now have to add what must be essentially painful memories. This is really a complex question, partly bound up with looking back over one's whole life, trying to pick out what has been important or valuable. The additional material has been thought pertinent because the background is closely related to all that has happened before; the chronology follows on directly from the end of the war; and it illuminates starkly what the war was about. The visit to Holland in 1947 links up with the visit to Germany only three years later. I suppose, in a way, I was favoured to gain brief insights into how the war had affected two very different families in Europe – insights which illustrated only too poignantly how fortunate my own family had been. But perhaps the most compelling motive is that I feel I owe it to the people involved, though it is hard, at times, to find the inner resolve to tie up all the threads.

It all began with the letter to *Picture Post*. In November 1939 *Picture Post* magazine had run a series of features about war aims as seen both by leading personalities and by ordinary readers. In a fit of youthful idealism I had tried to express what I thought our war aims should be. This letter appeared in the issue of 11 November 1939, and read as follows:

'We are fighting this war as much for the liberation of the German people as for that of the Poles and Czechs, and for the preservation of our own liberty. We must see that a sane system of government is established in Germany. Then, when Europe is free from the fear of aggression, we can begin to construct a United States of Europe and, eventually, a United States of the World.

'If we want to achieve this end, we must not let it be obscured by hatred, whatever atrocities may be committed. War cannot be humanised, but it is the fact that most of us want it to be that gives hope for a new, Christian civilisation.'
(See diary entry for Feb. 6, 1940)

Letters From Holland
There is no diary, then, after June 1945, but there is a bundle of letters, still in my possession, which at first glance might appear to be a bundle of love-letters. Perhaps, in a sense, they are, although the contents are not at all intimate. In the Spring of 1946, less than a year after the end of the European war, I unexpectedly received a letter from a girl in Holland. The letter of mine to *Picture Post* had been read, long afterwards, by a Dutch girl living in Rotterdam. What was I thinking about

things now the war was over? she wanted to know. Could I imagine what my feelings would be, if my father and brother had been shot by the Germans? as her own father and brother had been in February 1945, only three months before the war ended.

This first letter was a short one – it had been sent to my old home address – but it was the beginning of quite a long correspondence and led to my paying a visit to Holland in 1947 and, in the end, to considerable heartache for both of us.

Nelly Visser turned out to be an attractive blonde girl of 22 in 1946, but she was certainly not a dumb blonde, though a little shortsighted and wore spectacles. Indeed, her letters were composed in beautiful English, with a fine literary style and an almost poetic expression. I never ceased to be amazed at her command of a foreign language. She was working as a telephonist at a large bank in Rotterdam and she, her mother, and younger sister and brother, lived in the southern part of the city, some distance from the centre. Though about four years younger than myself, she seemed more mature. Nevertheless, it appeared that what I wrote helped her to come to terms, up to a point, with the cruel deaths of her father and brother. I don't know exactly what I replied, except that I tried to avoid conventional platitudes. Someone who had taken the trouble to read my letter in *Picture Post*, who had thought about it, and had written to me in my own language, had to be somebody special and required a special answer. Since my own father and brother were still alive, as I have stated previously, I was not really well equipped to handle the question. I don't know who was. The shooting of two people was an exemplar for the killing of millions for no particular reason, and who could cope with such enormity?

The family was not Jewish; her older brother, she said, had been keen on the Oxford Movement before the war. The actual circumstances cannot now be disentangled from the turmoil of war as the Germans retreated before the Allied offensive on the Siegfried Line in February 1945. There had been a German concentration camp at Oud-Leusden, near the small Dutch town of Amersfoort (and not a long distance from Arnhem), and it is

326

ertain that before they left the Germans killed as many men of military age as possible. Among these were the father and brother of my correspondent in Holland. 'My dear father and brother now sleep forever between woods of fir trees at Rusthof,' she wrote in a moving account in her second letter. The country is beautiful because it is so simple that we can think sanely again.' Her letters were so literate for somebody writing in a foreign language that I was astounded. My knowledge of the Dutch language, needless to say, was nonexistent – though I suppose that was understandable and forgivable – but it did not seem to matter.

The entries in my diary during the early months of 1945 are evidence of my genuine sympathy for the plight of the people of Holland. Some areas of the country were by-passed by the British attack further south, and they were desperately unlucky to be among the last places liberated. The Dutch population had suffered unspeakably at the hands of the Germans and many were dying of starvation by the time the war ended.

Letter followed letter; eventually we exchanged nearly 40 letters, as well as various postcards, greetings cards, and occasional small gifts. Some letters contained snapshots. We told each other about our families, our work, our pastimes, our hopes and fears. I also learned something of the sufferings of one Dutch family.

Letter dated 9 May 1946: '...have gone to Amersfoort, where a monument was unveiled for them who were executed by shooting by the Germans at Feb. 5th, 1945. The shooting took place in the garden of a villa near the station. The shot-holes in the wall could still easily be seen. Now a monument with the names of the 20 men, among whom my father and brother, has been masoned in that wall. The unveiling of it was very ceremonial...'

'After that we walked to the cemetery "Rusthof" at Oud-Leusden, that is one hour's walk ... flowers on all the graves of the war-victims and on those of the English and American flyers too...'

'There was hardly no food, only 400gr bread in a week ...

[you] could sometimes buy potatoes and you had to eat them fo
breakfast, lunch, and dinner, for there was nothing else. [Ann
Frank, in Amsterdam, tells a similar story of living on one kin
of vegetable, usually potatoes or beans, day after day.] German
could come and take away our husbands and sons to kill ther
... Secretly we listened to the English news...'

This letter was accompanied by postcards which showed th
cemetery at Rusthof and the site of the concentration camp
they could have been normal postcard views of a quiet country
side – but two aerial views of the same area in Rotterdam, on
taken before 1940, the second in 1946, provided a startlin
contrast. A vast expanse of what had once been a thriving cit
was now flattened to the ground; much of this had been due t
the German bombardment in 1940, but it had also suffered fror
Allied bombing.

A letter of 13 July 1946 tells more of the hard times they wer
going through. She has only one pair of shoes, needing repair. '
have not another pair and they are also not to obtain. Then the
cannot repair, because I have not any coupon... You see, ver
hopeless. Tomorrow, Perhaps I am able then to glue the sherd
of this day.' I had to admire this sentence; no novelist coul
have phrased it better. 'Sherds' is not a word in common usage
how did she come to find it? And the thought seemed to fit m
own failures only too well: how often indeed do I seem to b
trying to glue the sherds of many days?

She goes on to mention Mr Jansen of the cemetery Rustho
... [who] receives many letters from the relations of the Englist
Canadian, and American flyers who are buried in that cemetery
I help to translate these letters for him...' There were othe
miscellaneous items of information, such as that 'I live near th
[football] stadium of Rotterdam' and, more unenviably, 'Not fo
six weeks we have had sugar.'

She had also met other English, American, and Canadia
people. 4 August 1946: '...Mr and Mrs Barlow from Essex
They were here last week for a few days to visit the grave o
their son, who was a flyer and was brought down in his plan
near Amersfoort in 1943.' She always used the word 'flyer'
rather than 'pilot'.

'It is such a lovely Sunday morning and so calm that it becomes tangible.'

4 June 1946   Apparently I sent some English cigarettes, presumably for her birthday in early June. Attitudes to smoking were much more tolerant then; there was no anti-smoking pressure as there is today – it was largely a matter of individual choice. I was never a heavy smoker myself, but I seldom smoked cigarettes; mostly I smoked a pipe. 'My compliments for the good packing, they were unviolated. Everybody is envious of me for the real English cigarettes.' I was always charmed by her choice of words.

'From my mother I got a pair of spectacles for my birthday. You must laugh?'

21 Aug. 1946   'What a fine letter you wrote me last time. I thought it like a glass of mineral water, so sparkling and made me glad.' I have no idea what I had written.

Generally her English was more or less faultless, but there were occasional lapses, occasional 'howlers' which could be hilarious at times. 'Mr S (from Scotland) did not even wear a petticoat (is that right).' She meant 'a kilt'.

I must have taken pity on her lack of footwear, for from a letter dated *17/18 October 1946* it seems that I had found a pair of shoes to send, but have no recollections of doing so. Nelly also mentions a letter I had written on a 'stuttering typewriter', which afforded her 'rollicking fun'.

The rest of the letter was far more sombre in tone. 'We have been to the consecration of death-cell 601 of the prison at Scheveningen, which is called "Oranjehotel". During the occupation by the Germans those who were condemned to death were confined in these cells. Probably my father and brother must have been there too.' Music of Grieg and Bach was played and cell no. 601 was opened. 'Here the light will always burn as a symbol of the luminous example they gave us ... All was so full of emotion, that we felt very tired going home again.'

Her letters were always carefully laid out and perfectly

legible and, as I have indicated, her English could have put many natives of England to shame. This letter, however, unusually in green ink on green paper, was a little difficult to read.

2 Nov. 1946   'No doubt at first sight from whom the letter is! (it smells of the hospital).'

'I read your diary and thought it very nice. Your descriptions are so clear, that your own life is shut out for a moment.' I cannot recall how I sent my diary, since it was quite lengthy – did I send carbon copies? 'Once I took it with me to read it in lunchtime.'

'I could really never have thought there are boys like you. This is not to flatter, for it is true. You try to understand my ideas and thoughts and do not shift them from you, before [because] I am only a girl, even a foreigner.' In this respect she reminds me a little of Anne Frank.

'You are so very kind in trying to obtain another pair of shoes.' (Where on earth did I get them? – my memory is a blank on the shoes.)

Christmas Day 1946   'Since yesterday the cross upon the church opposite our house is lightened. A marvellous green cross high up in the dark sky.'

Some letters, like this one, were several pages in length, but all immaculately written.

4 Jan. 1947   New Year thoughts – 'Our dreams of the future are so nice. But future is not lovely in reality.' This was a typical Nelly Visser remark: she could be very realistic, probably as a result of harsh wartime experience.

At other times she showed her good nature. When dancing with an awkward partner, 'With a shy smile I tried to agree, to dance not so well, nevertheless my toes glowed with indignation' – one could hardly improve on this description.

She was often self-critical, however. 'I realise my egoism by talking of myself and my problems any time without asking for your life. Excuse me, but I think your answers always so

mportant. They help me to find my way...' and so on. At least
was doing something right.

et at the beginning of 1947 (letter dated 9 January 1947) I
eceived a severe telling-off for writing that at Christmas,
omewhat untypically, I had imbibed too freely and had become
ather tipsy. Perhaps I had exaggerated a little for the sake of
ffect, for I was as moderate in drinking as in smoking. Up to
hen Nelly's letters had been quite lengthy, many of them
vritten in green ink on pink notepaper, but this time it was
imply a curt note in black ink on bank stationery. 'How can you
e such a fool?' she wanted to know. She was furious, – but she
vas right, and I respected her for it. It was also an indication that
 deeper relationship was developing ... and she was worried
fterwards that she might have ruined everything.

I think I recognised the justice of her comments and I must
ave replied quickly to reassure her, for on 13 January 1947 she
vrote me a long letter in red ink on pink paper. I sometimes
vondered whether the different colours of ink or paper had
ome conscious or subconscious significance.

On my birthday in February I received a specially drawn
reetings.

6 Feb. 1947   Some talk of my visiting Holland. I am not
ure how the subject arose, but I was informed that 'Mam said
ou are welcome at our home.' The letter finished, 'Tell me
oon your plans according to your summer holidays. It will be
vonderful to meet you personnally (sic).'

2 Mar. 1947   'So kind of you to surprise me in sending
hat nice little brooch. I appreciate it very much as it is charming
nd apart. My heartfelt thanks for the quite unexpected present.'
 cannot now remember the brooch, or my reason for sending it,
ut we exchanged small gifts at Christmas and birthdays
hrough the post. I am sure the brooch could not have been very
xpensive.

She often contrasts good intentions with actual deeds, calls
erself 'a coward who even does not try to leap over the

331

troubles.' Some of this was connected with a proposed visit to England for a holiday. '[in my last letter] Intentionally I did not want to say any word. Of course, you will be astonished now. Well Ted, there are some troubles. Still I like to go to England for I am not a little child. Oh you will not understand much of it. Does not matter...' This suggested to me some family disagreement. But she goes on, 'You are welcome in Rotterdam [from 12–26 July].'

Her mood sounded a little gloomy in this letter, partly because the weather had been very cold and they had no coal. 'It is 12 o'clock midnight and I am as cold as ice.' 'Everywhere these days one can hear the word: Hopeless!'

18 Mar. 1947   'We are looking for our own kind of happiness in our own way.' 'Of course, you don't know me and my circumstances.' There were always hints of mysterious troubles and difficulties in her life, which may possibly have been the result of the loss of her father and brother, or perhaps something entirely different.

28 Mar. 1947   It seems that I had tried to write something in Dutch. 'Our language is rather difficult, mind you. Likely the new spelling will become the official one this year. I think you possess a book in the old spelling, which is not so simple.' (!) I had felt it necessary to prepare for my visit by learning a little of the language. I must have written several sentences in Dutch – today I can hardly remember a word.

The letter passes on to other matters. '... why did you guess that I did not like to tell? It's true, at present I am unhappy ... I cannot tell you the troubles ... But then I have to tell you the reason why I do not want you know them. Especially you, mind you.' I could only presume that the 'troubles' concerned some previous attachment.

15 Apr. 1947   The next letter continued in much the same vein. Foreseeing a problem, 'Let us not entertain too high hopes of each other. Try to understand we may not do so ... our letters merely show the best and nicest side of ourselves. In that glance

332

ne would idealise each other too soon.' – a shrewd observation, nd not a little prophetic, as it happened. And later, 'Suppose I hould tell all those problems to another person. I am sure what ould be the usual conventional replies. Oh, as compared with ours, you are so different.'

This letter was written in green ink on blue paper, suggesting 'blue' mood, I suppose.

May 1947   An extremely long letter, eight pages. 'You now, I am fond of scenery. But fear, if I have to be in a little ull place for all my life, that in spite of the lovely environs, here will often be the strong longing for the busy exciting life f a big town.' A fair comment, which I more or less reciproated, and an indication of the way her mind was working.

'Cigarettes are rationed here; men get 100 fortnightly and we 0.' This refers to Dutch brands; English or American cigarttes, though not rationed, were simply unaffordable.

Amongst many other details, Nelly reveals that she had lied to er mother about how she first wrote to me because of my letter n *Picture Post*. She says that her mother would not understand ... 'And I lied – "Somebody gave me his address".'

'Ted, you think me the most wonderful girl.' (I must have old her this in one of my letters.) 'I smile.' She was also hinking about coming to England and mentioned some rather ague plans for doing so. 'I shall stay with family Barlow at Harold Wood' and there was also somebody at Birmingham vhom she hoped to visit.

This letter also includes an account of the ceremony at Rusthof' on 3 May, to commemorate the dead in the war. It was a solemn occasion and afterwards they placed flowers on the graves. And the letter ends, 'Perhaps you don't know that your ext letter will be the 25th one ... I cannot imagine they will come no longer.'

6 May 1947   A short letter, wholly in Dutch, thanking me or some magazines I had sent.

5 June 1947   'I wondered why I thought your last letter so

wonderful.' Beginning during the war I had been trying my
hand at writing poetry, and had evidently sent her one of my
poems called 'Speedboat'. Nelly, in return, was offering to send
me a little book of Dutch poems by a poet named Tony de
Ridder. This arrived in due course, with an inscription in penci
in the fly leaf:

> And build together,
> What none shall sever,
> Bridges from man to man,
> The whole round earth to span.

The source of this quotation was not given, but it may have been
something culled from her dead brother's Oxford Group litera
ture.

27 June 1947   We had spoken on the phone the day before
she having phoned me at the hospital. It was the only way to do
it, for there was no telephone at my lodgings; in fact few
working-class homes at that time did possess telephones. A
letter followed – 'I hope you did not misunderstand me in regard
to the soap . . . The soap situation is very bad here at present. In a
long time we have not had any ration.'

'. . . When you get this letter, I guess you will be in a nervous
fit. For you have to go to Cambridge next week, have not you'
(Her English was a little pedantic in this respect; she rarely
employed contractions such as 'haven't' or 'isn't'.) This time
you must succeed, Ted.' This referred to the fact that I was re
sitting my bacteriology final (and this time passed).

1 July 1947   Having sent a photograph of myself working in
the laboratory at Clare Hall Hospital – 'Looking at the snaps
hardly cannot believe that person is Ted. So strange in that white
coat and among so many bottles.'

8 July 1947   The time of my visit to Holland was approach
ing, and there were final arrangements for meeting at the station.
It was the last letter to be received before the actual journey

'Mam, Jopie, and Bob are looking forward to see you too. My mother's only trouble is whether you will like the Dutch food.

'P.S. I enclose a snap of myself because this will help you not to run past me, instead of to say "How do you do?"' As if it was likely!

11–12 July 1947   I travelled to Holland by boat from Harwich to Hook of Holland. This was, in any case, my first trip abroad, and there were many new experiences to cope with, apart from the fact that I was to stay with a strange family whose language I did not speak. I was understandably nervous, but was looking forward, at least, to seeing something of another country.

I was met by Nelly at Rotterdam station and was taken to their home. They lived in a rather small apartment, and with myself there were five people in the house. I was given a small room at the top, which I presume was once her elder brother's room. It was quite adequate for me, but generally they were rather cramped for space, and not knowing their habits and customs I often felt awkward and ill-at-ease when the whole family was present.

Nelly and I got on very well together, and most days we went out to see the sights of Holland. However, we were rarely alone together, whether at home or on days out, since her brother Bob was on holiday from school and accompanied us on several occasions. He was a friendly enough youth, but he spoke little English. Their mother was a rather solid, domineering woman and, although at first she was kind and pleasant, it soon appeared that she did not like me very much, her disapproval became more obvious each day, and the language barrier was too difficult to surmount in the time available. I was a victim of the classical 'mother-in-law' syndrome really, before even any thought of marriage.

It was perhaps not an auspicious time to go. After two years the ravages of war were still much in evidence, not only in Rotterdam but in the country as a whole. Much of the city centre in Rotterdam was still a wasteland, where amidst a vast empty space the ruin of the cathedral still stood defiantly. Transport services were getting back to normal reasonably well, as far as I could tell, and we were able to visit several Dutch towns without too much trouble.

A visit to Amsterdam and a boat trip around the maze of canals was almost obligatory – you never know what you are going to see round the next bend. In Rotterdam itself we went to the famous Museum Boymans, which has a fine art gallery. Another day we visited the cemetery at Rusthof, to pay our respects to the two men of the family who had lost their lives through German savagery. In 1947 I do not think the cemetery had been laid out properly – I remember a field in the woods with Allied flags flying over it. We walked there from Amersfoort on a glorious summer's day; in fact we had lovely weather most of the time I was there.

Prior to the trip to Holland I had bought a cheap secondhand camera from a friend. It was a simple roll-film camera (though not a box type) and was not in good condition; it was the first camera I ever owned. In those days only relatively well-off people could afford 35mm cameras. One also had to be economical with roll film because most popular cameras produced only eight exposures on a film, so there was not much latitude for error, as there is today. Anyway, this camera accompanied me to Holland and the pictures I took there were some of the first I ever took. It was to be the beginning of a lifelong interest in photography as a hobby, and partly due to this, a few photographic records of my visits to Holland and Germany have survived. Nonetheless, it is something of a miracle that any of my first efforts were worth printing and even more of a miracle that the negatives of the portraits of Nelly, myself, and her brother had not been lost or thrown out. In fact the prints made from them well over 40 years later are by no means unpleasing; these were taken somewhere along the way to the cemetery at Oud-Leusden.

Thanks to Nelly's help, I was able to see a hospital at Haarlem and the beach at Scheveningen. Another memorable trip took us to Arnhem, where I was able to cross over the Army bridge, which was still in position. It gave me quite a thrill to walk over the bridge where the fateful battle had been fought only three years before, even though our attempt to cross the river had then been abortive. It had been a bridge too far in a military sense, and for me too it came to represent a final obstacle to my purpose in coming to Holland.

This is not meant to be an autobiography, nor was the original diary. It is meant as a continuation of the diary – a record of the immediate post-war period as it affected a certain family, written only partly with hindsight. But since it also affected me, inevitably some personal history enters into it. I came from a conventional family background and from a generation whose respectable aims were to marry, settle down, and bring up a family. Like most of my friends and acquaintances, I was looking for a girl to marry, and this talented Dutch blonde seemed to be the answer to my quest. In the rather fraught and enclosed family atmosphere and unusual circumstances of the holiday there were few, if any, opportunities for passion. We had kissed once or twice when her mother was out, but the highlight of those days occurred when we travelled to Delft, surely one of the most enchanting towns in Europe and where I bought my sister a brooch of Delftware. With its little tree-lined canals and mellow old buildings and its atmosphere of calm, it is the perfect place for romantic dalliance. For once we had been left alone and there, by the bank of a canal, on a sunny afternoon in Delft, we kissed and embraced passionately. That was about as far as it could go then, but we walked back hand in hand and I was walking on air. There was an overpowering sense of freedom, which almost as soon as I got back to England I tried to recapture in a short poem. It may have no great merit as poetry, but it is a true emotional record from that phase of my life and still expresses a sense of exhilaration and liberation. It is a memory of a certain time and place in my own words – banal perhaps, but authentic.

FOR N.A.V.: A Memory.

There is nothing more to know,
Nothing better in the heart

337

> Than this – to break the chains
> That tighten round our days.
> We found our freedom;
> We escaped, those sunny afternoons,
> From time, from words, from numbers
> And machines.
>
> Only the bright sky and the trees
> Blessed us, who loved so much.
> I heard your heart's wild beating,
> – And the world vanished;
> There was only you and I,
> And happiness.

During my stay there I had received a belated birthday gift which Nelly had been unable to send through the post. It was a copy of Mary Webb's novel, *Precious Bane* (a book which has been televised in recent years). I do not think there was any significance in the choice: the bookshop probably had only a very limited range of suitable titles. Yet the story of a girl whose beauty was flawed again seems symbolic of some baneful influence which was threatening our relationship.

From a purely factual 'touristic' angle my visit had been quite successful, but it became clear after I had returned to England that I had not matched up to expectations, at least as far as her mother was concerned, though why this was so I could not understand. There was no reason that I could think of. I was polite and well-behaved, and there was virtually no difference in social class. In appearance I was quite personable, except that in those years I was very thin. I was no ignoramus and I had a worthwhile job with decent prospects. I simply did not know what her mother had against me. I had been at some disadvantage as a foreigner, but what had I done or not done to incur her dislike? It was a puzzle to which I never discovered an answer.

Nelly and I were both sincere people, I believe, and I had come back to England thinking that the relationship would develop and blossom, yet a few days after my return came a short note in pencil on plain paper; it had been written the day following my departure.

338

Rotterdam, 28-7-47.

My dear Ted,

   If you write me, please to the following address:
     Miss N. A. Visser,
     c/o Amsterdamsche Bank,
     [address of bank].

Yours, Nelly.

I sensed straightaway that something was wrong. Whatever went wrong, though, I do not blame myself; I have to blame the mother for interfering, even though in doing so I am adopting a selfish standpoint. It has to be borne in mind that at this time Nelly was the main bread-winner in the family. Having lost the two chief sources of income with the deaths by execution of her husband and son, it was understandable that Mrs Visser would not take kindly to losing another. I never knew the occupations of the two men who were shot, or even whether they were in continuous employment. From Nelly's letters, I gathered that they were a fairly stable family who had somehow managed to survive through the war years. Her younger sister, Jopie, had an office job and was presumably contributing something to the family income, while the younger son, Bob, was approaching wage-earning age. The family finances, therefore, must have been rather vulnerable.

My own finances were not in a much better state. The £160 in my savings account had grown to about £200 by 1947, but as I had withdrawn £50 for the trip to Holland, I was barely marking time as regards money. I suppose I was earning £7 or £8 a week at this time, though I now had a secure job with reasonably good prospects. But I was still living in lodgings. I could not see my way to bringing a girl over to England, even if she had been able to escape her mother's antagonism. I was not in a position for anything adventurous. When I visited Germany in 1950, I was still not earning more than about £10 a week.

The next letter I received was not until about four months later. It was dated *27 November 1947*, written in blue ink on cream notepaper. She said she was sorry for not having written sooner, but if she had done so unwanted 'complications' would have arisen. I could only guess that the complications were connected with her mother. The crucial paragraph said, 'To be honest, I have to tell you, Mam dislikes our correspondence. Why? Ted, you and I we made a great mistake. You had better done not to come to Holland. All was like a dream. *You were my ideal.* It is not easy to describe, but since your holidays here something has changed.' (Yes, she changed her mind!) 'Oh, perhaps I had written you much earlier if I was not such a coward. I am afraid Mam will read your letters.' – yet her mother could not read English. And surely there was something radically wrong somewhere if she could not receive letters without fear of interception. Yet strangely, this is the first letter which contained any kind of endearment, muted though it was.

4 Dec. 1947   I had written to Mr Jansen, as I had heard nothing for four months and was becoming quite worried about her welfare. This was not well received, but at least elicited a reply. 'Oh, fool that you are! writing to everybody you know,' she scolded me in her forthright manner. 'If I am right, my mother has sent a letter to you last night. That is why I ask you now not to tell her, I have written you last week. She thinks I have not done so. Please, don't make more complications. Kindest regards, Yours, Nelly.'

I never received any letter from her mother. In any case, I was intrigued to know, what could she have said? And how could her mother, who knew no English, have written to me? Likewise, how could I have told her mother anything? She seemed to be in fear of her mother. As far as I was concerned, the whole business was completely inexplicable.

I received another letter for the New Year. *1 January 1948*: 'Dear Ted, My best wishes for a happy 1948,' but then she tells me of 'my boyfriend of Amsterdam, who is in the service (i.e. forces) at present and was so lucky to be able to come to Laag-Soeren,' (near Arnhem). '...soon we shall have a party when my boyfriend will be demobbed.' ... 'Oh, you will have guessed already, I falled (sic) in love at first sight. He is such a nice boy

340

Then I have had much sorrow, for our love' [whose love? ours?
theirs?] 'may not insist, (persist, last) mind you.' This passage
struck me as rather ambiguous. Indeed, her last letters were
increasingly difficult to interpret. Then came a hint that she
might not write any more, but did not want to hurt me. It was
already too late to say this, as I felt strongly that I had not been
given a fair chance. Still, two or three more letters followed, as
neatly written and well composed as ever. One for my birthday
was in green ink on pink paper again.

12 Feb. 1948   It begins, 'Many letters I have written to you
and so many ones I have torn to pieces too.' I wondered, later,
what she had been struggling to express in the torn-up letters.
There is a softness, a tone of regret, about the last letters (which,
after all, she need not have written at all), which convinced me
that if she had been in this country, there might have been a
different ending. Here she seems depressed. 'We always make a
mistake by thinking our dreams are the future. The reality is
quite different however. I only can cry.' But she continues,
'Here are my best congratulations and a sincere kiss. If I lived in
England, I would have visited you tonight with many tulips of
the most beautiful colours. We should have talked and laughed
. . Yes, if.' That little 'Yes, if' seemed so full of meaning. And
further, 'I have not heard from you in such a long time. Are you
angry?' (What did she expect? I was not angry, but deep down I
was badly hurt.) But even then there was a ray of hope, 'My
boy, it is the best to end this letter, I am too cheerless . . . Please,
will you write me soon to the Bank?' Couldn't she understand I
did not want a sort of platonic friendship?

I must have written back, for the last letter is addressed to
Shenley Hospital, where I had recently moved, and . not to
Potters Bar. It is written in black ink on white paper, dated 31
March 1948. Nelly tells me some small items of news, about the
new fashion with long skirts, for instance, the 'New Look'. Also
'Mam, Jopie and Bob are quite well. I never talk of you to them,
for this is the best.' She tells me about their Easter and her plans
for the summer holidays. But then, half guiltily, half wistfully,

'Sometimes I wonder, what you are thinking of me.' It was becoming difficult to know *what* to think! And more to the point, perhaps, what was she thinking of me? 'You were my ideal,' she had said. I suppose I was flattered (and still am) that anyone could consider me their ideal! – but it placed me in an impossible position. Had I really been such a disappointment in person?

Letter continued on 2 April. 'This morning I had a strange sensation for my left ear is deaf. I cannot hear anything' (almost symbolic, one would think), 'Have I already told you I have started to play tennis this year? It is a fine sport.' finishing 'Dear boy, this is all for the present. Many greetings. Yours, Nelly.'

I don't know if I replied. I believe one year I sent a Christmas card.

I never thought badly of her, on the contrary, but there did not now seem any point in continuing the correspondence. But I kept all the letters. In the end there were 38 letters, some postcards, and a few other mementoes. It was impossible to throw them away. Some of them were written with an intensity and a sensibility worthy of Anne Frank or Karen Blixen (an author I discovered much later). I never heard any more, but today Nelly would have only just turned 70 and could well be still living in Holland. I hope she found happiness. Perhaps I will try to find out.

Time is a great healer, they say, and as the years passed all this was submerged in a variety of other interests and experiences. The letters were put in the back of a cupboard, and there they remained. In reviewing my past life, however, I realised that they represented a significant episode from the war. Indirectly perhaps, we were casualties of war – lives that had been damaged or blighted by war, even though surviving it. What happened, did happen. The past cannot be altered.

POSTSCRIPT

The Visser family of Rotterdam, Holland, in 1947:

Father, ——— Visser, first name not known, shot by Germans in February 1945. Age probably in late 40s.

Mother, ——— Visser, first name not known, still living in 1947.

Son, Ary Visser, shot by Germans in February 1945, age 23 or 24.

Daughter, Nelly Visser, age (in 1947) 23, telephone operator at bank in Rotterdam, wrote to me in 1946 as a result of reading a letter I had written to *Picture Post* magazine in November 1939.

Daughter, Jo or Jopie, age about 21, working in an office.

Son, Robert (Bob) Visser, age 17 , in 1946 still a student.

A subsequent visit to Rusthof revealed that the Visser parents were a little older than previously estimated. According to the dates on the gravestone the father, Johan (?) Visser, was 55 years old at the time of his death; the son, Ary, was 24 years old. The mother, who is buried nearby, died in 1960, just short of her 69th birthday.

I also discovered that the 20 men who died were shot as a reprisal for the death of one German. It also emerged that an even later reprisal on 20 March 1945 took place in another part of Amersfoort, where a further 10 Dutch civilians lost their lives. Some are said to have been members of the Dutch Resistance. The bullet holes are still visible in the wall.

Thus at least 30 men in one small town alone were killed in acts of vengeance.

INTERLUDE: NEW PHASES

Life, in my experience, goes in phases. Within the context of that phase of my life as it was in 1947, and without prejudice to another phase that was still some years away – in the shape of a hospital nurse, a vivacious dark-haired girl with the most radiant smile, whom I wanted to marry and, perhaps more astonishingly, wanted to marry me – my journey to Holland has to be regarded as a disastrous mistake. Of course, as a holiday break it was not a complete failure, and the majority of people did not know the background to it. It was easy to say that it had been a pleasant holiday and leave it at that.

At this period I had still not obtained my final professional qualifications, and besides my busy hospital life I had many cultural interests. In our letters Nelly and I had not discussed the subject of religion very seriously, though I know that in one letter I had touched on it briefly. I was looking for a religion in which I could believe honestly. In fact, after the war was over I had become interested in Quakerism and the way in which it worked through practical agencies. Towards the end of 1947, after the trip to Holland, I became a member of the Society of Friends at Barnet Meeting. I was impressed with its international outlook, while there was not too much emphasis on religious dogma. For some years I was taken up with the activities of Friends and was attending talks and retreats and earnest discussion groups, though in the end this turned out to be another phase. I now perceive that I was possibly too preoccupied with vague generalities and not enough with individual human nature.

Though the diary had to be abandoned, from an early age it had been an idiosyncrasy of mine to keep lists of all the books I read, many of the films seen, theatre and concert visits, art exhibitions, sporting events, and almost any art-form which attracted me, all going back to about 1935. These lists make a good substitute for a diary. My wartime diary suggests how frequently I went to the cinema or theatre, though many visits were not recorded. In the search for wholeness, it may be that I was trying to absorb too many experiences, and in this post-war period my spiritual, emotional, and intellectual wires were in danger of becoming inextricably tangled.

At the age of 15 I was enjoying a whole range of literature, from thrillers and adventure stories, through detective fiction to novels and classics, mostly borrowed from the public library, but occasionally bought in cheap editions. I had even read many of Shakespeare's plays, though this was probably a case of running before I could walk. I liked the sound of the words. When war came I was reading more serious novels, biography, travel books, and books of humour, as well as more popular fiction. By 1947 or 1948 my reading habits had changed somewhat (temporarily, at least), and I was confining myself mainly to poetry and drama (some of it religious), mystical and Quaker writers – including the *Journal of George Fox* – with only an occasional novel. One novel which influenced me enormously was *The Voyage* by Charles Morgan. I also greatly admired the life and writings of Albert Schweitzer.

Music was also becoming an increasingly important source of renewal to me, though I could never read music or play an instrument. I attended several of the concerts for young people conducted by Dr Ernest Read, as well as performances by more famous orchestras and conductors. I haunted the Promenade Concerts, which in those days were usually under the baton of Sir Adrian Boult or Basil Cameron, and people like Moura Lympany (piano) and Ida Haendel (violin) were performing. In 1949 I heard Elgar's *Dream of Gerontius* for the first time: Elgar had strong associations with Shenley through the Speyer family. Towards the end of that year there was a memorable *Messiah*, with a choir of 1000 conducted by Malcolm Sargent, the soloists including Kathleen Ferrier and Heddle Nash. Another unforgettable concert was given by the Vienna Philharmonic under Bruno Walter. Though not really an opera-lover, I went to hear *The Mastersingers* at Covent Garden.

In between times I paid fairly regular visits to the London art galleries. An outstanding exhibition of early 1948 was the Tate Gallery's 'Paintings and Drawings by Vincent van Gogh'. Later came an Exhibition of Indian Art at the Royal Academy, and the following year I enjoyed 'Masterpieces from Munich' at the National Gallery, the annual Royal Academy Summer Exhibition, and the Tate Gallery showed 'Art Treasures from Vienna'. In 1950, amongst other joys, I saw both the film and the play of *The Heiress*, and another successful play, *The Lady's Not For Burning*. I had a multitude of enthusiasms, which have given me many pleasant memories.

In 1948, too, I moved to a new job at Shenley Hospital, only two miles or so from where I had been working before. I had gained my Associateship in 1947, and in the autumn of 1948 I achieved the Fellowship of my profession. It was in the same year that the National Health Service was introduced. There were new phases and new faces. Now, both at work and in leisure time, I was meeting various new people, and somehow or other I succeeded in putting the unhappy Dutch episode behind me. But it was not plain sailing in this respect, and two or three other courtships with members of hospital staff ended unsatisfactorily during this period.

In the two decades after the end of the war Shenley Hospital was in its heyday. There was a large influx of foreign workers, beginning with French, Belgian, and Dutch nurses. The usual English and Irish contingents were soon augmented by Spanish, Portuguese, and a few Norwegian as well. Most of these came as female nursing or domestic staff. On the male side the changes were not so marked, but when I went there there were a fair sprinkling of Poles, mainly on the kitchen or garden staff. They were survivors in some way or other of the Polish Resistance Forces – tough, likeable, and adaptable characters, some of whom knew hardly any English, but who were reliable and hard-working types. I came to have a great respect for them. In later years staff began to be recruited from even further afield; nurses both male and female came from several Oriental countries, including the Philippines, from Mauritius, from the West Indies, and there were even one or two from South America. The hospital was caring for about 1800 mentally ill patients and, taking into account two day shifts and the night shift, there were something like 500 on the nursing staff and the medical staff consisted of at least 12 doctors, together with numerous other staff – medical auxiliaries, engineers, cooks and caterers, clerical staff, and artisans.

Among this thriving community of patients and staff were people of all races and creeds. Shenley Hospital (and some of the other hospitals roundabout) became a veritable United Nations in itself. As far as I am aware, there were never any political difficulties.

AFTERMATH II

On the face of it, the visit to Holland and that to Germany three years later had entirely different motives. In the first case I saw at first-hand the effects on a Dutch family who had lost a father and brother (or from the mother's point of view, husband and son) by ruthless killing; while the second journey brought me in contact with a couple who had suffered much hardship because of their religious beliefs. The Dutch family were relatively young, the German couple elderly, though they had a daughter in England, then married, but who had been sent to school in England just before the war. Yet they both typified, in diverse circumstances, what had been at stake during the war. During those five post-war years, what I had written to *Picture Post* as a youth of 19 became crystallised in what I learned of what the war had done to Europe as a whole.

At the age of 19 or 20 I could not have had much idea of the political and economic complexities involved in a 'United States of Europe', though it is fair to say that I had begun to read political books such as George Orwell's *The Road to Wigan Pier*, *Spanish Testament* by Arthur Koestler, and John Gunther's *Inside Europe*, amongst others. When I used the expression 'United States of Europe', I do not think I envisaged anything like the European Community today, but rather a loose co-operative of sovereign nation states. In 1939, of course, it was a vastly different world in which we lived. However, Winston Churchill himself used the expression in a later speech. Therefore, both my travels, which were intended as holidays, but turned out to be much more than that, sprang out of a basic ideological desire to help 'win the peace'.

This is what had lain behind my decision to join the Society of Friends, and it was as a direct result of my connection with Quakers that I paid a visit to Germany. In the immediate post-war years, motivated by humanitarian beliefs, I sent a few food parcels to Germany (and much later, to Poland), and received letters back from two recipients. Then in 1950, having seen an advertisement for paying guests, I went to stay with Mary and Leonhard Friedrich in Bad Pyrmont, which is in the Hanover district of Germany. Mary was an English woman married to a German, who was a small publisher of religious books. They were both Quakers and had lived in Germany since the early 1920s. There I gained an inkling of what it had been like to live under the Nazi tyranny.

In contrast to the story from Holland, which is based on letters written to me, I can draw on a diary kept during my stay, which records some of the grim wartime experiences of the Friedrichs. I was learning more about photography and had with me (and still have) a pocket-book to record technical data, and I used this to jot down every day all that I was told in conversation. These notes, made rather hurriedly, have been transcribed word for word, and really they speak for themselves. Therefore they are included exactly as written, some holiday observations mixed up with an account which seemed to me so important that I thought I had better write it all down while still fresh in my mind. Fortunately too, some photographs have survived.

My journey took me across part of West Germany; it was only five years after the end of the war, and the view from the train was instructive. I gazed upon acres and acres of ruined towns, reduced to rubble by incessant bombing, which had been partly cleared in some areas prior to the reconstruction which was only just beginning. Just as in Holland, and indeed in many parts of Britain, the devastation of war aroused sombre thoughts.

There are really two strands to the story of the Friedrichs: Leonhard's sufferings in Buchenwald and Mary's harrowing experiences at home in Bad Pyrmont. Mr and Mrs Friedrich were both in their sixties when I stayed with them. Mary was not of great physical stature; she had rather severe features and was sometimes severe in manner. She usually wore rimless spectacles and was simply and neatly dressed.

Leonhard, too, was only of medium height, going rather bald, but had a rounder face and mostly wore a benevolent expression in spite of all his terrible treatment. He was not very talkative, however, and left his wife to do the talking. Since she was English, this was probably the most convenient arrangement. I believe it was a long time before he could bear to speak about life – and death – in Buchenwald.

It must be understood that when I went there I had no knowledge of their previous history, and I was not aware that Leonhard had spent three years in a concentration camp. But the horrific pictures which had emerged at the end of the war from camps such as Auschwitz, Belsen, and Buchenwald had affected me profoundly, as I noted in the war diary. They reminded one of scenes from Dante's *Inferno* and it was with such images in mind that I wrote a poem, which was the best I could do. Likewise the gruesome chronicle of the refugee family which was billeted on Mary while Leonhard was away is like something out of a Greek tragedy – but this was only one episode towards the end of the war. In fact they had been committed to helping Jewish families from as early as as 1937, and there had been at least three years of unrelenting persecution by the Gestapo, following Leonhard's arrest in 1942.

This has been authoritatively described by their daughter, Brenda Bailey, in her story of their lives, *A Quaker Couple in Nazi Germany* (published 1994). Some sort of instinct prompted me to make notes of my observations and all that I was told during the fortnight I was there; by the same token, I have kept these notes safe in the intervening years. One chapter in Brenda Bailey's book confirms my account.

351

uchenwald Concentration Camp

he bitter bones, the martyred flesh.
Their pale eclipse did not console, for life's slow merge
With death's so stealthily mingling mesh
No final gesture made, but like some fading dirge,
Passed, insensibly, from night to nothingness.

See, here are the twisted lips, the anguished eyes
That saw a hideous world, reeking with murder-foetid air.
No peace was ever here, no human sympathies;
Here flourished the cruel cancer of despair,
Too strong for courage, too vile for dignity.

See, here the cadaverous limbs, the bloodless wounds
Of those once noble, once humane, once wondrously
    alive,
Now carved savagely in shame, to ghastly sculptures
    ground,
Fixed in all death's attitudes, like souls in Dante's hellish
    hive;
But their purgatory's done, they no more know its bounds.

See, here are the blackened skulls, the charred remains –
Ashes of humiliation, the lowest pitch of fate
Brought to men by brutes, whose poisoned brains
Envenomed multitudes, and who, so sterile to create,
Destroyed; and on our age left their accursed stains.

Their crimes are embodied here. These spectral forms cry
    out,
Are vocal with a stark and wrathful warning;
A giant accusation shrouds them all about.
Their tragic shades shall haunt our brightest dawning
With grey miasmas from the years of doubt.

Poem written by Edward Stebbing in May 1945, five years
before meeting a survivor from Buchenwald.

A Visit to Germany (notes written daily).

Aug. 12th 1950
Left Victoria 8.46. Arrive Dover 10.45.
Fine and sunny. Smooth crossing. Lunch on boat – 9/5d!
Dep. Ostend 5.30. Arr. Brussels 7.00.
Very warm, seats hard. Belgium – flat fields, little haystacks, long lines of trees. People working in fields – ploughing, harvest. Passengers predominantly English.
Long wait near frontier and again at Aachen (over 1 hour). Oh, for a cup of tea!
Arrive Cologne 1.20. Depart 3.00.

Aug. 13th
Stopped at Essen, Bochum, Hamm, in the night – names remembered from reports of air-raids.
Early Sun. morning – still going on through pleasant wooded countryside.
Arrive Hanover 8.30. Had breakfast.
Depart Hanover 10.24.
Arrive Bad Pyrmont 11.35. Surprised to see shops open.
Had lunch at Quakerhaus with Young Friends.
Lovely surroundings.
Visited Leonhard and Mary Friedrich (with whom I was to stay) in the afternoon. Went for walk in early evening. Bad Pyrmont laid out as a spa town with many formal walks, but surroundings have much natural beauty – wooded hills, etc. – straightness of the pines, like telegraph poles. Came back for final meeting of Young Friend.
　　Discussion on procedure at future gatherings – questions of limiting numbers, whether a certain theme should be set, how much should be prepared, how free time be spent, etc. (A German boy sat beside me and translated everything that was said.)

Aug. 14th
I was very tired after travelling and got up just before 12.00.
Bread dark and somewhat rubbery – sugar very scarce and not

353

very sweet – tea very dear and has a queer taste – meat and butter dear, fruit and vegetables fairly cheap.

In afternoon went into town, went down Hauptallee, lovely in the sun, with cafes with tables outside and shady trees and a fountain at the bottom. Saw the Schloss.

After tea went for another walk. Visited Dr Otto Buchinger's (a Friend) clinic, where people go for fasting treatment, but the doctor wasn't there. Also saw Quaker rest-house where Displaced Persons and others in need of a rest are looked after. The place is run by Friends' Service Council (originally for those persecuted by the Nazis) with two Friend hostesses, but all housework, etc. is done by Catholic sisters and novitiates! (FSC took it over from Catholics). The wardens were out.

Aug. 15th
Morning – in town. Had glass of spring-water (10pfg).
Afternoon – went in Kurpark, listened to music.
The town swarms with doctors and dentists – every few yards a doctor's name-plate. Many cripples and people with sticks about (many looked as if they could throw their sticks away and walk perfectly well without them).

Have heard several tragic stories from Mary Friedrich about people's experiences during and since the war. For many it is a hard life.

Aug. 16th
Morning – went for walk up to top of Bomberg hill – went up viewing tower (with MF and ES).
MF told us of her husband's experiences in Buchenwald – three years there – poor food, cotton clothes (no underclothes), crowded sleeping quarters, heavy work digging. One day he was whipped across the face for wearing gloves and he almost fainted with the pain of it into the trench he was digging. He came round, however, to hear the guard say 'Take him to the sick-bay,' and he knew this would mean being given an injection from which there would be no return, so he pulled himself together sufficiently to carry on with his work. At the end of the day he was told to report to the SS man. He was very frightened,

354

for he knew this usually meant a flogging and he saw several others flogged, but when his turn came he was not told to strip. Instead, the SS man asked him why he was there. 'Because I am a Quaker, I suppose.' 'Look,' said the guard, 'I'd like to help you. I owe my life to Quakers. My mother told me, if it hadn't been for Quaker food (after 1914–18 war) I wouldn't have lived. All you've got to do is to sign this paper to become a member of the National Socialist party.' Leonhard: 'I couldn't do that after all I've been through. Besides, I wouldn't be able to do the kind of work you'd want me to do.' A few days later he was offered a munitions job, but he again refused on pacifist grounds. Eventually he was given a job as a storekeeper, where he could have a stove and eat food sent him, wash, etc. But there was no comradeship in the sleeping-huts; men were killed by others for stealing bread – even priests stole. He kept that job till the end of the war. When the end was near the Germans tried to disperse Buchenwald – tried to bring gas-chambers from Auschwitz, but these were delayed – tried to march prisoners away, but many died on the way. In the end many SS men were made prisoners by the inmates until the Americans came.

For the first one-and-a-half years years while L was away the Gestapo came twice a week to search their house and the Quakerhaus and to ask questions. MF had refugees billeted with her (why she was allowed to remain there I still can't understand, but she stayed there, an English woman with Germans living in the rooms beneath her, all through the war) and had a harrowing time. Here is the dreadful story of the refugees:

It begins in America, where a woman was born of Jewish parents from Vienna. She married a man in Germany, who took on the Jewish religion (which was worse than being born a Jew in Nazi eyes). They had four children – two boys, two girls. One child, however, was not the woman's, but born of a servant because the husband wanted to disprove the race-theory by showing that the half-brother would be no different from the other children. I don't know much of their pre-war history, but when war came the parents were terrified of being discovered Jews, so burnt all their identification papers. The children did not know they were Jews.

Later, presumably because things were getting too difficult, man and wife attempted suicide by cutting the arteries in their wrists, while laying in bed. The eldest girl discovered them unconscious, so the attempt was unsuccessful, but the woman was left with a lame hand and the man had scars on his arm. The girl then found out she was a Jew.

The woman came to Pyrmont, to Dr Buchinger, for a cure of her hand. She was scared to go back to Bremen, so Dr Buchinger let her stay, but eventually she had to leave and went to Mrs Friedrich together with one of her boys. Her husband came to see her, for a weekend, but said he had slipped on the way and injured himself, so asked to stay. During the night he started raving and sobbing. MF got up and told him to be quiet, but he would not. Next day she told his wife and they changed rooms and the man stayed there.

The next thing was that they said their other son (aged about eight) was very lonely and had threatened to take his life, if he couldn't come to his parents. This, Mrs F realised afterwards, must have been untrue, but at the time she was taken in and the boy came.

Then a story was told about the elder daughter, that she had a baby in an incubator, born before its time; her husband was away fighting in Russia. It was said she could not leave the baby, but she turned up alone one day with hardly any luggage. Her father went back with her, but when she got back she disappeared for about a week. She apparently had a vision and went to Berlin to see Hitler to warn him about something. The man was looking for her and caring for the baby; she was in trouble with the police as well. He told them the Quakers in Pyrmont would look after her and the baby. The police were glad to be rid of her and let them go. So they returned with the baby, a child of three months.

This child, it turned out, was the child of her own father.* He was a strange, terrible character, a hypnotist. He hypnotised both his wife and his daughter.

One day he thrashed the girl for saying something about him.

---

* i.e. by an act of incest.

Hearing screams, MF went to see what was happening and told him she could not allow that conduct. He threatened her too, but she managed to quieten him and later sent for the police, but they did not give any satisfaction.

Later, the girl tried to commit suicide by taking sleeping-tablets. She was unconscious for about a week before she recovered. (At that time one did not send for a doctor for such things.) She was often in a stuporose condition, as though drugged (hypnotised?), and neglected the child.

A pretext was found to bring the younger daughter, a pretty girl, to Pyrmont, and she and the two boys went to stay with Dr Buchinger. One morning the woman and girl went out without feeding or washing the baby and did not return till midday. They said they had been to see the priest, as the girl had something on her mind which she wanted to confess, though they were not Catholics. However, they had not been able to see the priest. In the afternoon they again went out without caring for the baby. This time they saw the priest, but without much satisfaction. They returned in the evening, the girl in a highly nervous state, and said they were going to see a doctor later that evening. Before they went out, the girl went in the bathroom and was in there a long time. The mother was worried and said, 'I hope nothing has happened in there.' The girl came out, however, with her coat wrapped round her and looking as pale as death. They went out.

MF went into the bathroom and found blood everywhere. In the WC, she said, 'was something horrible' – she thought it might have been a miscarriage or something – she didn't look closely, but flushed it down and cleaned the place up. Later it was discovered that the girl had cut her breasts off and put them in the lavatory pan.

The two women went to a doctor, but he wouldn't see them. (The town was full of wounded German soldiers.) They went to the police; the girl asked to be locked up, said she was out of her mind and wanted to be put away, she couldn't put up with life any longer. They wouldn't take any notice, told her to go back to Frau Friedrich, who was kind and would look after her. She undid her coat and showed her underclothes saturated with blood. Then they knew something was really wrong and took her to the hospital. They had no room for her there, but put her in a room down in the basement, where she stayed some time. She tried to end her life by banging her head against the walls. All her hair came out and her head became dreadfully swollen.

There she stayed until the Americans came, when her mental symptoms vanished. They treated her until she was well enough to return to MF's flat. The other daughter also spent a lot of time there. American doctors came and stayed a long time twice a week. MF mentioned it to one, who said, 'Oh, yes, I am psycho-analysing her,' and warned her that the girl was an advanced case of syphilis. But other American soldiers came up too and finally MF discovered that the mother, at her husband's sugges-tion, was procuring her younger daughter to make money to live on; the other girl was helping too. MF told the doctor not to come any more or she would go to his CO. That stopped the doctors coming. But others continued to come. One day another woman – another refugee who was living with M – came to her and said that the parents were out, but there were two men with the girls, two in one room, two in another, and no sound was coming from them. M wouldn't interfere, but the other woman went into one room (which by chance had been left unlocked) and found man and girl naked. The mother returned and was angry with M for allowing the other woman (who also, M afterwards found, had been consistently stealing from her) to go into one of her rooms without knocking – she paid rent, her rooms were private, etc. etc. But M said she knew what the rooms were being used for and gave them two hours to clear out, the whole lot. (The man had already gone, suddenly, early one morning.) They went, but Ruth (the older girl) returned, said there was no bed or anything where they had gone – could she stay? M let her stay another week, helped her get a mattress, etc., then she, too, went.

Evening – report on Germany Yearly Meeting, held in Berlin, followed by Monthly Meeting – Emil Fuchs free and comfort-able in his new position, students glad to come and talk to him.

Membership seems to be mostly middle-aged women – only six men. Young people leave district when they reach a certain age, for they can't study and there is little scope for careers in Pyrmont. A children's class at the Meeting – yet two or three children of the *class-teachers* have recently been confirmed into the Lutheran Church. Another daughter of a Friend had a child by a married Catholic man; she knew he was married, but persisted in the relationship. How will the Meeting flourish in this way? What does it say for Quaker influence and teaching?

Aug. 17th
Made acquaintance with refugee girl by giving her a bar of chocolate for her little boy of three. She has another baby and lives with her husband in two rooms at the top of the house, where I am. It is a poor existence – they have to go downstairs and outside for water, toilet, etc. The owners of the house are very unkind to them. How will they come to have any belief in the decency of human nature if they are treated like this? And they are probably much better off than many in the big towns.

Morning – walked to Holzhausen, a pleasant, peaceful country village. Farming appears to be the main occupation.

Afternoon – walked over to Friedensthal. Had coffee, waffeln, (waffles), and cake (DM 2.64). Some nice new houses being built.

Thunderstorm in evening.

Aug. 18th
Morning – walked in Kurpark and town with doctor staying at rest-house.. He earns less money than I do; wants to emigrate. Speaks quite good English. Spent three years in a Russian camp near Archangel, learnt English and Russian while there. Some of his fellows performed Shaw's *Devil's Disciple* there!

Afternoon – in Kurpark again.
A newspaper costs about 4d. here.
German people seem very sober and proper here: seem lacking in humour. In Pyrmont many look prosperous and well-dressed, but that is because only well-off folk can afford to come for the 'cure'; they are not representative of the average German.

There are many refugees here, however. In the Western Zone there are ten million, a tremendous problem.

Aug. 19th

A fine morning. Walked to Lügde with Werner Malz, the doctor. He told me some more of his experiences with the Russians. At first, when they came to his town, the soldiers were a bad sort and committed atrocities – destroyed buildings, raped women, including little girls and old women. Later a hospital was set up for POWs, where he worked. There he found many of the Russian doctors and sisters very good-natured; some would give him things secretly. Then he was moved to a place near Archangel, at first in a hospital, then in a camp. Very cold there. Civilians were not too badly disposed, because they were people forced to live there because they would not adhere to the Communist doctrine. In the camp conditions were worse – had to work digging drains on a starvation diet; some of the guards were brutal. But the general picture was not quite so bad as in Buchenwald. His experiences did not appear to have made him bitter; he was a very charming and friendly person and humourous too. He came from somewhere near Oldenburg, but I think he was a native of Breslau.

Lügde is a very attractive Westphalian village. The houses are mainly old and of a type not found in England. There's a very old church, on a site formerly used for heathen rites. We had coffee and a plate of delicious whipped cream with cake at a small eating-house. My friend called Lügde 'a dreamt village' – and so it is.

Afternoon – went out, got caught in heavy rain.

Had a bath – water heated in a large boiler by a fire lit underneath, more trouble than a gas-boiler, but has the supreme advantage of heating the room, nor can anything much go wrong with it.

Aug. 20th (Sunday)

Meeting for Worship – about 50 people present. Meeting-house rather bare, rather like a small concert-hall, with long rows of tip-up seats and modernistic lights which throw the light up to the ceiling – no table with flowers on. But spacious and bright, in surroundings of trees.

Strolled in pine-forest afterwards with a boy from Berlin. If

360

you stand still in the pine forest it is absolutely silent, nothing stirs. The only life I saw were some very large orange slugs.

Afternoon – went for a walk with Leonhard. How beautiful the forest is, with the sunlight filtering through the graceful tree-trunks of pine, beech, and sycamore.

We came to a road where pieces of broken-up Jewish tombstones had been used as rough paving-stones. One could read parts of the inscriptions on them. What would Quakers think if their burial-grounds were desecrated in this way? Such signs of Nazi barbarity will take a long time to disappear.

M said the Germans are not disposed to invite people to their homes. They can't let themselves go like the English. But they are hard-working and try to keep up a good appearance.

Have had some bananas, which is a treat.

Evening – went for a walk after dark with Werner Malz. Went in Kurpark, saw illuminated fountains.

Aug. 21st

Went to Hanover, most of which seems to be in ruins. Went for a trip on the Machsee – a large boating lake.

My best achievement with the language: asked for a bottle of orangeade and got a hot sausage and a bread-roll! But I've never tasted such a good sausage in England. And the orangeade was iced.

Aug. 22nd

In the morning went to Hamelin with Neville Macfarlane. A charming town full of old houses and picturesque side-streets. The Pied Piper legend is much in evidence. Explored town and climbed up the Klüt and up the tower on top, from which a marvellous view is obtained. Came down, missed the train, and had a meal in the town. We had *Fleischbruhe mit Ei*, which turned out to be meat-broth with a raw egg served separately – some indecision on how to eat it. Also a glass of tea, served as a bag of tea on a piece of string on a glass rod, in hot water. (The tea cost about 10d.)

From the train-windows the land looks very well cultivated.

There seem to be more people working on the land than in England and they work hard, including womenfolk.

Aug. 23rd
Afternoon – coach-trip to Hermanns-Denkmal, through Detmold, Bad Meinberg, and the Externesteine, where are some huge outcrops of stone, the site of former heathen practices, later becoming Christian. A primitive chapel is hewn out of the rock and baptisms were done there; outside is a very early carving of the Crucifixion.

Hermanns-Denkmal is a colossal monument on top of a hill, visible for miles. From the hill a wonderful view is obtained, Sampled German beer.

Evening – talk by Muriel Lester at Quakerhaus on the colour problem in South Africa and on Gandhi's way of dealing with it. A fine talk, emphasising the mystical approach.

Aug. 24th
Morning – went to Meeting at Josefshaus at 9 o'clock with Muriel Lester and Mary Friedrich. Afterwards in town, shopping.

Afternoon – coach-trip to Polle, then on paddle-boat to Bodenwerder (along the Weser), then coach back to Pyrmont, stopping at Grohnde.

At Pyrmont had a Bockwurst (sausage a foot long) and beer, sitting at table on pavement.

Extraordinary number of barber's shops in German towns.

Aug. 25th
Morning – Kurpark and town, taking photographs.

Afternoon – walked to Lügde with Stella Johnson.

Evening – MF told us something of how Nazi brutality and persecution of the Jews was gradually built up and became accepted by the German people through continual compromise.

Aug. 26th
12.20 Left Pyrmont for Cologne.

The Ruhr rather flat and uninteresting. Much evidence of bombing in the towns. Wuppertal a wilderness of ruins.

Arrive Cologne 5.45. Saw cathedral and a little bit of the town, dreadfully battered, but full of life.

Stayed night at the Quaker Jugendheim, where fine work is being done. Children are sent for two months for building up, rest, good meals. Unorganised youth have a club in the evenings and there is a sewing-room where unemployed girls learn needlework and mothers of several children come to use the sewing-machines; and there is a shoe-maker's shop, where poor people can get shoes repaired cheaply, paying only for time, as leather is a gift from FSC. The staff-house was sent from Norway, a present from Norwegian Friends, who sent Norwegians to put it up – a strong, comfortable, wooden house. Food comes mostly from America. The club-house is another wooden hut – to be pulled down and rebuilt. One English FSC girl there, one English Fellowship of Reconciliation girl part-time, two Germans (young man and woman), and several come in each day. It is truly an oasis in the desert, but many more are needed. I was given tea and grapes (!) on arrival, talked to the residents, and slept on a camp-bed in the meeting-room where Cologne Friends meet.

Aug. 27th
Left Koln 6.27. – caught train by the skin of my teeth.
Arrive Ostend 1.35. Arrive Dover 6.15 – good crossing.
Arrive Victoria 10. It's good to be in England again.

Naturally Mary and Leonhard Friedrich were the central characters in the scenario of my German visit, but I also met other interesting people. One was a survivor from a Russian prison-camp, and it was particularly valuable to compare his descriptions with those of Leonhard, as relayed by Mary. Nearly at the end of my holiday another notable peace-worker came to give a talk at the Quakerhaus. This was Muriel Lester, who had travelled the world on behalf of the Fellowship of Reconciliation, trying to persuade political leaders to use non-violent methods of solving their problems. She was not a Quaker herself, but a Nonconformist Christian and a disciple of Gandhi. She was almost the same age as Mary Friedrich, but unmarried; I only met her very briefly during the two days she was there, but I certainly remember her steadfast sincerity.

I managed to capture them all in one photo on the balcony at Bismarckstrasse: two who had risked their lives in opposing the Hitler regime, one of them an ex-inmate of Buchenwald; a dedicated peace-worker who practised what she preached; a survivor of about my own age from a Russian prisoner-of-war camp; and another visitor from England, a paying guest like myself. In the corresponding photo I took the place of Werner Malz, and I feel doubly honoured to be portrayed with most of them. How much history had been packed into those four lives! I was really just an onlooker, I thought.

The Friedrichs and Muriel Lester all lived to old age in England; they richly deserved their years of peaceful retirement, though their health was sometimes poor. At the time 1 met them, in 1950, very little had been published in the way of first-hand accounts of wartime experiences, but many have appeared in succeeding years. By coincidence the lives of Mary and Leonhard and of Muriel have appeared quite recently within a year of each other. A fine biography of Muriel Lester has been written by Jill Wallis, under the title *Mother of World Peace* (1993), which does great justice to her work; in the following year the book about the Friedrichs by their daughter, already mentioned, appeared.

In my own case the story goes on. We must not be allowed to forget what happened. In the light of certain news reports and articles concerning, for example, Oskar Schindler, subject of a major film, it has become my personal mission to have the names of Mary and Leonhard Friedrich entered on the roll of non-Jews as Righteous Among the Nations. That would be a fitting memorial. Towards the end of 1994 I made contact with Yad Vashem in Jerusalem and have been in touch with the Israeli Embassy about it. For what happens we will have to wait and see.

As regards the message preached by Muriel Lester, I do not think now that I could go all the way along that path, nor all the way with the Quaker peace testimony. Much as I admired her personality and unshakeable pacifist beliefs and her untiring efforts, I came to a point where I could not agree. There were too many contrary forces to be reconciled. The conflict between pacifism and patriotism cannot be dismissed lightly. The dilemma had occupied my mind frequently during the war, but ultimately I could not see how Hitler could have been stopped except by force, and if he had not been stopped there would have been no vestige of liberal culture left in Europe, no place for people like Muriel Lester. (This, of course, is said with the benefit of hindsight.) Somehow the Friedrichs seemed to be made of sterner stuff – they stood their ground and suffered for it. Yet they would not have thought themselves heroic. I sometimes wonder how I would have acted in similar circumstances.

Looking back nearly half a century, I ask myself how I, an ordinary quiet sort of man, came to be mixed up in such traumatic events, albeit not at the sharp end, almost by proxy, one might say. Some of it reads like a novel. During the war itself I always felt that I was only on the margin of things, but on reflection, perhaps this was taking a too narrow view. In what I have called the Aftermath, I was given unexpected insights into the thoughts and feelings of a young woman in a bereaved family, met a survivor from a German concentration camp and another from a Russian camp, listened to a woman who had to cope with so many terrible situations, and heard from another who had met Gandhi and many other figures of her day. But regardless of my role, what happened, *did* happen, and has to be told. What has it all meant? is another question.

The legacy of the Second World War is incalculable. One hears the opinion that, after 50 years, it may be time to forget the inhumanities of the dictators. I am a peace-loving person and am willing to think well of the new generation, who have inherited such a fearful legacy. But the passage of time is not enough in itself, and I fail to see why the Germans as a nation under Hitler, who had terrorised most of Europe for 12 nightmare years (1933–1945), should somehow be exonerated from condemnation and allowed to play a dominant role in European politics.

On the other hand, it is greatly to the credit of *this* nation that it did not stand idly by and let ourselves, too, be herded into the gas-chambers.

Fifty years is not long, not long enough to forget or forgive. But there *were* some, as my story shows, who, when it came to the point, did not shirk the consequences of resisting Nazi oppression. If I can be instrumental in honouring the names of two of them, that will be an achievement I shall be proud of. I have learned an inescapable lesson of history: the past, whether good or evil, cannot be altered.